Wintergreen

Cross-Leaved

Heath

HEATH

Alder

FAMILY

Sloe

Grass

Geranium

Rowan

Ash

Trefoil

TYPES of

FRUIT

Strawberry

Medlar

Bell Heather

Beech

CATKIN

Willow

Oak

MINT

FAMILY

Thyme

Corn-Mint

Marjoram

Self-Heal

Ground Ivy

DICOTYLEDONS

THE WEEK-END BOOK

The
Week-End
Book

*A new edition: the former features
revised and amplified and six
new sections; all freshly
embellished*

*Editor: Francis Meynell
advised by Sylvia Mulvey and Gerald Barry*

❖❖❖❖❖❖❖❖❖❖❖❖❖❖❖❖❖❖❖❖❖❖❖❖❖❖❖❖

The Nonesuch Press   *and*   Random House Inc.
London   New York

Made and printed in England at The Stellar Press
Library of Congress Catalogue Card Number 55-10804
This edition first published 1955
All rights reserved

WEEK-END

The train! The twelve o'clock for paradise.
Hurry, or it will try to creep away.
Out in the country everyone is wise:
We can be only wise on Saturday.
There you are waiting, little friendly house:
Those are your chimney-stacks with you between,
Surrounded by old trees and strolling cows,
Staring through all your windows at the green.
Your homely floor is creaking for our tread;
The smiling tea-pot with contented spout
Thinks of the boiling water, and the bread
Longs for the butter. All their hands are out
To greet us, and the gentle blankets seem
Purring and crooning: 'Lie in us, and dream'.

Harold Monro.

THE CONTENTS

DEDICATION

'TO ONE WHO HAS BEEN LONG IN CITY PENT...'

THE PREFACE

In its infancy The Week-End Book proclaimed, perhaps a
little arrogantly, that it needed no explanation, no introduction. With this new edition there is more occasion for
commentary: a change of the well-known is more challenging
than what is entirely new.

First let me say that the new edition has enjoyed (and I too
have enjoyed) the advice and help of Sylvia Mulvey and
Gerald Barry. They have brought it into touch with generations junior to mine. With what result?

All the old features are here, though some are a little lopped
and others much expanded. The biggest change is in the
addition of six new sections. Of these the *Late Poems* (late in
the sense of recent) makes a contemporary anthology: like
Great Poems, a very personal choice without regard to reputation or protocol; and without the embarrassment of the
label 'Great'. Since living poets have their own views of
greatness (taste, as Mr Nicholas Bentley has said, is after all
only a matter of taste) and many have lived a long life, the
qualifying birth-date for the poets of the *Great Poems* anthology ends in the 'eighties of the last century. In this section
my original principle persists: it is a strictly *un*representative
anthology. For two reasons. The first has already been
mentioned – it is a personal, an idiosyncratic choice. The
second is that it nearly always eschews the regular anthology
pieces – for the intention is to make it a supplement to, not a
competitor with, the 'Oxford Book of English Verse', doubtless carried in another pocket. (In earlier editions the plan
was made plain by 'A List of Great Poems not in this book'.)
In this scheme I can but hope that I am still with my
readers, my readers with me. Of all sections in the earlier
editions, *Great Poems* proved to be prime favourite. Many
additions and a few omissions have now been made. The net
gain of poems throughout the book is nearly a hundred.

But the main effect of the new sections, and of the revisions
to the old, is to give expression to that growth of interest in
nature subjects which is an outstanding feature of this century. This enlarged interest is catered for by the sections *All
Creatures that on Earth do Dwell; The Green and Pleasant
Land, and how it came to be so; The Fields, and the Beasts
thereof; A Kalendar of Wild Flowers*. In the same spirit, the

ix

Bird Song at Morning section is enlarged, elaborated and made a practical tool for the week-end observer. It records in musical notation some common bird-songs which the in-expert find hard of recognition by means of 'cheep-cheep' or other onomatopoeic effects. Again, a concept of space-time which has been developed in the last quarter-century is inter-preted for the layman in the new version of *Starshine at Night*. *Etiquette* is a cheerful collection of glints from the past and hints from the present. It acknowledges and encourages the hopeful new interest in penmanship. The jokes of yesteryear are not the jokes of today, and *First Aid* and *The Law* have now less whimsy and more utility. Similarly 'Travels with a Donkey' gives place to *Weights and Weathers*. Community Singing, which the earlier editions did much to foster, is less appealing today than family singing: and so a new collection of *Rounds* takes the place of most of the old song section.

More specialised help has been commanded for this edition than for any of its predecessors. Thus Mr John Moore is responsible for everything but a sentence or two in *All Creatures that on Earth do Dwell; The Green and Pleasant Land; The Fields, and the Beasts thereof;* Mrs Rosemary Russell for all but the musical notation of *Bird Song at Morning*, which is the work of Mr Percy Edwards and Mr Charles Tovey; Mrs Caroe for the drawings and text (but not the inexact title) of *A Kalendar of Wild Flowers* (with a bouquet for its prototype, the delightful series of advertise-ments by Shell-Mex and B.P. Ltd.). Mr J. M. Richards has brought pubs into *Architecture*, in which the relevant new drawings are by Mr Colin Milne; Dr Fred Hoyle has set the *Stars* in their fresh firmament; Mrs Evelyn Forbes has re-lated to the habits of our day the *Food and Drink* section, with a thesis presented by Mr Martin Zander on coffee-making; Mr C. R. Hewitt has limpified the *Law*; Mr R. S. Read, of the Royal Meteorological Society, has made the *Weather* scientific; Miss Cynthia Meynell has given first aid to *First Aid;* Mr Peter Eden has rounded up the *Rounds*. I am par-ticularly grateful to Mr Paul Gallico (who walks a Bentley Countryman) first for his temper- and life-saving injunctions for motorists, and secondly for permission to reprint them from 'Esquire'. The end-papers are by Mrs Caroe, and the sectional headpieces are by Mr Philip Burgoyne.

Francis Meynell.

GREAT POEMS

As certain also of your own poets have said.
The Acts of the Apostles.

. . . those brave translunary things
That the first poets had.
Marlowe.

Oft, in the public roads
Yet unfrequented, while the morning light
Was yellowing the hill tops, I went abroad
With a dear friend, and for the better part
Of two delightful hours we strolled along
By the still borders of the misty lake,
Repeating favourite verses with one voice.
William Wordsworth.

The poetry of earth is never dead.
Keats.

Great Poems

'As certain also of your own poets have said'

O WESTERN WIND

O WESTERN wind, when wilt thou blow,
  That the small rain down can rain?
Christ, that my love were in my arms
  And I in my bed again!

Anonymous.

¶

ADAM lay ybounden,
  Bounden in a bond;
Four thousand winter
  Thought he not too long;
And all was for an appil,
  An appil that he took,
As clerkès finden
  Wretten in their book.
Ne hadde the appil taken been,
  The appil taken been,
Ne hadde never our Lady
  A-been hevenè Queene.
Blessèd be the time
  That appil taken was.
Therefore we moun sing
  'Deo Gracias'.

Anonymous.

JOLY JOLY WAT

THE shepherd upon a hill he sat;
He had on him his tabard and his hat,
His tarbox, his pipe, and his flagat;
His name was called Joly Joly Wat,

3

For he was a good herdes boy
            Ut hoy!
  For in his pipe he made so much joy.

The shepherd upon a hill was laid;
His dog to his girdle was tied;
He had not slept but a little braid,
But '*Gloria in excelsis*' was to him said.
            Ut hoy!
  For in his pipe he made so much joy.

The shepherd on a hill he stood;
Round about him his sheep they yode;
He put his hand under his hood,
He saw a star as red as blood.
            Ut hoy!
  For in his pipe he made so much joy.

The shepherd said anon right,
'I will go see yon farly sight,
Whereas the angel singeth on height,
And the star that shineth so bright.'
            Ut hoy!
  For in his pipe he made so much joy.

'Now farewell, Moll, and also Will!
For my love go ye all still
Unto I come again you till,
And evermore, Will, ring well thy bell.'
            Ut hoy!
  For in his pipe he made so much joy.

'Now must I go there Christ was born;
Farewell! I come again to morn.
Dog, keep well my sheep from the corn,
And warn well "Warroke" when I blow my horn!'
            Ut hoy!
  For in his pipe he made so much joy.

When Wat to Bethlehem come was,
He sweat, he had gone faster than a pace;
He found Jesu in a simple place,
Between an ox and an ass.
            Ut hoy!
  For in his pipe he made so much joy.

'Jesu, I offer to thee here my pipe,
My skirt, my tarbox, and my scrip;
Home to my fellows now will I skip,
And also look unto my sheep.'
> Ut hoy!
> For in his pipe he made so much joy.

'Now farewell, mine own herdsman Wat!'
'Yea, for God, lady, even so I hight;
Lull well Jesu in thy lap,
And farewell, Joseph, with thy round cape!'
> Ut hoy!
> For in his pipe he made so much joy.

'Now may I well both hope and sing,
For I have been at Christ's bearing;
Home to my fellows now will I fling,
Christ of heaven to his bliss us bring!'
> Ut hoy!
> For in his pipe he made so much joy.

Anonymous.

5

I SING of a maiden
> That is makeless.
King of all kinges
> To her son she ches.

He came all so stille
> There his mother was
As dew in Aprille
> That falleth on grass.

He came all so stille
> To his mother's bower,
As dew in Aprille
> That falleth on the flower.

He came all so stille
> There his mother lay,
As dew in Aprille
> That falleth on the spray.

Mother and maiden
> Was never none but she;
Well may such a lady
> Godès mother be!

Anonymous.

5

JOLLY GOOD ALE AND OLD

I CANNOT eat but little meat,
    My stomach is not good;
But sure I think that I can drink
    With him that wears a hood.
Though I go bare, take ye no care,
    I nothing am a-cold;
I stuff my skin so full within
    Of jolly good ale and old.
        Back and side go bare, go bare;
        Both foot and hand go cold;
        But, belly, God send thee good ale enough,
Whether it be new or old.

I love no roast but a nut-brown toast,
    And a crab laid in the fire;
A little bread shall do me stead;
    Much bread I not desire.
No frost nor snow, no wind, I trow,
    Can hurt me if I wold;
I am so wrapped and thoroughly lapped
    Of jolly good ale and old.
        Back and side go bare, go bare, etc.

And Tib, my wife, that as her life
    Loveth well good ale to seek,
Full oft drinks she till ye may see
    The tears run down her cheek:
Then doth she trowl to me the bowl
    Even as a maltworm should,
And saith, 'Sweetheart, I took my part
    Of this jolly good ale and old.'
        Back and side go bare, go bare, etc.

Now let them drink till they nod and wink,
    Even as good fellows should do;
They shall not miss to have the bliss
    Good ale doth bring men to;
And all poor souls that have scoured bowls
    Or have them lustily trolled,
God save the lives of them and their wives,
    Whether they be young or old.
        Back and side go bare, go bare;
        Both foot and hand go cold;
        But, belly, God send thee good ale enough,
        Whether it be new or old.
        John Still (Bishop of Bath and Wells).

WALY, WALY

O W A L Y , waly, up the bank,
  And waly, waly, doun the brae,
And waly, waly, yon burn-side,
  Where I and my Love wont to gae!
I lean'd my back unto an aik,
  I thocht it was a trustie tree;
But first it bow'd and syne it brak –
  Sae my true love did lichtlie me.

O waly, waly, gin love be bonnie
  A little time while it is new!
But when 'tis auld it waxeth cauld,
  And fades awa' like morning dew.
O wherefore should I busk my heid,
  O wherefore should I kame my hair?
For my true Love has me forsook,
  And says he'll never lo'e me mair.

Now Arthur's Seat sall be my bed,
  The sheets sall ne'er be 'filed by me;
Saint Anton's well sall be my drink,
  Since my true Love has forsaken me;
Marti'mas wind, when wilt thou blaw,
  And shake the green leaves aff the tree?
O gentle Death, when wilt thou come?
  For of my life I am wearie.

'Tis not the frost, that freezes fell,
  Nor blawing snaw's inclemencie,
'Tis not sic cauld that makes me cry;
  But my Love's heart grown cauld to me.
When we cam in by Glasgow toun,
  We were a comely sicht to see;
My Love was clad in the black velvet,
  And I mysel in cramasie.

But had I wist, before I kist,
  That love had been sae ill to win,
I had lock'd my heart in a case o' gowd,
  And pinn'd it wi' a siller pin.
And O! if my young babe were born,
  And set upon the nurse's knee;
And I mysel were dead and gane,
  And the green grass growing over me!
                              Anonymous.

HELEN OF KIRCONNELL

I WISH I were where Helen lies,
Night and day on me she cries;
O that I were where Helen lies,
   On fair Kirconnell lea!

Curst be the heart that thought the thought,
And curst the hand that fired the shot,
When in my arms burd Helen dropt,
   And died to succour me!

O think na ye my heart was sair,
When my Love dropp'd and spak nae mair!
There did she swoon wi' meikle care,
   On fair Kirconnell lea.

As I went down the water side,
None but my foe to be my guide,
None but my foe to be my guide,
   On fair Kirconnell lea;

I lighted down my sword to draw,
I hacked him in pieces sma',
I hacked him in pieces sma',
   For her sake that died for me.

O Helen fair, beyond compare!
I'll mak a garland o' thy hair,
Shall bind my heart for evermair,
   Until the day I die!

O that I were where Helen lies!
Night and day on me she cries;
Out of my bed she bids me rise,
   Says, 'Haste, and come to me!'

O Helen fair! O Helen chaste!
If I were with thee, I'd be blest,
Where thou lies low and taks thy rest,
   On fair Kirconnell lea.

I wish my grave were growing green,
A winding-sheet drawn owre my e'en,
And I in Helen's arms lying,
   On fair Kirconnell lea.

I wish I were where Helen lies!
Night and day on me she cries;
And I am weary of the skies,
    For her sake that died for me.

                        Anonymous.

THE QUEEN'S MARIE

MARIE HAMILTON's to the kirk gane,
    Wi' ribbons in her hair;
The King thought mair o' Marie Hamilton
    Than ony that were there.

Marie Hamilton's to the kirk gane
    Wi' ribbons on her breast;
The King thought mair o' Marie Hamilton
    Than he listen'd to the priest.

Marie Hamilton's to the kirk gane,
    Wi' gloves upon her hands;
The King thought mair o' Marie Hamilton
    Than the Queen and a' her lands.

She hadna been about the King's court
    A month but barely one,
Till she was beloved by a' King's court
    And the King the only man.

She hadna been about the King's court
    A month, but barely three,
Till frae the King's court Marie Hamilton,
    Marie Hamilton durstna be.

The King is to the Abbey gane,
    To pu' the Abbey tree,
To scale the babe frae Marie's heart
    But the thing it wadna be.

O she has row'd it in her apron,
    And set it on the sea –
'Gae sink ye or swim ye, bonny babe,
    Ye'se get nae mair o' me.'

Word is to the kitchen gane,
    And word is to the ha',
And word is to the noble room
    Amang the ladies a',

9

That Marie Hamilton's brought to bed,
  And the bonny babe's miss'd and awa'.

Scarcely had she lain down again,
  An scarcely fa'en asleep,
When up and started our gude Queen
  Just at her bed-feet;
Saying –'Marie Hamilton, where's your babe ?
  For I am sure I heard it greet.'

'O no, O no, my noble Queen!
  Think no sic thing to be;
'Twas but a stitch into my side,
  And sair it troubles me!'

'Get up, get up, Marie Hamilton:
  Get up and follow me;
For I am going to Edinburgh town,
  A rich wedding for to see.'

O slowly, slowly rase she up,
  And slowly put she on;
And slowly rade she out the way
  Wi' mony a weary groan.

The Queen was clad in scarlet,
  Her merry maids all in green;
And every town that they cam to,
  They took Marie for the Queen.

'Ride hooly, hooly, gentlemen,
  Ride hooly now wi' me!
For never, I am sure, a wearier burd
  Rade in your companie.'–

But little wist Marie Hamilton,
  When she rade on the brown,
That she was gaen to Edinburgh town
  And a' to be put down.

'Why weep ye so, ye burgess wives,
  Why look ye so on me ?
O I am going to Edinburgh town,
  A rich wedding to see.'

When she gaed up the tolbooth stairs,
  The corks frae her heeels did flee;
And lang or e'er she cam down again,
  She was condemn'd to die.

When she cam to the Netherbow port,
   She laugh'd loud laughters three;
But when she came to the gallows foot
   The tears blinded her e'e.

'Yestreen the Queen had four Maries.
   The night she'll hae but three;
There was Marie Seaton, and Marie Beaton,
   And Marie Carmichael, and me.

'O often have I dress'd my Queen
   And put gowd upon her hair;
But now I've gotten for my reward
   The gallows to be my share.

'Often have I dress'd my Queen
   And often made her bed;
But now I've gotten for my reward
   The gallows tree to tread.

'I charge ye all, ye mariners,
   When ye sail owre the faem,
Let neither my father nor mother get wit
   But that I'm coming hame.

'I charge ye all, ye mariners,
   That sail upon the sea,
That neither my father nor mother get wit
   The dog's death I'm to die.

'For if my father and mother got wit,
   And my bold brethren three,
O mickle wad be the gude red blude
   This day wad be spilt for me!

'O little did my mother ken,
   The day she cradled me
The lands I was to travel in
   Or the death I was to die!'

                 Anonymous.

THE SONG OF SONGS, WHICH IS SOLOMON'S

L E T him kiss me with the kisses of his mouth: for thy love is
better than wine.
Because of the savour of thy good ointments thy name is as
ointment poured forth, therefore do the virgins love thee.

Draw me, we will run after thee: the king hath brought me into his chambers: we will be glad and rejoice in thee, we will remember thy love more than wine: the upright love thee.

I am black, but comely, O ye daughters of Jerusalem, as the tents of Kedar, as the curtains of Solomon.

Look not upon me, because I am black, because the sun hath looked upon me: my mother's children were angry with me; they made me the keeper of the vineyards; but mine own vineyard have I not kept.

Tell me, O thou whom my soul loveth, where thou feedest, where thou makest thy flock to rest at noon: for why should I be as one that turneth aside by the flocks of thy companions?

If thou know not, O thou fairest among women, go thy way forth by the footsteps of the flock, and feed thy kids beside the shepherds' tents.

I have compared thee, O my love, to a company of horses in Pharaoh's chariots.

Thy cheeks are comely with rows of jewels, thy neck with chains of gold.

We will make thee borders of gold with studs of silver.

While the king sitteth at his table, my spikenard sendeth forth the smell thereof.

A bundle of myrrh is my wellbeloved unto me; he shall lie all night betwixt my breasts.

My beloved is unto me as a cluster of camphire in the vineyards of En-gedi.

Behold, thou art fair, my love; behold, thou art fair; thou hast doves' eyes.

Behold, thou art fair, my beloved, yea, pleasant; also our bed is green.

The beams of our house are cedar, and our rafters of fir.

II

I AM the rose of Sharon, and the lily of the valleys.

As the lily among thorns, so is my love among the daughters.

As the apple tree among the trees of the wood, so is my beloved among the sons. I sat down under his shadow with great delight, and his fruit was sweet to my taste.

He brought me to the banqueting house, and his banner over me was love.

Stay me with flagons, comfort me with apples; for I am sick of love.

His left hand is under my head, and his right hand doth embrace me.

I charge you, O ye daughters of Jerusalem, by the roes, and by the hinds of the field, that ye stir not up, nor awake my love, till he please.

The voice of my beloved! behold, he cometh leaping upon the mountains, skipping upon the hills.

My beloved is like a roe or a young hart: behold, he standeth behind our wall, he looketh forth at the windows, shewing himself through the lattice.

My beloved spake, and said unto me, Rise up, my love, my fair one, and come away.

For, lo, the winter is past, the rain is over and gone;

The flowers appear on the earth; the time of the singing of birds is come, and the voice of the turtle is heard in our land;

The fig tree putteth forth her green figs, and the vines with the tender grape give a good smell. Arise, my love, my fair one, and come away.

O my dove, that art in the clefts of the rock, in the secret places of the stairs, let me see thy countenance, let me hear thy voice; for sweet is thy voice, and thy countenance is comely.

Take us the foxes, the little foxes, that spoil the vines: for our vines have tender grapes.

My beloved is mine, and I am his: he feedeth among the lilies.

Until the day break and the shadows flee away, turn, my beloved, and be thou like a roe or a young hart upon the mountains of Bether.

III

BY night on my bed I sought him whom my soul loveth: I sought him but I found him not.

I will rise now, and go about the city in the streets, and in the broad ways I will seek him whom my soul loveth: I sought him, but I found him not.

The watchmen that go about the city found me: to whom I said, Saw ye him whom my soul loveth?

It was but a little that I passed from them, but I found him whom my soul loveth: I held him, and would not let him go, until I had brought him into my mother's house, and into the chamber of her that conceived me.

I charge you, O ye daughters of Jerusalem, by the roes, and by the hinds of the field, that ye stir not up, nor awake my love, till he please.

Who is this that cometh out of the wilderness like pillars of smoke, perfumed with myrrh and frankincense, with all powders of the merchant?

13

Behold his bed, which is Solomon's; threescore valiant men are about it, of the valiant of Israel.

They all hold swords, being expert in war: every man hath his sword upon his thigh because of fear in the night.

King Solomon made himself a chariot of the wood of Lebanon.

He made the pillars thereof of silver, the bottom thereof of gold, the covering of it of purple, the midst thereof being paved with love, for the daughters of Jerusalem.

Go forth, O ye daughters of Zion, and behold king Solomon with the crown wherewith his mother crowned him in the day of his espousals, and in the day of the gladness of his heart.

IV

BEHOLD, thou art fair, my love; behold, thou art fair; thou hast doves' eyes within thy locks: thy hair is as a flock of goats, that appear from mount Gilead.

Thy teeth are like a flock of sheep that are even shorn, which came up from the washing; whereof every one bear twins, and none is barren among them.

Thy lips are like a thread of scarlet, and thy speech is comely: thy temples are like a piece of a pomegranate within thy locks.

Thy neck is like the tower of David builded for an armoury, whereon there hang a thousand bucklers, all shields of mighty men.

Thy two breasts are like two young roes that are twins, which feed among the lilies.

Until the day break, and the shadows flee away, I will get me to the mountain of myrrh, and to the hill of frankincense.

Thou art all fair, my love; there is no spot in thee.

Come with me from Lebanon, my spouse, with me from Lebanon: look from the top of Amana, from the top of Shenir and Hermon, from the lion's dens, from the mountains of the leopards.

Thou hast ravished my heart, my sister, my spouse; thou hast ravished my heart with one of thine eyes, with one chain of thy neck.

How fair is thy love, my sister, my spouse! how much better is thy love than wine! and the smell of thine ointments than all spices!

Thy lips, O my spouse, drop as the honeycomb: honey and milk are under thy tongue; and the smell of thy garments is like the smell of Lebanon.

A garden inclosed is my sister, my spouse; a spring shut up, a fountain sealed.

Thy plants are an orchard of pomegranates, with pleasant fruits; camphire, with spikenard.

Spikenard and saffron; calamus and cinnamon, with all trees of frankincense; myrrh and aloes, with all the chief spices:

A fountain of gardens, a well of living waters, and streams from Lebanon.

Awake, O north wind; and come, thou south; blow upon my garden, that the spices thereof may flow out. Let my beloved come into his garden, and eat his pleasant fruits.

V

I AM come into my garden, my sister, my spouse: I have gathered my myrrh with my spice; I have eaten my honeycomb with my honey; I have drunk my wine with my milk; eat, O friends; drink, yea, drink abundantly, O beloved.

I sleep, but my heart waketh: it is the voice of my beloved that knocketh, saying, Open to me, my sister, my love, my dove, my undefiled: for my head is filled with dew, and my locks with the drops of the night.

I have put off my coat; how shall I put it on ? I have washed my feet; how shall I defile them ?

My beloved put in his hand by the hole of the door, and my bowels were moved for him.

I rose up to open to my beloved; and my hands dropped with myrrh, and my fingers with sweet-smelling myrrh, upon the handles of the lock.

I opened to my beloved; but my beloved had withdrawn himself, and was gone: my soul failed when he spake: I sought him, but I could not find him; I called him, but he gave me no answer.

The watchmen that went about the city found me, they smote me, they wounded me; the keepers of the walls took away my veil from me.

I charge you, O daughters of Jerusalem, if ye find my beloved, that ye tell him, that I am sick of love.

What is thy beloved more than another beloved, O thou fairest among women ? what is thy beloved more than another beloved, that thou dost so charge us ?

My beloved is white and ruddy, the chiefest among ten thousand.

His head is as the most fine gold, his locks are bushy and black as a raven.

His eyes are as the eyes of doves by the rivers of waters, washed with milk, and fitly set.

His cheeks are as a bed of spices, as sweet flowers: his lips like lilies, dropping sweet smelling myrrh.
His hands are as gold rings set with the beryl: his belly is as bright ivory overlaid with sapphires.
His legs are as pillars of marble, set upon sockets of fine gold: his countenance is as Lebanon, excellent as the cedars.
His mouth is most sweet: yea, he is altogether lovely. This is my beloved, and this is my friend, O daughters of Jerusalem.

VI

WHITHER is thy beloved gone, O thou fairest among women? whither is thy beloved turned aside? that we may seek him with thee.
My beloved is gone down into his garden, to the beds of spices, to feed in the gardens, and to gather lilies.
I am my beloved's, and my beloved is mine: he feedeth among the lilies.
Thou art beautiful, O my love, as Tirzah, comely as Jerusalem, terrible as an army with banners.
Turn away thine eyes from me, for they have overcome me: thy hair is as a flock of goats that appear from Gilead.
Thy teeth are as a flock of sheep which go up from the washing, whereof every one beareth twins, and there is not one barren among them.
As a piece of a pomegranate are thy temples within thy locks.
There are threescore queens, and fourscore concubines, and virgins without number.
My dove, my undefiled is but one; she is the only one of her mother, she is the choice one of her that bare her. The daughters saw her, and blessed her; yea, the queens and the concubines, and they praised her.
Who is she that looketh forth as the morning, fair as the moon, clear as the sun, and terrible as an army with banners?
I went down into the garden of nuts to see the fruits of the valley, and to see whether the vine flourished, and the pomegranates budded.
Or ever I was aware, my soul made me like the chariots of Ammi-nadib.
Return, return, O Shulamite; return, return, that we may look upon thee. What will ye see in the Shulamite? As it were the company of two armies.

VII

HOW beautiful are thy feet with shoes, O prince's daughter! the joints of thy thighs are like jewels, the work of the hands of a cunning workman.

Thy navel is like a round goblet, which wanteth not liquor: thy belly is like an heap of wheat set about with lilies.

Thy two breasts are like two young roes that are twins.

Thy neck is as a tower of ivory; thine eyes like the fishpools in Heshbon, by the gate of Bath-rabbim: thy nose is as the tower of Lebanon which looketh towards Damascus.

Thine head upon thee is like Carmel, and the hair of thine head like purple; the king is held in the galleries.

How fair and how pleasant art thou, O love, for delights!

This thy stature is like to a palm tree, and thy breasts to clusters of grapes.

I said, I will go up to the palm tree, I will take hold of the boughs thereof: now also thy breasts shall be as clusters of the vine, and the smell of thy nose like apples;

And the roof of thy mouth like the best wine for my beloved, that goeth down sweetly, causing the lips of those that are asleep to speak.

I am my beloved's, and his desire is toward me.

Come, my beloved, let us go forth into the field; let us lodge in the villages.

Let us get up early to the vineyards; let us see if the vine flourish, whether the tender grape appear, and the pomegranates bud forth: there will I give thee my loves.

The mandrakes give a smell, and at our gates are all manner of pleasant fruits, new and old, which I have laid up for thee, O my beloved.

VIII

O THAT thou wert as my brother, that sucked the breasts of my mother! when I should find thee without, I would kiss thee; yea, I should not be despised.

I would lead thee, and bring thee into my mother's house, who would instruct me: I would cause thee to drink of spiced wine of the juice of my pomegranate.

His left hand should be under my head, and his right hand should embrace me.

I charge you, O daughters of Jerusalem, that ye stir not up, nor awake my love, until he please.

Who is this that cometh up from the wilderness, leaning upon her beloved? I raised thee up under the apple tree: there thy mother brought thee forth: there she brought thee forth that bare thee.

Set me as a seal upon thine heart, as a seal upon thine arm: for love is strong as death; jealousy is cruel as the grave: the coals thereof are coals of fire, which hath a most vehement flame.

Many waters cannot quench love, neither can the floods drown it: if a man would give all the substance of his house for love, it would utterly be contemned.

We have a little sister, and she hath no breasts: what shall we do for our sister in the day when she shall be spoken for?

If she be a wall, we will build upon her a palace of silver: and if she be a door, we will inclose her with boards of cedar.

I am a wall, and my breasts like towers: then was I in his eyes as one that found favour.

Solomon had a vineyard at Baal-hamon; he let out the vineyard unto keepers; everyone for the fruit thereof was to bring a thousand pieces of silver.

My vineyard, which is mine, is before me: thou, O Solomon, must have a thousand, and those that keep the fruit thereof two hundred.

Thou that dwellest in the gardens, the companions hearken to thy voice: cause me to hear it.

Make haste, my beloved, and be thou like to a roe or to a young hart upon the mountains of spices.

The Authorised Version.

TOM OF BEDLAM'S SONG

FROM the hag and hungry goblin
That into rags would rend ye,
　　All the spirits that stand
　　By the naked man
In the book of moons, defend ye.

That of your five sound senses
You never be forsaken,
　　Nor wander from
　　Yourselves with Tom
Abroad to beg your bacon.

With a thought I took for Maudlin,
And a cruse of cockle pottage,
　　With a thing thus tall,
　　Sky bless you all,
I befell into this dotage.

I slept not since the Conquest,
Till then I never wakèd,
　　Till the roguish boy
　　Of love where I lay
Me found and stript me naked.

18

The moon's my constant mistress,
And the lonely owl my marrow;
  The flaming drake
  And the night-crow make
Me music to my sorrow.

I know more than Apollo,
For oft, when he lies sleeping,
  I see the stars
  At mortal wars
In the wounded welkin weeping,

The moon embrace her shepherd,
And the queen of love her warrior,
  While the first doth horn
  The star of morn,
And the next the heavenly farrier.

With an host of furious fancies,
Whereof I am commander,
  With a burning spear
  And a horse of air
To the wilderness I wander;

By a knight of ghosts and shadows
I summoned am to tourney
  Ten leagues beyond
  The wide world's end –
Methinks it is no journey.

Anonymous.

¶

L O V E not me for comely grace,
  For my pleasing eye or face,
Nor for any outward part,
No, nor for a constant heart:
  For these may fail or turn to ill,
    So thou and I shall sever:
Keep, therefore, a true woman's eye,
And love me still but know not why –
  So hast thou the same reason still
    To doat upon me ever!

Anonymous.

THE CONCLUSION

EVEN such is Time, that takes in trust
   Our youth, our joys, our all we have,
And pays us but with earth and dust;
   Who, in the dark and silent grave,
When we have wandered all our ways,
Shuts up the story of our days.
But from this earth, this grave, this dust,
My God shall raise me up, I trust.
Walter Raleigh.

A FAREWELL TO ARMS

MY golden locks Time hath to silver turn'd;
   O Time too swift, O swiftness never ceasing!
My youth 'gainst age, and age 'gainst time, hath spurn'd,
   But spurn'd in vain; youth waneth by increasing:
Beauty, strength, youth, are flowers but fading seen;
Duty, faith, love, are roots, and ever green.

My helmet now shall make an hive for bees,
   And lover's sonnets turn to holy psalms;
A man-at-arms must now serve on his knees,
   And feed on prayers, which are old age his alms:
But though from court to cottage I depart,
My saint is sure of my unspotted heart.

And when I saddest sit in homely cell,
   I'll teach my swains this carol for a song, –
'Blest be the hearts that wish my sovereign well,
   Curst be the souls that think her any wrong!'
Goddess, allow this aged man his right
To be your beadsman now that was your knight.
George Peele.

SONG

WHENAS the rye reach to the chin,
And chopcherry, chopcherry ripe within,
Strawberries swimming in the cream,
And schoolboys playing in the stream;
Then oh, then oh, then oh, my true Love said,
Till that time come again
She could not live a maid.
George Peele.

THE PARTING

S I N C E there's no help, come, let us kiss and part –
Nay, I have done, you get no more of me;
And I am glad, yea glad with all my heart,
That thus so cleanly I myself can free.
Shake hands for ever, cancel all our vows,
And, when we meet at any time again,
Be it not seen in either of our brows
That we one jot of former love retain.
Now at the last gasp of Love's latest breath,
When, his pulse failing, Passion speechless lies,
When Faith is kneeling by his bed of death,
And Innocence is closing up his eyes –
    Now if thou wouldst, when all have given him over,
    From death to life thou might'st him yet recover.
                        Michael Drayton.

SONNET

Y O U ' R E not alone when you are still alone;
O God! from you that I could private be!
Since you one were, I never since was one,
Since you in me, myself since out of me.
Transported from myself into your being,
Though either distant, present yet to either;
Senseless with too much joy, each other seeing
And only absent when we are together.
Give me my self, and take your self again!
Devise some means but how I may forsake you!
So much is mine that doth with you remain,
That taking what is mine, with me I take you.
    You do bewitch me! O that I could fly
    From my self you, or from your own self I!
                        Michael Drayton.

SONNET

W H E N first I ended, then I first began;
Then more I travelled further from my rest.
Where most I lost, there most of all I won;
Pinèd with hunger, rising from a feast.
Methinks I fly, yet want I legs to go,
Wise in conceit, in act a very sot,

Ravished with joy amidst a hell of woe,
What most I seem that surest am I not.
I build my hopes a world above the sky,
Yet with the mole I creep into the earth;
In plenty I am starved with penury,
And yet I surfeit in the greatest dearth.
  I have, I want, despair, and yet desire,
  Burned in a sea of ice, and drowned amidst a fire.
                                        Michael Drayton.

SONG

TAKE, O take those lips away
That so sweetly were forsworn,
And those eyes, the break of day,
Lights that do mislead the morn:
But my kisses bring again,
          Bring again –
Seals of love, but sealed in vain,
          Sealed in vain!

Hide, O hide those hills of snow,
  Which thy frozen bosom bears,
On whose tops the pinks that grow
  Are of those that April wears.
But first set my poor heart free
Bound in those icy chains by thee.
                                William Shakespeare.

LXV

SINCE brass nor stone, nor earth, nor boundless sea,
But sad mortality o'ersways their power,
How with this rage shall beauty hold a plea,
Whose action is no stronger than a flower?
O, how shall summer's honey breath hold out
Against the wreckful siege of battering days,
When rocks impregnable are not so stout,
Nor gates of steel so strong, but time decays?
O fearful meditation! where, alack,
Shall Time's best jewel from Time's quest lie hid?
Or what strong hand can hold his swift foot back?
Or who his spoil of beauty can forbid?
  O, none, unless this miracle have might,
  That in black ink my love may still shine bright.
                                William Shakespeare.

CXXVIII

H O W oft, when thou, my music, music play'st,
Upon that blessèd wood whose motion sounds
With thy sweet fingers, when thou gently sway'st
The wiry concord that mine ear confounds,
Do I envy those jacks that nimble leap
To kiss the tender inward of thy hand,
Whilst my poor lips, which should that harvest reap,
At the wood's boldness by thee blushing stand!
To be so tickled, they would change their state
And situation with those dancing chips,
O'er whom thy fingers walk with gentle gait,
Making dead wood more blest than living lips.
   Since saucy jacks so happy are in this,
     Give them thy fingers, me thy lips to kiss.
William Shakespeare.

CXXIX

T H E expense of spirit in a waste of shame
Is lust in action; and till action, lust
Is perjured, murderous, bloody, full of blame,
Savage, extreme, rude, cruel, not to trust,
Enjoy'd no sooner but despised straight,
Past reason hunted, and no sooner had
Past reason hated, as a swallow'd bait
On purpose laid to make the taker mad;
Mad in pursuit and in possession so;
Had, having, and in quest to have, extreme;
A bliss in proof, and proved, a very woe;
Before, a joy proposed; behind, a dream.
   All this the world well knows; yet none knows well
     To shun the heaven that leads men to this hell.
William Shakespeare.

CXXX

M Y mistress' eyes are nothing like the sun;
Coral is far more red than her lips red;
If snow be white, why then her breasts are dun;
If hairs be wires, black wires grow in her head.

23

I have seen roses damask'd, red and white,
But no such roses see I in her cheeks;
And in some perfumes is there more delight
Than in the breath that from my mistress reeks.
I love to hear her speak, yet well I know
That music hath a far more pleasing sound;
I grant I never saw a goddess go;
My mistress, when she walks, treads on the ground:
   And yet, by heaven, I think my love as rare
   As any she belied with false compare.

William Shakespeare.

CANZONET

SEE, see, mine own sweet jewel,
See what I have here for my darling:
A robin-redbreast and a starling.
These I give both, in hope to move thee –
And yet thou say'st I do not love thee.

Anonymous.

MADRIGAL

MY Love in her attire doth show her wit,
   It doth so well become her;
For every season she hath dressings fit,
   For winter, spring, and summer.

No beauty she doth miss
When all her robes are on;
But Beauty's self she is
When all her robes are gone.

Anonymous.

SPRING

SPRING, the sweet Spring, is the year's pleasant king;
Then blooms each thing, then maids dance in a ring,
Cold doth not sting, the pretty birds do sing –
   Cuckoo, jug-jug, pu-we, to-witta-woo!

The palm and may make country houses gay,
   Lambs frisk and play, the shepherds pipe all day,
And we hear aye birds tune this merry lay –
   Cuckoo, jug-jug, pu-we, to-witta-woo!

The fields breathe sweet, the daisies kiss our feet,
Young lovers meet, old wives a-sunning sit,
In every street these tunes our ears do greet –
  Cuckoo, jug-jug, pu-we, to-witta-woo!
    Spring, the sweet Spring!

Thomas Nashe.

IN TIME OF PESTILENCE

A D I E U, farewell earth's bliss!
This world uncertain is:
Fond are life's lustful joys,
Death proves them all but toys.
None from his darts can fly;
I am sick, I must die –
  Lord, have mercy on us!

Rich men, trust not in wealth,
Gold cannot buy you health;
Physic himself must fade;
All things to end are made;
The plague full swift goes by;
I am sick, I must die –
  Lord, have mercy on us!

Beauty is but a flower
Which wrinkles will devour;
Brightness falls from the air;
Queens have died young and fair;
Dust hath clos'd Helen's eye;
I am sick, I must die –
  Lord, have mercy on us!

Strength stoops unto the grave,
Worms feed on Hector brave;
Swords may not fight with fate;
Earth still holds ope her gate;
Come, Come! the bells do cry;
I am sick, I must die –
  Lord, have mercy on us!

Wit with his wantonness
Tasteth death's bitterness;
Hell's executioner
Hath no ears for to hear
What vain art can reply;
I am sick, I must die –
  Lord, have mercy on us!

Haste therefore each degree
To welcome destiny;
Heaven is our heritage,
Earth but a player's stage.
Mount we unto the sky;
I am sick, I must die –
   Lord, have mercy on us!

Thomas Nashe.

¶

K I N D are her answers,
  But her performance keeps no day.;
Breaks time, as dancers
  From their own music when they stray:
  All her free favours
And smooth words wing my hopes in vain.
O did ever voice so sweet but only feign?
  Can true love yield such delay,
  Converting joy to pain?

Lost is our freedom,
  When we submit to women so:
Why do we need them,
  When in their best they work our woe?
  There is no wisdom
Can alter ends, by Fate prefixed.
O why is the good of man with evil mixed?
  Never were days yet call'd two,
  But one night went betwixt.

Thomas Campion.

JACK AND JOAN

J A C K and Joan they think no ill,
But loving live, and merry still;
Do their week-days' work, and pray
Devoutly on the holy day:
Skip and trip it on the green,
And help to choose the Summer Queen;
Lash out, at a country feast,
Their silver penny with the best.

Well can they judge of nappy ale,
And tell at large a winter tale;
Climb up to the apple loft,
And turn the crabs till they be soft.

Tib is all the father's joy,
And little Tom the mother's boy
And all their pleasure is Content,
And care, to pay their yearly rent.

Joan can call by name her cows,
And deck her window with green boughs;
She can wreaths and tutties make,
And trim with plums a bridal cake.
Jack knows what brings gain or loss;
And his long flail can stoutly toss:
Makes the hedge, which others break;
And ever thinks what he doth speak.

Now, you courtly dames and knights,
That study only strange delights;
Though you scorn the homespun gray,
And revel in your rich array:
Though your tongues dissemble deep,
And can your heads from danger keep;
Yet, for all your pomp and train,
Securer lives the silly swain.

Thomas Campion.

THE TRIUMPH

S E E the Chariot at hand here of Love,
    Wherein my Lady rideth!
Each that draws is a swan or a dove,
    And well the car Love guideth.
As she goes, all hearts do duty
        Unto her beauty;
And enamour'd do wish, so they might
        But enjoy such a sight,
That they still were to run by her side,
Through swords, through seas, whither she would
                            [ride.
Do but look on her eyes, they do light
    All that Love's world compriseth!
Do but look on her hair, it is bright
    As Love's star when it riseth!
Do but mark, her forehead's smoother
        Than words that soothe her;
And from her arch'd brows such a grace
        Sheds itself through the face,
As alone there triumphs to the life
All the gain, all the good, of the elements' strife.

27

Have you seen but a bright lily grow
  Before rude hands have touch'd it?
Have you mark'd but the fall of the snow
  Before the soil hath smutch'd it?
Have you felt the wool of beaver,
    Or swan's down ever?
Or have smelt of the bud of the brier,
    Or the nard in the fire?
Or have tasted the bag of the bee?
O so white, O so soft, O so sweet is she!

Ben Jonson.

THE GOOD-MORROW

I WONDER, by my troth, what thou and I
Did, till we loved? were we not wean'd till then?
But suck'd on country pleasures, childishly?
Or snorted we in the Seven Sleepers' den?
'Twas so; but this, all pleasures fancies be;
If ever any beauty I did see,
Which I desired, and got, 'twas but a dream of thee.

And now good-morrow to our waking souls,
Which watch not one another out of fear;
For love all love of other sights controls,
And makes one little room an everywhere.
Let sea-discoverers to new worlds have gone;
Let maps to other worlds on worlds have shown;
Let us possess one world; each hath one, and is one.

My face in thine eye, thine in mine appears,
And true plain hearts do in the faces rest;
Where can we find two better hemispheres
Without sharp north, without declining west?
Whatever dies, was not mix'd equally;
If our two loves be one, or thou and I
Love so alike that none can slacken, none can die.

John Donne.

THE SUN RISING

BUSY old fool, unruly Sun,
  Why dost thou thus,
Through windows, and through curtains, call on us?
Must to thy motions lovers' seasons run?

Saucy pedantic wretch, go chide
    Late school-boys and sour prentices,
Go tell court-huntsmen that the king will ride,
    Call country ants to harvest offices;
Love, all alike, no season knows nor clime,
Nor hours, days, months, which are the rags of time.

    Thy beams so reverend and strong
        Why shouldst thou think?
I could eclipse and cloud them with a wink,
But that I would not lose her sight so long.
    If her eyes have not blinded thine,
    Look, and to-morrow late tell me,
    Whether both th' Indias of spice and mine
        Be where thou left'st them, or lie here with me.
Ask for those kings whom thou saw'st yesterday,
And thou shalt hear, 'All here in one bed lay.'

    She's all states, and all princes I;
        Nothing else is;
Princes do but play us; compared to this,
All honour's mimic, all wealth alchemy.
    Thou, Sun, art half as happy as we,
    In that the world's contracted thus;
    Thine age asks ease, and since thy duties be
        To warm the world, that's done in warming us.
Shine here to us, and thou art everywhere;
This bed thy centre is, these walls thy sphere.

                                        John Donne.

LOVE'S DEITY

I LONG to talk with some old lover's ghost,
    Who died before the god of love was born.
I cannot think that he, who then loved most,
    Sunk so low as to love one which did scorn.
But since this god produced a destiny,
And that vice-nature, custom, lets it be,
    I must love her that loves not me.

Sure, they which made him god, meant not so much,
    Nor he in his young godhead practised it.
But when an even flame two hearts did touch,
    His office was indulgently to fit
Actives to passives. Correspondency
Only his subject was; it cannot be
    Love, till I love her, who loves me.

But every modern god will now extend
   His vast prerogative as far as Jove.
To rage, to lust, to write to, to commend,
   All is the purlieu of the god of love.
O! were we waken'd by this tyranny
To ungod this child again, it could not be
   I should love her, who loves not me.

Rebel and atheist too, why murmur I,
   As though I felt the worst that love could do?
Love might make me leave loving, or might try
   A deeper plague, to make her love me too;
Which, since she loves before, I'm loth to see.
Falsehood is worse than hate; and that must be,
   If she whom I love, should love me.

                            John Donne.

THE DREAM

D E A R love, for nothing less than thee
Would I have broke this happy dream;
     It was a theme
For reason, much too strong for fantasy.
Therefore thou waked'st me wisely; yet
My dream thou brokest not, but continued'st it.
Thou art so true that thoughts of thee suffice
To make dreams truths, and fables histories;
Enter these arms, for since thou thought'st it best,
Not to dream all my dream, let's act the rest.

As lightning, or a taper's light,
Thine eyes, and not thy noise waked me;
     Yet I thought thee
– For thou lov'st truth – an angel, at first sight;
But when I saw thou saw'st my heart,
And knew'st my thoughts beyond an angel's art,
When thou knew'st what I dreamt, when thou knew'st
Excess of joy would wake me, and camest then, [when
I must confess, it could not choose but be
Profane, to think thee any thing but thee.

Coming and staying show'd thee, thee,
But rising makes me doubt, that now
     Thou art not thou.

That love is weak where fear's as strong as he;
'Tis not all spirit, pure and brave,
If mixture it of fear, shame, honour have;
Perchance as torches, which must ready be,
Men light and put out, so thou deal'st with me;
Thou cam'st to kindle, go'st to come; then I
Will dream that hope again, but else would die.

John Donne.

LOVE'S GROWTH

I SCARCE believe my love to be so pure
    As I had thought it was,
    Because it doth endure
Vicissitude, and season, as the grass;
Methinks I lied all winter, when I swore
My love was infinite, if spring make it more.

But if this medicine, love, which cures all sorrow
    With more, not only be no quintessence,
    But mix'd of all stuffs, vexing soul, or sense,
And of the sun his active vigour borrow,
Love's not so pure and abstract as they use
To say, which have no mistress but their Muse;
But as all else, being elemented too,
Love sometimes would contemplate, sometimes do.

And yet no greater, but more eminent,
    Love by the spring is grown;
    As in the firmament
Stars by the sun are not enlarged, but shown,
Gentle love deeds, as blossoms on a bough,
From love's awaken'd root do bud out now.

If, as in water stirr'd more circles be
    Produced by one, love such additions take,
    Those like so many spheres but one heaven make,
For they are all concentric unto thee;
And though each spring do add to love new heat,
As princes do in times of action get
New taxes, and remit them not in peace,
No winter shall abate this spring's increase.

John Donne.

THE ECSTACY

WHERE, like a pillow on a bed,
  A pregnant bank swell'd up, to rest
The violet's reclining head,
  Sat we two, one another's best.

Our hands were firmly cémented
  By a fast balm, which thence did spring;
Our eye-beams twisted, and did thread
  Our eyes upon one double string.

So to'entergraft our hands, as yet
  Was all the means to make us one;
And pictures in our eyes to get
  Was all our propagation.

As, 'twixt two equal armies, Fate
  Suspends uncertain victory,
Our souls – which to advance their state,
  Were gone out – hung 'twixt her and me.

And whilst our souls negotiate there,
  We like sepulchral statues lay;
All day, the same our postures were,
  And we said nothing, all the day.

If any, so by love refined,
  That he soul's language understood,
And by good love were grown all mind,
  Within convenient distance stood,

He – though he knew not which soul spake,
  Because both meant, both spoke the same –
Might thence a new concoction take,
  And part far purer than he came.

This ecstasy doth unperplex
  (We said) and tell us what we love;
We see by this, it was not sex;
  We see, we saw not, what did move:

But as all several souls contain
  Mixture of things they know not what,
Love these mix'd souls doth mix again,
  And makes both one, each this and that.

A single violet transplant,
   The strength, the colour, and the size –
All which before was poor and scant –
   Redoubles still, and multiplies.

When love with one another so
   Interinanimates two souls,
That abler soul, which thence doth flow,
   Defects of loneliness controls.

We then, who are this new soul, know,
   Of what we are composed and made,
For th'atomies of which we grow
   Are souls, whom no change can invade.

But, O alas! so long, so far,
   Our bodies why do we forbear?
They are ours, though they're not we; we are
   Th'intelligences, they the spheres.

We owe them thanks, because they thus
   Did us, to us, at first convey,
Yielded their forces, sense, to us,
   Nor are dross to us, but allay.

On man heaven's influence works not so,
   But that it first imprints the air;
So soul into the soul may flow,
   Though it to body first repair.

As our blood labours to beget
   Spirits, as like souls as it can;
Because such fingers need to knit
   That subtle knot, which makes us man;

So must pure lovers' souls descend
   To affections, and to faculties,
Which sense may reach and apprehend,
   Else a great prince in prison lies.

To our bodies turn we then, that so
   Weak men on love reveal'd may look;
Love's mysteries in souls do grow,
   But yet the body is his book.

And if some lover, such as we,
   Have heard this dialogue of one,
Let him still mark us, he shall see
   Small change when we're to bodies gone.
                          John Donne.

33

DIVINE POEM

BATTER my heart, three personed God; for you
As yet but knock, breathe, shine, and seek to mend.
That I may rise and stand, o'erthrow me and bend
Your force to break, blow, burn and make me new.
I, like an usurped town, to another due,
Labour to admit you, but Oh, to no end;
Reason, your viceroy in me, me should defend,
But is captived and proves weak or untrue.
Yet dearly I love you and would be loved fain,
But am betrothed unto your enemy:
Divorce me, untie or break that knot again,
Take me to you, imprison me, for I
Except you enthrall me, never shall be free,
Nor ever chaste, except you ravish me.

John Donne.

OBERON'S FEAST

SHAPCOT! to thee the Fairy State
I with discretion, dedicate.
Because thou prizest things that are
Curious and unfamiliar,
Take first the feast; these dishes gone,
We'll see the Fairy Court anon.
A little mushroom-table spread,
After short prayers, they set on bread;
A moon-parch'd grain of purest wheat,
With some small glittering grit, to eat
His choice bits with; then in a trice
They make a feast less great than nice.
But all this while his eye is serv'd,
We must not think his ear was starv'd
But that there was in place to stir
His spleen, the chirring Grasshopper,
The merry Cricket, puling Fly,
The piping Gnat for minstrelsy.
And now, we must imagine first,
The Elves present to quench his thirst
A pure seed-pearl of infant dew,
Brought and besweetened in a blue
And pregnant violet; which done,
His kitling eyes begin to run
Quite through the table, where he spies
The horns of papery Butterflies:

Of which he eats, and tastes a little
Of that we call the cuckoo's spittle.
A little fuzz-ball pudding stands
By, yet not blessed by his hands,
That was too coarse; but then forthwith
He ventures boldly on the pith
Of sugared rush, and eats the sag
And well bestrutted Bee's sweet bag:
Gladding his palate with some store
Of Emit's eggs; what would he more?
But beards of Mice, a Newt's stew'd thigh,
A roasted Earwig, and a Fly;
With the red-capp'd Worm, that's shut
Within the concave of a nut,
Brown as his tooth. A little Moth,
Late fattened in a piece of cloth:
With wither'd cherries; Mandrake's ears;
Mole's eyes; to these, the slain Stag's tears;
The unctuous dewlaps of a Snail;
The broke heart of a Nightingale
O'ercome in music; with a wine,
Ne'er ravish'd from the flattering vine,
But gently press'd from the soft side
Of the most sweet and dainty bride,
Brought in a dainty daisy, which
He fully quaffs up to bewitch
His blood to height; this done, commended
Grace by his Priest: *The feast is ended.*
Robert Herrick.

THE ARGUMENT OF HIS BOOK

I SING of Brooks, of Blossoms, Birds, and Bowers;
Of April, May, of June, and July-Flowers.
I sing of May-poles, Hock-carts, Wassails, Wakes,
Of Bridegrooms, Brides, and of their Bridal cakes.
I write of Youth, of Love, and have access
By these, to sing of cleanly Wantonness.
I sing of Dews, of Rains, and piece by piece
Of Balme, of Oil, of Spice, and Amber-Greece.
I sing of Time's trans-shifting; and I write
How Roses first came red, and Lilies white.
I write of Groves, of Twilights, and I sing
The Court of Mab, and of the Fairy-King.
I write of Hell; I sing (and ever shall)
Of Heaven, and hope to have it after all.
Robert Herrick.

EXEQUY ON HIS WIFE

ACCEPT, thou shrine of my dead saint,
Instead of dirges this complaint;
And for sweet flowers to crown thy hearse
Receive a strew of weeping verse
From thy grieved Friend, whom thou might'st see
Quite melted into tears for thee.
   Dear loss! since thy untimely fate,
My task hath been to meditate
On thee, on thee! Thou art the book,
The library whereon I look,
Tho' almost blind. For thee, loved clay,
I languish out, not live, the day,
Using no other exercise
But what I practise with mine eyes:
By which wet glasses I find out
How lazily time creeps about
To one that mourns: this, only this,
My exercise and business is:
So I compute the weary hours,
With sighs dissolved into showers.
No wonder if my time go thus
Backward and most preposterous;
Thou hast benighted me; thy set
This eve of blackness did beget,
Who wast my day (tho' overcast
Before thou hadst thy noontide past):
And I remember must in tears
Thou scarce hadst seen so many years
As day tells hours. By thy clear sun
My love and fortune first did run;
But thou wilt never more appear
Folded within my hemisphere,
Since both thy light and motion,
Like a fled star, is fall'n and gone,
And 'twixt me and my soul's dear wish
The earth now interposed is,
Which such a strange eclipse doth make
As ne'er was read in Almanack.
   I could allow thee for a time
To darken me and my sad clime;
Were it a month, a year, or ten,
I would thy exile live till then,
And all that space my mirth adjourn –
So thou wouldst promise to return,

And putting off thy ashy shroud
At length disperse this sorrow's cloud.
   But woe is me! the longest date
Too narrow is to calculate
These empty hopes: never shall I
Be so much blest as to descry
A glimpse of thee, till that day come
Which shall the earth to cinders doom,
And a fierce fever must calcine
The body of this world – like thine,
My little world! That fit of fire
Once off, our bodies shall aspire
To our soul's bliss: then we shall rise
And view ourselves with clearer eyes
In that calm region where no night
Can hide us from each other's sight.
   Meantime thou hast her, earth: much good
May my harm do thee! Since it stood
With Heaven's will I might not call
Her longer mine, I give thee all
My short-lived right and interest
In her whom living I loved best:
With a most free and bounteous grief
I give thee what I could not keep.
Be kind to her, and prithee look
Thou write into thy Doomsday book
Each parcel of this rarity
Which in thy casket shrin'd doth lie:
See that thou make thy reck'ning straight,
And yield her back again by weight;
For thou must audit on thy trust
Each grain and atom of this dust
As thou wilt answer Him that lent –
Not gave – thee my dear monument.
So close the ground, and 'bout her shade
Black curtains draw; my bride is laid.
   Sleep on, my Love, in thy cold bed
Never to be disquieted!
My last good night! Thou wilt not wake
Till I thy fate shall overtake:
Till age, or grief, or sickness must
Marry my body to that dust
It so much loves; and fill the room
My heart keeps empty in thy tomb.
Stay for me there: I will not fail
To meet thee in that hollow vale,
And think not much of my delay:

37

I am already on the way,
And follow thee with all the speed
Desire can make, or sorrows breed.
Each minute is a short degree
And every hour a step towards thee.
At night when I betake to rest,
Next morn I rise nearer my West
Of life, almost by eight hours' sail,
Than when sleep breath'd his drowsy gale.
  Thus from the Sun my bottom steers
And my day's compass downward bears:
Nor labour I to stem the tide
Through which to thee I swiftly glide.
  'Tis true – with shame and grief I yield –
Thou, like the van, first took'st the field;
And gotten hast the victory
In thus adventuring to die
Before me, whose more years might crave
A just precedence in the grave.
But hark! my pulse, like a soft drum,
Beats my approach, tells thee I come;
And slow howe'er my marches be
I shall at last sit down by thee.
The thought of this bids me go on
And wait my dissolution
With hope and comfort. Dear – forgive
The crime – I am content to live
Divided, with but half a heart,
Till we shall meet and never part.

Henry King.

THE SURRENDER

M Y once dear Love; hapless that I no more
Must call thee so: the rich affections store
That fed our hopes, lies now exhaust and spent,
Like sums of treasure unto bankrupts lent.
  We that did nothing study but the way
To love each other, with which thoughts the day
Rose with delight to us, and with them set,
Must learn the hateful art, how to forget.
  We that did nothing wish that Heav'n could give
Beyond ourselves, nor did desire to live
Beyond that wish, all these now cancel must
As if not writ in faith, but words and dust.

Yet witness those clear vows which lovers make,
Witness the chaste desires that never break
Into unruly heats; witness that breast
Which in thy bosom anchor'd his whole rest,
'Tis no default in us, I dare acquit
Thy maiden faith, thy purpose fair and white
As thy pure self. Cross planets did envy
Us to each other, and Heaven did untie
Faster than vows could bind. O that the stars,
When lovers meet, should stand oppos'd in wars!
    Since then some higher Destinies command,
Let us not strive, nor labour to withstand
What is past help. The longest date of grief
Can never yield a hope of our relief;
And though we waste ourselves in moist laments,
Tears may drown us, but not our discontents.
    Fold back our arms, take home our fruitless loves,
That must new fortunes try, like turtle doves
Dislodgèd from their haunts. We must in tears
Unwind a love knit up in many years.
In this last kiss I here surrender thee
Back to thy self, so thou again art free.
Thou in another, sad as that, resend
The truest heart that lover ere did lend.
    Now turn from each. So fare our sever'd hearts
As the divorc'd soul from her body parts.
                                        Henry King.

THE PULLEY

WHEN God at first made man,
Having a glass of blessings standing by –
Let us (said he) pour on him all we can;
Let the world's riches, which dispersed lie,
    Contract into a span.

So strength first made a way,
Then beauty flow'd, then wisdom, honour, pleasure:
When almost all was out, God made a stay,
Perceiving that, alone of all his treasure,
    Rest in the bottom lay.

For if I should (said he)
Bestow this jewel also on my creature,
He would adore my gifts instead of me,
And rest in nature, not the God of nature:
    So both should losers be.

B   39

Yet let him keep the rest,
But keep them with repining restlessness;
Let him be rich and weary, that at least,
If goodness lead him not, yet weariness
    May toss him to my breast.

George Herbert.

DISCIPLINE

T H R O W away thy rod,
  Throw away thy wrath;
    O my God,
Take the gentle path.

For my heart's desire
  Unto thine is bent;
    I aspire
To a full consent.

Not a word or look
  I affect to own,
    But by book,
And thy book alone.

Though I fail, I weep;
  Though I halt in pace,
    Yet I creep
To the throne of grace.

Then let wrath remove,
  Love will do the deed;
    For with love
Stony hearts will bleed.

Love is swift of foot;
  Love's a man of war,
    And can shoot,
And can hit from far.

Who can 'scape his bow?
  That which wrought on thee,
    Brought thee low,
Needs must work on me.

Throw away thy rod:
Though man frailties hath,
        Thou art God;
Throw away thy wrath.
                    George Herbert.

DECAY

S W E E T were the days, when thou didst lodge with Lot,
Struggle with Jacob, sit with Gideon,
Advise with Abraham, when thy power could not
Encounter Moses' strong complaints and moan.
    Thy words were then, *Let me alone.*

One might have sought and found thee presently
At some fair oak, or bush, or cave, or well:
Is my God this way? No, they would reply:
He is to Sinai gone, as we heard tell:
    List, ye may hear great Aaron's bell.

But now thou dost thyself immure and close
In some one corner of a feeble heart:
Where yet both Sin and Satan, thy old foes,
Do pinch and straiten thee, and use much art
    To gain thy thirds and little part.

I see the world grows old, whenas the heat
Of thy great love once spread, as in an urn,
Doth closet up itself, and still retreat,
Cold sin still forcing it, till it return,
    And calling Justice, all things burn.
                    George Herbert.

REDEMPTION

H A V I N G been Tenant long to a rich Lord,
    Not thriving, I resolvèd to be bold,
    And make a suit unto him to afford
A new small-rented lease, and cancel th'old.

In Heaven at his manor I him sought,
    They told me there, that he was lately gone
    About some land, which he had dearly bought
Long since on Earth, to take possession.

I straight return'd, and knowing his great birth,
  Sought him accordingly in great resorts,
  In cities, theatres, gardens, parks, and courts:
At length I heard a ragged noise and mirth
  Of thieves and murderers. There I him espied,
  Who straight, *Your suit is granted*, said, and died.
                                        George Herbert.

SONG

A S K me no more where Jove bestows,
When June is past, the fading rose;
For in your beauty's orient deep
These flowers, as in their causes, sleep.

Ask me no more whither do stray
The golden atoms of the day;
For in pure love heaven did prepare
Those powders to enrich your hair.

Ask me no more whither doth haste
The nightingale when May is past;
For in your sweet dividing throat
She winters and keeps warm her note.

Ask me no more where those stars 'light
That downwards fall in dead of night;
For in your eyes they sit, and there
Fixèd become as in their sphere.

Ask me no more if east or west
The phœnix builds her spicy nest;
For unto you at last she flies,
And in your fragrant bosom dies.
                                        Thomas Carew.

A DEVOUT LOVER

I H A V E a mistress, for perfections rare
In every eye, but in my thoughts most fair.
Like tapers on the altar shine her eyes;
Her breath is the perfume of sacrifice;
And whersoe'er my fancy would begin,
Still her perfection lets religion in.
We sit and talk, and kiss away the hours
As chastely as the morning dews kiss flowers:
I touch her, like my beads, with devout care,
And come unto my courtship as my prayer.
                                        Thomas Randolph.

UPON A WEDDING

I TELL thee, Dick, where I have been,
Where I the rarest things have seen;
    O, things without compare!
Such sights again cannot be found
In any place on English ground,
    Be it at wake or fair.

At Charing Cross, hard by the way,
Where we, thou know'st, do sell our hay,
    There is a house with stairs;
And there did I see coming down
Such folk as are not in our town,
    Forty at least, in pairs.

Amongst the rest, one pest'lent fine
(His beard no bigger though than thine)
    Walked on before the rest:
Our landlord looks like nothing to him:
The King (God bless him) 'twould undo him,
    Should he go still so drest.

At Course-a-Park, without all doubt,
He should have first been taken out
    By all the maids i' th' town:
Though lusty Roger there had been,
Or little George upon the Green,
    Or Vincent of the Crown.

But wot you what? the youth was going
To make an end of all his wooing;
    The parson for him stay'd:
Yet by his leave, for all his haste,
He did not so much wish all past,
    Perchance, as did the maid.

The maid (and thereby hangs a tale),
For such a maid no Whitsun-ale
    Could ever yet produce:
No grape, that's kindly ripe, could be
So round, so plump, so soft as she,
    Nor half so full of juice.

Her finger was so small, the ring
Would not stay on, which they did bring,
    It was too wide a peck:
And to say truth (for out it must)
It looked like the great collar, just,
    About our young colt's neck.

Her feet beneath her petticoat,
Like little mice, stole in and out,
    As if they fear'd the light:
But O she dances such a way!
No sun upon an Easter-day
    Is half so fine a sight.

He would have kissed her once or twice,
But she would not, she was so nice,
    She would not do't in sight,
And then she looked as who should say:
I will do what I list to-day,
    And you shall do't at night.

Her cheeks so rare a white was on,
No daisy makes comparison,
    Who sees them is undone;
For streaks of red were mingled there,
Such as are on a Catherine pear,
    The side that's next the sun.

Her lips were red, and one was thin,
Compar'd to that was next her chin
    (Some bee had stung it newly);
But, Dick, her eyes so guard her face;
I durst no more upon them gaze
    Than on the sun in July.

Her mouth so small, when she does speak,
Thou'dst swear her teeth her words did break,
    That they might passage get;
But she so handled still the matter,
They came as good as ours, or better,
    And are not spent a whit.

If wishing should be any sin,
The parson himself had guilty been,
    She look'd that day so purely;
And did the youth so oft the feat
At night, as some did in conceit,
    It would have spoiled him surely.

Just in the nick the cook knocked thrice,
And all the waiters in a trice
　　His summons did obey;
Each serving-man, with dish in hand,
Marched boldly up, like our trained band,
　　Presented, and away.

When all the meat was on the table,
What man of knife or teeth was able
　　To stay to be intreated?
And this the very reason was,
Before the parson could say grace,
　　The company was seated.

The business of the kitchen's great,
For it is fit that men should eat,
　　Nor was it there denied –
Passion o' me, how I run on!
There's that that would be thought upon,
　　I trow, besides the bride.

Now hats fly off, and youths carouse;
Healths first go round, and then the house,
　　The bride's came thick and thick:
And when 'twas nam'd another's health,
Perhaps he made it hers by stealth;
　　And who could help it, Dick?

On the sudden up they rise and dance;
Then sit again and sigh, and glance:
　　Then dance again and kiss:
Thus several ways the time did pass,
Whilst ev'ry woman wished her place,
　　And every man wished his.

By this time all were stol'n aside
To counsel and undress the bride;
　　But that he must not know:
But yet 'twas thought he guess'd her mind,
And did not mean to stay behind
　　Above an hour or so.

When in he came, Dick, there she lay
Like new-fall'n snow melting away
　　('Twas time, I trow, to part)
Kisses were now the only stay,
Which soon she gave, as who would say,
　　God b' w' ye, with all my heart.

But, just as Heaven would have, to cross it,
In came the bridesmaids with the posset:
   The bridegroom ate in spite;
For had he left the women to 't,
It would have cost two hours to do 't,
   Which were too much that night.

At length the candle's out, and now
All that they had not done they do.
   What that is, who can tell?
But I believe it was no more
Than thou and I have done before
   With Bridget and with Nell.

                John Suckling.

DRINKING

T H E thirsty earth soaks up the rain,
And drinks and gapes for drink again;
The plants suck in the earth, and are
With constant drinking fresh and fair;
The sea itself (which one would think
Should have but little need of drink)
Drinks twice ten thousand rivers up,
So fill'd that they o'erflow the cup.
The busy Sun (and one would guess
By's drunken fiery face no less)
Drinks up the sea, and when he's done,
The Moon and Stars drink up the Sun:
They drink and dance by their own light,
They drink and revel all the night:
Nothing in Nature's sober found,
But an eternal health goes round.
Fill up the bowl, then, fill it high,
Fill all the glasses there – for why
Should every creature drink but I?
Why, man of morals, tell me why?

                Abraham Cowley.

LOVE

I ' L L sing of Heroes, and of Kings;
In mighty numbers, mighty things,
Begin, my Muse; but lo, the strings
To my great song rebellious prove;
The strings will sound of nought but Love.

I broke them all, and put on new;
'Tis this or nothing sure will do.
These sure (said I) will me obey;
These, sure, heroic notes will play.
Straight I began with thund'ring Jove,
And all th' immortal Powers, but Love.
Love smil'd, and from my enfeebled lyre
Came gentle airs, such as inspire
Melting love, and soft desire.
Farewell then Heroes, farewell Kings,
And mighty numbers, mighty things;
Love tunes my heart just to my strings.
                                   Abraham Cowley.

§

*And she washed his feet with her tears, and
wiped them with the hairs of her head.*

THE proud Egyptian Queen, her Roman guest,
(T'express her love in height of state, and pleasure)
     With Pearl dissolv'd in Gold, did feast –
          Both Food, and Treasure.

And now (dear Lord!) thy Lover, on the fair
And silver tables of thy feet, behold!
     Pearl in her tears, and in her hair
          Offers thee gold.
                                   Edward Sherburne.

TO HIS COY MISTRESS

HAD we but world enough, and time,
This coyness, lady, were no crime.
We would sit down, and think which way
To walk, and pass our long love's day.
Thou by the Indian Ganges' side
Should'st rubies find: I by the tide
Of Humber would complain. I would
Love you ten years before the Flood,
And you should, if you please, refuse
Till the conversion of the Jews.
My vegetable love should grow
Vaster than empires, and more slow.
An hundred years should go to praise
Thine eyes, and on thy forehead gaze:

47

Two hundred to adore each breast:
But thirty thousand to the rest;
An age at least to every part,
And the last age should shew your heart.
For, lady, you deserve this state,
Nor would I love at lower rate.
   But at my back I always hear
Time's wingèd chariot hurrying near:
And yonder all before us lie
Deserts of vast eternity.
Thy beauty shall no more be found;
Nor, in thy marble vault, shall sound
My echoing song; then worms shall try
That long-preserv'd virginity:
And your quaint honour turn to dust,
And into ashes all my lust.
The grave's a fine and private place,
But none, I think, do there embrace.
   Now, therefore, while the youthful hue
Sits on thy skin like morning dew,
And while thy willing soul transpires
At every pore with instant fires,
Now let us sport us while we may;
And now, like amorous birds of prey,
Rather at once our Time devour,
Than languish in his slow-chapt power.
Let us roll all our strength and all
Our sweetness up into one ball,
And tear our pleasures with rough strife
Thorough the iron gates of life.
Thus, though we cannot make our Sun
Stand still, yet we will make him run.

Andrew Marvell.

THE FAIR SINGER

T O make a final conquest of all me,
Love did compose so sweet an enemy,
In whom both beauties to my death agree,
Joining themselves in fatal harmony;
That, while she with her eyes my heart does bind,
She with her voice might captivate my mind.

I could have fled from one but singly fair:
My disentangled soul itself might save,
Breaking the curlèd trammels of her hair.

But how should I avoid to be her slave,
Whose subtle art invisibly can wreathe
My fetters of the very air I breathe?

It had been easy fighting in some plain,
Where victory might hang in equal choice,
But all resistance against her is vain,
Who has the advantage both of eyes and voice;
And all my forces needs must be undone,
She having gainèd both the wind and sun.
                              Andrew Marvell.

THE GARDEN

H O W vainly men themselves amaze
To win the palm, the oak, or bays;
And their incessant labours see
Crowned from some single herb, or tree,
Whose short and narrow-verged shade
Does prudently their toils upbraid;
While all flow'rs and all trees do close
To weave the garlands of repose.

Fair Quiet, have I found thee here,
And Innocence, thy sister dear?
Mistaken long, I sought you then
In busy companies of men.
Your sacred plants, if here below,
Only among the plants will grow;
Society is all but rude
To this delicious solitude.

No white nor red was ever seen
So amorous as this lovely green.
Fond lovers, cruel as their flame,
Cut in these trees their mistress' name:
Little, alas! they know or heed
How far these beauties hers exceed!
Fair trees! wheres'e'er your barks I wound
No name shall but your own be found.

When we have run our passion's heat,
Love hither makes his best retreat.
The Gods, that mortal beauty chase,
Still in a tree did end their race;
Apollo hunted Daphne so,
Only that she might laurel grow;

And Pan did after Syrinx speed,
Not as a nymph, but for a reed.

What wondrous life is this I lead!
Ripe apples drop about my head;
The luscious clusters of the vine
Upon my mouth do crush their wine;
The nectaren, and curious peach,
Into my hands themselves do reach;
Stumbling on melons, as I pass,
Insnared with flowers, I fall on grass.

Meanwhile, the mind, from pleasure less,
Withdraws into its happiness:
The mind, that ocean where each kind
Does straight its own resemblance find;
Yet it creates, transcending these,
Far other worlds, and other seas;
Annihilating all that's made
To a green thought in a green shade.

Here at the fountain's sliding foot,
Or at some fruit-tree's mossy root,
Casting the body's vest aside,
My soul into the boughs does glide:
There like a bird it sits, and sings,
Then whets and claps its silver wings;
And, till prepared for longer flight,
Waves in its plumes the various light.

Such was that happy garden-state,
While man there walked without a mate:
After a place so pure and sweet,
What other help could yet be meet!
But 'twas beyond a mortal's share
To wander solitary there:
Two paradises 'twere in one,
To live in paradise alone.

How well the skilful gardener drew
Of flowers, and herbs, this dial new;
Where, from above, the milder sun
Does through a fragrant zodiac run;
And, as it works, the industrious bee
Computes its time as well as we.
How could such sweet and wholesome hours
Be reckon'd but with herbs and flowers!

Andrew Marvell.

MOURNING

Y O U, that decipher out the fate
Of human offsprings from the skies,
What mean these infants which of late
Spring from the stars of *Chlora's* eyes?

Her eyes confus'd, and doubled o'er,
With tears suspended ere they flow,
Seem bending upwards, to restore
To Heaven, whence it came, their woe;

When, moulding of the watery spheres,
Slow drops untie themselves away;
As if she, with those precious tears,
Would strow the ground where *Strephon* lay.

Yet some affirm, pretending art,
Her eyes have so her bosom drown'd,
Only to soften near her heart
A place to fix another wound.

And, while vain pomp does her restrain
Within her solitary bower,
She courts herself in am'rous rain;
Herself both Danäe and the shower.

Nay others, bolder, hence esteem
Joy now so much her master grown,
That whatsoever does but seem
Like grief, is from her windows thrown.

Nor that she pays, while she survives,
To her dead love this tribute due;
But casts abroad these donatives,
At the installing of a new.

How wide they dream! The Indian slaves
That sink for pearl through seas profound,
Would find her tears yet deeper waves
And not of one the bottom sound.

I yet my silent judgement keep,
Disputing not what they believe:
But sure as oft as women weep,
It is to be suppos'd they grieve.

Andrew Marvell.

THE DEFINITION OF LOVE

M Y Love is of a birth as rare
As 'tis for object strange and high:
It was begotten by Despair
Upon Impossibility.

Magnanimous Despair alone
Could show me so divine a thing,
Where feeble Hope could ne'er have flown
But vainly flapt its tinsel wing.

And yet I quickly might arrive
Where my extended soul is fixt,
But Fate does iron wedges drive,
And always crowds itself betwixt.

For Fate with jealous eye does see
Two perfect loves; nor lets them close:
Their union would her ruin be,
And her tyrannic power depose.

And therefore her decrees of steel
Us as the distant poles have placed,
(Though love's whole world on us doth wheel)
Not by themselves to be embraced

Unless the giddy Heaven fall,
And earth some new convulsion tear;
And, us to join, the world should all
Be cramped into a *planisphere*.

As lines, so loves *oblique* may well
Themselves in every angle greet:
But ours so truly *parallel*,
Though infinite can never meet.

Therefore the love which us doth bind,
But Fate so enviously debars,
Is the conjunction of the mind,
And opposition of the stars.

Andrew Marvell.

THE REVIVAL

UNFOLD, unfold! take in his light,
Who makes thy cares more short than night.
The joys which with his day-star rise
He deals to all but drowsy eyes;
And (what the men of this world miss)
Some drops and dews of future bliss.

Hark, how his winds have chang'd their note,
And with warm whispers call thee out.
The frosts are past, the storms are gone,
And backward life at last comes on.
The lofty groves in express joys
Reply unto the turtle's voice;
And here in dust and dirt, O here
The lilies of his love appear!

Henry Vaughan.

THE ECLIPSE

WHITHER, O whither didst thou fly
When I did grieve thine holy eye,
When thou didst mourn to see me lost,
And all thy care and counsels crost.
O do not grieve, where'er thou art!
Thy grief is an undoing smart,
Which doth not only pain, but break
My heart, and makes me blush to speak.
Thy anger I could kiss, and will:
But O thy grief, thy grief doth kill!

Henry Vaughan.

THE WORLD

I SAW Eternity the other night,
Like a great Ring of pure and endless light,
        All calm, as it was bright;
And round beneath it, Time in hours, days, years,
        Driven by the spheres
Like a vast shadow moved; in which the world
        And all her train were hurled.
The doting lover in his quaintest strain
        Did there complain;

Near him, his lute, his fancy, and his flights,
    Wit's sour delights,
With gloves, and knots, the silly snares of pleasure,
    Yet his dear treasure,
All scattered lay, while he his eyes did pour
    Upon a flower.

The darksome statesman, hung with weights and woe,
Like a thick midnight-fog, moved there so slow,
    He did not stay, nor go;
Condemning thoughts – like sad eclipses – scowl
    Upon his soul,
And clouds of crying witnesses without
    Pursu'd him with one shout.
Yet digg'd the mole, and lest his ways be found,
    Worked under ground,
Where he did clutch his prey; (But one did see
    That policy);
Churches and altars fed him; perjuries
    Were gnats and flies;
It rained about him blood and tears; but he
    Drank them as free.

The fearful miser on a heap of rust
Sate pining all his life there, did scarce trust
    His own hands with the dust,
Yet would not place one piece above, but lives
    In fear of thieves.
Thousands there were as frantic as himself
    And hugged each one his pelf;
The downright epicure placed heaven in sense
    And scorn'd pretence,
While others, slipp'd into a wide excess,
    Said little less;
The weaker sort slight, trivial wares enslave,
    Who think them brave;
And poor, despised Truth sate counting by
    Their victory.

Yet some, who all this while did weep and sing,
And sing, and weep, soared up into the Ring;
    But most would use no wing.
O fools (said I) thus to prefer dark night
    Before true light!
To live in grots and caves, and hate the day
    Because it shows the way,

The way, which from this dead and dark abode
    Leads up to God,
A way where you might tread the sun, and be
    More bright than he.
But as I did their madness so discuss,
    One whisper'd thus,
This Ring the Bridegroom did for none provide,
    But for his bride.

                  Henry Vaughan.

THE NIGHT

    T H R O U G H that pure virgin-shrine,
That sacred veil drawn o'er thy glorious noon,
That men might look and live, as glow-worms shine
    And face the moon:
    Wise Nicodemus saw such light
    As made him know his God by night.

    Most blest believer he!
Who in that land of darkness and blind eyes
Thy long-expected healing wings could see
    When thou didst rise,
    And, what can never more be done,
    Did at midnight speak with the Sun!

    O who will tell me, where
He found thee at that dead and silent hour?
What hallowed solitary ground did bear
    So rare a flower
    Within whose sacred leaves did lie
    The fulness of the Deity?

    No mercy-seat of gold,
No dead and dusty cherub, nor carved stone,
But his own living works did my Lord hold
    And lodge alone;
    Where trees and herbs did watch and peep
    And wonder, while the Jews did sleep.

    Dear night! this world's defeat;
The stop to busy fools; care's check and curb;
The day of spirits; my soul's calm retreat
    Which none disturb!
    Christ's progress, and his prayer-time;
    The hours to which high Heaven doth chime.

God's silent, searching flight:
When my Lord's head is fill'd with dew and all
His locks are wet with the clear drops of night;
    His still, soft call;
  His knocking-time; the soul's dumb watch,
  When spirits their fair kindred catch.

    Were all my loud, evil days
Calm and unhaunted as is thy dark tent,
Whose peace but by some angel's wing or voice
    Is seldom rent;
  Then I in heaven all the long year
  Would keep, and never wander here.

    But living where the sun
Doth all things wake, and where all mixt and tire
Themselves and others, I consent and run
    To every mire;
  And by this world's ill-guiding light,
  Err more than I can do by night.

    There is in God (some say)
A deep, but dazzling darkness; as men here
Say it is late and dusky, because they
    See not all clear.
  O for that night! where I in him
  Might live invisible and dim.
                Henry Vaughan.

THE DAWNING

A H ! what time wilt thou come ? when shall that cry
'*The Bridegroom's coming !*' fill the sky ?
Shall it in the evening run
When our words and works are done ?
Or will thy all-surprising light
    Break at midnight,
When either sleep, or some dark pleasure
Possesseth mad man without measure ?
Or shall these early, fragrant hours
    Unlock thy bowers
And with their blush of light descry
Thy locks crowned with eternity ?
Indeed, it is the only time
That with thy glory doth best chime;

All now are stirring, ev'ry field
  Full hymns doth yield,
The whole Creation shakes off night,
And for thy shadow looks the light;
Stars now vanish without number,
Sleepy planets set and slumber,
The pursy clouds disband and scatter,
All except some sudden matter;
Not one beam triumphs, but from far
  That morning-star.
Oh at what time soever thou,
Unknown to us, the heavens wilt bow,
And with thy angels in the van,
Descend to judge poor careless man,
Grant I may not like puddle lie
In a corrupt security,
Where, if a traveller water crave,
He finds it dead, and in a grave.
But as this restless, vocal spring
All day and night doth run, and sing,
And though here born, yet is acquainted
Elsewhere, and flowing keeps untainted;
So let me all my busy age
In thy free services engage;
And though (while here) of force I must
Have commerce sometimes with poor dust,
And in my flesh, though vile and low,
As this doth in her channel, flow,
Yet let my course, my aim, my love
And chief acquaintance be above;
So when that day and hour shall come,
In which thyself will be the sun,
Thou'lt find me dress'd and on my way,
Watching the break of thy great day.
     Henry Vaughan.

ANGUISH

M Y God and King! to Thee
  I bow my knee;
I bow my troubled soul, and greet
With my foul heart thy holy feet.
Cast it, or tread it! it shall do
Even what thou wilt, and praise thee too.

My God, could I weep blood,
  Gladly I would,
Or if thou wilt give me that art,
Which through the eyes pours out the heart,
I will exhaust it all, and make
Myself all tears, a weeping lake.

O! 'tis an easy thing
  To write and sing;
But to write true, unfeigned verse
Is very hard! O God, disperse
These weights, and give my spirit leave
To act as well as to conceive!

  O my God, hear my cry;
    Or let me die! . . .
                        Henry Vaughan.

PHILLADA FLOUTS ME

O WHAT a plague is love!
  How shall I bear it?
She will inconstant prove,
  I greatly fear it.
She so torments my mind
  That my strength faileth,
And wavers with the wind
  As a ship saileth.
Please her the best I may,
She loves still to gainsay;
Alack and well-a-day!
  Phillada flouts me.

At the fair yesterday
  She did pass by me;
She look'd another way
  And would not spy me:
I woo'd her for to dine,
  But could not get her;
Will had her to the wine –
  He might entreat her.
With Daniel she did dance,
On me she look'd askance:
O thrice unhappy chance!
  Phillada flouts me.

Fair maid, be not so coy,
  Do not disdain me!
I am my mother's joy:
  Sweet, entertain me!
She'll give me, when she dies,
  All that is fitting:
Her poultry and her bees,
  And her goose sitting,
A pair of mattress beds,
And a bag full of shreds;
And yet, for all these goods,
  Phillada flouts me.

She hath a clout of mine
  Wrought with blue coventry,
Which she keeps for a sign
  Of my fidelity:
But i' faith, if she flinch
  She shall not wear it;
To Tib, my t'other wench,
  I mean to bear it.
And yet it grieves my heart
So soon from her to part:
Death strike me with his dart!
  Phillada flouts me.

Thou shalt eat crudded cream
  All the year lasting,
And drink the crystal stream
  Pleasant in tasting;
Whig and whey whilst thou lust,
  And bramble-berries,
Pie-lid and pastry-crust,
  Pears, plums, and cherries.
Thy raiment shall be thin,
Made of a weevil's skin —
Yet all's not worth a pin!
  Phillada flouts me.

In the last month of May
  I made her posies;
I heard her often say
  That she loved roses.
Cowslips and gillyflowers
  And the white lily
I brought to deck the bowers
  For my sweet Philly.

But she did all disdain,
And threw them back again;
Therefore 'tis flat and plain
   Philllada flouts me.

Fair maiden, have a care,
   And in time take me;
I can have those as fair
   If you forsake me:
For Doll the dairy-maid
   Laugh'd at me lately,
And wanton Winifred
   Favours me greatly.
One throws milk on my clothes,
T'other plays with my nose;
What wanting signs are those?
   Phillada flouts me.

I cannot work nor sleep
   At all in season:
Love wounds my heart so deep,
   Without all reason.
I 'gin to pine away
   In my love's shadow,
Like as a fat beast may,
   Penn'd in a meadow,
I shall be dead, I fear,
Within this thousand year:
And all for that my dear
   Phillada flouts me.

Anonymous.

POVERTY

A s in the house I sate
   Alone & desolate,
No creature but the fire & I,
The chimney & the stool, I lift mine eye
    Up to the wall,
   And in the silent hall
    Saw nothing mine
But some few cups & dishes shine,
The table & the wooden stools
   Where people used to dine:
   A painted cloth there was
Wherein some ancient story wrought
A little entertain'd my thought
Which light discover'd through the glass.

I wonder'd much to see
That all my wealth should be
Confin'd in such a little room,
Yet hope for more I scarcely durst presume.
It griev'd me sore
That such a scanty store
Should be my all:
For I forgot my ease & health,
Nor did I think of hands or eyes,
Nor soul nor body prize;
I neither thought the sun,
Nor moon, nor stars, nor people, *mine*,
Tho' they did round about me shine;
And therefore was I quite undone.

Some greater things I thought
Must needs for me be wrought,
Which till my craving mind could see
I ever should lament my poverty:
I fain would have
Whatever bounty gave;
Nor could there be
Without, or love or deity:
For, should not he be infinite
Whose hand created me?
Ten thousand absent things
Did vex my poor & wanting mind,
Which, till I be no longer blind,
Let me not see the King of kings.

His love must surely be
Rich, infinite, & free;
Nor can he be thought a God
Of grace & pow'r, that fills not his abode,
His holy court,
In kind & liberal sort;
Joys & pleasures,
Plenty of jewels, goods, & treasures,
(To enrich the poor, cheer the forlorn)
His palace must adorn,
And given all to me:
For till *his* works *my* wealth became,
No love, or peace, did me enflame:
But now I have a DEITY.

Thomas Traherne.

UPON NOTHING

N O T H I N G! thou elder brother ev'n to Shade,
Thou hadst a being e'er the world was made,
And (well fixt) art alone of ending not afraid.

E'er time and place were, time and place were not,
When primitive Nothing something straight begot,
Then all proceeded from the great united – What.

Something the gen'ral attribute of all,
Sever'd from thee, its sole original,
Into thy boundless self must undistinguish'd fall.

Yet something did thy mighty pow'r command,
And from thy fruitful emptiness's hand,
Snatch'd men, beasts, birds, fire, air and land.

Matter, the wickedest off-spring of thy race,
By Form assisted, flew from thy embrace,
And rebel Light obscur'd thy reverend dusky face.

With Form, and Matter, Time and Place did join,
Body, thy foe, with thee did leagues combine,
To spoil thy peaceful realm, and ruin all thy line.

But turn-coat Time assists the foe in vain,
And, brib'd by thee, assists thy short-liv'd reign,
And to thy hungry womb drives back thy slaves again.

Tho' mysteries are barr'd from laick eyes,
And the Divine alone, with warrant, pries
Into thy bosom, where the truth in private lies,

Yet this of thee the wise may freely say,
Thou from the virtuous nothing tak'st away,
And to be part with thee the wicked wisely pray.

Great Negative, how vainly would the wise
Enquire, define, distinguish, teach, devise,
Didst thou not stand to point their dull philosophies ?

Is, or *is not,* the two great ends of fate,
And, true or false, the subject of debate,
That perfect, or destroy, the vast designs of fate.

When they have rack'd the politician's breast,
Within thy bosom must securely rest,
And, when reduc'd to thee, are least unsafe and best.

But, Nothing, why does Something still permit
That sacred monarchs should at council sit,
With persons highly thought, at best, for nothing fit.

Whilst weighty Something modestly abstains,
From prince's coffers, and from statesmen's brains,
And nothing there like stately Nothing reigns.

Nothing, who dwell'st with fools in grave disguise,
For whom they reverend shapes, and forms devise,
Lawn sleeves, and furs, and gowns, when they like thee
    look wise.

French truth, Dutch prowess, British policy,
Hibernian learning, Scotch civility,
Spaniards' dispatch, Danes' wit, are mainly seen in thee.

The great man's gratitude to his best friend,
King's promises, whores' vows, towards thee they bend,
Flow swiftly into thee, and in thee ever end.
                                John Wilmot, Earl of Rochester.

THE CHOICE

G R A N T me, indulgent Heaven! a rural seat,
    Rather contemptible than great!
Where, though I taste Life's sweets, still I may be
    Athirst for Immortality!
I would have business; but exempt from strife!
    A private, but an active, life!
A Conscience bold, and punctual to his charge!
    My stock of Health; or Patience large!
Some books I'd have, and some acquaintance too;
    But very good, and very few!
Then (if one mortal two such grants may crave!)
    From silent life, I'd steal into my grave!
                                Nahum Tate.

THE SOLDIER'S DEATH

T R A I L all your pikes, dispirit every drum,
March in a slow procession from afar,
Ye silent, ye dejected men of war!
Be still the hautboys, and the flute be dumb!

63

Display no more, in vain, the lofty banner;
For see! where on the bier before ye lies
The pale, the fall'n, th' untimely Sacrifice
To your mistaken Shrine, to your false Idol Honour.
                    Anne, Countess of Winchilsea.

THE POET

L E S T you should think that verse shall die,
    Which sounds the silver Thames along,
Taught on the wings of truth to fly
    Above the reach of vulgar song;

Though daring Milton sits sublime,
    In Spenser native Muses play;
Nor yet shall Waller yield to time,
    Nor pensive Cowley's moral lay.

Sages and chiefs long since had birth
    Ere Caesar was, or Newton named;
These raised new empires o'er the earth,
    And those, new heavens and systems framed.

Vain was the chief's, the sage's pride!
They had no poet, and they died.
In vain they schemed, in vain they bled!
They had no poet, and are dead.
                    Alexander Pope.

ON THE RECEIPT OF MY
MOTHER'S PICTURE

O T H A T those lips had language! Life has pass'd
With me but roughly since I heard thee last.
Those lips are thine – thy own sweet smile I see,
The same that oft in childhood solaced me;
Voice only fails, else how distinct they say,
'Grieve not, my child, chase all thy fears away!'
The meek intelligence of those dear eyes
(Blest be the art that can immortalize,
The art that baffles Time's tyrannic claim
To quench it) here shines on me still the same.
    Faithful remembrancer of one so dear,
O welcome guest, though unexpected here!
Who bidst me honour with an artless song,
Affectionate, a mother lost so long.

I will obey, not willingly alone,
But gladly, as the precept were her own:
And, while that face renews my filial grief,
Fancy shall weave a charm for my relief,
Shall steep me in Elysian reverie,
A momentary dream, that thou art she.
    My mother! when I learn'd that thou wast dead,
Say, wast thou conscious of the tears I shed?
Hover'd thy spirit o'er thy sorrowing son,
Wretch even then, life's journey just begun?
Perhaps thou gav'st me, though unfelt, a kiss;
Perhaps a tear, if souls can weep in bliss –
    Ah, that maternal smile! it answers – Yes.
I heard the bell toll'd on thy burial day,
I saw the hearse that bore thee slow away,
And, turning from my nursery window, drew
A long, long sigh, and wept a last adieu!
But was it such? – It was. – Where thou art gone
Adieus and farewells are a sound unknown.
May I but meet thee on that peaceful shore,
The parting word shall pass my lips no more!
Thy maidens, grieved themselves at my concern,
Oft gave me promise of thy quick return.
What ardently I wish'd, I long believed,
And, disappointed still, was still deceived;
By expectation every day beguiled,
Dupe of tomorrow even from a child.
Thus many a sad tomorrow came and went,
Till, all my stock of infant sorrows spent,
I learn'd at last submission to my lot,
But, though I less deplored thee, ne'er forgot.
    Where once we dwelt our name is heard no more,
Children not thine have trod my nursery floor;
And where the gardener Robin, day by day,
Drew me to school along the public way,
Delighted with my bauble coach, and wrapp'd
In scarlet mantle warm, and velvet capp'd,
'Tis now become a history little known,
That once we call'd the pastoral house our own.
Shortlived possession! but the record fair,
That memory keeps of all thy kindness there,
Still outlives many a storm, that has effaced
A thousand other themes less deeply traced.
Thy nightly visits to my chamber made,
That thou mightst know me safe and warmly laid;
Thy morning bounties ere I left my home,
The biscuit, or confectionary plum;

The fragrant waters on my cheeks bestow'd
By thy own hand, till fresh they shone and glow'd:
All this, and more endearing still than all,
Thy constant flow of love, that knew no fall,
Ne'er roughen'd by those cataracts and breaks,
That humour interposed too often makes;
All this still legible in memory's page,
And still to be so to my latest age,
Adds joy to duty, makes me glad to pay
Such honours to thee as my numbers may;
Perhaps a frail memorial, but sincere,
Not scorn'd in Heaven, though little noticed here.
      Could Time, his flight reversed, restore the hours,
When, playing with thy vesture's tissued flowers,
The violet, the pink, and jessamine,
I pricked them into paper with a pin
(And thou wast happier than myself the while,
Wouldst softly speak, and stroke my head, and smile),
Could those few pleasant days again appear,
Might one wish bring them, would I wish them here?
I would not trust my heart – the dear delight
Seems so to be desired, perhaps I might.–
But no – what here we call our life is such,
So little to be loved, and thou so much,
That I should ill requite thee to constrain
Thy unbound spirit into bonds again.
      Thou, as a gallant bark from Albion's coast
(The storms all weather'd and the ocean cross'd)
Shoots into port at some well haven'd isle,
Where spices breathe, and brighter seasons smile,
There sits quiescent on the floods, that show
Her beauteous form reflected clear below,
While airs impregnated with incense play
Around her, fanning light her streamers gay;
So thou, with sails how swift! hast reach'd the shore,
'Where tempests never beat nor billows roar;'
And thy loved consort on the dangerous tide
Of life long since has anchor'd by thy side.
But me, scarce hoping to attain that rest,
Always from port withheld, always distress'd –
Me howling blasts drive devious, tempest-toss'd,
Sails ripp'd, seams opening wide, and compass lost,
And day by day some current's thwarting force
Sets me more distant from a prosperous course.
      Yet O the thought, that thou art safe, and he!
That thought is joy, arrive what may to me.

My boast is not that I deduce my birth
From loins enthroned, and rulers of the earth;
But higher far my proud pretensions rise –
The son of parents pass'd into the skies.
    And now, farewell – Time unrevoked has run
His wonted course, yet what I wish'd is done.
By contemplation's help, not sought in vain,
I seem to have lived my childhood o'er again;
To have renew'd the joys that once were mine,
Without the sin of violating thine;
And, while the wings of fancy still are free,
And I can view this mimic show of thee,
Time has but half succeeded in his theft –
Thyself removed, thy power to soothe me left.
                              William Cowper.

LOVE'S SECRET

N E V E R seek to tell thy love,
    Love that never told can be;
For the gentle wind does move
    Silently, invisibly.

I told my love, I told my love,
    I told her all my heart;
Trembling, cold, in ghastly fears,
    Ah! she did depart!

Soon as she was gone from me,
    A traveller came by,
Silently, invisibly:
    He took her with a sigh.
                      William Blake.

THE DIVINE IMAGE

T O Mercy, Pity, Peace, and Love
All pray in their distress;
And to these virtues of delight
Return their thankfulness.

For Mercy, Pity, Peace, and Love
Is God, our father dear,
And Mercy, Pity, Peace, and Love
Is Man, his child and care.

67

For Mercy has a human heart,
Pity a human face,
And Love, the human form divine,
And Peace, the human dress.

Then every man, of every clime,
That prays in his distress,
Prays to the human form divine,
Love, Mercy, Pity, Peace.

And all must love the human form,
In heathen, turk, or jew;
Where Mercy, Love, & Pity dwell
There God is dwelling too.

William Blake.

INFANT JOY

'I HAVE no name:
I am but two days old.'
What shall I call thee?
'I happy am,
Joy is my name.'
Sweet joy befall thee!

Pretty joy!
Sweet joy but two days old,
Sweet joy I call thee:
Thou dost smile,
I sing the while,
Sweet joy befall thee!

William Blake.

¶

I LAID me down upon a bank
Where love lay sleeping;
I heard among the rushes dank
Weeping, Weeping.

Then I went to the heath and the wild
To the thistles and thorns of the waste;
And they told me how they were beguil'd,
Driven out, and compel'd to be chaste.

William Blake.

AUGURIES OF INNOCENCE

T O see a World in a Grain of Sand
And a Heaven in a Wild Flower,
Hold Infinity in the palm of your hand
And Eternity in an hour.

A Robin Red breast in a Cage
Puts all Heaven in a Rage.
A dove house fill'd with Doves & Pigeons
Shudders Hell thro' all its regions.
A dog starv'd at his Master's Gate
Predicts the ruin of the State.
A Horse misus'd upon the Road
Calls to Heaven for Human blood.
Each outcry of the hunted Hare
A fibre from the Brain does tear.
A Skylark wounded in the wing,
A Cherubim does cease to sing.
The Game Cock clip'd & arm'd for fight
Does the Rising Sun affright.
Every Wolf's & Lion's howl
Raises from Hell a Human Soul.
The wild Deer, wand'ring here & there,
Keeps the Human Soul from Care.
The Lamb misus'd breeds Public Strife
And yet forgives the Butcher's Knife.
The Bat that flits at close of Eve
Has left the Brain that won't Believe.
The Owl that calls upon the Night
Speaks the Unbeliever's fright.
He who shall hurt the little Wren
Shall never be belov'd by Men.
He who the Ox to wrath has mov'd
Shall never be by Woman lov'd.
The wanton Boy that kills the Fly
Shall feel the Spider's enmity.
He who torments the Chafer's Sprite
Weaves a Bower in endless Night.
The Caterpiller on the Leaf
Repeats to thee thy Mother's grief.
Kill not the Moth nor Butterfly,
For the Last Judgment draweth nigh.
He who shall train the Horse to War
Shall never pass the Polar Bar.
The Beggar's Dog & Widow's Cat,
Feed them & thou wilt grow fat.

The Gnat that sings his Summer's Song
Poison gets from Slander's tongue.
The poison of the Snake & Newt
Is the sweat of Envy's Foot.
The Poison of the Honey Bee
Is the Artist's Jealousy.
The Prince's Robes & Beggar's Rags
Are Toadstools on the Miser's Bags.
A Truth that's told with bad intent
Beats all the Lies you can invent.
It is right it should be so;
Man was made for Joy & Woe;
And when this we rightly know
Thro' the World we safely go.
Joy & Woe are woven fine,
A Clothing for the Soul divine;
Under every grief & pine
Runs a joy with silken twine.
The Babe is more than Swadling Bands;
Throughout all these Human Lands
Tools were made, & Born were hands,
Every Farmer understands.
Every Tear from Every Eye
Becomes a Babe in Eternity;
This is caught by Females bright,
And return'd to its own delight.
The Bleat, the Bark, Bellow & Roar
Are Waves that Beat on Heaven's Shore.
The Babe that weeps the Rod beneath
Writes Revenge in realms of Death.
The Beggar's Rags, fluttering in Air,
Does to Rags the Heavens tear.
The Soldier, arm'd with Sword & Gun,
Palsied strikes the Summer's Sun.
The poor Man's farthing is worth more
Than all the Gold on Afric's Shore.
One Mite wrung from the Lab'rer's hands
Shall buy and sell the Miser's Lands:
Or, if protected from on high,
Does the whole Nation sell & buy.
He who mocks the Infant's Faith
Shall be mock'd in Age & Death.
He who shall teach the Child to Doubt
The rotting Grave shall ne'er get out.
He who respects the Infant's faith
Triumphs over Hell & Death.
The Child's Toys & the Old Man's Reasons

Are the Fruits of the Two Seasons.
The Questioner, who sits so sly,
Shall never know how to Reply.
He who replies to words of Doubt
Doth put the Light of Knowledge out.
The Strongest Poison ever known
Came from Cæsar's Laurel Crown.
Nought can deform the Human Race
Like to the Armour's iron brace.
When Gold & Gems adorn the Plow
To peaceful Arts shall Envy Bow.
A Riddle or the Cricket's Cry
Is to Doubt a fit Reply.
The Emmet's Inch & Eagle's Mile
Make Lame Philosophy to smile.
He who Doubts from what he sees
Will ne'er Believe, do what you Please.
If the Sun & Moon should Doubt,
They'd immediately Go Out.
To be in a Passion you Good may do,
But no Good if a Passion is in you.
The Whore & Gambler, by the State
Licenc'd, build that Nation's Fate.
The Harlot's cry from Street to Street
Shall weave Old England's winding Sheet.
The Winner's Shout, the Loser's Curse,
Dance before dead England's Hearse.
Every Night & every Morn
Some to Misery are Born.
Every Morn and every Night
Some are Born to Sweet Delight.
Some are Born to Sweet Delight,
Some are Born to Endless Night.
We are led to Believe a Lie
When we see not Thro' the Eye,
Which was Born in a Night to perish in a Night
When the Soul Slept in Beams of Light.
God appears & God is Light
To those poor Souls who dwell in Night,
But does a Human Form Display
To those who Dwell in Realms of day.

William Blake.

MUTABILITY

FROM low to high doth dissolution climb,
And sink from high to low, along a scale

Of awful notes, whose concord shall not fail;
A musical, but melancholy chime,
Which they can hear who meddle not with crime,
Nor avarice, nor over-anxious care.
Truth fails not; but her outward forms that bear
The longest date do melt like frosty rime,
That in the morning whitened hill and plain
And is no more; drop like the tower sublime
Of yesterday, which royally did wear
His crown of weeds, but could not even sustain
Some casual shout that broke the silent air,
Or the unimaginable touch of Time.

William Wordsworth.

HUMAN LIFE

I F dead, we cease to be; if total gloom
    Swallow up life's brief flash for ay, we fare
As summer-gusts, of sudden birth and doom,
    Whose sound and motion not alone declare,
But are their whole of being! If the breath
    Be Life itself, and not its task and tent,
If even a soul like Milton's can know death;
    O Man! thou vessel purposeless, unmeant,
Yet drone-hive strange of phantom purposes!
    Surplus of nature's dread activity,
Which, as she gazed on some nigh-finish'd vase,
Retreating slow, with meditative pause,
    She form'd with restless hands unconsciously!
Blank accident! nothing's anomaly!

If rootless thus, thus substanceless thy state,
Go, weigh thy dreams, and be thy hopes, thy fears,
The counter-weights! – Thy laughter and thy tears
    Mean but themselves, each fittest to create,
And to repay the other! Why rejoices
    Thy heart with hollow joy for hollow good?
    Why cowl thy face beneath the mourner's hood,
Why waste thy sighs, and thy lamenting voices,
    Image of Image, Ghost of Ghostly Elf,
That such a thing as thou feel'st warm or cold?
Yet what and whence thy gain, if thou withhold
    These costless shadows of thy shadowy self?
Be sad! be glad! be neither! seek, or shun!
Thou hast no reason why! Thou canst have none;
Thy being's being is contradiction.

S. T. Coleridge.

72

JENNY KISS'D ME

JENNY kiss'd me when we met,
  Jumping from the chair she sat in;
Time, you thief, who love to get
  Sweets into your list, put that in!
Say I'm weary, say I'm sad,
  Say that health and wealth have miss'd me,
Say I'm growing old, but add
  Jenny kiss'd me.

Leigh Hunt.

WE'LL GO NO MORE A-ROVING

SO, we'll go no more a-roving
  So late into the night,
Though the heart be still as loving,
  And the moon be still as bright.

For the sword outwears its sheath,
  And the soul wears out the breast,
And the heart must pause to breathe,
  And love itself have rest.

Though the night was made for loving,
  And the day returns too soon,
Yet we'll go no more a-roving
  By the light of the moon.

Byron.

TO NIGHT

SWIFTLY walk o'er the western wave,
    Spirit of Night!
Out of the misty eastern cave,
Where, all the long and lone day-light,
Thou wovest dreams of joy and fear,
Which make thee terrible and dear –
    Swift be thy flight!

Wrap thy form in a mantle gray,
    Star-inwrought!
Blind with thine hair the eyes of Day;
Kiss her until she be wearied out,
Then wander o'er city, and sea, and land
Touching all with thine opiate wand –
    Come, long-sought!

73

When I arose and saw the dawn,
   I sighed for thee;
When light rode high, and the dew was gone,
And noon lay heavy on flower and tree,
And the weary day turned to his rest,
Lingering like an unloved guest,
   I sighed for thee.

Thy brother Death came, and cried,
   Wouldst thou me?
Thy sweet child Sleep, the filmy-eyed,
Murmured like a noontide bee,
Shall I nestle near thy side?
Wouldst thou me? – And I replied,
   No, not thee!

Death will come when thou art dead,
   Soon, too soon –
Sleep will come when thou art fled;
Of neither would I ask the boon
I ask of thee, belovéd Night –
Swift be thine approaching flight,
   Come soon, soon!

P. B. Shelley.

§

A WIDOW bird sate mourning for her love
   Upon a wintry bough;
The frozen wind crept on above,
   The freezing stream below.

There was no leaf upon the forest bare,
   No flower upon the ground,
And little motion in the air
   Except the mill-wheel's sound.

P. B. Shelley.

SONG TO THE MEN OF ENGLAND

MEN of England, wherefore plough
For the lords who lay ye low?
Wherefore weave with toil and care
The rich robes your tyrants wear?

Wherefore feed, and clothe, and save,
From the cradle to the grave,
Those ungrateful drones who would
Drain your sweat – nay, drink your blood?

Wherefore, Bees of England, forge
Many a weapon, chain, and scourge,
That these stingless drones may spoil
The forced produce of your toil?

Have ye leisure, comfort, calm,
Shelter, food, love's gentle balm?
Or what is it ye buy so dear
With your pain and with your fear?

The seed ye sow, another reaps;
The wealth ye find, another keeps;
The robes ye weave, another wears;
The arms ye forge, another bears.

Sow seed,– but let no tyrant reap;
Find wealth,– let no impostor heap;
Weave robes,– let not the idle wear;
Forge arms,– in your defence to bear.

Shrink to your cellars, holes, and cells;
In halls ye deck another dwells.
Why shake the chains ye wrought? Ye see
The steel ye tempered glance on ye.

With plough and spade, and hoe and loom,
Trace your grave, and build your tomb,
And weave your winding-sheet, till fair
England be your sepulchre.

P. B. Shelley.

THE HOUR OF DEATH

LEAVES have their time to fall,
And flowers to wither at the north wind's breath,
    And stars to set – but all,
Thou hast *all* seasons for thine own, O Death!

    Day is for mortal care;
Eve, for glad meetings round the joyous hearth;
    Night, for the dreams of sleep, the voice of prayer –
But all for thee, thou Mightiest of the earth!

75

The banquet hath its hour,
Its feverish hour of mirth, and song, and wine;
    There comes a day for grief's o'erwhelming power,
A time for softer tears – but all are thine.

Youth and the opening rose
May look like things too glorious for decay,
    And smile at thee! – but thou art not of those
That wait the ripened bloom to seize their prey.

Leaves have their time to fall,
And flowers to wither at the north wind's breath,
    And stars to set – but all,
Thou hast *all* seasons for thine own, O Death!

We know when moons shall wane,
When summer birds from far shall cross the sea,
    When autumn's hue shall tinge the golden grain –
But who shall teach us when to look for thee?

Is it when spring's first gale
Comes forth to whisper where the violets lie?
    Is it when roses in our paths grow pale?
They have one season – all are ours to die!

Thou art where billows foam,
Thou art where music melts upon the air;
    Thou art around us in our peaceful home,
And the world calls us forth – and thou art there.

Thou art where friend meets friend,
Beneath the shadow of the elm to rest;
    Thou art where foe meets foe, and trumpets rend
The skies, and swords beat down the princely crest.

Leaves have their time to fall,
And flowers to wither at the north wind's breath,
    And stars to set – but all,
Thou hast *all* seasons for thine own, O Death!
                                        Felicia Hemans.

WRITTEN IN THE FIELDS

T O one who has been long in city pent,
'Tis very sweet to look into the fair
And open face of heaven,– to breathe a prayer
Full in the smile of the blue firmament.

Who is more happy, when, with heart's content,
Fatigued he sinks into some pleasant lair
Of wavy grass, and reads a debonair
And gentle tale of love and languishment?
Returning home at evening, with an ear
Catching the notes of Philomel,– an eye
Watching the sailing cloudlet's bright career,
He mourns that day so soon has glided by:
E'en like the passage of an angel's tear,
That falls through the clear ether silently.

John Keats.

ON THE ELGIN MARBLES

MY spirit is too weak; mortality
    Weighs heavily on me like unwilling sleep,
    And each imagined pinnacle and steep
Of godlike hardship tells me I must die
Like a sick eagle looking at the sky.
    Yet 'tis a gentle luxury to weep,
    That I have not the cloudy winds to keep
Fresh for the opening of the morning's eye.
Such dim-conceived glories of the brain,
    Bring round the heart an indescribable feud;
So do these wonders a most dizzy pain,
    That mingles Grecian grandeur with the rude
Wasting of old Time – with a billowy main
    A sun, a shadow of a magnitude.

John Keats.

DAYS

DAUGHTERS of Time, the hypocritic Days,
Muffled and dumb like barefoot dervishes
And marching single in an endless file,
Bring diadems and faggots in their hands.
To each they offer gifts after his will –
Bread, kingdoms, stars, and sky that holds them all.
I, in my pleached garden, watch'd the pomp,
Forgot my morning wishes, hastily
Took a few herbs and apples, and the day
Turn'd and departed silent. I, too late,
Under her solemn fillet saw the scorn.

Ralph Waldo Emerson.

77

5

G O from me. Yet I feel that I shall stand
Henceforward in thy shadow. Nevermore
Alone upon the threshold of my door
Of individual life, I shall command
The uses of my soul, nor lift my hand
Serenely in the sunshine as before,
Without the sense of that which I forbore –
Thy touch upon the palm. The widest land
Doom takes to part us, leaves thy heart in mine
With pulses that beat double. What I do
And what I dream include thee, as the wine
Must taste of its own grapes. And when I sue
God for myself, He hears that name of thine,
And sees within my eyes the tears of two.
                    Elizabeth Barrett Browning.

from IN MEMORIAM

B E near me when my light is low,
    When the blood creeps, and the nerves prick
    And tingle; and the heart is sick,
And all the wheels of Being slow.

Be near me when the sensuous frame
    Is rack'd with pangs that conquer trust;
    And Time, a maniac scattering dust,
And Life, a Fury slinging flame.

Be near me when my faith is dry,
    And men the flies of latter spring,
    That lay their eggs, and sting and sing
And weave their petty cells and die.

Be near me when I fade away,
    To point the term of human strife,
    And on the low dark verge of life
The twilight of eternal day.

                    Tennyson.

TWO IN THE CAMPAGNA

I W O N D E R do you feel to-day
    As I have felt since, hand in hand,
We sat down on the grass, to stray
    In spirit better through the land,
This morn of Rome and May?

For me, I touched a thought, I know,
  Has tantalized me many times,
(Like turns of thread the spiders throw
  Mocking across our path) for rhymes
To catch at and let go.

Help me to hold it! First it left
  The yellowing fennel, run to seed
There, branching from the brickwork's cleft,
  Some old tomb's ruin; yonder weed
Took up the floating weft,

Where one small orange cup amassed
  Five beetles – blind and green they grope
Among the honey-meal; and last,
  Everywhere on the grassy slope
I traced it. Hold it fast!

The champaign with its endless fleece
  Of feathery grasses everywhere!
Silence and passion, joy and peace,
  An everlasting wash of air –
Rome's ghost since her decease.

Such life here, through such length of hours,
  Such miracles performed in play,
Such primal naked forms of flowers,
  Such letting Nature have her way
While Heaven looks from its towers!

How say you? Let us, O my dove,
  Let us be unashamed of soul,
As earth lies bare to heaven above!
  How is it under our control
To love or not to love?

I would that you were all to me,
  You that are just so much, no more,
Nor yours, nor mine, nor slave nor free!
  Where does the fault lie? What the core
Of the wound, since wound must be?

I would I could adopt your will,
  See with your eyes, and set my heart
Beating by yours, and drink my fill
  At your soul's springs,– your part my part
In life, for good and ill.

No. I yearn upward, touch you close,
   Then stand away. I kiss your cheek,
Catch your soul's warmth – I pluck the rose
   And love it more than tongue can speak –
Then the good minute goes.

Already how am I so far
   Out of that minute? Must I go
Still like the thistle-ball, no bar,
   Onward, whenever light winds blow,
Fixed by no friendly star?

Just when I seemed about to learn!
   Where is the thread now? Off again!
The old trick! Only I discern –
   Infinite passion, and the pain
Of finite hearts that yearn.

Robert Browning.

POPULARITY

S T A N D still, true poet that you are,
   I know you; let me try and draw you.
Some night you'll fail us. When afar
   You rise, remember one man saw you,
Knew you, and named a star.

My star, God's glow-worm! Why extend
   That loving hand of His which leads you,
Yet locks you safe from end to end
   Of this dark world, unless He needs you –
Just saves your light to spend?

His clenched Hand shall unclose at last
   I know, and let out all the beauty.
My poet holds the future fast,
   Accepts the coming ages' duty,
Their present for this past.

That day, the earth's feast-master's brow
   Shall clear, to God the chalice raising;
'Others give best at first, but Thou
   For ever set'st our table praising,–
Keep'st the good wine till now.'

Meantime, I'll draw you as you stand,
  With few or none to watch and wonder.
I'll say – a fisher (on the sand
  By Tyre the Old) his ocean-plunder,
A netful, brought to land.

Who has not heard how Tyrian shells
  Enclosed the blue, that dye of dyes
Whereof one drop worked miracles,
  And coloured like Astarte's eyes
Raw silk the merchant sells?

And each bystander of them all
  Could criticise, and quote tradition
How depths of blue sublimed some pall,
  To get which, pricked a king's ambition;
Worth sceptre, crown and ball.

Yet there's the dye,– in that rough mesh,
  The sea has only just o'er-whispered!
Live whelks, the lip's-beard dripping fresh,
  As if they still the water's lisp heard
Through foam the rock-weeds thresh.

Enough to furnish Solomon
  Such hangings for his cedar-house,
That when gold-robed he took the throne
  In that abyss of blue, the Spouse
Might swear his presence shone

Most like the centre-spike of gold
  Which burns deep in the blue-bell's womb,
What time, with ardours manifold,
  The bee goes singing to her groom,
Drunken and overbold.

Mere conchs! not fit for warp or woof!
  Till art comes,– comes to pound and squeeze
And clarify,– refines to proof
  The liquor filtered by degrees,
While the world stands aloof.

And there's the extract, flasked and fine,
  And priced, and saleable at last!
And Hobbs, Nobbs, Stokes and Nokes combine
  To paint the future from the past,
Put blue into their line.

Hobbs hints blue,– straight he turtle eats.
   Nobbs prints blue,– claret crowns his cup.
Nokes outdares Stokes in azure feats,–
   Both gorge. Who fished the murex up?
What porridge had John Keats?

                     Robert Browning.

from THE PRISONER

'HE comes with western winds, with evening's wandering airs,
With that clear dusk of heaven that brings the thickest stars;
Winds take a pensive tone and stars a tender fire
And visions rise and change which kill me with desire –

'Desire for nothing known in my maturer years
When joy grew mad with awe at counting future tears;
When, if my spirit's sky was full of flashes warm,
I knew not whence they came, from sun or thunderstorm;

'But first a hush of peace, a soundless calm descends;
The struggle of distress and fierce impatience ends;
Mute music soothes my breast – unuttered harmony
That I could never dream till earth was lost to me.

'Then dawns the Invisible, the Unseen its truth reveals;
My outward sense is gone, my inward essence feels –
Its wings are almost free, its home, its harbour found;
Measuring the gulf it stoops and dares the final bound!

'Oh dreadful is the check – intense the agony
When the ear begins to hear and the eye begins to see;
When the pulse begins to throb, the brain to think again;
The soul to feel the flesh and the flesh to feel the chain!'

                     Emily Brontë.

BEAT! BEAT! DRUMS!

BEAT! beat! drums! – blow! bugles! blow!
Through the windows – through doors – burst like a ruthless
    force,
Into the solemn church, and scatter the congregation,
Into the school where the scholar is studying;
Leave not the bridegroom quiet – no happiness must he
    have now with his bride,
Nor the peaceful farmer any peace, ploughing his field or
    gathering his grain,
So fierce you whirr and pound you drums – so shrill you
    bugles blow.

Beat! beat! drums! – blow! bugles! blow!
Over the traffic of cities – over the rumble of wheels in the
    streets;
Are beds prepared for sleepers at night in the houses? no
    sleepers must sleep in those beds,
No bargainers' bargains by day – no brokers or speculators –
    would they continue?
Would the talkers be talking? would the singer attempt to
    sing?
Would the lawyer rise in the court to state his case before the
    judge?
Then rattle quicker, heavier drums – you bugles wilder blow.

Beat! beat! drums! – blow! bugles! blow!
Make no parley – stop for no expostulation,
Mind not the timid – mind not the weeper or prayer,
Mind not the old man beseeching the young man,
Let not the child's voice be heard, nor the mother's en-
    treaties,
Make even the trestles to shake the dead where they lie
    awaiting the hearses,
So strong you thump O terrible drums – so loud you bugles
    blow.

Walt Whitman.

GROWING OLD

WHAT is it to grow old?
Is it to lose the glory of the form,
The lustre of the eye?
Is it for beauty to forego her wreath?
– Yes, but not this alone.

Is it to feel our strength –
Not our bloom only, but our strength – decay?
Is it to feel each limb
Grow stiffer, every function less exact,
Each nerve more loosely strung?

Yes, this, and more; but not
Ah, 'tis not what in youth we dream'd 'twould be!
'Tis not to have our life
Mellow'd and soften'd as with sunset-glow,
A golden day's decline.

'Tis not to see the world
As from a height, with rapt prophetic eyes,
And heart profoundly stirr'd;
And weep, and feel the fulness of the past,
The years that are no more.

It is to spend long days
And not once feel that we were ever young;
It is to add, immured
In the hot prison of the present, month
To month with weary pain.

It is to suffer this,
And feel but half, and feebly, what we feel.
Deep in our hidden heart
Festers the dull remembrance of a change,
But no emotion – none.

It is – last stage of all –
When we are frozen up within, and quite
The phantom of ourselves,
To hear the world applaud the hollow ghost
Which blamed the living man.
                              Matthew Arnold.

MAGNA EST VERITAS

HERE, in this little Bay,
Full of tumultous life and great repose,
Where, twice a day,
The purposeless, glad ocean comes and goes,
Under high cliffs, and far from the huge town,
I sit me down.
For want of me the world's course will not fail:
When all its work is done, the lie shall rot;
The truth is great, and shall prevail,
When none cares whether it prevail or not.
                              Coventry Patmore.

A FAREWELL

WITH all my will, but much against my heart,
We two now part.
My Very Dear,
Our solace is, the sad road lies so clear.

84

It needs no art,
With faint, averted feet
And many a tear,
In our opposed paths to persevere.
Go thou to East, I West.
We will not say
There's any hope, it is so far away.
But, O, my Best,
When the one darling of our widowhead,
The nursling Grief,
Is dead,
And no dews blur our eyes
To see the peach-bloom come in evening skies,
Perchance we may,
Where now this night is day,
And even through faith of still averted feet,
Making full circle of our banishment,
Amazed meet;
The bitter journey to the bourne so sweet
Seasoning the termless feast of our content
With tears of recognition never dry.

Coventry Patmore.

WINTER

I, singularly moved
To love the lovely that are not beloved,
Of all the Seasons, most
Love Winter, and to trace
The sense of the Trophonian pallor on her face.
It is not death, but plenitude of peace;
And the dim cloud that does the world enfold
Hath less the characters of dark and cold
Than warmth and light asleep,
And correspondent breathing seems to keep
With the infant harvest, breathing soft below
Its eider coverlet of snow.
Nor is in field or garden anything
But, duly look'd into, contains serene
The substance of things hoped for, in the Spring,
And evidence of Summer not yet seen.
On every chance-mild day
That visits the moist shaw,
The honeysuckle, 'sdaining to be crost
In urgence of sweet life by sleet or frost,

'Voids the time's law
With still increase
Of leaflet new, and little, wandering spray;
Often, in sheltering brakes,
As one from rest disturb'd in the first hour,
Primrose or violet bewilder'd wakes,
And deems 'tis time to flower;
Though not a whisper of her voice he hear,
The buried bulb does know
The signals of the year,
And hails far Summer with his lifted spear.
The gorse-field dark, by sudden, gold caprice,
Turns, here and there, into a Jason's fleece;
Lilies, that soon in Autumn slipp'd their gowns of green,
And vanish'd into earth,
And came again, ere Autumn died, to birth,
Stand full-array'd, amidst the wavering shower,
And perfect for the Summer, less the flower;
In nook of pale or crevice of crude bark,
Thou canst not miss,
If close thou spy, to mark
The ghostly chrysalis,
That, if thou touch it, stirs in its dream dark;
And the flush'd Robin, in the evenings hoar,
Does of Love's Day, as if he saw it, sing;
But sweeter yet than dream or song of Summer or Spring
Are Winter's sometime smiles, that seem to well
From infancy ineffable;
Her wandering, languorous gaze,
So unfamiliar, so without amaze,
On the elemental, chill adversity,
The uncomprehended rudeness; and her sigh
And solemn, gathering tear,
And look of exile from some great repose, the sphere
Of ether, moved by ether only, or
By something still more tranquil.

Coventry Patmore.

LOVE SIGHT

WHEN do I see thee most, beloved one?
  When in the light the spirits of mine eyes
  Before thy face, their altar, solemnize
The worship of that Love through thee made known?

Or when, in the dusk hours, (we two alone,)
　　Close-kissed and eloquent of still replies
　　Thy twilight-hidden glimmering visage lies,
And my soul only sees thy soul its own?

O love, my love! if I no more should see
Thyself, nor on the earth the shadow of thee,
　　Nor image of thine eyes in any spring,—
How then should sound upon Life's darkening slope
The ground-whirl of the perish'd leaves of Hope,
　　The wind of Death's imperishable wing?
　　　　　　　　　　Dante Gabriel Rossetti.

THE WOODSPURGE

T H E wind flapped loose, the wind was still,
Shaken out dead from tree and hill:
I had walk'd on at the wind's will,—
I sat now, for the wind was still.

Between my knees my forehead was,—
My lips, drawn in, said not Alas!
My hair was over in the grass,
My naked ears heard the day pass.

My eyes, wide open, had the run
Of some ten weeds to fix upon;
Among those few, out of the sun,
The woodspurge flowered, three cups in one.

From perfect grief there need not be
Wisdom or even memory:
One thing then learnt remains to me,—
The woodspurge has a cup of three.
　　　　　　　　　　Dante Gabriel Rossetti.

MODERN LOVE

XLVII

W E saw the swallows gathering in the sky,
And in the osier-isle we heard them noise.
We had not to look back on summer joys,
Or forward to a summer of bright dye:
But in the largeness of the evening earth
Our spirits grew as we went side by side.
The hour became her husband and my bride.

Love that had robbed us so, thus blessed our dearth!
The pilgrims of the year waxed very loud
In multitudinous chatterings, as the flood
Full brown came from the West, and like pale blood
Expanded to the upper crimson cloud.
Love that had robbed us of immortal things,
This little moment mercifully gave,
Where I have seen across the twilight wave
The swan sail with her young beneath her wings.
                                        George Meredith.

SEED-TIME

FLOWERS of the willow-herb are wool;
Flowers of the briar berries red;
Speeding their seed as the breeze may rule.
Flowers of the thistle loosen the thread.
Flowers of the clematis drip in beard,
Slack from the fir-tree youngly climbed;
Chaplets in air, flies foliage seared;
Heeled upon earth, lie clusters rimed.

Where were skies of the mantle stained
Orange and scarlet, a coat of frieze
Travels from North till day has waned,
Tattered, soaked in the ditch's dyes;
Tumbles the rook under grey or slate;
Else enfolding us, damps to the bone;
Narrows the world to my neighbour's gate;
Paints me Life as a wheezy crone.

Now seems none but the spider lord;
Star in circle his web waits prey,
Silvering bush-mounds, blue brushing sward;
Slow runs the hour, swift flits the ray.
Now to his thread-shroud is he nigh,
Nigh to the tangle where wings are sealed,
He who frolicked the jewelled fly;
All is adroop on the down and the weald.

Mists more lone for the sheep-bell enwrap
Nights that tardily let slip a morn
Paler than moons, and on noontide's lap
Flame dies cold, like the rose late born.
Rose born late, born withered in bud! –
I, even I, for a zenith of sun
Cry, to fulfil me, nourish my blood:
O for a day of the long light, one!

Master the blood, nor read by chills,
Earth admonishes: Hast thou ploughed,
Sown, reaped, harvested grain for the mills,
Thou hast the light over shadow of cloud.
Steadily eyeing, before that wail
Animal-infant, thy mind began,
Momently nearer me: should sight fail,
Plod in the track of the husbandman.

Verily now is our season of seed,
Now in our Autumn; and Earth discerns
Them that have served her in them that can read,
Glassing, where under the surface she burns,
Quick at her wheel, while the fuel, decay,
Brightens the fire of renewal: and we?
Death is the word of a bovine-day,
Know you the breast of the springing To-be.
                              George Meredith.

MIRAGE

THE hope I dreamed of was a dream,
    Was but a dream; and now I wake,
Exceeding comfortless, and worn, and old,
    For a dream's sake.

I hang my harp upon a tree,
    A weeping willow in a lake;
I hang my silent harp there, wrung and snapt
    For a dream's sake.

Lie still, lie still, my breaking heart;
    My silent heart, lie still and break:
Life, and the world, and mine own self, are changed
    For a dream's sake.
                              Christina Rossetti.

LIFE

    I ASKED no other thing,
    No other was denied.
    I offered Being for it;
    The mighty merchant smiled.

    Brazil? He twirled a button,
    Without a glance my way:
    'But, madam, is there nothing else
    That we can show to-day?'
                              Emily Dickinson.

THE SHOW

T H E show is not the show,
But they that go.
Menagerie to me
My neighbours be.
Fair play –
Both went to see.

Emily Dickinson.

❡

I T A S T E a liquor never brewed,
From tankards scooped in pearl;
Not all the vats upon the Rhine
Yield such an alcohol!

Inebriate of air am I,
And debauchee of dew,
Reeling, through endless summer days,
From inns of molten blue.

When landlords turn the drunken bee
Out of the foxglove's door,
When butterflies renounce their drams,
I shall but drink the more!

Till seraphs swing their snowy hats,
And saints to windows run,
To see the little tippler
Leaning against the sun!

Emily Dickinson.

❡

I B E N D E D unto me a bough of May,
That I might see and smell:
It bore it in a sort of way,
It bore it very well.
But when I let it backward sway,
Then it were hard to tell

With what a toss, with what a swing,
The dainty thing
Resumed its proper level,
And sent me to the devil.
I know it did – you doubt it ?
I turned, and saw them whispering about it.

T. E. Brown.

THE BRISTOL CHANNEL

T H I S sea was Lazarus, all day
At Dives' gate he lay,
And lapped the crumbs.
Night comes;
The beggar dies –
Forthwith the Channel, coast to coast,
Is Abraham's bosom; and the beggar lies
A lovely ghost.

T. E. Brown.

SUNSET AT CHAGFORD

HOMO LOQUITUR

I S it ironical, a fool enigma,
This sunset show?
The purple stigma,
Black mountain cut upon a saffron glow –
Is it a mammoth joke,
A riddle put for me to guess,
Which, having duly honoured, I may smoke,
And go to bed,
And snore,
Having a soothing consciousness
Of something red?
Or is it more?
Ah, is it, is it more?

A dole, perhaps?
The scraps
Tossed from the table of the revelling gods? –
What odds!
I taste them – Lazarus
Was nourished thus!
But, all the same, it surely is a cheat –
Is this the stuff they eat?
A cheat! a cheat!
Then let the garbage be –
Some pig-wash! let it vanish down the sink
Of night! 'tis not for me.
I will not drink
Their draff,
While, throned on high, they quaff
The fragrant sconce –
Has Heaven no cloaca for the nonce?

Say 'tis an anodyne –
It never shall be mine.
I want no opiates –
The best of all their cates
Were gross to balk the meanest sense;
I want to be co-equal with their fates;
I will not be put off with temporal pretence:
I want to be awake, and know, not stand
And stare at waving of a conjuror's hand.

But is it speech
Wherewith they strive to reach
Our poor inadequate souls?
The round earth rolls;
I cannot hear it hum –
The stars are dumb –
The voices of the world are in my ear
A sensuous murmur. Nothing speaks
But man, my fellow – him I hear,
And understand; but beasts and birds
And winds and waves are destitute of words.
What is the alphabet
The gods have set?
What babbling! what delusion!
And in these sunset tints
What gay confusion!
Man prints
His meaning, has a letter
Determinate. I know that it is better
Than all this cumbrous hieroglyph –
The *For*, the *If*
Are growth of man's analysis:
The gods in bliss
Scrabble a baby jargon on the skies
For us to analyse!
Cumbrous? nay, idiotic –
A party-coloured symbolism,
The fragments of a shivered prism:
Man gives the swift demotic.

'Tis good to see
The economy
Of poor upstriving man!
Since time began,
He has been sifting
The elements; while God, on chaos drifting,
Sows broadcast all His stuff.

92

Lavish enough,
No doubt; but why this waste?
See! of these very sunset dyes
The virgin chaste
Takes one, and in a harlot's eyes
Another rots. They go by billion billions:
Each blade of grass
Ignores them as they pass;
The spiders in their foul pavilions,
Behold this vulgar gear,
And sneer;
Dull frogs
In bogs
Catch rosy gleams through rushes,
And know that night is near;
Wrong-headed thrushes
Blow bugles to it;
And a wrong-headed poet
Will strut, and strain the cogs
Of the machine, he blushes
To call his Muse, and maunder;
And, marvellous to relate!
These pseudo-messengers of state
Will wander
Where there is no intelligence to meet them,
Nor even a sensorium to greet them.
The very finest of them
Go where there's naught to love them
Or notice them: to cairns, to rocks
Where ravens nurse their young,
To mica-splints from granite-boulders wrung
By channels of the marsh, to stocks
Of old dead willows in a pool as dead.
Can anything be said
To these? The leech
Looks from its muddy lair,
And sees a silly something in the air –
Call you this *speech?*
O God, if it be speech,
Speak plainer,
If Thou would'st teach
That I shall be a gainer!
The age of picture-alphabets is gone:
We are not now so weak;
We are too old to con
The horn-book of our youth. Time lags –

O, rip this obsolete blazon into rags!
And speak! O, speak!

But, if I be a spectacle
In Thy great theatre, then do Thy will:
Arrange Thy instruments with circumspection;
Summon Thine angels to the vivisection!
But quick! O, quick!
For I am sick,
And very sad.
Thy pupils will be glad.
'See', Thou exclaim'st, 'this ray!
How permanent upon the retina!
How odd that purple hue!
The pineal gland is blue.
I stick this probe
In the posterior lobe –
Behold the cerebellum
A smoky yellow, like old vellum!
Students will please observe
The structure of the optic nerve.
See! nothing could be finer –
That film of pink
Around the hippocampus minor.
Behold!
I touch it, and it turns bright gold.
Again! – as black as ink.
Another lancet – thanks!
That's Manx –
Yes, the delicate pale sea-green
Passing into ultra-marine –
A little blurred – in fact
This brain seems packed
With sunsets. Bring
That battery here; now put your
Negative pole beneath the suture –
That's just the thing.
Now then the other way –
I say! I say!
More chloroform!
(A little more will do no harm).
Now this is the most instructive of all
The phenomena, what in fact we may call
The most obvious justification
Of vivisection in general.
Observe (once! twice!
That's very nice) –

Observe, I say, the incipient relation
Of a quasi-moral activity
To this physical agitation!
Of course, you see. . . .'
Yes, yes, O God,
I feel the prod
Of that dissecting knife.
Instructive, say the pupil angels, *very:*
And some take notes, and some take sandwiches
    and sherry;
And some are prying
Into the very substance of my brain –
I feel their fingers!
(My life! my life!)
Yes, yes! it lingers!
The sun, the sun –
Go on! go on!
Blue, yellow, red!
But please remember that I am not dead,
Nor even dying.

SUNSET AT CHAGFORD

RESPONDET δημιουργος

Yes, it is hard, but not for you alone.
You speak of cup and throne,
And all that separates Me from you.
It is not that you don't believe:
It is but that you misconceive
The work I have to do.

No throne, no cup
Nor down, but likest up,
As from a deep black shaft, I look to see
The fabric of My own immensity.
You have the temporal activity, and rejoice
In sweet, articulate voice –
Tunes, songs.
To Me no less
Belongs
The fixed, sad fashion of productiveness.
You think that I am wise,
Or cunning, clever as a man is clever.
You think all knowledge with Me lies,
From Me must flow.
I know not if I know –

But this I know, I will work on for ever.
You fret because you are not this and that,
And so you die;
But I,
Who have not sat
Since first into the void I swam,
Obeying Mine own laws,
Persist, because
I am but what I am.

I am old and blind;
I have no speech
'Wherewith to reach'
Your quick-selecting ears.
And yet I mark your tears;
And yet I would be kind.
And so I strain
To speak, as now;
And, in more cheerful vein,
You haply will allow
I make My meaning fairly plain.
Therefore it is I store
Such beauty in the clouds, and on the shore
Make foam-flakes glisten; therefore you have seen
This sunset; therefore 'tis the green
And lusty grass
Hath come to pass
And flame
Lies sparkling in the dews –
And yet I cannot choose
But do the same!

I am no surgeon,
I have no lancet, but I mingle
Sap for the buds, that they may burgeon,
And tingle
With soft sweet throes
Of parturition vegetal.
And so to all
The surfaces
I outward press,
And hold the very brink
Of speech, that I would think
Speech must come next.
But I can do no more: wherefore I am not vexed;
But you are, being perplexed
With suppositions, scribbling o'er the text
Of natural life. And, seeing that this is so,

And that I cannot know
The innumerous ills,
Therefore I strew the hills
And vallies with delight,
That, day or night,
In sad or merry plight,
You may catch sight
Of some sweet joy that thrills
Your heart.
And what if I impart
The same to frog or newt,
What if I steep the root
Of some old stump in bright vermilion,
And if the spider in his quaint pavilion
Catches a sunbeam where he thought a fly,
Ah, why
Should I not care for such?
I, Who make all things, know it is not much.
And, by analogy I must suppose
They have their woes
Like you:
Therefore I still must strew
Joys that may wait for centuries,
And light at last on Socrates,
Or on the frog, whose eyes
You may have noticed full of bright surprise –
Or have you not? Ah, then
You only think of men!
But I would have no single creature miss
One possible bliss.
And this
Is certain: never be afraid!
I love what I have made.
I know this is not wit,
This is not to be clever,
Or anything whatever.
You see, I am a servant, that is it:
You've hit
The mark – a servant: for the other word –
Why, you are Lord, if any one is Lord.

T. E. Brown.

WEATHERS

T H I S is the weather the cuckoo likes,
    And so do I;
When showers betumble the chestnut spikes,
    And nestlings fly;
And the little brown nightingale bills his best,
And they sit outside the 'Traveller's Rest',
And maids come forth sprig-muslin drest,
And citizens dream of the South and West,
    And so do I.

This is the weather the shepherd shuns,
    And so do I:
When beeches drip in browns and duns,
    And thresh, and ply;
And hill-hid tides throb, throe on throe,
And meadow rivulets overflow,
And drops on gate-bars hang in a row,
And rooks in families homeward go,
    And so do I.   *Thomas Hardy.*

¶

I L O O K into my glass,
And view my wasting skin,
And say, 'Would God it came to pass
My heart had shrunk as thin!'

For then, I, undistrest
By hearts grown cold to me,
Could lonely wait my endless rest
With equanimity.

But Time, to make me grieve,
Part steals, lets part abide;
And shakes this fragile frame at eve
With throbbings of noontide.

          Thomas Hardy.

THE SLEEP-WORKER

W H E N wilt thou wake, O Mother, wake and see –
As one who, held in trance, has laboured long
By vacant rote and prepossession strong –
The coils that thou hast wrought unwittingly;

Wherein have place, unrealized by thee,
Fair growths, foul cankers, right enmeshed with wrong,
Strange orchestras of victim-shriek and song,
And curious blends of ache and ecstasy ? –

Should that morn come, and show thy opened eyes
All that Life's palpitating tissues feel,
How wilt thou bear thyself in thy surprise ? –

Wilt thou destroy, in one wild shock of shame,
Thy whole high heaving firmamental frame,
Or patiently adjust, amend, and heal ?

Thomas Hardy.

AT A LUNAR ECLIPSE

T H Y shadow, Earth, from Pole to Central Sea,
Now steals along upon the Moon's meek shine
In even monochrome and curving line
Of imperturbable serenity.

How shall I link such sun-cast symmetry
With the torn troubled form I know as thine,
That profile, placid as a brow divine,
With continents of moil and misery ?

And can immense Mortality but throw
So small a shade, and Heaven's high human scheme
Be hemmed within the coasts yon arc implies ?

Is such the stellar gauge of earthly show,
Nation at war with nation, brains that teem,
Heroes, and women fairer that the skies ?

Thomas Hardy.

THE LEADEN ECHO AND THE GOLDEN ECHO

THE LEADEN ECHO

H O W to kéep – is there ány any, is there none such, nowhere
known some, bow or brooch or braid or brace, láce, latch
or catch or key to keep
Back beauty, keep it, beauty, beauty, beauty, . . . from
vanishing away ?
Ó is there no frowning of these wrinkles, rankèd wrinkles
deep,

Dówn? no waving off of these most mournful messengers,
    still messengers, sad and stealing messengers of grey?
No there's none, there's none, O no there's none,
Nor can you long be, what you now are, called fair,
Do what you may do, what, do what you may,
And wisdom is early to despair:
Be beginning; since, no, nothing can be done
To keep at bay
Age and age's evils, hoar hair,
Ruck and wrinkle, drooping, dying, death's worst, winding
    sheets, tombs and worms and tumbling to decay;
So be beginning, be beginning to despair.
O there's none; no no no there's none:
Be beginning to despair, to despair,
Despair, despair, despair, despair.

THE GOLDEN ECHO

    Spare!
There ís one, yes I have one (Hush there!);
Only not within seeing of the sun,
Not within the singeing of the strong sun,
Tall sun's tingeing, or treacherous the tainting of the earth's
    air,
Somewhere elsewhere there is ah well where! one,
Óne. Yes I cán tell such a key, I dó know such a place,
Where whatever's prized and passes of us, everything that's
    fresh and fast flying of us, seems to us sweet of us and
    swiftly away with, done away with, undone,
Úndone, done with, soon done with, and yet dearly and
    dangerously sweet
Of us, the wimpled-water-dimpled, not-by-morning-
    matchéd face,
The flower of beauty, fleece of beauty, too too apt to, ah! to
    fleet,
Never fleets móre, fastened with the tenderest truth
To its own best being and its loveliness of youth: it is an
    ever-lastingness of, O it is an all youth!
Come then, your ways and airs and looks, locks, maiden
    gear, gallantry and gaiety and grace,
Winning ways, airs innocent, maiden manners, sweet looks,
    loose locks, long locks, lovelocks, gaygear, going gallant,
    girlgrace –
Resign them, sign them, seal them, send them, motion
    them with breath,

And with sighs soaring, soaring síghs deliver
Them; beauty-in-the-ghost, deliver it, early now, long be-
    fore death
Give beauty back, beauty, beauty, beauty, back to God,
    beauty's self and beauty's giver.
See; not a hair is, not an eyelash, not the least lash lost; every
    hair
Is, hair of the head, numbered.
Nay, what we had lighthanded left in surly the mere mould
Will have waked and have waxed and have walked with the
    wind what while we slept,
This side, that side hurling a heavyheaded hundredfold
What while we, while we slumbered.
O then, weary then whý should we tread? O why are we so
    haggard at the heart, so care-coiled, care-killed, so
    fagged, so fashed, so cogged, so cumbered,
When the thing we freely fórfeit is kept with fonder a care,
Fonder a care kept than we could have kept it, kept
Far with fonder a care (and we, we should have lost it) finer,
    fonder
A care kept.– Where kept? Do but tell us where kept,
    where.–
Yonder.– What high as that! We follow, now we follow.–
    Yonder, yes yonder, yonder,
Yonder.
                        Gerard Manley Hopkins.

***

¶

    THE idle life I lead
    Is like a pleasant sleep,
    Wherein I rest and heed
    The dreams that by me sweep.

    And still of all my dreams
    In turn so swiftly past,
    Each in its fancy seems
    A nobler than the last.

    And every eve I say,
    Noting my step in bliss,
    That I have known no day
    In all my life like this.
                      Robert Bridges.

CHRIST IN THE UNIVERSE

W I T H this ambiguous earth
His dealings have been told us. These abide:
The signal to a maid, the human birth,
The lesson, and the young Man crucified.

But not a star of all
The innumerable host of stars has heard
How He administered this terrestrial ball.
Our race have kept their Lord's entrusted Word.

Of His earth-visiting feet
None knows the secret, cherished, perilous,
The terrible, shamefast, frightened, whispered, sweet,
Heart-shattering secret of His way with us.

No planet knows that this
Our wayside planet, carrying land and wave,
Love and life multiplied, and pain and bliss,
Bears, as chief treasure, one forsaken grave.

Nor, in our little day,
May His devices with the heavens be guessed,
His pilgrimage to thread the Milky Way,
Or His bestowals there be manifest.

But, in the eternities,
Doubtless we shall compare together, hear
A million alien Gospels, in what guise
He trod the Pleiades, the Lyre, the Bear.

Oh, be prepared, my soul!
To read the inconceivable, to scan
The million forms of God those stars unroll
When, in our turn, we show to them a Man.
                                    Alice Meynell.

TO THE BODY

T H O U inmost, ultimate
Council of judgment, palace of decrees,
Where the high senses hold their spiritual state,
     Sued by earth's embassies,
And sign, approve, accept, conceive, create;

Create – thy senses close
With the world's pleas. The random odours reach
Their sweetness in the place of thy repose,
  Upon thy tongue the peach,
And in thy nostrils breathes the breathing rose.

  To thee, secluded one,
The dark vibrations of the sightless skies,
The lovely inexplicit colours run;
  The light gropes for those eyes.
O thou august! thou dost command the sun.

  Music, all dumb, hath trod
Into thine ear her one effectual way;
And fire and cold approach to gain thy nod,
  Where thou call'st up the day,
Where thou awaitest the appeal of God.
                              Alice Meynell.

THE RAINY SUMMER

THERE'S much afoot in heaven and earth this year;
  The winds hunt up the sun, hunt up the moon,
Trouble the dubious dawn, hasten the drear
  Height of a threatening noon.

No breath of boughs, no breath of leaves, of fronds,
  May linger or grow warm; the trees are loud;
The forest, rooted, tosses in her bonds,
  And strains against the cloud.

No scents may pause within the garden-fold;
  The rifled flowers are cold as ocean-shells;
Bees, humming in the storm, carry their cold
  Wild honey to cold cells.
                              Alice Meynell.

¶

MY body, which my dungeon is,
And yet my parks and palaces: –
  Which is so great that there I go
All the day long to and fro,
And when the night begins to fall
Throw down my bed and sleep, while all
The building hums with wakefulness –

Even as a child of savages
When evening takes her on her way,
(She having roamed a summer's day
Along the mountain-sides and scalp)
Sleeps in the antre of that alp: –
    Which is so broad and high that there,
As in the topless field of air,
My fancy soars like to a kite
And faints in the blue infinite: –
    Which is so strong, my strongest throes
And the rough world's besieging blows
Not break it, and so weak withal,
Death ebbs and flows in its loose wall
As the green sea in fishers' nets,
And tops its topmost parapets: –
    Which is so wholly mine that I
Can wield its whole artillery,
And mine so little, that my soul
Dwells in perpetual control,
And I but think and speak and do
As my dead fathers move me to: –
    If this born body of my bones
The beggared soul so barely owns,
What money passed from hand to hand,
What creeping custom of the land,
What deed of author or assign,
Can make a house a thing of mine ?

                   R. L. Stevenson.

¶

O N Wenlock Edge the wood's in trouble;
  His forest fleece the Wrekin heaves;
The gale, it plies the saplings double,
  And thick on Severn snow the leaves.

'Twould blow like this through holt and hanger
  When Uricon the city stood:
'Tis the old wind in the old anger,
  But then it threshed another wood.

Then, 'twas before my time, the Roman
  At yonder heaving hill would stare:
The blood that warms an English yeoman,
  The thoughts that hurt him, they were there.

There, like the wind through woods in riot,
  Through him the gale of life blew high;
The tree of man was never quiet:
  Then 'twas the Roman, now 'tis I.

The gale, it plies the saplings double,
  It blows so hard, 'twill soon be gone:
To-day the Roman and his trouble
  Are ashes under Uricon.

A. E. Housman.

¶

    F R O M far, from eve and morning
      And yon twelve-winded sky,
    The stuff of life to knit me
      Blew hither: here am I.

    Now – for a breath I tarry
      Nor yet disperse apart –
    Take my hand quick and tell me,
      What have you in your heart.

    Speak now, and I will answer;
      How shall I help you, say;
    Ere to the wind's twelve quarters
      I take my endless way.

A. E. Housman.

A FALLEN YEW

I T seemed corrival of the world's great prime,
  Made to un-edge the scythe of Time,
    And last with stateliest rhyme.

No tender Dryad ever did indue
  That rigid chiton of rough yew,
    To fret her white flesh through:

But some god, like to those grim Asgard lords,
  Who walk the fables of the hordes
    From Scandinavian fjords,

Upheaved its stubborn girth, and raised unriven,
  Against the whirl-blast and the levin,
    Defiant arms to Heaven.

105

When doom puffed out the stars, we might have said,
    It would decline its heavy head,
      And see the world to bed.

For this firm yew did from the vassal leas,
    And rain and air, its tributaries,
      Its revenues increase,

And levy impost on the golden sun,
    Take the blind years as they might run,
      And no fate seek or shun.

But now our yew is strook, is fallen – yea,
    Hacked like dull wood of every day
      To this and that, men say.

Never! – To Hades' shadowy shipyards gone,
    Dim barge of Dis, down Acheron
      It drops, or Lethe wan.

Stirred by its fall – poor destined bark of Dis! –
    Along my soul a bruit there is
      Of echoing images,

Reverberations of mortality:
    Spelt backward from its death, to me
      Its life reads saddenedly.

Its breast was hollowed as the tooth of eld;
    And boys there creeping, unbeheld,
      A laughing moment dwelled.

Yet they, within its very heart so crept,
    Reached not the heart that courage kept
      With winds and years beswept.

And in its boughs did close and kindly nest
    The birds, as they within its breast,
      By all its leaves caressed.

But bird nor child might touch by any art
    Each other's or the tree's hid heart,
      A whole God's breadth apart;

The breadth of God, the breadth of death and life!
  Even so, even so, in undreamed strife
    With pulseless Law, the wife,—

The sweetest wife on sweetest marriage-day,—
  Their soul at grapple in mid-way,
    Sweet to her sweet may say:

'I take you to my inmost heart, my true!'
  Ah, fool! but there is one heart you
    Shall never take him to!

The hold that falls not when the town is got,
  The heart's heart, whose immurèd plot
    Hath keys yourself keep not!

Its ports you cannot burst — you are withstood —
  For him that to your listening blood
    Sends precepts as he would.

Its gates are deaf to Love, high summoner;
  Yea, Love's great warrant runs not there:
    You are your prisoner.

Yourself are with yourself the sole consortress
  In that unleaguerable fortress;
    It knows you not for portress.

Its keys are at the cincture hung of God;
  Its gates are trepidant to His nod;
    By Him its floors are trod.

And if His feet shall rock those floors in wrath,
  Or blest aspersion sleek His path,
    Is only choice it hath.

Yea, in that ultimate heart's occult abode
  To lie as in an oubliette of God,
    Or in a bower untrod,

Built by a secret Lover for His Spouse; —
  Sole choice is this your life allows,
    Sad tree, whose perishing boughs
      So few birds house!

                              Francis Thompson.

ARAB LOVE SONG

THE hunchèd camels of the night
Trouble the bright
And silver waters of the moon.
The Maiden of the Morn will soon
Through Heaven stray and sing,
Star gathering.

Now while the dark about our loves is strewn,
Light of my dark, blood of my heart, O come!
And night will catch her breath up, and be dumb.

Leave thy father, leave thy mother
And thy brother;
Leave the black tents of thy tribe apart!
Am I not thy father and thy brother,
And thy mother?
And thou – what needest with thy tribe's black tents
Who hast the red pavilion of my heart?
                                        Francis Thompson.

THE HEART

O NOTHING, in this corporal earth of man,
    That to the imminent heaven of his high soul
Responds with colour and with shadow, can
    Lack correlated greatness. If the scroll
Where thoughts lie fast in spell of hieroglyph
    Be mighty through its mighty habitants;
If God be in His Name; grave potence if
    The sounds unbind of hieratic chants;
All's vast that vastness means. Nay, I affirm
    Nature is whole in her least things exprest,
Nor know we with what scope God builds the worm.
    Our towns are copied fragments from our breast;
    And all man's Babylons strive but to impart
    The grandeurs of his Babylonian heart.
                                        Francis Thompson.

THE KINGDOM OF GOD
'In no Strange Land'

O WORLD invisible, we view thee,
O world intangible, we touch thee,
O world unknowable, we know thee,
Inapprehensible, we clutch thee!

Does the fish soar to find the ocean,
The eagle plunge to find the air –
That we ask of the stars in motion
If they have rumour of thee there?

Not where the wheeling systems darken,
And our benumbed conceiving soars! –
The drift of pinions, would we hearken,
Beats at our own clay-shuttered doors.

The angels keep their ancient places; –
Turn but a stone, and start a wing!
'Tis ye, 'tis your estrangèd faces,
That miss the many-splendoured thing.

But (when so sad thou canst not sadder)
Cry; – and upon thy so sore loss
Shall shine the traffic of Jacob's ladder
Pitched betwixt Heaven and Charing Cross.

Yea, in the night, my Soul, my daughter,
Cry,– clinging Heaven by the hems;
And lo, Christ walking on the water
Not of Gennesareth, but Thames!

Francis Thompson.

IMMORTALITY

s o I have sunk my roots in earth
Since that my pretty boys had birth;
And fear no more the grave and gloom,
I, with the centuries to come.

As the tree blossoms so bloom I,
Flinging wild branches to the sky;
Renew each year my leafy suit,
Strike with the years a deeper root;

Shelter a thousand birds to be,
A thousand herds give praise to me;
And in my kind and grateful shade
How many a weary head be laid.

To hear the cuckoo the first time,
And 'mid new roses in the prime
To read the poets newly. This,
Year after year, shall be my bliss.

Of me shall love be born anew;
I shall be loved and lover too;
Years after this poor body has died
Shall be the bridegroom and the bride.

And many million lights of home
Shall light for me the time to come.
Unto me much shall be forgiven,
I that make many souls for heaven.

Katharine Tynan.

'HE KNOWETH NOT THAT THE DEAD ARE THINE'

T H E weapon that you fought with was a word,
And with that word you stabbed me to the heart.
Not once but twice you did it, for the sword
    Made no blood start.

They have not tried you for your life. You go
Strong in such innocence as men will boast.
They have not buried me. They do not know
    Life from its ghost.

Mary Coleridge.

¶

E G Y P T ' S might is tumbled down
    Down a-down the deeps of thought;
Greece is fallen and Troy town,
    Glorious Rome hath lost her crown,
Venice' pride is nought.

But the dreams their children dreamed
    Fleeting, unsubstantial, vain,
Shadowy as the shadows seemed,
Airy nothing, as they deemed,
    These remain.

Mary Coleridge.

¶

C I T I E S and Thrones and Powers
    Stand in Time's eye,
Almost as long as flowers,
    Which daily die:

But, as new buds put forth
   To glad new men,
Out of the spent and unconsidered Earth
   The Cities rise again.

This season's Daffodil,
   She never hears
What change, what chance, what chill,
   Cut down last year's;
But with bold countenance,
   And knowledge small,
Esteems her seven days' continuance
   To be perpetual.

So Time that is o'er-kind
   To all that be,
Ordains us e'en as blind,
   As bold as she:
That in our very death,
   And burial sure,
Shadow to shadow, well persuaded, saith,
   'See how our works endure!'

Rudyard Kipling.

THAT THE NIGHT COME

S H E lived in storm and strife,
Her soul had such desire
For what proud death may bring
That it could not endure
The common good of life,
But lived as 'twere a king
That packed his marriage day
With banneret and pennon,
Trumpet and kettledrum,
And the outrageous cannon,
To bundle time away
That the night come.

W. B. Yeats.

EASTER, 1916

I H A V E met them at close of day
Coming with vivid faces
From counter or desk among grey
Eighteenth-century houses.

I have passed with a nod of the head
Or polite meaningless words,
Or have lingered awhile and said
Polite meaningless words,
And thought before I had done
Of a mocking tale or a gibe
To please a companion
Around the fire at the club,
Being certain that they and I
But lived where motley is worn:
All changed, changed utterly:
A terrible beauty is born.

That woman's days were spent
In ignorant good will,
Her nights in argument
Until her voice grew shrill.
What voice more sweet than hers
When young and beautiful
She rode to harriers?
This man had kept a school
And rode our wingèd horse;
This other his helper and friend
Was coming into his force;
He might have won fame in the end,
So sensitive his nature seemed,
So daring and sweet his thought.
This other man I had dreamed
A drunken, vain-glorious lout.
He had done most bitter wrong
To some who are near my heart,
Yet I number him in the song;
He, too, has resigned his part
In the casual comedy:
He, too, has been changed in his turn,
Transformed utterly:
A terrible beauty is born.

Hearts with one purpose alone
Through summer and winter seem
Enchanted to a stone
To trouble the living stream.
The horse that comes from the road,
The rider, the birds that range
From cloud to tumbling cloud,
Minute by minute they change;
As shadow of cloud on the stream
Changes minute by minute;

A horse-hoof slides on the brim,
And a horse plashes within it
Where long-legged moor-hens dive,
And hens to moor-cocks call.
Minute by minute they live:
The stone's in the midst of all.

Too long a sacrifice
Can make a stone of the heart.
O when may it suffice?
That is Heaven's part, our part
To murmur name upon name
As a mother names her child
When sleep at last has come
On limbs that had run wild.
What is it but nightfall?
No, no, not night but death;
Was it needless death after all?
For England may keep faith
For all that is done and said.
We know their dream; enough
To know they dreamed and are dead.
And what if excess of love
Bewildered them till they died?
I write it out in a verse –
MacDonagh and MacBride
And Connolly and Pearse
Now and in time to be,
Wherever green is worn,
Are changed, changed utterly:
A terrible beauty is born.

W. B. Yeats.

SOLOMON AND THE WITCH

A N D thus declared that Arab lady:
'Last night, where under the wild moon
On grassy mattress I had laid me,
Within my arms great Solomon,
I suddenly cried out in a strange tongue
Not his, not mine.'
                        And he that knew
All sounds by bird or angel sung
Answered: 'A crested cockerel crew
Upon a blossoming apply bough
Three hundred years before the Fall,
And never crew again till now,

And would not now but that he thought,
Chance being at one with Choice at last,
All that the brigand apple brought
And this foul world were dead at last.
He that crowed out eternity
Thought to have crowed it in again.
A lover with a spider's eye
Will find out some appropriate pain,
Aye, though all passion's in the glance,
For every nerve: lover tests lover
With cruelties of Choice and Chance;
And when at last that murder's over
Maybe the bride-bed brings despair,
For each an imagined image brings
And finds a real image there;
Yet the world ends when these two things,
Though several, are a single light,
When oil and wick are burned in one;
Therefore a blessed moon last night
Gave Sheba to her Solomon.'

'Yet the world stays':
                           'If that be so,
Your cockerel found us in the wrong
Although he thought it worth a crow.
Maybe an image is too strong
Or maybe is not strong enough.'

'The night has fallen; not a sound
In the forbidden sacred grove,
Unless a petal hit the ground,
Nor any human sight within it
But the crushed grass where we have lain;
And the moon is wilder every minute.
Oh, Solomon! let us try again.'
                                    W. B. Yeats.

THE PRECEPT OF SILENCE

I KNOW you: solitary griefs,
Desolate passions, aching hours!
I know you: tremulous beliefs,
Agonized hopes, and ashen flowers!

The winds are sometimes sad to me;
The starry spaces, full of fear;
Mine is the sorrow on the sea,
And mine the sigh of places drear.

Some players upon plaintive strings
Publish their wistfulness abroad:
I have not spoken of these things,
Save to one man, and unto God.

Lionel Johnson.

¶

BUT OH! not Lovely Helen, nor the pride
Of that most ancient Ilium matched with doom.
Men murdered Priam in his royal room
And Troy was burned with fire and Hector died.
For even Hector's dreadful day was more
Than all his breathing courage dared defend;
The armouréd light and bulwark of the war
Trailed his great story to the accustomed end.

He was the city's buttress, Priam's Son,
The Soldier, born in bivouac – praises great
And horns in double front of battle won,
Yet down he went: when unremembering fate
Felled him at last with all his armour on.
Hector: the horseman: in the Scæan Gate.

Hilaire Belloc.

LEISURE

WHAT is this life if, full of care,
We have no time to stand and stare.

No time to stand beneath the boughs
And stare as long as sheep or cows.

No time to see, when woods we pass,
Where squirrels hide their nuts in grass.

No time to see, in broad daylight,
Streams full of stars, like skies at night.

No time to turn at Beauty's glance,
And watch her feet, how they can dance.

115

No time to wait till her mouth can
Enrich that smile her eyes began.

A poor life this if, full of care,
We have no time to stand and stare.

W. H. Davies.

THE LIKENESS

W H E N I came forth this morn I saw
   Quite twenty cloudlets in the air;
And then I saw a flock of sheep,
   Which told me how those clouds came there.

That flock of sheep, on that green grass,
   Well might it lie so still and proud!
Its likeness had been drawn in heaven
   On a blue sky, in silvery cloud.

I gazed me up, I gazed me down,
   And swore, though good the likeness was,
'Twas a long way from justice done
   To such white wool, such sparkling grass.

W. H. Davies.

THE TWO CHILDREN

'A H, little boy! I see
   You have a wooden spade.
Into this sand you dig
   So deep – for what?' I said.
'There's more rich gold,' said he,
   'Down under where I stand,
Than twenty elephants
   Could move across the land.'

'Ah, little girl with wool! –
   What are you making now?'
'Some stockings for a bird,
   To keep his legs from snow.'
And there those children are,
   So happy, small, and proud:
The boy that digs his grave,
   The girl that knits her shroud.

W. H. Davies.

A GREAT TIME

S W E E T Chance, that led my steps abroad,
 Beyond the town, where wild flowers grow –
A rainbow and a cuckoo, Lord,
 How rich and great the times are now!
 Know, all ye sheep
 And cows, that keep
On staring that I stand so long
 In grass that's wet from heavy rain –
A rainbow and a cuckoo's song
 May never come together again;
 May never come
 This side the tomb.

W. H. Davies.

THE BELLS OF HEAVEN

 ' T W O U L D ring the bells of Heaven
 The wildest peal for years,
 If Parson lost his senses
 And people came to theirs,
 And he and they together
 Knelt down with angry prayers
 For tamed and shabby tigers
 And dancing dogs and bears,
 And wretched, blind pit ponies,
 And little hunted hares.

Ralph Hodgson.

¶

 T I M E, you old gipsy man,
 Will you not stay,
 Put up your caravan
 Just for one day?

 All things I'll give you
 Will you be my guest,
 Bells for your jennet
 Of silver the best,
 Goldsmiths shall beat you
 A great golden ring,
 Peacocks shall bow to you,
 Little boys sing,

Oh, and sweet girls will
Festoon you with may,
Time, you old gipsy,
Why hasten away?

Last week in Babylon,
Last night in Rome,
Morning, and in the crush
Under Paul's dome;
Under Paul's dial
You tighten your rein –
Only a moment,
And off once again;
Off to some city
Now blind in the womb,
Off to another
Ere that's in the tomb.

Time, you old gipsy man,
  Will you not stay,
Put up your caravan
  Just for one day?
                    Ralph Hodgson.

THE SCRIBE

W H A T lovely things
  Thy hand hath made:
The smooth-plumed bird
  In its emerald shade,
The seed of the grass,
  The speck of stone
Which the wayfaring ant
  Stirs – and hastes on!

Though I should sit
  By some tarn in thy hills,
Using its ink
  As the spirit wills
To write of Earth's wonders,
  Its live, willed things,
Flit would the ages
  On soundless wings
Ere unto Z
  My pen drew nigh;
Leviathan told,
  And the honey-fly:

And still would remain
  My wit to try –
My worn reeds broken,
  The dark tarn dry,
All words forgotten –
  Thou, Lord, and I.
                              Walter De la Mare.

ECCLESIASTES

T H E R E is one sin: to call a green leaf grey,
  Whereat the sun in heaven shuddereth.
There is one blasphemy: for death to pray,
  For God alone knoweth the praise of death.

There is one creed: 'neath no world-terror's wing
  Apples forget to grow on apple-trees.
There is one thing is needful – everything –
  The rest is vanity of vanities.
                              G. K. Chesterton.

THE PRAISE OF DUST

' W H A T of vile dust?' the preacher said.
  Methought the whole world woke,
The dead stone lived beneath my foot,
  And my whole body spoke.

'You, that play tyrant to the dust,
  And stamp its wrinkled face,
This patient star that flings you not
  Far into homeless space,

'Come down out of your dusty shrine
  The living dust to see,
The flowers that at your sermon's end
  Stand blazing silently.

'Rich white and blood-red blossom; stones,
  Lichens like fire encrust;
A gleam of blue, a glare of gold,
  The vision of the dust.

'Pass them all by: till, as you come
  Where, at a city's edge,
Under a tree – I know it well –
  Under a lattice ledge,

'The sunshine falls on one brown head.
  You, too, O cold of clay,
Eater of stones, may haply hear
  The trumpets of that day

'When God to all his paladins
  By his own splendour swore
To make a fairer face than heaven,
  Of dust and nothing more.'

                                    G. K. Chesterton.

MENDING WALL

SOMETHING there is that doesn't love a wall,
That sends the frozen-ground-swell under it,
And spills the upper boulders in the sun;
And makes gaps even two can pass abreast.
The work of hunters is another thing:
I have come after them and made repair
Where they have left not one stone on a stone,
But they would have the rabbit out of hiding,
To please the yelping dogs. The gaps I mean,
No one has seen them made or heard them made,
But at spring mending-time we find them there.
I let my neighbour know beyond the hill;
And on a day we meet to walk the line
And set the wall between us once again.
We keep the wall between us as we go.
To each the boulders that have fallen to each.
And some are loaves and some so nearly balls
We have to use a spell to make them balance:
'Stay where you are until our backs are turned!'
We wear our fingers rough with handling them.
Oh, just another kind of out-door game,
One on a side. It comes to little more:
There where it is we do not need the wall:
He is all pine and I am apple orchard.
My apple trees will never get across
And eat the cones under his pines, I tell him.
He only says, 'Good fences make good neighbours.'
Spring is the mischief in me, and I wonder
If I could put a notion in his head:
'Why do they make good neighbours? Isn't it
Where there are cows? But here there are no cows.
Before I built a wall I'd ask to know
What I was walling in or walling out,
And to whom I was like to give offence.

Something there is that doesn't love a wall,
That wants it down.' I could say 'Elves' to him,
But it's not elves exactly, and I'd rather
He said it for himself. I see him there
Bringing a stone grasped firmly by the top
In each hand, like an old-stone savage armed.
He moves in darkness as it seems to me,
Not of woods only and the shade of trees.
He will not go behind his father's saying,
And he likes having thought of it so well.
He says again, 'Good fences make good neighbours.'
                                        Robert Frost.

BY A BIER-SIDE

T H I S is a sacred city built of marvellous earth.
Life was lived nobly here to give such beauty birth.
Beauty was in this brain and in this eager hand:
Death is so blind and dumb Death does not understand.
Death drifts the brain with dust and soils the young limbs'
        glory,
Death makes justice a dream, and strength a traveller's story.
Death drives the lovely soul to wander under the sky,
Death opens unknown doors. It is most grand to die.
                                        John Masefield.

INVOCATION

O W A N D E R E R into many brains
O spark the emperor's purple hides,
You sow the dusk with fiery grains
When the gold horseman rides.
    O beauty on the darkness hurled,
    Be it through me you shame the world.
                                        John Masefield.

TO HIS MOTHER, C.L.M.

I N the dark womb where I began
My mother's life made me a man.
Through all the months of human birth
Her beauty fed my common earth.
I cannot see, nor breathe, nor stir,
But through the death of some of her.

121

Down in the darkness of the grave
She cannot see the life she gave.
For all her love, she cannot tell
Whether I use it ill or well,
Nor knock at dusty doors to find
Her beauty dusty in the mind.

If the grave's gates could be undone,
She would not know her little son,
I am so grown. If we should meet,
She would pass by me in the street,
Unless my soul's face let her see
My sense of what she did for me.

What have I done to keep in mind
My debt to her and womankind?
What woman's happier life repays
Her for those months of wretched days?
For all my mouthless body leech'd
Ere Birth's releasing hell was reach'd?

What have I done, or tried, or said
In thanks to that dear woman dead?
Men triumph over women still,
Men trample women's rights at will,
And man's lust roves the world untamed.

.   .   .   .

O grave, keep shut lest I be shamed.

John Masefield.

SONNETS

V

I COULD not sleep for thinking of the sky,
The unending sky, with all its million suns
Which turn their planets everlastingly
In nothing, where the fire-haired comet runs.
If I could sail that nothing, I should cross
Silence and emptiness with dark stars passing;
Then, in the darkness, see a point of gloss
Burn to a glow, and glare, and keep amassing,
And rage into a sun with wandering planets,
And drop behind; and then, as I proceed,
See his last light upon his last moon's granites
Die to a dark that would be night indeed:
Night where my soul might sail a million years
In nothing, not even Death, not even tears.

XIV

Y O U are too beautiful for mortal eyes,
You the divine unapprehended soul;
The red worm in the marrow of the wise
Stirs as you pass, but never sees you whole.
Even as the watcher in the midnight tower
Knows from a change in heaven an unseen star,
So from your beauty, so from the summer flower,
So from the light, one guesses what you are.
So in the darkness does the traveller come
To some lit chink, through which he cannot see
More than a light, nor hear, more than a hum,
Of the great hall where Kings in council be.
So, in the grave, the red and mouthless worm
Knows of the soul that held his body firm.

X V

I S it a sea on which the souls embark
Out of the body, as men put to sea?
Or do we come like candles in the dark
In the rooms in cities in eternity?
Is it a darkness that our powers can light?
Is this, our little lantern of man's love,
A help to find friends wandering in the night
In the unknown country with no star above?
Or is it sleep, unknowing, outlasting clocks
That outlast men, that, though the cockcrow ring,
Is but one peace, of the substance of the rocks;
Is but one space in the now unquickened thing;
Is but one joy, that, though the million tire,
Is one, always the same, one life, one fire?

XLIV

O L I T T L E self, within whose smallness lies
All that man was, and is, and will become,
Atom unseen that comprehends the skies
And tells the tracks by which the planets roam;
That, without moving, knows the joys of wings,
The tiger's strength, the eagle's secrecy,
And in the hovel can consort with kings,
Or clothe a God with his own mystery.
O with what darkness do we cloak thy light,
What dusty folly gather thee for food,

Thou who alone art knowledge and delight,
The heavenly bread, the beautiful, the good.
O living self, O God, O morning star,
Give us thy light, forgive us what we are.

LIX

I F Beauty be at all, if, beyond sense,
There be a wisdom piercing into brains,
Why should the glory wait on impotence,
Biding its time till blood is in the veins?
There is no beauty, but, when thought is quick,
Out of the noisy sickroom of ourselves
Some flattery comes to try to cheat the sick,
Some drowsy drug is groped for on the shelves.
There is no beauty, for we tread a scene
Red to the eye with blood of living things.
Thought is but joy from murder that has been,
Life is but brute at war upon its kings.
There is no beauty, nor could beauty care
For us, this dust, that men make everywhere.
John Masefield.

THE DANIEL JAZZ

Let the leader train the audience to roar like lions, to join in the refrain,
'Go chain the lions down', before he begins to lead them in this jazz.

D A R I U S the Mede was a king and a wonder. *Beginning*
His eye was proud, and his voice was thunder. *with a*
He kept bad lions in a monstrous den. *strain of*
He fed up the lions on Christian men. *'Dixie'.*

Daniel was the chief hired man of the land. *With a touch*
He stirred up the jazz in the palace band. *of*
He whitewashed the cellar. He shovelled in *'Alexander's*
  the coal. *Ragtime*
And Daniel kept a-praying: 'Lord, save my soul.' *Band'.*
Daniel kept a-praying: 'Lord, save my soul.'
Daniel kept a-praying: 'Lord, save my soul.'

Daniel was the butler, swagger and swell.
He ran upstairs. He answered the bell.
And *he* would let in whoever came a-calling:
Saints so holy, scamps so appalling.
'Old man Ahab leaves his card.
Elisha and the bears are a-waiting in the yard.

Here comes Pharoah and his snakes a-calling.
Here comes Cain and his wife a-calling.
Shadrach, Meshach and Abednego for tea.
Here comes Johah and the whale,
And the *Sea!*
Here comes St. Peter and his fishing-pole.
Here comes Judas and his silver a-calling.
Here comes old Beelzebub a-calling.'
And Daniel kept a-praying: 'Lord, save my soul.'
Daniel kept a-praying: 'Lord, save my soul.'
Daniel kept a-praying: 'Lord, save my soul.'

His sweetheart and his mother were Christian and meek.
They washed and ironed for Darius every week.
One Thursday he met them at the door:
Paid them as usual, but acted sore.
He said: 'Your Daniel is a dead little pigeon.
He's a good hard worker, but he talks religion.'
And he showed them Daniel in the lion's cage.
Daniel standing quietly, the lions in a rage.

His good old mother cried: –
'Lord, save him.'
And Daniel's tender sweetheart cried: –
'Lord, save him.'

And she was a golden lily in the dew.
And she was as sweet as an apple on the tree.
And she was as fine as a melon in the corn-field,
Gliding and lovely as a ship on the sea,
Gliding and lovely as a ship on the sea.

And she prayed to the Lord: –
'*Send* Gabriel. *Send* Gabriel.'

King Darius said to the lions: –
'Bite Daniel. Bite Daniel.
Bite him. Bite him. Bite him!'

Thus roared the lions: –
'We want Daniel, Daniel, Daniel,
We want Daniel, Daniel, Daniel.
Grrrrrrrrrrrrrrrrrrrrrrrrrrrrrrrrrrrrrrrrrrrr   *Here the audience roars*
Grrrrrrrrrrrrrrrrrrrrrrrrrrrrrrrrrrrrrrrrrrrr'   *with the leader.*

And Daniel did not frown,
Daniel did not cry.
He kept on looking at the sky.

And the Lord said to Gabriel: –
'Go chain the lions down,
Go chain the lions down.
Go chain the lions down.
Go chain the lions down.'
And *Gabriel* chained the lions,
And *Gabriel* chained the lions,
And *Gabriel* chained the lions,
And Daniel got out of the den,
And Daniel got out of the den,
And Daniel got out of the den.
And Darius said: 'You're a Christian child,'
Darius said: 'You're a Christian child,'
Darius said: 'You're a Christian child,'
And gave him his job again,
And gave him his job again,
And gave him his job again.

The audience sings this with the leader, to the old negro tune.

Nicholas Vachel Lindsay.

HOW SAMSON
BORE AWAY THE GATES OF GAZA

(*A Negro Sermon*)

ONCE, in a night as black as ink,
She drove him out when he would not drink.
Round the house there were men in wait
Asleep in rows by the Gaza gate.
But the Holy Spirit was in this man.
Like a gentle wind he crept and ran.
('It is midnight,' said the big town clock.)

He lifted the gates up, post and lock.
The hole in the wall was high and wide
When he bore away old Gaza's pride
Into the deep of the night: –
The bold Jack Johnson Israelite,–
Samson –
The Judge,
The Nazarite.

The air was black, like the smoke of a dragon.
Samson's heart was as big as a wagon.
He sang like a shining golden fountain.
He sweated up to the top of the mountain.
He threw down the gates with a noise like judgment.
And the quails all ran with the big arousement.

But he wept –'I must not love tough queens,
And spend on them my hard-earned means.
I told that girl I would drink no more.
Therefore she drove me from her door.
Oh sorrow!
Sorrow!
I cannot hide.
Oh Lord look down from your chariot side.
You make me Judge, and I am not wise.
I am weak as a sheep for all my size.'

Let Samson
Be coming
Into your mind.

The moon shone out, the stars were gay.
He saw the foxes run and play.
He rent his garments, he rolled around
In deep repentance on the ground.
Then he felt a honey in his soul,
Grace abounding made him whole.
Then he saw the Lord in a chariot blue.
The gorgeous stallions whinnied and flew.
The iron wheels hummed an old hymn-tune
And crunched in thunder over the moon.
And Samson shouted to the sky:
'My Lord, my Lord is riding high.'

Like a steed, he pawed the gates with his hoof.
He rattled the gates like rocks on the roof,
And danced in the night
On the mountain top,
Danced in the deep of the night:
The Judge, the holy Nazarite,
Whom ropes and chains could never bind.

Let Samson
Be coming
Into your mind.

Whirling his arms, like a top he sped.
His long black hair flew round his head
Like an outstretched net of silky cord,
Like a wheel of the chariot of the Lord.

Let Samson
Be coming
Into your mind.

Samson saw the sun anew.
He left the gates in the grass and dew.
He went to a country-seat a-nigh.
Found a harlot proud and high:
Philistine that no man could tame –
Delilah was her lady-name.
Oh sorrow,
Sorrow,
She was too wise.
She cut off his hair,
She put out his eyes.

Let Samson
Be coming
Into your mind.

Nicholas Vachel Lindsay.

OUR STORY

THERE was a young king who was sad,
    And a young queen who was lonely;
They lived together their busy life,
    Known to each other only,–

Known to each other with strange love,
    But with sighs for the king's vain sorrow
And for the queen's vain loneliness
    And vain forethought of the morrow.

After a barren while they died,
    In death they were not parted:
Now in their grave perhaps they know
    Why they were broken-hearted.

Thomas MacDonagh.

LATE POEMS

And here the poet meets his favouring muse.
Crabbe.

It is a pretty poem, Mr Pope, but you must
not call it Homer.
Richard Bentley.

I wish you would read a little poetry sometimes. Your ignorance cramps my conversation.
Anthony Hope.

Late
'And here Poems
the poet meets his favouring muse'

IN THE POPPY FIELD

MAD Patsy said, he said to me,
That every morning he could see
An angel walking on the sky;
Across the sunny skies of morn
He threw great handfuls far and nigh
Of poppy seed among the corn;
And then, he said, the angels run
To see the poppies in the sun.

A poppy is a devil weed,
I said to him – he disagreed;
He said the devil had no hand
In spreading flowers tall and fair
Through corn and rye and meadow land,
By garth and barrow everywhere:
The devil has not any flower,
But only money in his power.

And then he stretched out in the sun
And rolled upon his back for fun:
He kicked his legs and roared for joy
Because the sun was shining down:
He said he was a little boy
And would not work for any clown:
He ran and laughed behind a bee,
And danced for very ecstasy.

James Stephens.

THE SNARE

I HEAR a sudden cry of pain!
   There is a rabbit in a snare:
Now I hear the cry again,
   But I cannot tell from where.

131

But I cannot tell from where
  He is calling out for aid;
Crying on the frightened air,
  Making everything afraid.

Making everything afraid,
  Wrinkling up his little face,
As he cries again for aid;
  And I cannot find the place!

And I cannot find the place
  Where his paw is in the snare:
Little one! Oh, little one!
  I am searching everywhere.
James Stephens.

TO A POET A THOUSAND YEARS HENCE

I WHO am dead a thousand years,
  And wrote this sweet archaic song,
Send you my words for messengers
  The way I shall not pass along.

I care not if you bridge the seas,
  Or ride secure the cruel sky,
Or build consummate palaces
  Of metal or of masonry.

But have you wine and music still,
  And statues and a bright-eyed love,
And foolish thoughts of good or ill,
  And prayers to them who sit above?

How shall we conquer? Like a wind
  That falls at eve our fancies blow,
And old Mæonides the blind
  Said it three thousand years ago.

O friend unseen, unborn, unknown,
  Student of our sweet English tongue,
Read out my words at night, alone:
  I was a poet, I was young.

Since I can never see your face,
  And never shake you by the hand,
I send my soul through time and space
  To greet you. You will understand.
James Elroy Flecker.

THE BIRDS

WITHIN mankind's duration, so they say,
Khephren and Ninus lived but yesterday.
Asia had no name till man was old
And long had learned the use of iron and gold;
And æons had passed, when the first corn was planted,
Since first the use of syllables was granted.

Men were on earth while climates slowly swung,
Fanning wide zones to heat and cold, and long
Subsidence turned great continents to sea,
And seas dried up, dried up interminably,
Age after age; enormous seas were dried
Amid wastes of land. And the last monsters died.

Earth wore another face. O since that prime
Man with how many works has sprinkled time!
Hammering, hewing, digging tunnels, roads;
Building ships, temples, multiform abodes.
How for his body's appetites, his toils
Have conquered all earth's products, all her soils;
And in what thousand thousand shapes of art
He has tried to find a language for his heart!

Never at rest, never content or tired:
Insatiate wanderer, marvellously fired,
Most grandly piling and piling into the air
Stones that will topple or arch he knows not where.
And yet did I, this spring, think it more strange,
More grand, more full of awe, than all that change,
And lovely and sweet and touching unto tears,
That through man's chronicled and unchronicled years,
And even into that unguessable beyond,
The water-hen has nested by a pond,
Weaving dry flags, into a beaten floor,
The one sure product of her only lore.
Low on a ledge above the shadowed water
Then, when she heard no men, as Nature taught her,
Plashing around with busy scarlet bill
She built that nest, her nest, and builds it still.

O let your strong imagination turn
The great wheel backward, until Troy unburn,
And then unbuild, and seven Troys below
Rise out of death, and dwindle, and outflow,
Till all have passed, and none has yet been there:
Back, ever back. Our birds still crossed the air;

133

Beyond our myriad changing generations
Still built, unchanged, their known inhabitations.
A million years before Atlantis was
Our lark sprang from some hollow in the grass,
Some old soft hoof-print in a tussock's shade;
And the wood-pigeon's smooth snow-white eggs were laid
High, amid green pines' sunset-coloured shafts,
And rooks their villages of twiggy rafts
Set on the tops of elms, where elms grew then,
And still the thumbling tit and perky wren
Popped through the tiny doors of cosy balls
And the blackbird lined with moss his high-built walls.
A round mud cottage held the thrush's young,
And straws from the untidy sparrow's hung.
And, skimming forktailed in the evening air,
When man first was were not the martens there?
Did not those birds some human shelter crave,
And stow beneath the cornice of his cave
Their dry tight cups of clay? And from each door
Peeped on a morning wiseheads three or four.
Yes, daw and owl, curlew and crested hern,
Kingfisher, mallard, water-rail and tern,
Chaffinch and greenfinch, warbler, stonechat, ruff,
Pied wagtail, robin, fly-catcher and chough,
Missel-thrush, magpie, sparrow-hawk, and jay,
Built, those far ages gone, in this year's way.
And the first man who walked the cliffs of Rame,
As I this year, looked down and saw the same
Blotches of rusty red on ledge and cleft
With grey-green spots on them, while right and left
A dizzying tangle of gulls were floating and flying,
Wheeling and crossing and darting, crying and crying,
Circling and crying, over and over and over,
Crying with swoop and hover and fall and recover.
And below on a rock against the grey sea fretted,
Pipe-necked and stationary and silhouetted,
Cormorants stood in a wise, black, equal row
Above the nests and long blue eggs we know.

O delicate chain over all ages stretched,
O dumb tradition from what far darkness fetched:
Each little architect with its one design
Perpetual, fixed and right in stuff and line,
Each little ministrant who knows one thing,
One learned rite to celebrate the spring.
Whatever alters else on sea or shore,
These are unchanging: man must still explore.

J. C. Squire.

ADDRESS TO MY SOUL

M Y soul, be not disturbed
By planetary war;
Remain securely orbed
In this contracted star.

Fear not, pathetic flame;
Your sustenance is doubt:
Glassed in translucent dream
They cannot snuff you out.

Wear water, or a mask
Of unapparent cloud;
Be brave and never ask
A more defunctive shroud.

The universal points
Are shrunk into a flower;
Between its delicate joints
Chaos keeps no power.

The pure integral form,
Austere and silver-dark,
Is balanced on the storm
In its predestined arc.

Small as a sphere of rain
It slides along the groove
Whose path is furrowed plain
Among the suns that move.

The shapes of April buds
Outlive the phantom year:
Upon the void at odds
The dewdrop falls severe.

Five-petalled flame, be cold:
Be firm, dissolving star:
Accept the stricter mould
That makes you singular.

Elinor Wylie.

ILIAD

F A L S E dreams, all false,
mad heart, were yours.
The word, and nought else,
in time endures.

Not you long after,
perished and mute,
will last, but the defter
viol and lute.
Sweetly they'll trouble
the listeners
with the cold dropped pebble
of painless verse.
Not you will be offered,
but the poet's false pain.
Mad heart, you have suffered,
and loved in vain.
What joy doth Helen
or Paris have
where these lie still in
a nameless grave?
Her beauty's a wraith,
and the boy Paris
muffles in death
his mouth's cold cherries.
Aye! these are less,
that were love's summer,
than one gold phrase
of old blind Homer!
Not Helen's wonder
nor Paris stirs,
but the bright untender
hexameters.
And thus, all passion
is nothing made,
but a star to flash in
an Iliad.
Mad heart, you were wrong!
No love of yours,
but only what is sung,
when love's over, endures.

Humbert Wolfe.

KILLED BY A HAWK

I STIR them with my stick,
   These trembling feathers left behind
To show a hawk was sick,
   No more to fly except on the loose wind.

How beautiful they are
    Scattered by death yet speaking of
Quick flight and precious care
    Of those great gems, the nest-eggs, warm with love.

Feathers without a bird!
    As though the bird had flown away
From its own feathers, fired
    By strange desire for some immortal spray.
Andrew Young.

THE COUNTRY BEDROOM

M Y room's a square and candle-lighted boat,
In the surrounding depths of night afloat.
My windows are the portholes, and the seas
The sound of rain on the dark apple-trees.

Sea monster-like beneath, an old horse blows
A snort of darkness from his sleeping nose,
Below, among drowned daisies. Far off, hark!
Far off one owl amidst the waves of dark.
Frances Cornford.

IN MEMORIAM D.O.M.

C H E S T N U T candles are lit again
For the dead that died in spring:
Dead lovers walk the orchard ways,
And the dead cuckoos sing.

Is it they who live and we who are dead?
Hardly the springtime knows
For which today the cuckoo calls
And the white blossom blows.

Listen and hear the happy wind
Whisper and lightly pass:
Your love is sweet as hawthorn is,
Your hope green as the grass.

The hawthorn's faint and quickly gone,
The grass in autumn dies;
Put by your life, and see the spring
With everlasting eyes.
William Kerr.

A SONG TO COURT A LADY WITH

Come, live with me and be my love,
And we, to whom occasions prove
Mere wandering shadows, here may see
The shadow of stability.

If our too thoughtful days are spent
In solitude and discontent;
If man's an alien thing; and, worse,
If the whole granite universe,

Towers, pinnacles, and heavy trees,
All natural bulks, all masonries,
All stuff, all bone and sinew, thaw,
Till we see nothing childhood saw,

Till time's a mock and mist; how, then,
Poor harried strays, can we regain
A world that will not shake or move?
Come live with me and be my love.

For notably we'll play this part
Of eager love, and with fresh heart,
No longer thoughtful now being wise,
Build a pragmatic paradise.

I'll swear the world grows happy, and
The great millennium's at hand;
I'll swear there's none so loved as you:
And *you* shall swear, and all come true.

Mankind shall grow conversable
And smile in witness of good will.
No two could rival, they'll confess,
Our comradeship, our kindliness.

Dearest, I've beggared all my store
Of words: I cannot promise more.
If these delights your mind may move
Come, live with me and be my love.

Alan Porter.

TO AN OLD LADY DEAD

O L D lady, when last year I sipped your tea
And wooed you with my deference to discuss
The elegance of your embroidery,
I felt no forethought of our meeting thus.

Last week your age was 'almost eighty-three'.
Today you own the eternal over-plus.
These moments are 'experience' for me;
But not for you; not for a mutual 'us'.

I visit you unwelcomed; you've no time
Left to employ in afternoon politeness.
You've only Heaven's great stairway now to climb,
And your long load of years has changed to lightness.
     When Oxford belfries chime you do not hear,
     Nor in this mellow-toned autumnal brightness
Observe an English-School-like atmosphere . . .
     You have inherited everlasting whiteness.

You lived your life in grove and garden shady
Of social Academe, good talk and taste:
But now you are a very quiet old lady,
Stiff, sacrosanct, and alabaster-faced.
     And, while I tip-toe awe-struck from your room,
     I fail to synthesize your earth-success
With this, your semblance to a sculptured tomb
That clasps a rosary of nothingness.
                              Siegfried Sassoon.

THE SICK BOY

'TOMORROW he will be better.'– It's too long,
Dumb lips, pitiful eyes, too long to leave.
O for a dawn tonight! for a bird's song,
A dew, a freshness, a new sun at eve!
A bright east for your sake, a disarray
Of all the heavens to bring your break of day.
                              Viola Meynell.

THE HILL

BREATHLESS, we flung us on the windy hill,
Laughed in the sun, and kissed the lovely grass.
You said, 'Through glory and ecstasy we pass;
Wind, sun, and earth remain, the birds sing still,
When we are old, are old . . .' 'And when we die
All's over that is ours; and life burns on
Through other lovers, other lips,' said I,
'Heart of my heart, our heaven is now, is won!'

'We are Earth's best, that learnt her lesson here.
Life is our cry. We have kept the faith!' we said;
'We shall go down with unreluctant tread
Rose-crowned into the darkness!' . . . Proud we were,
And laughed, that had such brave true things to say.
– And then you suddenly cried, and turned away.

Rupert Brooke.

THE BUSY HEART

N O W that we've done our best and worst, and parted,
I would fill my mind with thoughts that will not rend.
(O heart, I do not dare go empty-hearted)
I'll think of Love in books, Love without end;
Women with child, content; and old men sleeping;
And wet strong ploughlands, scarred for certain grain;
And babes that weep, and so forget their weeping;
And the young heavens, forgetful after rain;
And evening hush, broken by homing wings;
And Song's nobility, and Wisdom holy,
That live, we dead. I would think of a thousand things,
Lovely and durable, and taste them slowly,
One after one, like tasting a sweet food.
I have need to busy my heart with quietude.

Rupert Brooke.

THE DEAD

T H E S E hearts were woven of human joys and cares,
    Washed marvellously with sorrow, swift to mirth.
The years had given them kindness. Dawn was theirs,
    And sunset, and the colours of the earth.
These had seen movement, and heard music; known
    Slumber and waking; loved; gone proudly friended;
Felt the quick stir of wonder; sat alone;
    Touched flowers and furs and cheeks. All this is ended.

There are waters blown by changing winds to laughter
And lit by the rich skies, all day. And after,
    Frost, with a gesture, stays the waves that dance
And wandering loveliness. He leaves a white
    Unbroken glory, a gathered radiance,
A width, a shining peace, under the night.

Rupert Brooke.

THE LITTLE GHOST WHO DIED FOR LOVE

Deborah Churchill, born 1678, was hanged 1708 for shielding her lover after a duel in which he killed his opponent and then fled to Holland. According to the law at the time she was hanged* in his stead. It is recorded that: 'Though she died at peace with God, this malefactor could never understand the justice of her sentence, to the last moment of her life.'

' F E A R not, O maidens, shivering
As bunches of the dew-drenched leaves
In the calm moonlight . . . it is the cold sends quivering
My voice, a little nightingale that grieves.

Now Time beats not, and dead Love is forgotten . . .
The spirit too is dead and dank and rotten,

And I forget the moment when I ran
Between my lover and the sworded man –
Blinded with terror lest I lose his heart.
The sworded man dropped, and I saw depart

Love and my lover and my life . . . he fled
And I was strung and hung upon the tree.
It is so cold now that my heart is dead
And drops through time . . . night is too dark to see

Him still . . . But it is spring; upon the fruit-boughs of
          your lips,
Young maids, the dew like India's splendour drips.
Pass by among the strawberry beds, and pluck the berries
Cooled by the silver moon; pluck boughs of cherries
That seem the lovely lucent coral bough
(From streams of starry milk those branches grow)
That Cassiopeia feeds with her faint light,
Like Ethiopia ever jewelled bright.

Those lovely cherries do enclose
Deep in their hearts the silver snows,

And the small budding flowers upon the trees
Are filled with sweetness like the bags of bees.

Forget my fate . . . but I, a moonlight ghost,
Creep down the strawberry paths and seek the lost
World, the apothecary at the Fair.
I, Deborah, in my long cloak of brown
Like the small nightingale that dances down
The cherried boughs, creep to the doctor's bare
Booth . . . cold as ivy in the air,
And, where I stand, the brown and ragged light
Holds something still beyond, hid from my sight.

Once, plumaged like the sea, his swanskin head
Had wintry white quills . . . "Hearken to the Dead . . .
I was a nightingale, but now I croak
Like some dark harpy hidden in night's cloak,
Upon the walls; among the Dead, am quick.
Oh, give me medicine, for the world is sick;
Not medicines planet-spotted like fritillaries
For country sins and old stupidities,
Nor potions you may give a country maid
When she is lovesick . . . love in earth is laid,
Grown dead and rotten". . . . so I sank me down,
Poor Deborah in my long cloak of brown.

Though cockcrow marches crying of false dawns
Shall bury my dark voice, yet still it mourns
Among the ruins,– for it is not I
But this old world, is sick and soon must die!'

Edith Sitwell.

THE RETURN

THE veteran Greeks came home
Sleepwandering from the war.
We saw the galleys come
Blundering over the bar.
Each soldier with his scar
In rags and tatters came home.

Reading the wall of Troy
Ten years without a change
Was such intense employ
(Just out of the arrows' range),
All the world was strange
After ten years of Troy.

Their eyes knew every stone
In the huge heartbreaking wall
Year after year grown
Till there was nothing at all
But an alley steep and small,
Tramped earth and towering stone.

Now even the hills seemed low
In the boundless sea and land,
Weakened by distance so.
How could they understand
Space empty on every hand
And the hillocks squat and low?

And when they arrived at last
They found a childish scene
Embosomed in the past,
And the war lying between –
A child's preoccupied scene
When they came home at last.

But everything trite and strange,
The piece, the parcelled ground,
The vinerows – never a change!
The past and the present bound
In one oblivious round
Past thinking trite and strange.

But for their grey-haired wives
And their sons grown shy and tall
They would have given their lives
To raise the battered wall
Again, if this was all
In spite of their sons and wives.

Penelope in her tower
Looked down upon the show
And saw within an hour
Each man to his wife go,
Hesitant, sure and slow:
She, alone in her tower.

Edwin Muir.

THE TIME UPON MY WRIST

T H E time upon my wrist
May tell how far the sun,
Since punctual he cleared the mist,
Over his clockwork universe has run;
Yet the smooth hours that chime
His even march of days
May nothing tell of that unmeasured time,
That inward pulse, my urgent heart obeys.

The time upon my wrist,
Before the white moon rise,
May tell the pin-eyed scientist
Where now she lights Antipodean skies;
Yet this it may not show,
What lunar dream lies curled
Within my mind, and lights, how far below,
A shore unknown to me of my own world:

143

Nor may it prophesy when
That moon of dream shall break
On the hither shore – and then, oh! then
Above dark seas my lucid passion wake,
Till singing words of light
In that rich plenilune
Sprinkle with images a summer night
And change this earth's December to my June.
                                    G. Rostrevor Hamilton.

MORTALITY

I N the green quiet wood, where I was used,
    In summer, to a welcome calm and dark,
I found the threat of murder introduced
    By scars of white paint on the wrinkled bark.

How few old friends were to be spared! And now
    I see my friends with new eyes here in town
– Men as trees walking, and on every brow
    A pallid scar, and all to be cut down.
                                    Gerald Gould.

WHISPERS OF IMMORTALITY

W E B S T E R was much possessed by death
And saw the skull beneath the skin;
And breastless creatures under ground
Leaned backward with a lipless grin.

Daffodil bulbs instead of balls
Stared from the sockets of the eyes!
He knew that thought clings round dead limbs
Tightening its lusts and luxuries.

Donne, I suppose, was such another
Who found no substitute for sense,
To seize and clutch and penetrate;
Expert beyond experience,

He knew the anguish of the marrow
The ague of the skeleton;
No contact possible to flesh
Allayed the fever of the bone.

Grishkin is nice: her Russian eye
Is underlined for emphasis;
Uncorseted, her friendly bust
Gives promise of pneumatic bliss.

The couched Brazilian jaguar
Compels the scampering marmoset
With subtle effluence of cat;
Grishkin has a maisonette;

The sleek Brazilian jaguar
Does not in its arboreal gloom
Distil so rank a feline smell
As Grishkin in a drawing-room.

And even the Abstract Entities
Circumambulate her charm;
But our lot crawls between dry ribs
To keep our metaphysics warm.

T. S. Eliot.

WINTER REMEMBERED

T W O evils, monstrous either one apart,
Possessed me, and were long and loath at going:
A cry of Absence, Absence, in the heart,
And in the wood the furious winter blowing.

Think not, when fire was bright upon my bricks,
And past the tight boards hardly a wind could enter,
I glowed like them, the simple burning sticks,
Far from my cause, my proper heat and centre.

Better to walk forth in the murderous air
And wash my wound in the snows; that would be healing;
Because my heart would throb less painful there,
Being caked with cold, and past the smart of feeling.

And where I went, the hugest winter blast
Would have this body bowed, these eyeballs streaming,
And though I think this heart's blood froze not fast
It ran too small to spare one drop for dreaming.

Dear love, these fingers that had known your touch,
And tied our separate forces first together,
Were ten poor idiot fingers not worth much,
Ten frozen parsnips hanging in the weather.

John Crowe Ransom.

145

THE SEED SHOP

HERE in a quiet and dusty room they lie,
Faded as crumbled stone or shifting sand,
Forlorn as ashes, shrivelled, scentless, dry –
Meadows and gardens running through my hand.

In this brown husk a dale of hawthorn dreams,
A cedar in this narrow cell is thrust
That will drink deeply of a century's streams,
These lilies shall make summer on my dust.

Here in their safe and simple house of death,
Sealed in their shells a million roses leap;
Here I can blow a garden with my breath,
And in my hand a forest lies asleep.

Muriel Stuart.

NEW COUNTRYMAN

What do I know now, that I did not know?
Cow does not smell of milk, milk smells of cow.
Stubble, the brighter for autumnal haze,
Is half a summer's suns in afterglow.
Rain is a mortal friend, that was a foe.
'Sear', 'rathe', 'a-cold' are words of common grace.
Winter's thin landscape brings the beacon-brow
Comforting close, emptying the middle space
(A painter's trick): not features now, but face.
Within the roofless cottage, the broken base,
How quickly, quickly grass resumes its ways.

What eagers most the eye? Rain-gleam of plough.
What hurries, not harries, the heart? Fall, flow
Of leaves. Not mournful, no, no, no:
A sequined curtain shaken down to show
Singled twig, sprung branch, bough –
The bones of building sculptured into lace.
What heartens hope? Winter wheat in snow
Showing its ringes? But all, all the year's phase:
Charge, change, provision, deaths, decays,
The natural thrift: garner, store, stow
Of residue, each to its occasion, purpose, place
– So extending Time, his dear delays,
That I, growing old, have length, yes length, of days.

These things, before unknown to me, I know
                And praise, praise.

Francis Meynell.

from THE LAND

SUMMER

N O W be you thankful, who in England dwell,
That to the starving trees and thirsty grass
Even at summer's height come cloudy fleets
Moist from the wastes of the Atlantic swell,
To spill their rain, and pass,
While fields renew their sweets.
Not as the Arab watches in despair
The scrannel promise of his harvest parch
Even before the sun climbs high in March
And only dust-motes dim the scorching air.
He who must yoke to wooden water-wheel
The bullock or the camel, turning slow
But constant in the round and trodden groove,
Slumberous as hypnotics move,
To the lamentation of the whining cogs,
While in the runnels rapid waters flow,
Lapped by the timid tongue of pariah dogs,
And in the trenches spread, to quench and heal.
Or as the Persian from his hills of snow
Gathers the freshet to the jealous pool,
And floods his garden with a hundred streams
Under the plane-trees when the evening's cool,
But still for all his pains
Sees roses languish with returning noon,
And in the heat of June
The leaves already flutter from the planes.

Such arid months as only exiles know,
With longing for the smell of English rains,
Some drops to lay the dust, some shower to stir
The earthy redolence of soaking loam,
Some saddening of the sky before the shower,
Some dew to hold a footprint for an hour;
When through the stones the lizard and the snake
Rustle their brittle length, and crickets chirr
Day after day, and broom-pods crackling break,
Scavenger kites hang waiting for the dead
Over the old and solitary ram,
And the mule picks his way up the dried river-bed,–
This know, and know then how the heart can ache
With pining for the woods and clouds of home.

If I could take my England, and could wring
One living moment from her simple year,

147

One moment only, whether of place or time,
– One winter coppice feathery with rime,
One shred of dawn in spring,–
Then should my voice find echo in English ear;
Then might I say, 'That which I love, I am.'

Full summer comes; June brings the longest day.
All country-dwellers know the small despair
Of the year's summit; but the yeoman now
Has little time for vain regrets to spare.
There's work enough for him and all his folks;
He watches for the flowering of his hay;
Knows that cleared land is ready for the plough;
Washes his empty sheds with cleansing lime
While herds at pasture fatten to their prime,
With frisking tails in shade beneath the oaks.

V. Sackville-West.

¶

A L L ignorance toboggans into know
and trudges up to ignorance again:
but winter's not forever, even snow
melts; and if spring should spoil the game, what then?

all history's a winter sport or three:
but were it five, i'd still insist that all
history is too small for even me;
for me and you, exceedingly too small.

Swoop (shrill collective myth) into thy grave
merely to toil the scale to shrillerness
per every madge and mabel dick and dave
– tomorrow is our permanent address

and there they'll scarcely find us (if they do,
we'll move away still further: into now

E. E. Cummings.

FIFTH PHILOSOPHER'S SONG

A M I L L I O N million spermatozoa,
    All of them alive:
Out of their cataclysm but one poor Noah
    Dare hope to survive.

And among that billion minus one
    Might have chanced to be
Shakespeare, another Newton, a new Donne –
    But the One was Me.

Shame to have ousted your betters thus,
    Taking ark while the others remained outside!
Better for all of us, froward Homunculus,
    If you'd quietly died!
                Aldous Huxley.

THUNDER AT NIGHT

RESTLESS and hot two children lay
    Plagued with uneasy dreams,
Each wandered lonely through false day
    A twilight torn with screams.

True to the bed-time story, Ben
    Pursued his wounded bear,
Ann dreamed of chattering monkey men,
    Of snakes twined in her hair . . .

Now high aloft above the town
    The thick clouds gather and break,
A flash, a roar, and rain drives down:
    Aghast the young things wake.

Trembling for what their terror was,
    Surprised by instant doom,
With lightning in the looking glass,
    Thunder that rocks the room.

The monkeys' paws patter again,
    Snakes hiss and flash their eyes:
The bear roars out in hideous pain:
    Ann prays: her brother cries.

They cannot guess, could not be told
    How soon comes careless day,
With birds and dandelion gold,
    Wet grass, cool scents of May.
                Robert Graves.

LOST LOVE

H I S eyes are quickened so with grief,
He can watch a grass or leaf
Every instant grow; he can
Clearly through a flint wall see,
Or watch the startled spirit flee
From the throat of a dead man:
Across two counties he can hear,
And catch your words before you speak;
The woodlouse or the maggot's weak
Clamour rings in his sad ear;
And noise so slight it would surpass
Credence: – drinking sound of grass;
Worm talk, clashing jaws of moth
Chumbling holes in cloth:
The groan of ants who undertake
Gigantic loads for honour's sake,
Their sinews creak, their breath comes thin:
Whir of spiders when they spin,
And minute whispering, mumbling, sighs
Of idle grubs and flies.
This man is quickened so with grief,
He wanders god-like or like thief
Inside and out, below, above,
Without relief seeking lost love.

Robert Graves.

HAPPINESS

E V E R again to breathe pure happiness,
The happiness our mother gave us, boys?
To smile at nothings, needing no caress?
Have we not laughed too often since with joys?
Have we not wrought too sick and sorrowful wrongs
For their hands' pardoning? The sun may cleanse,
And time, and starlight. Life will sing sweet songs,
And gods will show us pleasures more than men's.

Yet heaven looks smaller than the old doll's-home,
No nestling place is left in bluebell bloom,
And the wide arms of trees have lost their scope.
The former happiness is unreturning:
Boys' griefs are not so grievous as our yearning,
Boys have no sadness sadder than our hope.

Wilfred Owen.

§

L O V E is not all: it is not meat nor drink
Nor slumber nor a roof against the rain;
Nor yet a floating spar to men that sink
And rise and sink and rise and sink again;
Love can not fill the thickened lung with breath,
Nor clean the blood, nor set the fractured bone;
Yet many a man is making friends with death
Even as I speak, for lack of love alone.
It well may be that in a difficult hour,
Pinned down by pain and clamouring for release,
Or nagged by want past resolution's power,
I might be driven to sell your love for peace,
Or trade the memory of this night for food.
It well may be. I do not think I would.
                              Edna St. Vincent Millay.

§

W H E N we are old and these rejoicing veins
Are frosty channels to a muted stream,
And out of all our burning there remains
No feeblest spark to fire us, even in dream,
This be our solace: that it was not said
When we were young and warm and in our prime,
Upon our couch we lay as lie the dead,
Sleeping away the unreturning time.
O sweet, O heavy-lidded, O my love,
When morning strikes her spear upon the land,
And we must rise and arm us and reprove
The insolent daylight with a steady hand,
Be not discountenanced if the knowing know
We rose from rapture but an hour ago.
                              Edna St. Vincent Millay.

§

I F I should learn, in some quite casual way,
That you were gone, not to return again –
Read from the back-page of a paper, say,
Held by a neighbour in a subway train,
How at the corner of this avenue
And such a street (so are the papers filled)
A hurrying man, who happened to be you,
At noon today had happened to be killed,

I should not cry aloud – I could not cry
Aloud, or wring my hands in such a place –
I should but watch the station lights rush by
With a more careful interest on my face;
Or raise my eyes and read with greater care
Where to store furs and how to treat the hair.
                    Edna St. Vincent Millay.

¶

N O T in a silver casket cool with pearls
Or rich with red corundum or with blue,
Locked, and the key withheld, as other girls
Have given their loves, I give my love to you;
Not in a lovers'-knot, not in a ring
Worked in such fashion, and the legend plain –
Semper fidelis, where a secret spring
Kennels a drop of mischief for the brain:
Love in the open hand, no thing but that,
Ungemmed, unhidden, wishing not to hurt,
As one should bring you cowslips in a hat
Swung from the hand, or apples in her skirt,
I bring you, calling out as children do:
'Look what I have! – And these are all for you.'
                    Edna St. Vincent Millay.

PASSER MORTUUS EST

D E A T H devours all lovely things;
    Lesbia with her sparrow
Shares the darkness,– presently
    Every bed is narrow.

Unremembered as old rain
    Dries the sheer libation,
And the little petulant hand
    Is an annotation.

After all, my erstwhile dear,
    My no longer cherished,
Need we say it was not love,
    Now that love is perished?
                    Edna St. Vincent Millay.

THE SHOWER

s o here we stand beneath the dripping trees,
The drooping trees, and listen to the rain.
It has been dropping now for hours, it seems. The bees,
The flies, the rabbits, will never be seen again;
They must be drowned in the streaming grass, and thrust
Down the swift torrents, bubbling over the dust.
First on one foot, then on the other, we stand;
And sigh, and lean against the knobby trunk;
And catch the jewels in a chilly hand;
And wonder how far down the rain has sunk,
How far down to wash the earth from the roots
And bleach them white, and make the sap run thin.
All the world is filled with bogs, and newts,
Mushrooms, moss, and frogs, and boys kept in
Because of the rain.　　　But look! It is giving over!
The drops come slower, the leaves shiver and shake,
And a watery eye blinks out from the sky. Birds wake,
The shadow lifts, the lark flushes up from the clover,
And the purple shines, and the green, and every stone
Glitters and flashes, and the road steams in the sun;
The butterfly preens her wings; the bee has already flown.
Good-bye, old friendly tree, don't you wish you could run ?
　　　　　　　　　　　　　　　　Richard Church.

¶

so　still the world this winter noon,
So sparkling-cold and still,
Of quietness the heart
Could take her fill.

Upon the shallow snow
Clear rang my careful tread.
Summer had died, long ago,
But was not dead

While from the lattice thorn,
To chide my lingering doubt,
Lively with faith and fear
A feather'd eye looked out,

And on the powder'd verge,
Where road gives way to grass
For others' coming and going,
Many a printing was

Of blackbird, of wren:
Who burn away their blood,
Even as we,
To ends not understood.

So rare the fallen fleece of sky,
So far the noise of men,
Myself for a musing moment
Was blackbird, was wren.

Gerald Bullett.

THE IMMIGRANT

W H E N Ruth was old
She'd take her children's children on her knee.
They never wearied to be told
Tales of her girlhood in a far country.

For though her eyes grew dim
Men said of her: 'Her heart is always young,'
And Boaz, while she spoke to him,
Loved the faint accent of a foreign tongue.

Frank Kendon.

FOREFATHERS

H E R E they went with smock and crook,
   Toiled in the sun, lolled in the shade,
Here they mudded out the brook
   And here their hatchet cleared the glade:
Harvest-supper woke their wit,
Huntsman's moon their wooings lit.

From this church they led their brides,
   From this church themselves were led
Shoulder-high; on these waysides
   Sat to take their beer and bread.
Names are gone – what men they were
These their cottages declare.

Names are vanished, save the few
   In the old brown Bible scrawled;
These were men of pith and thew,
   Whom the city never called;
Scarce could read or hold a quill,
Built the barn, the forge, the mill.

On the green they watched their sons
   Playing till too dark to see,
As their fathers watched them once,
   As my father once watched me;
While the bat and beetle flew
On the warm air webbed with dew.

Unrecorded, unrenowned,
   Men from whom my ways begin,
Here I know you by your ground
   But I know you not within –
There is silence, there survives
Not a moment of your lives.

Like the bee that now is blown
   Honey-heavy on my hand,
From his toppling tansy-throne
   In the green tempestuous land –
I'm in clover now, nor know
Who made honey long ago.

                            Edmund Blunden.

TIME

WHERE is my field, my wood, my morning dew?
Where are my savage spoils, my singular
And holy blessedness, my pretty husks
And berries, my delight in apple-rind,
My clouds, and where my brooks of quietness?
Where is my fighting anger? Gone, all gone,
Or shrunk to poverty. What have you done
With the fair emerald worm that I so loved;
What with the tinselled fly that I thought angel?
Where is my bread that was the bread of heaven?
Exchanged for harms, unquiet thoughts, and doubts.
What else itches your talons? leave to me
Contempt of luxury, and eyes to see
My way to some new joy to make these good,
Or, usurer, I will make insurrection
(For you are prettily hated in the town);
I'll raze your dirty mansion, it needs purging,
And wring your neck until your head comes off,
And burn your remnant. Foul and greedy Time,
See, your hoard rots apace, and all who have
Some true wealth, and the wisdom to preserve it,
Fly from your precinct into Eternity –
A city that I wish I had not left.

                            Ruth Pitter.

THE COMET

O STILL withhold thyself, be not possessed:
Hyperbola, the dread uncharted line,
Debase not into orbit; still make shine
Portentous rays of arrowy unrest
Among the earthy planets. Know not law,
Here are too many who lie straitly bound:
Fly all but in the sun, and shooting round
Dart to the outer darkness of our awe:
And if there be incalculable return,
Come in another shape with monstrous hair
Or triple train enclosing half the skies:
Still let thy face with various omens burn,
Still shun the reasoned pathways to despair,
Nor answerable be to earthly eyes.

Ruth Pitter.

¶

N O W that I am clean again,
Now I've slept and fed,
How shall I remember when
I was someone dead?

Now the balm has worked its art
And the gashes dry,
And the lizard at my heart
Has a sleepy eye,

How shall I remember yet
Freezing underground,
With the wakened lizard set
To the living wound?

Do not ponder the offence
Nor reject the sore,
Do not tear the cerements
Flesh may need once more.

Cold comes back and pain comes back
And the lizard, too.
And the burden in the sack
May be meant for you.

Do not play the risen dunce
With unrisen men.
Lazarus was risen once
But earth gaped again.
                    Stephen Vincent Benét.

¶

W H A T things shall be said of you,
Terrible beauty in armour?
What things shall be said of you,
Horses riding the sky?
The fleetness, the molten speed,
The rhythm rising like beaten
Drums of barbaric gold
Until fire mixes with fire?

The night is a sparkling pit
Where Time no longer has power
But only vast cadence surging
Toward an instant of tiny death.
Then, with the slow withdrawal
Of seas from a rock of moonlight,
The clasping bodies unlock
And the lovers have little words.

What is this spear, this burnished
Arrow in the deep waters
That is not quenched by them
Until it has found its mark?
What is this beating of wings
In the formless heart of the tempest?
This wakening of a sun
That was not wakened before?

They have dragged you down from the sky
And broken you with an ocean
Because you carried the day,
Phaeton, charioteer.
But still you loose from the cloud
The matched desires of your horses
And sow on the ripened earth
The quickened, the piercing flame.

What things shall be said of you,
Terrible beauty in armour?
Dance that is not a dance,
Brief instant of welded swords.

157

For a moment we strike the black
Door with a fist of brightness.
And then it is over and spent,
And we sink back into life.

Back to the known, the sure,
The river of sleep and waking,
The dreams floating the river,
The nearness, the conquered peace.
You have come and smitten and passed,
Poniard, poniard of sharpness.
The child sleeps in the planet.
The blood sleeps again.

Stephen Vincent Benét.

THE TRAITORS

A CRY of ruin strides the sky
Tonight above our burdened fields
That lift the weight of summer high
Like trophy on their glittering shields.

Wings tread night's silent noon, and words
Of peril fall from straining bills
Where loud with prophecy the birds
Call startled sleepers to their sills,

While windows swing and iron chains
Strangle the hound's uproarious throat,
To see on farms and silver skeins
Of brooks the moon-live shadows float.

The geese bear windward to the south
Arousing panic as they ride,
Their treachery the first, their mouth
The first to shake earth's drowsing pride,

Till fear assails the eyes that scan
The troubled night whose breath the frost
Will stiffen, and the bravest man
Surrenders and the world is lost.

Their treason threads the sleeping grove
Whose swallows hear the cry and stir,
Till summer waits alone, to love
The thief who comes to plunder her.

Morton Dauwen Zabel.

THE FLOWER

L E T no light word your silence mar:
This one red flame be all you say,
Between the old and new desire
A solitary point of fire,
The hesitation of a star
Between the twilight and the day.

So rich the pollen of your breath
It is sufficient to be dumb,
Foreknowing, as the moment slips,
That in the parting of our lips
The hour has slain a rose whose death
Will colour all our days to come.
                                        Roy Campbell.

A WOMAN WITH CHILD

N O W she is like the white tree-rose
That takes a blessing from the sun:
Summer has filled her veins with light,
And her warm heart is washed with noon.

Or as a poplar, ceaselessly
Gives a soft answer to the wind:
Cool on the light her leaves lie sleeping,
Folding a column of sweet sound.

Powder the stars. Forbid the night
To wear those brilliants for a brooch.
So soon, dark death, you may close down
The mines that made this beauty rich.

Her thoughts are pleiads, stooping low
O'er glades where nightingale has flown:
And like the luminous night around her
She has at heart a certain dawn.
                                        C. Day Lewis.

THE SHELL

W H O could devise
But the dark sea this thing
Of depth, of dyes
Claws of weed cling,

Whose colour cries:
'I am of water, as of air the wing',
Yet holds the eyes
As though they looked on music perishing?

Yet the shell knows
Only its own dark chamber
Coiled in repose
Where without number
One by one goes
Each blind wave, feeling mother-of-pearl and amber,
Flooding, to close
A book all men might clasp, yet none remember.

Too far away
For thought to find the track,
Sparkling with spray
Rose, green and black,
The colours play,
Strained by the ebb, revealing in the wrack
The myth of day,
A girl too still to call her bridegroom back.

There falls the weight
Of glory unpossessed;
There the sands late
Hold the new guest
Whose ponderous freight
Draws the pool's hollow like a footprint pressed.
Its outcast state
Suddenly seems miraculous and blest.

Turn it; now hold
Its ancient heart. How fair
With lost tales told
In sea-salt air
Light's leaf-of-gold
Leaps from the threshold up the spiral stair,
Then lost, is cold,
Bound in a flash to rock with Ariadne's hair.
                                                Vernon Watkins.

ESSEX

' T H E vagrant visitor erstwhile,
My colour-plate book says to me,
'Could wend by hedgerow-side and stile,
From Benfleet down to Leigh-on-Sea.'

160

And as I turn the colour-plates
Edwardian Essex opens wide,
Mirrored in ponds and seen through gates,
Sweet uneventful countryside.

Like streams the little by-roads run
Through oats and barley round a hill
To where blue willows catch the sun
By some white weather-boarded mill.

'A Summer Idyll Matching Tye'
' At Havering-atte-Bower, the Stocks'
And cobbled pathways lead the eye
To cottage doors and hollyhocks.

Far Essex,– fifty miles away
The level wastes of sucking mud
Where distant barges high with hay
Come sailing in upon the flood.

Near Essex of the River Lea
And anglers out with hook and worm
And Epping Forest glades where we
Had beanfeasts with my father's firm.

At huge and convoluted pubs
They used to set us down from brakes
In that half-land of football clubs
Which London near the Forest makes.

Then deepest Essex few explore
Where steepest thatch is sunk in flowers
And out of elm and sycamore
Rise flinty fifteenth-century towers.

I see the little branch line go
By white farms roofed in red and brown,
The old Great Eastern winding slow
To some forgotten country town.

Now yarrow chokes the railway track,
Brambles obliterate the stile,
No motor coach can take me back
To that Edwardian 'erstwhile'.

John Betjeman.

9

WILL you turn a deaf ear
To what they said on the shore,
Interrogate their poises
In their rich houses;

Of stork-legged heaven-reachers
Of the compulsory touchers
The sensitive amusers
And masked amazers?

Yet wear no ruffian badge
Nor lie behind the hedge
Waiting with bombs of conspiracy
In arm-pit secrecy;

Carry no talisman
For germ or the abrupt pain
Needing no concrete shelter
Nor porcelain filter?

Will you wheel death anywhere
In his invalid chair,
With no affectionate instant
But his attendant?

For to be held for friend
By an undeveloped mind
To be joke for children is
Death's happiness:

Whose anecdotes betray
His favourite colour as blue
Colour of distant bells
And boys' overalls.

His tales of the bad lands
Disturb the sewing hands;
Hard to be superior
On parting nausea;

To accept the cushions from
Women against martyrdom.
Yet applauding the circuits
Of racing cyclists.

Never to make signs
Fear neither maelstrom nor zones
Salute with soldiers' wives
When the flag waves;

Remembering there is
No recognized gift for this;
No income, no bounty,
No promised country.

But to see brave sent home
Hermetically sealed with shame
And cold's victorious wrestle
With molten metal.

A neutralizing peace
And an average disgrace
Are honour to discover
For later other.

W. H. Auden.

MEETING POINT

T I M E was away and somewhere else,
There were two glasses and two chairs
And two people with the one pulse
(Somebody stopped the moving stairs):
Time was away and somewhere else.

And they were neither up nor down,
The stream's music did not stop
Flowing through heather, limpid brown,
Although they sat in a coffee shop
And they were neither up nor down.

The bell was silent in the air
Holding its inverted poise –
Between the clang and clang a flower,
A brazen calyx of no noise:
The bell was silent in the air.

The camels crossed the miles of sand
That stretched around the cups and plates;
The desert was their own, they planned
To portion out the stars and dates:
The camels crossed the miles of sand.

Time was away and somewhere else.
The waiter did not come, the clock
Forgot them and the radio waltz
Came out like water from a rock:
Time was away and somewhere else.

Her fingers flicked away the ash
That bloomed again in tropic trees:
Not caring if the markets crash
When they had forests such as these,
Her fingers flicked away the ash.

God or whatever means the Good
Be praised that time can stop like this,
That what the heart has understood
Can verify in the body's peace
God or whatever means the Good.

Time was away and she was here
And life no longer what it was,
The bell was silent in the air
And all the room a glow because
Time was away and she was here.
Louis Macneice.

PRAYER

T H E laws of blind unrest, not art,
Have built this room in time and space,
The furniture of human sense
That bounds my sorrow, curbs delight.

But to the grail, these fragile walls
Are thinner than a floating dream,
And here the heart's full measure fills
With what is worldwide, yet within.

And gathering round me those I know
In the close circle of a prayer,
The sleepers, the forgetful, grow
In love, though not in presence, near.

My distant ones, this heart on fire
Is for a candle in your night,
While you lie safe within that care
Whose dark is sleep, whose waking, light.
Kathleen Raine.

164

THE FEBRUARY HEDGE

T H E ash-tree's saplings spring and pour
With falling water's power and curve
As if the sky called them, the sky their floor,
The sun's the gravity they serve.

Bow of water; scythe's arc
To part the air.– O see the metal-light
And smooth stem seeking the bud's lustreless dark,
There pouring out of sight.

E. J. Scovell.

¶

S I N C E we are what we are, what shall we be
But what we are? We are, we have
Six feet and seventy years, to see
The light, and then resign it for the grave.
We are not worlds, no, nor infinity,
We have no claims on stone, except to prove
In the invention of the human city
Ourselves, our breath, our death, our love.
   The tower we build soars like an arrow
From the earth's rim towards the sky's,
Upwards-downwards in a star-filled pond,
Climbing and diving from our world, to narrow
The gap between the world shut in the eyes
And the receding world of light beyond.

Stephen Spender.

PAN AND SYRINX

A C R O S S the heavy sands running they came,
She like his shadow shot on before him,
But bit by bit it shortened to full stop
And noonday dot. Then, just within his gasp
She faded, in the sunburst of his joy
Expunged. He had not time to countermand
His smirk of pride, or blandly to run on
As if the running were his only ploy
And she a by-play. Stupidly he stood
Looking in every flaw of air for her,
And staring close at every bird that rose
Out of the reeds, his shock eyes jumping on
From place to place of her nonentity.

Where had she gone, the hussy? Had she flown
Clean out of time and space? A dream? But no,
For still her nestlings' beaks gaped after her,
And still his nostrils quivered and fanned wide
Like twanged elastic in an ecstasy;
Ear and eye still gonged her striking image.

He called her loudly, then: 'Syrinx! Syrinx!'
But nothing blinked: the ignorant ox browsed on,
And the reflective river brassily
Slewed by without a pause. At his foot
Out of the bearded iris rose the bee
In drizzling sibilance. But angrily
Pan stood, and stamped the sudden edge, his hands
Chawed savagely at the sedge. But what, what
Was this they held so closely choked? A reed?
Was ever reed like this one, coolest green,
And blue as if the ice-roots ran in it?
He opened his hands, and looked. O now he knew
The subterfuge of flesh. So this was how
She gave the slip to his lubricity.
He broke into a goat, the Spirit gone:
The Spirit flown, *she* split into a reed:
Green reed, red animal were complements,
And neither could the other venerate.
Her he could feel, but never enter now:
Him she could enter, but could never feel:
So red and green must wrangle endlessly.
Ah, why had he come here? Was it to see
Grass shaken by the wind? Would nothing ease
The nettle-tease of flesh, the salted taws
Of lust?

Grief crowded in his eyes and looked at her,
Till, fogged by too-long thought, he turned away
Lugubriously, lugging the bruised reed:
And with no backward look he went
With bold subtracting steps across the plain
And vanished in the upland groves and haze.
And afterwards was heard
His starving flute crying in stony places,
Calling for love, for love the heavenly rain,
To fall and make his green reed nymph again.
And still he cried 'Syrinx', and still he drew
Her only answer from the reed he blew.

W. R. Rodgers.

166

AT RICHMOND

A T Richmond the river is running for the city:
Though the tall houses on the hill and hotels
In white paint hint of the cliffs and broader sea,
He cannot falter nor alter from his nature.
Lord, neither let falsity my days dissipate.
I have been weak and injudicious in many things,
Have made my tongue an irritant against my intention,
Was calm only in convalescence after sin,
And have frequently feared. Then forgive
Yet once, bless and beckon to the broken city.
                                        Anne Ridler.

JUDGING DISTANCES
[In the Army]

N O T only how far away, but the way that you say it
Is very important. Perhaps you may never get
The knack of judging a distance, but at least you know
How to report on a landscape: the central sector,
The right of arc and that, which we had last Tuesday,
    And at least you know

That maps are of time, not place, so far as the army
Happens to be concerned – the reason being,
Is one which need not delay us. Again, you know
There are three kinds of tree, three only, the fir and the
    poplar,
And those which have bushy tops to; and lastly
    That things only seem to be things.

A barn is not called a barn, to put it more plainly,
Or a field in the distance, where sheep may be safely grazing.
You must never be over-sure. You must say, when reporting:
At five o'clock in the central sector is a dozen
Of what appear to be animals; whatever you do,
    Don't call the bleeders *sheep.*

I am sure that's quite clear; and suppose, for the sake of
    example,
The one at the end, asleep, endeavours to tell us
What he sees over there to the west, and how far away,
After first having come to attention. There to the west,
On the fields of summer the sun and the shadows bestow
    Vestments of purple and gold.

F   167

The still white dwellings are like a mirage in the heat,
And under the swaying elms a man and a woman
Lie gently together. Which is, perhaps, only to say
That there is a row of houses to the left of arc,
And that under some poplars a pair of what appear to be
    humans
    Appear to be loving.

Well that, for an answer, is what we might rightly call
Moderately satisfactory only, the reason being,
Is that two things have been omitted, and those are
    important.
The human beings, now: in what direction are they,
And how far away, would you say? And do not forget
    There may be dead ground in between.

There may be dead ground in between; and I may not have
    got
The knack of judging a distance; I will only venture
A guess that perhaps between me and the apparent lovers,
(Who, incidentally, appear by now to have finished,)
At seven o'clock from the houses, is roughly a distance
    Of about one year and a half.

                                            Henry Reed.

POEM FOR EPIPHANY

Three Kings stepped out of my body,
Walked across the sand by the wild sea
From December into January.

A King stepped out of my head,
And before him the sand was red
And the sea gold,
And he beheld
The landscape like an empire and found in
Even a sycamore leaf the plan of his domain.
And he offered the gold of his sight
The regimen of his thought
To the Child born that night.

A King stepped out of my breast
Who had the bearing of a priest.
To him the moon's movement
Was a sacrament,

And the taste of water and of wine,
The touch of bread and the weight of a stone.
And he offered the frankincense of the heart,
Prayer swung in the censer on the charcoal alight,
To the Child born that night.

A King stepped out of my loins,
And black as grapes were his skin and his veins.
In him was the anger of sex
Where the blood like a sea on the shingle breaks,
The pride of living, the longing for further birth
Because of the presentiment of death.
And he offered the myrrh of tiredness, the untight-
 'ning of the fingers from the nerve's root
To the Child born that night.

Three Kings stepped out of my body
But only my two eyes between the three –
Only my two eyes and the wild skies to see.

Norman Nicholson.

¶

T H E force that through the green fuse drives the flower
Drives my green age; that blasts the roots of trees
Is my destroyer.
And I am dumb to tell the crooked rose
My youth is bent by the same wintry fever.

The force that drives the water through the rocks
Drives my red blood; that dries the mouthing streams
Turns mine to wax.
And I am dumb to mouth unto my veins
How at the mountain spring the same mouth sucks.

The hand that whirls the water in the pool
Stirs the quicksand; that ropes the blowing wind
Hauls my shroud sail.
And I am dumb to tell the hanging man
How of my clay is made the hangman's lime.

The lips of time leech to the fountain head;
Love drips and gathers, but the fallen blood
Shall calm her sores.
And I am dumb to tell a weather's wind
How time has ticked a heaven round the stars.

And I am dumb to tell the lover's tomb
How at my sheet goes the same crooked worm.

Dylan Thomas.

169

A TOUGH GENERATION

T O grow unguided at a time when none
Are sure where they should plant their sprig of trust;
When sunshine has no special mission to endow
With gold the rustic rose, which will run wild
And ramble from the garden to the wood
To train itself to climb the trunks of trees
If the old seedsman die and suburbs care
For sentimental cottage-flowers no more;
To grow up in a wood of rotted trees
In which it is not known which tree will be
First to disturb the silent sultry grove
With crack of doom, dead crackling and dread roar –
Will be infallibly to learn that first
One always owes a duty to oneself;
This much at least is certain: one must live.
And one may reach, without having to search
For much more lore than this, a shrewd maturity,
Equipped with adult aptitude to ape
All customary cant and current camouflage;
Nor be a whit too squeamish where the soul's concerned,
But hold out for the best black market price for it
Should need remind one that one has to live.
Yet just as sweetly, where no markets are,
An unkempt rose may for a season still
Trust its own beauty and disclose its heart
Even to the woodland shade, and as in sacrifice
Renounce its ragged petals one by one.

David Gascoyne.

SONG

T H E R E is no joy in water apart from the sun,
There is no beauty not emphasized by death,
No meaning in home if exile were unknown;
A man who lives in a thermostat lives beneath
A bell of glass alone with the smell of death.

There is no beauty like that seen from a cliff;
The beauty of women comes and goes with a breath;
A man must offer the beauty of his wife
In sacrifice to give his children breath –
The children will walk on their folded hands of death.

Nothing in life is near and nothing far
Apart from love; a man can live beneath
His roof more lonely than an outer star;
And know a woman's beauty, a flower's breath
Walking alone in the valley of the shadow of death.

R. N. Currey.

THE ABANDONED SHADE

WALKING the abandoned shade
of childhood's habitations,
my ears remembering chime,
hearing their buried voices.

Hearing original summer,
the birdlit banks of dawn,
the yellow-hammer beat of blood
gilding my cradle eyes.

Hearing the tin-moon rise
and the sunset's penny fall,
the creep of frost and weep of thaw
and bells of winter robins.

Hearing again the talking house
and the four vowels of the wind,
and midnight monsters whispering
in the white throat of my room.

Season and landscape's liturgy,
badger and sneeze of rain,
the bleat of bats, and bounce of rabbits
bubbling under the hill:

Each old and echo-salted tongue
sings to my backward glance;
but the voice of the boy, the boy I seek,
within my mouth is dumb.

Laurie Lee.

HATE POEMS

Up, Lord, disappoint him and cast him
  down.
Psalm XVII.

Hence, ye profane; I hate ye all;
Both the great vulgar, and the small.
Abraham Cowley.

The dupe of friendship, and the fool of love;
have I not reason to hate and despise myself? Indeed I do; and chiefly for not having
hated and despised the world enough.
William Hazlitt.

Now hatred is by far the longest pleasure;
Men love in haste, but they detest at leisure.
Byron.

Hate Poems

'up, Lord, disappoint him and cast   him down'

¶

G U P, Scot,
Ye blot:
Laudate
Caudate,
Set in better
Thy pentameter.
This Dundas,
This Scottish ass,
He rymes and railes
That Englishmen have tailes.
   Skeltonus laureatus,
Anglicus natus,
Provocat Musas
Contra Dundas
Spurcussimum Scotum,
Undique notum,
Rustice fotum,
Vapide potum.
Skelton laureat
After this rate
Defendeth with his pen
All Englysh men
Agayn Dundas,
That Scottish ass.
Shake thy tayle, Scot, like a cur,
For thou beggest at every man's dur:
Tut, Scot, I sey,
To shake thy dog, hey!
Dundas of Galaway
With thy versyfyeng rayles
How they have tayles.

By Jesu Christ,
Fals Scot, thou lyest:
But behynd in our hose
We bere there a rose
For thy Scottyshe nose,
A spectacle case
To cover thy face,
With trey, deuce, ace.
A tolman to blot,
A rough foted Scot!
Dundas, sir knave,
Why dost thou deprave
This royall reame,
Whose radiant beame
And relucent light
Thou hast in despite,
Thou donghyll knyght?
But thou lakest might
Dundas, dronken and drowsy,
Skabed, scurvy and lowsy,
Of unhappy generacion
And most ungracious nacion.
Dundas,
That dronke asse,
That ratis and rankis,
That prates and prankes
On Huntley bankes,
Take this our thankes;
Dunde, Dunbar,
Walke Scot,
Walke, sot,
Rayle not to far.

John Skelton.

ON ROBERT DUDLEY, EARL OF LEICESTER

H E R E lieth the worthy warrior
Who never blooded sword;
Here lieth the noble councillor,
Who never held his word;
Here lieth his excellency,
Who ruled all the state;
Here lieth the Earl of Leicester
Whom all the world did hate.

Anon., 1588.

THE CURSE

WHOEVER guesses, thinks, or dreams he knows
Who is my mistress, wither by this curse;
  Him, only for his purse,
  May some dull whore to love dispose,
And she yield then to all that are his foes;
  May he be scorned by one, whom all else scorn,
  Forswear to others, what to her he hath sworn,
  With fear of missing, shame of getting, torn.

Madness his sorrow, gout his cramp, may he
Make, by but thinking, who hath made him such;
  And may he feel no touch
  Of conscience, but of fame, and be
Anguished, not that 'twas sin, but that 'twas she;
  In early and long scarceness may he rot,
  For land which had been his, if he had not
  Himself incestuously an heir begot.

May he dream treason, and believe that he
Meant to perform it, and confess, and die,
  And no record tell why;
  His sons, which none of his may be,
Inherit nothing but his infamy;
  Or may he so long parasites have fed,
  That he would fain be theirs whom he hath bred,
  And at the last be circumcised for bread.

The venom of all stepdames, gamesters' gall,
What tyrants and their subjects interwish,
  What plants, mines, beasts, fowl, fish,
  Can contribute, all ill which all
Prophets or poets spake, and all which shall
  Be annexed in schedules unto this by me,
  Fall on that man; for if it be a she
  Nature beforehand hath out-cursed me.
         John Donne.

ON THE DUKE OF BUCKINGHAM

A MAN so various that he seemed to be
Not one, but all mankind's epitome.
Stiff in opinions, always in the wrong;
Was everything by starts, and nothing long;
But, in the course of one revolving moon,
Was chemist, fiddler, statesman and buffoon:
Then all for women, painting, rhyming, drinking:
Besides ten thousand freaks that died in thinking.

Blest madman, who could every hour employ,
With something new to wish, or to enjoy!
Railing and praising were his usual themes;
And both (to show his judgement) in extremes:
So over violent, or over civil,
That every man, with him, was god or devil.
In squandering wealth was his peculiar art:
Nothing went unrewarded, but desert.
Beggared by fools, whom still he found too late:
He had his jest, and they had his estate.

John Dryden.

TO SIDMOUTH AND CASTLEREAGH

A S from an ancestral oak
Two empty ravens sound their clarion,
Yell by yell, and croak by croak,
When they scent the noonday smoke
Of fresh human carrion:

As two gibbering night-birds flit
From their bowers of deadly yew
Through the night to frighten it,
When the moon is in a fit,
And the stars are none or few:

As a shark and dog-fish wait
Under an Atlantic isle,
For the negro-ship, whose freight
Is the theme of their debate,
Wrinkling their red gills the while –

Are ye, two vultures sick for battle,
Two scorpions under one wet stone,
Two bloodless wolves, whose dry throats rattle,
Two crows perched on the murrained cattle,
Two vipers tangled into one.

P. B. Shelley.

ODE

To a Pig while His Nose was being bored.

H A R K ! hark! that Pig – that Pig! the hideous note,
  More loud, more dissonant, each moment grows –
Would one not think the knife was in his throat ?
  And yet they are only boring through his nose.

178

Pig! 'tis your master's pleasure – then be still,
  And hold your nose to let the iron through!
Dare you resist your lawful Sovereign's will?
  Rebellious Swine! you know not what you do.

To man o'er beast the power was given;
  Pig, hear the truth, and never murmur more!
Would you rebel against the will of Heaven?
  You impious beast, be still, and let them bore!

The social Pig resigns his natural rights
  When first with man he covenants to live;
He barters them for safer stye delights,
  For grains and wash, which man alone can give.

Sure is provision on the social plan,
  Secure the comforts that to each belong!
Oh, happy Swine! the impartial sway of man
  Alike protects the weak Pig and the strong.

And you resist! you struggle now because
  Your master has thought fit to bore your nose!
You grunt in flat rebellion to the laws
  Society finds needful to impose!

Go to the forest, Piggy, and deplore
  The miserable lot of savage Swine!
See how young Pigs fly from the great Boar,
  And see how coarse and scantily they dine!

Behold their hourly danger, when who will
  May hunt or snare or seize them for his food!
Oh, happy Pig! whom none presumes to kill
  Till your protecting master thinks it good!

And when, at last, the closing hour of life
  Arrives (for Pigs must die as well as Man),
When in your throat you feel the long sharp knife,
  And the blood trickles to the pudding-pan;

And when, at last, the death wound yawning wide,
  Fainter and fainter grows the expiring cry,
Is there no grateful joy, no loyal pride,
  To think that for your master's good you die?
                                    Robert Southey.

9

ANOTHER Epic! Who inflicts again
More books of blank upon the sons of men?
Bœotian C O T T L E, rich Bristowa's boast,
Imports old stories from the Cambrian coast,
And sends his goods to market – all alive!
Lines forty thousand, Cantos twenty-five!
Fresh fish from Hippocrene! who'll buy? who'll buy?
The precious bargain's cheap – in faith, not I.
Your turtle-feeder's verse must needs be flat,
Though Bristol bloat him with the verdant fat;
If Commerce fills the purse, she clogs the brain,
And A M O S C O T T L E strikes the Lyre in vain.
In him an author's luckless lot behold!
Condemned to make the books which once he sold.
Oh, A M O S C O T T L E! – Phœbus! what a name
To fill the speaking-trump of future fame! –
Oh, A M O S C O T T L E! for a moment think
What meagre profits spring from pen and ink!
When thus devoted to poetic dreams,
Who will peruse thy prostituted reams?
Oh! pen perverted! paper misapplied!
Had C O T T L E still adorned the counter's side,
Bent o'er the desk, or, born to useful toils,
Been taught to make the paper which he soils,
Ploughed, delved, or plied the oar with lusty limb,
He had not sung of Wales, nor I of him.

Byron.

ON A POET LAUREATE

H E had written praises of a regicide;
　He had written praises of all kings whatever;
He had written for republics far and wide,
　And then against them bitterer than ever;
For pantisocracy he once had cried
　Aloud – a scheme less moral than 'twas clever;
Then grew a hearty anti-Jacobin –
Had turn'd his coat – and would have turn'd his skin.

He had sung against all battles, and again
　In their high praise and glory: he had call'd
Reviewing 'the ungentle craft', and then
　Become as base a critic as e'er crawl'd –
Fed, paid and pamper'd by the very men
　By whom his muse and morals had been maul'd:
He had written much blank verse, and blanker prose,
And more of both than anybody knows. *Byron.*

180

CROMEK

A PETTY sneaking knave I knew –
O! Mr Cromek, how do ye do?
                                William Blake.

SOLILOQUY OF THE SPANISH CLOISTER

G R – R – R – there go, my heart's abhorrence!
   Water your damned flower-pots, do!
If hate killed men, Brother Lawrence,
   God's blood, would not mine kill you!
What? your myrtle-bush wants trimming?
   Oh, that rose has prior claims –
Needs its leaden vase filled brimming?
   Hell dry you up with its flames!

At the meal we sit together;
   Salve tibi! I must hear
Wise talk of the kind of weather,
   Sort of season, time of year:
*Not a plenteous cork-crop: scarcely
   Dare we hope oak-galls, I doubt;*
What's the Latin name for 'parsley'?
   What's the Greek name for Swine's Snout?

Whew! We'll have our platter burnished,
   Laid with care on our own shelf!
With a fire-new spoon we're furnished,
   And a goblet for ourself,
Rinsed like something sacrificial
   Ere 'tis fit to touch our chaps –
Marked with L. for our initial!
   (He-he! There his lily snaps!)

Saint, forsooth! While brown Dolores
   Squats outside the Convent bank
With Sanchicha, telling stories,
   Steeping tresses in the tank,
Blue-black, lustrous, thick like horsehairs,
   – Can't I see his dead eye glow,
Bright as 'twere a Barbary corsair's?
   (That is, if he'd let it show!)

When he finishes refection,
   Knife and fork he never lays

Cross-wise, to my recollection,
  As do I, in Jesu's praise.
I, the Trinity illustrate,
  Drinking watered orange-pulp –
In three sips the Arian frustrate;
  While he drains his at one gulp!

Oh, those melons! If he's able
  We're to have a feast; so nice!
One goes to the Abbot's table,
  All of us get each a slice.
How go on your flowers? None double?
  Not one fruit-sort can you spy?
Strange! – And I, too, at such trouble,
  Keep them close-nipped on the sly!

There's a great text in Galatians,
  Once you trip on it, entails
Twenty-nine distinct damnations,
  One sure, if another fails;
If I trip him just a-dying,
  Sure of heaven as sure can be,
Spin him round and send him flying
  Off to hell, a Manichee?

Or, my scrofulous French novel
  On grey paper with blunt type!
Simply glance at it, you grovel
  Hand and foot in Belial's gripe;
If I double down its pages
  At the woeful sixteenth print,
When he gathers his greengages,
  Ope a sieve and slip it in't?

Or, there's Satan! – one might venture
  Pledge one's soul to him, yet leave
Such a flaw in the indenture
  As he'd miss till, past retrieve,
Blasted lay that rose-acacia
  We're so proud of! *Hy, Zy, Hine.* . . . .
'St, there's Vespers! *Plena gratia
  Ave, Virgo!* Gr-r-r – you swine!
                                  Robert Browning.

TO EDWARD FITZGERALD

I CHANCED upon a new book yesterday:
I opened it, and, where my finger lay

'Twixt page and uncut page, these words I read
– Some six or seven at most – and learned thereby
That you, Fitzgerald, whom by ear and eye
She never knew, 'thanked God my wife was dead.'
Ay, dead! and were yourself alive, good Fitz,
How to return you thanks would task my wits:
Kicking you seems the common lot of curs –
While more appropriate greeting lends you grace:
Surely to spit there glorifies your face –
Spitting from lips once sanctified by Hers.

Robert Browning.

THE REBEL

OH, I'm a good old Rebel,
   Now that's just what I am;
For this 'fair Land of Freedom'
   I do not care a dam.
I'm glad I fit against it –
   I only wish we'd won,
And I don't want no pardon
   For anything I've done.

I hates the Constitution,
   This great Republic, too;
I hates the Freedmen's Buro,
   In uniforms of blue.
I hates the nasty eagle,
   With all his brag and fuss;
The lyin', thievin' Yankees,
   I hates 'em wuss and wuss.

I hates the Yankee Nation
   And everything they do;
I hates the Declaration
   Of Independence, too.
I hates the glorious Union,
   'Tis dripping with our blood;
I hates the striped banner –
   I fit it all I could.

I followed old Mars' Robert
   For four year, near about,
Got wounded in three places,
   And starved at Pint Lookout.

183

I cotch the roomatism
   A-campin' in the snow,
But I killed a chance of Yankees
   I'd like to kill some mo'.

Three hundred thousand Yankees
   Is stiff in Southern dust;
We got three hundred thousand
   Before they conquered us.
They died of Southern fever
   And Southern steel and shot;
I wish it was three millions
   Instead of what we got.

I can't take up my musket
   And fight 'em now no more,
But I ain't agoin' to love 'em,
   Now that is sartin sure.
And I don't want no pardon
   For what I was and am;
I won't be reconstructed,
   And I don't care a dam.

Innes Randolph.

ON THE SITE OF A MULBERRY-TREE

Planted by Wm. Shakespeare: Felled
by the Rev. F. Gastrell.

T H I S tree, here fall'n, no common birth or death
   Shared with its kind. The world's enfranchised son,
   Who found the trees of Life and Knowledge one,
Here set it, frailer than his laurel-wreath.
Shall not the wretch whose hand it fell beneath
   Rank also singly – the supreme unhung?
   Lo! Sheppard, Turpin, pleading with black tongue
This viler thief's unsuffocated breath!
We'll search thy glossary, Shakespeare! whence almost,
   And whence alone, some name shall be revealed
     For this deaf drudge, to whom no length of ears
     Sufficed to catch the music of the spheres;
   Whose soul is carrion now,– too mean to yield
Some tailor's ninth allotment of a ghost.

Dante Gabriel Rossetti.

A PSALM OF MONTREAL

T H E *City of Montreal is one of the most rising and, in many respects, most agreeable on the American continent, but its inhabitants are as yet too busy with commerce to care greatly about the masterpieces of old Greek Art. In the Montreal Museum of Natural History I came upon two plaster casts, one of the Antinous and the other of the Discobolus – not the good one, but in my poem, of course, I intend the good one – banished from public view to a room where were all manner of skins, plants, snakes, insects, etc., and, in the middle of these, an old man stuffing an owl.*

'Ah,' said I, *'so you have some antiques here; why don't you put them where people can see them?'*

'Well, sir,' answered the custodian, *'you see they are rather vulgar.'*

He then talked a great deal and said his brother did all Mr Spurgeon's printing.

The dialogue – perhaps true, perhaps imaginary, perhaps a little of the one and a little of the other – between the writer and this old man gave rise to the lines that follow:

Stowed away in a Montreal lumber room
The Discobolus standeth and turneth his face to the wall;
Dusty, cobweb-covered, maimed and set at naught,
Beauty crieth in an attic and no man regardeth:
>   O God! O Montreal!

Beautiful by night and day, beautiful in summer and in
>   winter,
Whole or maimed, always and alike beautiful –
He preacheth gospel of grace to the skin of owls
And to one who seasoneth the skins of Canadian owls:
>   O God! O Montreal!

When I saw him I was wroth and I said, 'O Discobolus!
Beautiful Discobolus, a Prince both among gods and men!
What doest thou here, how camest thou hither, Discobolus,
Preaching thy gospel in vain to the skins of owls?'
>   O God! O Montreal!

And I turned to the man of skins and said unto him, 'O thou
>   man of skins,
Wherefore hast thou done thus to shame the beauty of the
>   Discobolus?'

185

But the Lord had hardened the heart of the man of skins
And he answered, 'My brother-in-law is haberdasher to Mr
    Spurgeon.'
                             O God! O Montreal!

'The Discobolus is put here because he is vulgar –
He has neither vest nor pants with which to cover his limbs;
I, Sir, am a person of most respectable connections –
My brother-in-law is haberdasher to Mr Spurgeon.'
                             O God! O Montreal!

Then I said, 'O brother-in-law to Mr Spurgeon's haber-
    dasher,
Who seasonest also the skins of Canadian owls,
Thou callest trousers 'pants', whereas I call them 'trousers',
Therefore thou art in hell-fire and may the Lord pity thee!'
                             O God! O Montreal!

'Preferrest thou the gospel of Montreal to the gospel of
    Hellas,
The gospel of thy connection with Mr Spurgeon's haber-
    dashery to the gospel of the Discobolus?'
Yet none the less blasphemed he beauty saying, 'The Dis-
    cobolus hath no gospel,
But my brother-in-law is haberdasher to Mr Spurgeon.'
                             O God! O Montreal!
                             Samuel Butler.

A PORTRAIT

I AM a kind of farthing dip,
    Unfriendly to the nose and eyes;
A blue-behinded ape, I skip
    Upon the trees of Paradise.

At mankind's feast I take my place
    In solemn sanctimonious state,
And have the air of saying grace
    While I defile the dinner plate.

I am 'the smiler with the knife',
    The battener upon garbage, I –
Dear Heaven, with such a rancid life,
    Were it not better far to die?

Yet still, about the human pale,
    I love to scamper, love to race,

To swing by my irreverent tail
   All over the most holy place;

And when at length, some golden day,
   The unfailing sportsman, aiming at,
Shall bag me – all the world shall say:
   Thank God, and there's an end of that !
                   R. L. Stevenson.

LINES TO A DON

REMOTE and ineffectual Don
That dared attack my Chesterton,
With that poor weapon, half-impelled,
Unlearnt, unsteady, hardly held,
Unworthy for a tilt with men –
Your quavering and corroded pen;
Don poor at Bed and worse at Table,
Don pinched, Don starved, Don miserable;
Don stuttering, Don with roving eyes,
Don nervous, Don of crudities;
Don clerical, Don ordinary,
Don self-absorbed and solitary;
Don here-and-there, Don epileptic;
Don puffed and empty, Don dyspeptic;
Don middle-class, Don sycophantic,
Don dull, Don brutish, Don pedantic;
Don hypocritical, Don bad,
Don furtive, Don three-quarters mad;
Don (since a man must make an end)
Don that shall never be my friend.

    .   .   .

Don different from those regal Dons!
With hearts of gold and lungs of bronze,
Who shout and bang and roar and bawl
The Absolute across the hall,
Or sail in amply bellowing gown
Enormous through the Sacred Town,
Bearing from College to their homes
Deep cargoes of gigantic tomes;
Dons admirable! Dons of Might!
Uprising on my inward sight
Compact of ancient tales, and port
And sleep – and learning of a sort.
Dons English, worthy of the land;
Dons rooted; Dons that understand.

Good Dons perpetual that remain
A landmark, walling in the plain –
The horizon of my memories –
Like large and comfortable trees.

    .   .   .

Don very much apart from these,
Thou scapegoat Don, thou Don devoted,
Don to thine own damnation quoted,
Perplexed to find thy trivial name
Reared in my verse to lasting shame.
Don dreadful, rasping Don and wearing,
Repulsive Don – Don past all bearing.
Don of the cold and doubtful breath,
Don despicable, Don of death;
Don nasty, skimpy, silent, level;
Don evil; Don that serves the devil.
Don ugly – that makes fifty lines.
There is a Canon which confines
A Rhymed Octosyllabic Curse
If written in Iambic Verse
To fifty lines. I never cut;
I far prefer to end it – but
Believe me I shall soon return.
My fires are banked, but still they burn
To write some more about the Don
That dared attack my Chesterton.

Hilaire Belloc.

BASE DETAILS

I F I were fierce, and bald, and short of breath,
  I'd live with scarlet Majors at the Base,
And speed glum heroes up the line to death.
  You'd see me with my puffy petulant face,
Guzzling and gulping in the best hotel,
  Reading the Roll of Honour. 'Poor young chap,'
I'd say –'I used to know his father well;
  Yes, we've lost heavily in this last scrap.'
And when the war is done and youth stone dead,
I'd toddle safely home and die – in bed.

Siegfried Sassoon.

AT THE HOUSE OF MRS KINFOOT

A T the house of Mrs Kinfoot
  Are collected

Men and women
Of all ages.
They are supposed
To sing, paint, or to play the piano.
In the drawing-room
The fireplace is set
With green tiles
Of an acanthus pattern.
The black curls of Mrs Kinfoot
Are symmetrical.
– Descended, it is said,
From the Kings of Ethiopia –
But the British bourgeoisie has triumphed.

Mr Kinfoot is bald
And talks
In front of the fireplace
With his head on one side,
And his right hand
In his pocket.
The joy of catching tame elephants,
And finding them to be white ones,
Still gleams from the jungle-eyes
Of Mrs Kinfoot,
But her mind is no jungle
Of Ethiopia,
But a sound British meadow.
Listen then to the gospel of Mrs Kinfoot:

The world was made for the British bourgeoisie,
They are its Swiss Family Robinson;
The world is not what it was.
We cannot understand all this unrest!

Adam and Eve were born to evening dress
In the southern confines
Of Belgravia.
Eve was very artistic, and all that,
And felt the fall
Quite dreadfully.
Cain was such a man of the world
And belonged to every club in London;
His father simply adored him,
– But had never really liked Abel,
Who was rather a milk-sop.
Nothing exists which the British bourgeoisie
Does not understand;

Therefore there is no death
– And, of course, no life.

The British bourgeoisie
Is not born,
And does not die,
But, if it is ill,
It has a frightened look in its eyes.

The War was splendid, wasn't it?
Oh yes, splendid, splendid.

Mrs Kinfoot is a dear,
And so artistic.

Osbert Sitwell.

SONNET WITH THE COMPLIMENTS OF THE SEASON.
To a Popular Leader much to be Congratulated on the Avoidance of a Strike at Christmas

I K N O W you. You will hail the huge release,
Saying the sheathing of thousand swords,
In silence and injustice, well accords
With Christmas bells. And you will gild with grease
The papers, the employers, the police,
And vomit up the void your windy words
To your New Christ; who bears no whip of cords
For them that traffic in the doves of peace.

The feast of friends, the candle-fruited tree,
I have not failed to honour. And I say
It would be better for such men as we,
And we be nearer Bethlehem, if we lay
Shot dead on scarlet snows for liberty,
Dead in the daylight upon Christmas Day.

G. K. Chesterton.

WISHES OF AN ELDERLY MAN
(WISHED AT A GARDEN-PARTY, JUNE, 1914)

I W I S H I loved the Human Race;
I wish I loved its silly face;
I wish I liked the way it walks;
I wish I liked the way it talks;
And when I'm introduced to one
I wish I thought *What Jolly Fun!*

Walter Raleigh.

TO A FAT LADY SEEN FROM THE TRAIN

O W H Y do you walk through the fields in gloves,
    Missing so much and so much?
O fat white woman whom nobody loves,
Why do you walk through the fields in gloves,
When the grass is soft as the breast of doves
    And shivering-sweet to the touch?
O why do you walk through the fields in gloves,
    Missing so much and so much?

Frances Cornford.

THE MOTOR BUS

W H A T is this that roareth thus?
Can it be a Motor Bus?
Yes, the smell and hideous hum
Indicat Motorem Bum!
Implet in the Corn and High
Terror me Motoris Bi:
Bo Motori clamitabo
Ne Motore caedar a Bo –
Dative be or Ablative
So thou only let us live –
Whither shall thy victims flee?
Spare us, spare us, Motor Be!
Thus I sang; and still anigh
Came in hordes Motores Bi,
Et complebat omne forum
Copia Motorum Borum.
How shall wretches live like us
Cincti Bis Motoribus?
Domine, defende nos
Contra hos Motores Bos!

A. Godley.

TO A CERTAIN ARCHBISHOP: *after hearing his broadcast
strictures on a Royal Personage fallen from power.*

My Lord Archbishop, what a scold you are!
And when your man is down how bold you are!
Of charity how oddly scant you are!
How Lang O Lord, how full of Cantuar!

Gerald Bullett.

THE TRAVELLER'S CURSE
AFTER MISDIRECTION
(From the Welsh)

MAY they wander stage by stage
Of the same vain pilgrimage,
Stumbling on, age after age,
Night and day, mile after mile,
At each and every step, a stile;
At each and every stile, withal,
May they catch their feet and fall;
At each and every fall they take,
May a bone within them break,
And may the bones that break within
Not be, for variation's sake,
Now rib, now thigh, now arm, now shin,
But always, without fail, THE NECK.

Robert Graves.

PRIG: EPITAPH

HERE lies a man who always thought
That he was acting as he ought.
He turned his cheek to every blow
And never said 'I told you so',
Nor claimed with any outward spite
The mean revenge of being right.
He died at three score years and ten
Detested by his fellow men
But conscious of a Heavenly Crown –

. . . . .

'Go *down!*' St. Peter said, 'GO DOWN!'

Colin Ellis.

NORA CRIONA

I HAVE looked him round and looked him through,
Know everything that he will do
In such a case, and such a case,
And when a frown comes on his face
I dream of it, and when a smile
I trace its sources in a while.

He cannot do a thing but I
Peep to find the reason why,

192

For I love him, and I seek,
Every evening in the week,
To peep behind his frowning eye
With little query, little pry,
And make him if a woman can
Happier than any man.

Yesterday he gripped her tight
And cut her throat – and serve her right!

James Stephens.

THE SOLDIER'S REPLY TO THE POET

(*'Will it be so again?'*)

S O the Soldier replied to the Poet,
Oh yes! it will all be the same,
But a bloody sight worse, and you know it
Since you have a hand in the game:
And you'll be the first in the racket
To sell us a similar dope,
Wrapped up in a rosier packet,
But noosed with as cunning a rope.
You coin us the catchwords and phrases
For which to be slaughtered; and then,
While thousands are blasted to blazes,
Sit picking your nose with your pen.
We know what you're bursting to tell us,
By heart. It is all very fine.
We must swallow the Bait that you sell us
And pay for your Hook and your Line.
But his pride for a soldier suffices
Since someone must carry the can;
In war, or depression, or crisis,
It's what you expect of a man.
But when we have come to the Isthmus
That bridges the Slump to the War,
We shall contact a new Father Christmas
Like the one we contacted before,
Deploring the one he replaces
Like you do (it's part of the show!)
But with those same mincing grimaces
And that mealy old kisser we know!
And he'll patent a cheap cornucopia
For all that our purse can afford,
And rent us a flat in Utopia
With dreams for our lodging and board.
And we'll hand in our Ammo and Guns

193

As we handed them in once before,
And he'll lock them up safe; till our sons
Are conscripted for Freedom once more.
We can die for our faith by the million
And laugh at our bruises and scars,
But hush! for the Poet-Civilian
Is weeping, between the cigars.
Mellifluous, sweeter than Cadbury's,
The M.O.I. Nightingale (Hush!)
Is lining his pockets with Bradburies
So his feelings come out with a rush,
For our woes are the cash in his kitty
When his voice he so kindly devotes
In sentiment, pathos and pity,
To bringing huge lumps to the throats
Of our widows, and sweethearts, and trollops,
Since it sells like hot cakes to the town
As he doles out the Goitre in dollops
And the public is gulping it down.
Oh well may he weep for the soldier
Who weeps at a guinea a tear,
For although his invention gets mouldier,
It keeps him his job in the rear.
When my Mrs the organ is wheeling
And my adenoids wheeze to the sky,
He will publish the hunger I'm feeling
And rake in his cheque with a sigh:
And when with a trayful of matches
And laces, you hawk in the street,
O comrades in tatters and patches,
Rejoice! since we're in for a treat:
For when we have died in the gutter
To safeguard his income and state,
Be sure that the Poet will utter
Some beautiful thoughts on our Fate!

Roy Campbell.

EPISODE OF DECAY

B E I N G very religious, she devoted most of her time to fear.
Under her calm visage, terror held her,
Terror of water, of air, of earth, of thought,
Terror lest she be disturbed in her routine of eating her husband.
She fattened on his decay, but she let him decay without pain.

194

And still she would ask, while she consumed him particle by
    particle,
'Do you wish me to take it, dear? Will it make you happier?'
And down the plump throat he went day after day in tidbits;
And he mistook the drain for happiness,
Could hardly live without the deadly nibbling . . .
She had eaten away the core of him under the shell,
Eaten his heart and drunk away his breath;
Till on Saturday, the seventeenth of April,
She made her breakfast on an edge of his mind.
He was very quiet that day, without knowing why.
A last valiant cell of his mind may have been insisting that
    the fault was not hers but his;
But soon he resumed a numbness of content;
The little cell may have been thinking that one dies sooner or
    later
And that one's death may as well be useful . . .
For supper, he offered her tea and cake from behind his left
    ear;
And after supper they took together the walk they always
    took together after supper.

Witter Bynner.

PARSLEY FOR VICE-PRESIDENT

I 'D like to be able to say a good word for parsley, but I can't,
And after all what can you find to say for something that
    even the dictionary dismisses as a biennial umbelliferous
    plant?
Speaking of which, I don't know how the dictionary figures
    it as biennial, it is biennial my eye, it is like the poor and
    the iniquitous,
Because it is always with us, because it is permanent and
    ubiquitous.
I will not venture to deny that it is umbelliferous,
I will only add that it is of a nasty green color, and faintly
    odoriferous,
And I hold by my complaint, though every cook and hostess
    in the land indict me for treason for it,
That parsley is something that as a rhymer I can find no
    rhyme for it and as an eater I can find no reason for it.
Well, there is one sin for which a lot of cooks and hostesses
    are some day going to have to atone,
Which is that they can't bear to cook anything and leave it
    alone.

No, they see food as something to base a lot of beautiful
    dreams and romance on,
Which explains lamb chops with pink and blue pants on.
Everything has to be all decorated and garnished
So the guests will be amazed and astarnished,
And whatever you get to eat, it's sprinkled with a lot of good
    old umbelliferous parsley looking as limp and as wistful
    as Lilian Gish,
And it is limpest, and wistfulest, and also thickest, on fish.
Indeed, I think maybe one reason for the disappearance of
    Enoch Arden
Was that his wife had an idea that mackerel tasted better if
    instead of looking like mackerel it looked like a garden.
Well, anyhow, there's the parsley cluttering up your food,
And the problem is to get it off without being rude,
And first of all you try to scrape it off with your fork,
And you might as well try to shave with a cork,
And then you surreptitiously try your fingers,
And you get covered with butter and gravy, but the parsley
    lingers,
And you turn red and smile at your hostess and compliment
    her on the recipe and ask her where she found it,
And then you return to the parsley and as a last resort you
    try to eat around it,
And the hostess says, Oh you are just picking at it, is there
    something wrong with it?
So all you can do is eat it all up, and the parsley along with it,
And now is the time for all good parsleyphobes to come to
    the aid of the menu and exhibit their gumption,
And proclaim that any dish that has either a taste or an ap-
    pearance that can be improved by parsley is *ipso facto* a
    dish unfit for human consumption.

                            Ogden Nash.

STATE POEMS

Permit the transports of a British muse
And pardon raptures that yourselves infuse.
*Nahum Tate, Poet Laureate, to
the new Parliament* (1701).

Praising all alike, is praising none.
John Gay.

The world, we believe, is pretty well agreed
in thinking that the shorter a prize poem
is, the better.
Macaulay.

State Poems

'Permit the transports of a British muse
And pardon raptures that yourselves infuse'

Robert Herrick on

THE KING (CHARLES I) AND QUEEN
UPON THEIR UNHAPPY DISTANCES

W O E , woe to them, who (by a ball of strife)
Doe, and have parted here a Man and Wife:
C H A R L S the best Husband, while M A R I A strives
To be, and is, the very best of Wives.

Colley Cibber (Poet Laureate):

B I R T H D A Y   O D E ,   1 7 3 2

L E T there be light!
Such was at once the word and work of heav'n,
   When from the void of universal night
   Free nature sprung to the Creator's sight,
And day to glad the new-born world was giv'n.

Succeeding days to ages roll'd,
And ev'ry age some wonder told:
At length arose this glorious morn!
   When, to extend his bounteous pow'r,
   High heav'n announc'd this instant hour
The best of monarchs shall be born!

   Around the royal table spread,
See how the beauteous branches shine!
   Sprung from the fertile genial bed
Of glorious G E O R G E and C A R O L I N E .

Anonymous, 1738:

ON QUEEN CAROLINE'S
SICKNESS AND DEATH

W H A T Pen th' Amazement can display,
Or Tongue describe the piercing Grief,
When Physick's Aid brought no Relief,
And *George* with all his blooming Race,
Tears trickling down each Royal Face,
Regardless of their Health and Rest,
Contended which should nurse her best,
Eager with pious Zeal to save
The Wife, the Mother, from the Grave?

. . . . .

Deep-piercing was the rude Alarm,
When she, who wont our Eyes to charm,
Our Ears with Musick to rejoice
When e'er she deigned to lift her Voice,
Who with a Smile each Heart could win,
Tho' Disappointment rag'd within,
Who with a Word could Passion chain,
And render all its Fury vain,
Withdrawn, and languishing in Bed,
Was more than once reported dead.

Like *Niobe*, one Speechless stood,
Insensible as Stone or Wood.
Her Anguish took a Root so deep,
She look'd amaz'd, but could not weep,
As if Affliction's wonted Train
Were inexpressive of her Pain.
Another, seiz'd with mortal Fright,
Sunk Lifeless at the killing Sight.
The Rest, in various Shapes, impart
The Symptoms of a wounded Heart.

Leigh Hunt addresses

THE INFANT PRINCESS ROYAL

W E L C O M E, bud beside the rose,
On whose stem our safety grows;
Welcome, little Saxon Guelph;
Welcome for thine own small self;
Welcome for thy father, mother,

Proud the one and safe the other;
Welcome to three kingdoms; nay,
Such is thy potential day,
Welcome, little mighty birth,
To our human star the earth.

Some have wish'd thee boy; and some
Gladly wait till boy shall come . . .

Alfred, Lord Tennyson writes of

THE EXHIBITION, 1862

UPLIFT a thousand voices full and sweet,
  In this wide hall with earth's invention stor'd,
  And praise th' invisible universal Lord,
Who lets once more in peace the nations meet,
  Where, Science, Art, and Labour have outpour'd
Their myriad horns of plenty at our feet.
O silent father of our Kings to be,
Mourn'd in this golden hour of jubilee,
For this, for all, we weep our thanks to thee!

Alfred Austin (Poet Laureate) goes

MAFEKING

ONCE again, banners, fly!
Clang again, bells, on high,
Sounding to sea and sky,
    Longer and louder,
Mafeking's glory with
Kimberley, Ladysmith,
Of our unconquered kith
    Prouder and prouder.

Hemmed in for half a year,
Still with no succour near,
Nor word of hope to cheer
    Wounded and dying,
Famished, and foiled of sleep
By the fierce cannon's leap,
They vowed still, still to keep
    England's Flag flying.

Nor was their mettle shown
By male and strong alone,
But, as intrepid grown,
    Fragile and tender
Without or tear or sigh
Echoed the brave old cry,
'We, too, would rather die,
    Die than surrender.'

As pressed the foe more near,
Only with naked spear,
Ne'er knowing what to fear,
    Parley, or blench meant,
Forward through shot and shell,
While still the foremost fell,
They with resistless yell
    Stormed his intrenchment.

Then, when hope dawned at last,
And fled the foe, aghast
At the relieving blast
    Heard in the melley,–
O our stout, stubborn kith!
Kimberley, Ladysmith,
Mafeking, wedded with
    Lucknow and Delhi!

Roy Dalziel celebrates

THE DIAMOND JUBILEE 1897

QUEEN VICTORIA sixty years the Monarch of our Realm
Shows the grand old lady has kept a steady helm.
She often tacked, she never backed, she always heaved her
    lead,
And never turned into her bunk when breakers were ahead.

Broadsheet sold in London streets

ON THE DEATH OF KING EDWARD VII

THE will of God we must obey.
Dreadful – our King taken away!
The greatest friend of the nation,
Mighty monarch and protection!

Heavenly Father, help in sorrow
Queen-Mother, and them to follow,
What to do without him who has gone!
Pray help! help! and do lead us on.

Greatest sorrow England ever had
When death took away our dear Dad;
A king was he from head to sole,
Loved by his people one and all.

His mighty work for the Nation,
Making peace and strengthening Union –
Always at it since on the throne:
Saved the country more than one billion.

EPIGRAMS

A box where sweets compacted lie.
George Herbert.

What is an Epigram? a dwarfish whole,
Its body brevity, and wit its soul.
Coleridge.

O be less beautiful, or be less brief.
Sir William Watson.

And if you find it wond'rous short,
It cannot hold you long.
Oliver Goldsmith.

Epigrams

'A box where sweets compacted lie'

ON THE PHRASE, 'TO KILL TIME'

T H E R E ' S scarce a point whereon mankind agree
So well, as in their boast of killing me:
I boast of nothing, but, when I've a mind,
I think I can be even with mankind.
        From *Voltaire: Dodd's* Select Epigrams.

RESPICE FINEM

M Y soul, sit thou a patient looker-on;
Judge not the play before the play is done:
Her plot hath many changes; every day
Speaks a new scene; the last act crowns the play.
        Francis Quarles.

GROWN-UP

W A S it for this I uttered prayers,
And sobbed and cursed and kicked the stairs,
That now, domestic as a plate,
I should retire at half-past eight?
        Edna St. Vincent Millay.

A CURE FOR POETRY

S E V E N wealthy towns contend for Homer dead
Thro' which the living Homer beg'd his bread.
        Thomas Seward.

THE PURITAN

T H E Puritan through Life's sweet garden goes
To pluck the thorn and cast away the rose,
And hopes to please by this peculiar whim
The God who fashioned it and gave it him.

Kenneth Hare.

LOVE

ALL love at first, like generous wine,
Ferments and frets, until 'tis fine;
But when 'tis settled on the lee,
And from the impurer matter free,
Becomes the richer still, the older,
And proves the pleasanter, the colder.

Samuel Butler.

A RIDDLE SOLVED

KIND souls, you wonder why, love you,
When you, you wonder why, love none.
We love, Fool, for the good we do,
Not that which unto us is done!

Coventry Patmore.

HOPE

POOR Hope sat on a grave, a very child,
  Blowing her rainbow bubbles; as she cast
Each one in the air, it broke. Yet still she smiled
Upon the latest one. 'Look! this will last.'

William James Linton.

TOO BAD

T H E heart of Man is capable of
  Forty ridiculous kinds of love,
And the heart of Woman is just an ocean
Of jealous, immoderate, damp devotion.

Clarence Day.

THE FIVE REASONS FOR DRINKING

I F all be true that I do think,
There are five reasons we should drink;
Good wine – a friend – or being dry –
Or lest we should be by and by –
Or any other reason why.

Henry Aldrich.

FREE-WILL AND PREDESTINATION

T H E R E was a young man who said 'Damn!
It appears to me now that I am
      Just a being that moves
      In predestinate grooves –
Not a bus, not a bus, but a tram.'

Maurice Hare.

TRIAL AND ERROR

A L A D Y is smarter than a gentleman, maybe.
She can sew a fine seam, she can have a baby,
She can use her intuition instead of her brain,
But she can't fold a paper on a crowded train.

Phyllis McGinley.

¶

M E N fall in love, and soar the skies
      From earth's profoundest prison:
O change the word as there it lies –
      Not fallen in love, but risen.

Wilfrid Meynell.

¶

N O ! not for those of women born,
      Not so unlike the die is cast;
For, after all our vaunt and scorn,
      How very small the odds at last!

Him, raised to Fortune's utmost top,
      With him beneath her feet compare;
And one has nothing more to hope,
      And one has nothing more to fear.

Samuel Wesley.

209

EPIGRAMS

OF TREASON

TREASON doth never prosper; what's the reason?
For if it prosper, none dare call it treason.

John Harington.

SPANIEL'S SERMONS

'TIS more than Spaniel's place is worth
To speak his masters ill:
As long as there is Peace on Earth
He teaches men goodwill.

But when the shells begin to fly
He calls our quarrel just
And bids us keep our powder dry
And place our God in trust.

Colin Ellis.

THE BALANCE OF EUROPE

NOW Europe balanced, neither side prevails;
For nothing's left in either of the scales.

Alexander Pope.

TO HIS LITTLE CHILD FROM THE TOWER

SWEET Benjamin, since thou art young,
And hast not yet the use of tongue,
Make it thy slave, while thou art free;
Imprison it, lest it do thee.

John Hoskins.

AGAINST PUBLISHING SATIRES

I MADE an armament to overcome
The embattled brutishness of Tweedledum,
Only to find that weapons forged by me
Upheld the brutish cause of Tweedledee.

Colin Ellis.

BAR AND BENCH

HOB in a pub drinks too much gin
While Nob takes too much wine at dinner:
Hob in the Bar commits a sin;
Nob on the Bench commits the Sinner.

Colin Ellis.

EPIGRAMS

ON INCLOSURES

'TIS bad enough in man or woman
To steal a goose from off a common;
But surely he's without excuse
Who steals the common from the goose.

Anonymous.

ENGLAND'S CRISIS

OF old, when empires tottered, none had skill
To diagnose the nature of their ill:
To us, more favoured, twenty doctors cry
'We understand your symptoms. You will die.'

Colin Ellis.

THE CRIMEAN HEROES

HAIL, ye indomitable heroes, hail!
Despite of all your generals ye prevail.

W. S. Landor.

BUNGALOID GROWTH

WHEN England's multitudes observed with frowns
That those who came before had spoiled the towns,
'This can no longer be endured!' they cried,
And set to work to spoil the countryside.

Colin Ellis.

ON A CERTAIN LORD'S GIVING SOME THOUSAND POUNDS FOR A HOUSE

SO many thousands for a house
For you, of all the world, Lord Mouse!
A little house would best accord
With you, my very little lord!
And then exactly match'd would be
Your house and hospitality.

David Garrick.

SHAM

I MIGHT endure his villa, quasi-Tudor,
His port-style wine, his bogus astrakhan,
Were not Sir Henry's bonhomie still cruder
And he so faint a typescript of a man.

G. Rostrevor Hamilton.

EPIGRAMS

ON SOME SOUTH AFRICAN NOVELISTS

Y O U praise the firm restraint with which they write –
    I'm with you there, of course:
They use the snaffle and the curb all right,
    But where's the bloody horse?

Roy Campbell.

¶

O F T have I wonder'd that, on Irish Ground
No poisonous reptiles ever yet were found:
Reveal'd the secret stands, of Nature's Work!
She saved her venom, to create a Burke.

Warren Hastings.

THE BETTER WAY

I F you desire to paralyse
Your enemy, don't 'damn his eyes';
From futile blasphemy desist;
Send him to Blank the oculist.

Walter Leaf (from *Nicharchus*).

ON A PROFESSOR'S VERSE

W H O forced the Muse to this alliance?
A Man of more degrees than parts –
The jilted Bachelor of Science
And Widower of Arts.

Roy Campbell.

¶

Y O U beat your pate, and fancy wit will come:
Knock as you please, there's nobody at home.

Alexander Pope.

ON THE MARTYRDOM OF F. GARCIA LORCA

N O T only did he lose his life
By shots assassinated:
But with a hatchet and a knife
Was after that – translated!

Roy Campbell.

EPIGRAMS

§

S W A N S sing before they die –'twere no bad thing
Should certain persons die before they sing.

S. T. Coleridge.

§

H O W did the party go in Portman Square?
I cannot tell you; Juliet was not there.
And how did Lady Gaster's party go?
Juliet was next me and I do not know.

Hilaire Belloc.

DIRCE

S T A N D close around, ye Stygian set,
  With Dirce in one boat conveyed,
Or Charon, seeing, may forget
  That he is old and she a shade.

W. S. Landor.

THE STATUE

W H E N we are dead, some Hunting-boy will pass
And find a stone half-hidden in tall grass
And grey with age: but having seen that stone
(Which was your image), ride more slowly on.

Hilaire Belloc.

CHLOE

B R I G H T as the day, and like the morning fair,
Such Chloe is – and common as the air.

Lansdowne.

UNFORGIVEN

W I T H Paul I have not lately dined:
My jokes were broader than his mind.

Colin Ellis.

LINGUA POTENTIOR ARMIS

T H A T speech surpasses force, is no new whim:
Jove caus'd the heav'ns to tremble; Juno him.

Anon. 1727.

EPIGRAMS

THE PROOF

H I S Lordship dines with him, I've heard Jock boast.
It proves a parasite may be a host.

G. Rostrevor Hamilton.

¶

L I E on! while my revenge shall be
To speak the very truth of thee.

Robert, Earl Nugent.

ON MR. PARTRIDGE

W H A T ! kill a partridge in the month of May!
Was that done like a sportsman ? Eh, Death, eh ?

Norfolk Epitaph, 1861.

EMINENT PHYSICISTS

I

N A T U R E , and Nature's laws, lay hid in night:
God said, *Let Newton be !* and all was light.

Alexander Pope.

I I

I T did not last: the Devil, howling *Ho !*
Let Einstein be ! restored the status quo.

J. C. Squire.

RELATIVITY

T H E R E was a young woman named Bright
Who travelled much faster than light.
   She started one day
   In a relative way,
And returned on the previous night.

Anonymous.

ON A DISTANT PROSPECT OF AN
ABSCONDING BOOKMAKER

A L A S ! what boots it that my noble steed,
   Chosen so carefully, the field outran ?
I did not reckon, bookie, on *your* speed:
   The proper study of mankind is man.

G. Rostrevor Hamilton.

EPIGRAMS

ON LADY POLTAGRUE, A PUBLIC PERIL

T H E Devil, having nothing else to do,
Went off to tempt My Lady Poltagrue.
My Lady, tempted by a private whim,
To his extreme annoyance, tempted him.

Hilaire Belloc.

THE FALSE ALARM

C H L O E proclaims full oft, she fears
The near approach of forty years.
Content thee, maiden; for in sooth
If parish registers tell truth,
That fatal age, their pages say,
Becomes more distant every day.

Anonymous.

A PORTRAIT PAINTER

G O O D Mr Fortune, A.R.A.,
    Rejoiced in twenty sons,
But even there he failed, they say,
    To get a likeness once.

G. Rostrevor Hamilton (from Lucillus).

THE KISS

' I S A W you take his kiss!' ' 'Tis true.'
'O, modesty!' ' 'Twas strictly kept:
He thought me asleep: at least, I knew
He thought I thought he thought I slept.'

Coventry Patmore.

REFLECTIONS ON ICE-BREAKING

CANDY
Is dandy
But liquor
Is quicker.

Ogden Nash.

A TRUE MAID

N O , no; for my virginity,
When I lose that, says Rose, I'll die:
Behind the elms, last night, cried Dick,
Rose, were you not extremely sick?

Matthew Prior.

EPIGRAMS

THE PHILANDERERS

SHE cheats her lover of his dues
And yet contrives to keep him tied,
At first deciding to refuse
And then – refusing to decide.

And he – to unexplored Thibet
And furthest Himalayan snow
He talks of going – to forget,
And, talking, he forgets to go.

Colin Ellis.

¶

'COME, come,' said Tom's father, 'at your time
    of life,
There's no longer excuse for thus playing the rake –
It is time you should think, boy, of taking a wife.'
'Why, so it is, father,– whose wife shall I take?'

Thomas Moore.

THE MENDELIAN THEORY

THERE was a young lady named Starky
Who had an affair with a darky.
    The result of her sins
    Was quadruplets, not twins:
One black, and one white, and two khaki.

Anonymous.

¶

MY Lord complains that Pope, stark mad with gardens,
Has cut three trees, the value of three farthings.
'But he's my neighbour,' cries the peer polite:
'And if he visit me, I'll waive the right.'
What! on compulsion, and against my will,
A lord's acquaintance? Let him file his bill!

Alexander Pope.

BYWAYS IN BIOGRAPHY

ALFRED de Musset
Used to call his cat Pusset.
His accent was affected.
That was to be expected.

Maurice Hare.

EPIGRAMS

YOU CAN'T PLEASE EVERYBODY

THE Duke of Rutland urged *The Times* to pray
For rain: the rain came down the following day.
The pious marvelled: sceptics murmured: 'Fluke!'
And farmers late with hay said: 'Damn that Duke!'
Quoted by E. V. Lucas.

DON'S HOLIDAY

PROFESSOR ROBINSON each summer beats
The fishing record of the world – such feats
As one would hardly credit from a lesser
Person than a history professor.
G. Rostrevor Hamilton.

BALLIOL RHYMES

FIRST come I, my name is Jowett,
There's no knowledge but I know it.
I am Master of this College,
What I don't know is not knowledge.

I am the Dean of Christ Church, sir,
This is my wife – look well at her.
She is the Broad; *I* am the High:
We are the University.

BURLESQUE

IF the man who turnips cries,
Cry not when his father dies,
'Tis a proof that he had rather
Have a turnip than his father.
Samuel Johnson.

MIND OVER MATTER

THERE was a faith-healer of Deal
Who said, 'Although pain isn't real,
  If I sit on a pin
  And it punctures my skin
I dislike what I fancy I feel.'
Anonymous.

EPIGRAMS

¶

H A D she told the dicks
How she got in that fix,
I would be much apter
To read the last chapter.

Ogden Nash.

THE POWER OF TIME

I F neither brass nor marble can withstand
The mortal force of Time's destructive hand;
If mountains sink to vales, if cities die,
And lessening rivers mourn their fountains dry;
When my old cassock (said a Welsh divine)
Is out at elbows, why should I repine?

Jonathan Swift.

TO SILENCE

W H Y the warning finger-tip
Pressed for ever on thy lip?
To remind the pilgrim Sound
That it moves on holy ground,
In a breathing-space to be
Hushed for all eternity.

J. B. Tabb.

ETERNITY

H E who bends to himself a Joy
Doth the wingèd life destroy;
But he who kisses the Joy as it flies
Lives in Eternity's sunrise.

William Blake.

¶

R E A S O N has moons, but moons not hers
Lie mirror'd on her sea,
Confounding her astronomers,
But oh, delighting me.

Ralph Hodgson.

AN INSCRIPTION

GRASS of levity,
Span in brevity,
Flowers' felicity,
Fire of misery,
Winds' stability,
Is mortality.

Anon. 1609.

¶

I FELT in such fine fettle,
I really could not settle,
It put me on my mettle;
I firmly grasped the nettle
Climbed Popocatepetl
And boiled my copper kettle.

Eleanor Dawson.

ON A SUNDIAL

LOSS and Possession, Death and Life are one.
There falls no shadow where there shines no sun.

Hilaire Belloc.

ON A BEAUTIFUL YOUTH STRUCK BLIND
WITH LIGHTNING

SURE, 'twas by Providence design'd
    Rather in pity than in hate,
That he should be, like Cupid, blind,
    To save him from Narcissus' fate.

Oliver Goldsmith.

UPON A GENTLEWOMAN
WITH A SWEET VOICE

SO long you did not sing, or touch your lute,
We knew 'twas Flesh and Blood, that there sat mute.
But when your playing, and your voice came in,
'Twas no more you then, but a *Cherubin*.

Robert Herrick.

219

EPIGRAMS

EPITAPH ON DRAKE

DRAKE, who the world hast conquered like a scrole;
Who saw'st the Arcticke and the Antarcticke Pole;
If men were silent, starres would make thee knowne:
Phoebus forgets not his companion.

Thomas Beedome.

ON DONNE'S POETRY

WITH Donne, whose muse on dromedary trots,
Wreathe iron pokers into true-love knots;
Rhyme's sturdy cripple, fancy's maze and clue,
Wit's forge and fire-blast, meaning's press and screw.

Coleridge.

ON THE TOILET TABLE
OF QUEEN MARIE-ANTOINETTE

THIS was her table, these her trim outspread
Brushes and trays and porcelain cups for red;
Here sate she, while her women tired and curled
The most unhappy head in all the world.

J. B. B. Nichols.

ON HIS SEVENTY-FIFTH BIRTHDAY

I STROVE with none; for none was worth my strife.
Nature I loved and, next to Nature, Art;
I warmed both hands before the fire of life;
It sinks, and I am ready to depart.

W. S. Landor.

MY OWN EPITAPH

LIFE is a jest, and all things show it;
I thought so once, but now I know it.

John Gay.

¶

MY candle burns at both ends;
It will not last the night;
But ah, my foes, and oh, my friends –
It gives a lovely light!

Edna St. Vincent Millay.

EPIGRAMS

¶

H E R E dead lie we because we did not choose
　To live and shame the land from which we sprung.
Life, to be sure, is nothing much to lose;
　But young men think it is, and we were young.
A. E. Housman.

DEATH STANDS ABOVE ME

D E A T H stands above me, whispering low
　I know not what into my ear:
Of his strange language all I know
　Is, there is not a word of fear.
W. S. Landor.

ON SIR JOHN VANBRUGH, ARCHITECT

U N D E R this stone, reader, survey
Dead Sir John Vanbrugh's house of clay.
Lie heavy on him, earth! for he
Laid many heavy loads on thee.
Abel Evans.

AN EPITAPH

(Twopence coloured, *penny plain*)

H E worshipped at the altar of Romance
(*Tried to seduce a woman half his age*)
And dared to stake his fortune on a chance
(*Gambled away his children's heritage*).

He valued only what the world held cheap
(*Refused to work, from laziness and pride*):
Dreams were his refuge and he welcomed sleep
(*He failed in business, took to drink and died*).
Colin Ellis.

ON CHARLES II

H E R E lies our sovereign Lord the King,
　Whose word no man relies on,
Who never said a foolish thing
　Nor ever did a wise one.
Rochester.

EPIGRAMS

ON PETER ROBINSON

H E R E lies the preacher, judge and poet, Peter,
Who broke the laws of God, and man, and metre.

Francis Jeffrey.

A GENTLEMAN OF THE OLD SCHOOL

H E R E lies a man of wealth and rank
Who hunted, whored, made bets and drank:
There is not much to tell beside
Except that he was born and died.

—AND OF THE NEW

H E R E lies his son, who lacked the skill
To live magnificently ill,
And loathed, while failing to avoid,
The follies that his sire enjoyed.

Colin Ellis.

UPON A CHILD

H E R E a pretty baby lies
Sung asleep with lullabies;
Pray be silent, and not stir
Th' easy earth that covers her.

Robert Herrick.

EPITAPH BY A SON

B E N E A T H this stone, in hopes of Zion,
Doth lie the landlord of the Lion;
His son keeps on the business still,
Resigned unto the heavenly will.

From *Fairley's Epitaphiana.*

ON THE DEATH OF SIR ALBERTUS AND LADY MORTON

H E first deceas'd – she, for a little, try'd
To live without him, lik'd it not, and dy'd.

Henry Wotton.

EPITAPH IN ELGIN CATHEDRAL

HERE lie I, Martin Elginbrodde:
Ha'e mercy o' my soul, Lord God,
As I wad do, were I Lord God
And ye were Martin Elginbrodde.

ON ELIZABETH THOMAS OB. 1808, AET. 27

SHE'D no fault save what travellers give the moon:
Her light was lovely, but she dies too soon.

SLIM CUNNING HANDS

SLIM cunning hands at rest, and cozening eyes –
Under this stone one loved too wildly lies;
How false she was, no granite could declare;
    Nor all earth's flowers, how fair.
                            Walter De la Mare.

UPON A VIRGIN

HERE a solemn fast we keep,
While all beauty lies asleep.
Hushed be all things, no noise here,
But the toning of a tear:
Or the sigh of such as bring
Cowslips for her covering.
                            Robert Herrick.

ON A DEFORMED PRIEST

BENEATH this yew, the shadow of a shade,
A little, humble, singing priest is laid.
He loved his life; of death was not afraid,
And loved his Maker, tho' so strangely made.
                            c. 1720.

¶

BLESSED Mary, pity me,
Who was a Virgin too, like thee;
But had, please God, no little son
To shower a lifetime's sorrows on.
                            Walter De la Mare.

223

SUFFOLK EPITAPH

STRANGER pass by and waste no time
On bad biography and careless rhyme.
For what I am, this humble dust encloses;
And what I was is no affair of yourses.

1870.

§

AFTER long thirty years re-met
I, William Clarke, and I, Jeanette
His wife, lie side by side once more;
But quieter than we lay before.

Sylvia Townsend Warner.

BLONDIE GOES TO HEAVEN

PAUL said and Peter said
    And all the saints alive or dead
Vowed she had the sweetest head
    Of yellow, yellow hair.

Anonymous.

EPITAPH FOR AN EXPLORER

TIGER, tiger, my mistake;
I thought that you were William Blake.

Ogden Nash.

THE JUNG IDEA

THE young things who frequent picture-palaces
Have no use for this psycho-analysis;
    And although Doctor Freud
    Is distinctly annoyed
The cling to their long-standing fallacies.

P.H.

THE MORON

SEE the happy moron,
He doesn't give a damn!
I wish I were a moron –
My God! Perhaps I am!

Anonymous.

THE ZOO

The living creature after his kind.
> *Genesis.*

Sporting the lion ramped, and in his paw,
Dandled the kid; bears, tigers, ounces, pards
Gamboll'd before them, th'unwieldly
   elephant
To make them mirth us'd all his might, and
   wreathed
His lithe proboscis.
> *Milton.*

Cows are my passion.
> *Charles Dickens.*

the Zoo

'the living creature after his kind'

THE BEASTS

I THINK I could turn and live with animals, they are so
    placid and self-contain'd;
I stand and look at them long and long.
They do not sweat and whine about their condition;
They do not lie awake in the dark and weep for their sins;
They do not make me sick discussing their duty to God;
Not one is dissatisfied – not one is demented with the mania
    of owning things;
Not one kneels to another, nor to his kind that lived
    thousands of years ago;
Not one is respectable or industrious over the whole earth.
Walt Whitman.

FOUR BEASTS

THERE be four things which are little upon the earth
But they are exceeding wise;
The ants are a people not strong,
Yet they prepare their meat in the summer;
The conies are but a feeble folk,
Yet they make their houses in the rocks;
The locusts have no king,
Yet they go forth all of them by bands;
The spider taketh hold with her hands,
And is in kings' palaces.
The Authorized Version.

JONAH AND THE WHALE

H E sported round the watery world.
His rich oil was a gloomy waveless lake
Within the waves. Affrighted seamen hurled
Their weapons in his foaming wake.

One old corroding iron he bore
Which journeyed through his flesh but yet had not
Found out his life. Another lance he wore
Outside him, pricking in a tender spot.

So distant were his parts that they
Sent but a dull faint message to his brain.
He knew not his own flesh, as great kings may
Not know the farther places where they reign.

His play made storm in a calm sea;
His very kindness slew what he might touch;
And wrecks lay scattered on his anger's lee.
The Moon rocked to and fro his watery couch.

His hunger cleared the sea. And where
He passed, the ocean's edge lifted its brim.
He skimmed the dim sea-floor to find if there
Some garden had its harvest ripe for him.

But in his sluggish brain no thought
Ever arose. His law was instinct blind.
No thought or gleam or vision ever brought
Light to the dark of his old dreamless mind.

Until one day sudden and strange
Half-hints of knowledge burst upon his sight.
Glimpses he had of Time, and Space, and Change,
And something greater than his might;

And terror's leap to imagine sin;
And blinding Truth half-bare unto his seeing.
It was the living man who had come in . . .
Jonah's thoughts flying through his being.

Viola Meynell.

Fish

HEAVEN

F I S H (fly-replete, in depth of June
Dawdling away their wat'ry noon)
Ponder deep wisdom, dark or clear,

THE ZOO

Each secret fishy hope or fear.
Fish say, they have their Stream and Pond
But is there anything Beyond?
This life cannot be All, they swear,
For how unpleasant, if it were!
One may not doubt that, somehow, good
Shall come of Water and of Mud;
And, sure, the reverent eye must see
A Purpose in Liquidity.
We darkly know, by Faith we cry,
The future is not Wholly Dry.
Mud unto Mud! – Death eddies near –
Not here the appointed End, not here!
But somewhere, beyond Space and Time,
Is wetter water, slimier slime!
And there (they trust) there swimmeth One
Who swam ere rivers were begun,
Immense, of fishy form and mind,
Squamous, omnipotent, and kind;
And under that Almighty Fin
The littlest fish may enter in.
Oh! never fly conceals a hook,
Fish say, in the Eternal Brook,
But more than mundane weeds are there,
And mud, celestially fair;
Fat caterpillars drift around,
And Paradisal grubs are found;
Unfading moths, immortal flies,
And the worm that never dies.
And in that Heaven of all their wish,
There shall be no more land, say fish.

Rupert Brooke.

THE TYGER

TYGER, Tyger, burning bright
In the forests of the night,
What immortal hand or eye
Dare frame thy fearful symmetry?

Burnt in distant deeps or skies
The cruel fire of thine eyes?
On what wings dare he aspire?
What the hand dare seize the fire?

And what shoulder and what art
Could twist the sinews of thy heart?
And when thy heart began to beat
What dread hand and what dread feet

Could fetch it from the furnace deep
And in thy horrid ribs dare steep?
In what clay and in what mould
Were thy eyes of fury roll'd?

Where the hammer? Where the chain?
In what furnace was thy brain?
What the anvil? What dread grasp
Dare its deadly terrors clasp?

When the stars threw down their spears
And water'd heaven with their tears
Dare he laugh his work to see?
Dare he who made the lamb make thee?

Tyger, tyger, burning bright
In the forests of the night,
What immortal hand and eye
Dare frame thy fearful symmetry?
William Blake.

MILK FOR THE CAT

WHEN the tea is brought at five o'clock,
And all the neat curtains are drawn with care,
The little black cat with bright green eyes
Is suddenly purring there.

At first she pretends, having nothing to do,
She has come in merely to blink by the grate,
But, though tea may be late or the milk may be sour,
She is never late.

And presently her agate eyes
Take a soft large, milky haze
And her independent casual glance
Becomes a stiff, hard gaze.

Then she stamps her claws or lifts her ears,
Or twists her tail and begins to stir,
Till suddenly all her lithe body becomes
One breathing, trembling purr.

The children eat and wriggle and laugh,
The two old ladies stroke their silk:
But the cat is grown small and thin with desire,
Transformed to a creeping lust for milk.

The white saucer like some full moon descends
At last from the clouds of the table above;
She sighs and dreams and thrills and glows,
Transfigured with love.

She nestles over the shining rim,
Buries her chin in the creamy sea;
Her tail hangs loose; each drowsy paw
Is doubled under each bending knee.

A long, dim ecstasy holds her life;
Her world is an infinite shapeless white,
Till her tongue has curled the last holy drop,
Then she sinks back into the night,

Draws and dips her body to heap
Her sleepy nerves in the great arm-chair,
Lies defeated and buried deep
Three or four hours unconscious there.
Harold Monro.

CATS AND KINGS

W I T H wide unblinking stare
    The cat looked; but she did not see the king.
She only saw a two-legged creature there
    Who, in due time, might have tit-bits to fling.

The king was on his throne.
    In his left hand he grasped the golden ball.
She looked at him with eyes of bright green stone,
    And thought, *What fun if he should let it fall.*

With swishing tail she lay
    And watched for happy accidents, while he,
The essential king, was brooding far away
    In his own world with hope and memory.

O, cats are subtle now,
    And kings are mice to many a modern mind;
And yet there throbbed behind that human brow
    The strangely simple thoughts that serve mankind.

H

The gulf might not be wide;
  But over it, at least, no cat could spring.
So once again an ancient adage lied.
  The cat looked; but she never saw the king.
                  Alfred Noyes.

THE MATRON-CAT'S SONG

s o once again the trouble's o'er
  And here I sit and sing;
Forgetful of my paramour
  And the pickle I was in;
Lord, lord, it is a trying time
  We bear when we're expecting,
When folk reproach us for the crime
  And frown with glance correcting.

So purra wurra, purra wurra, pronkum pronkum;
  Purra wurra pronkum, pronkum purr.

How much I feared my kits would be
  Slain in the hour of birth!
And so I sought a sanctuary
  Which causes me some mirth;
The surly cook, who hates all cats,
  Hath here a little closet,
And here we nest among her hats –
  Lord save me when she knows it!

Hey purra wurra, purra wurra, pronkum pronkum;
  Purra wurra pronkum, pronkum purr.

Four kits have I of aspect fair,
  Though usually but three;
Two female tabs, a charming pair,
  Who much resemble me;
Lord, lord, to think upon the sport
  Which doth await the hussies,
They'll be no better than they ought
  Nor worse than other pussies.

O purra wurra, purra wurra, pronkum pronkum;
  Purra wurra pronkum, pronkum purr.

Yet as becomes a mother fond
  I dote upon my boys,
And think they will excel beyond
  All other toms in noise;

How harsh their manly pelts will be,
  How stern and fixed each feature –
If they escape that cruelty
  Which man doth work on nature!

Ah purra wurra, purra wurra, pronkum pronkum;
  Purra wurra pronkum, pronkum purr.

Those eyes which now are sealèd fast
  Nine days against the light
Shall ere few months are overpast
  Like stars illume the night;
Those voices that with feeble squall
  Demand my whole attention,
Shall earn with rousing caterwaul
  Dishonourable mention.

Then purra wurra, purra wurra, pronkum pronkum;
  Purra wurra pronkum, pronkum purr.

But then, alas, I shall not care
  How flighty they may be,
For ere they're grown I'll have to bear
  Another four, or three;
And after all, they are the best
  While the whole crew reposes
With fast-shut eyes, weak limbs at rest,
  And little wrinkled noses.
So purra wurra, purra wurra, pronkum pronkum:
  Purra wurra pronkum, pronkum ryestraw;
Pronkum ryestraw, pronkum ryestraw,
  Pur-ra — wur-ra — pron-kum
Pronk . . . Foof. (She sleeps.)

                 Ruth Pitter.

Dog

THE SONG OF QUOODLE

T H E Y haven't got no noses,
  The fallen sons of Eve;
Even the smell of roses
  Is not what they supposes;
But more than mind discloses
  And more than men believe.

THE ZOO

The brilliant smell of water,
The brave smell of a stone,
The smell of dew and thunder,
The old bones buried under,
Are things in which they blunder
And err, if left alone.

The wind from winter forests,
The scent of scentless flowers,
The breath of brides' adorning,
The smell of snare and warning,
The smell of Sunday morning,
God gave to us for ours.

.   .   .   .

And Quoodle here discloses
All things that Quoodle can,
They haven't got no noses,
They haven't got no noses,
And goodness only knowses
The Noselessness of Man.

G. K. Chesterton

THE COW

THE friendly cow all red and white,
    I love with all my heart:
She gives me cream with all her might,
    To eat with apple-tart.

She wanders lowing here and there,
    And yet she cannot stray,
All in the pleasant open air,
    The pleasant light of day;

And blown by all the winds that pass
    And wet with all the showers,
She walks among the meadow grass
    And eats the meadow flowers.

R. L. Stevenson.

234

THE ZOO

Cow

THE LILY-POOL

W H A T sees our mailie in the lily-pool,
  What sees she with that large surprise?
What sees our mailie in the lily-pool
  With all the violet of her big eyes –
    Our mailie in the lily-pool?

She sees herself within the lily-pool,
  Herself in flakes of brown and white –
Herself beneath the slab that is the lily-pool,
  The green and liquid slab of light
  With cups of silver dight,
  Stem-rooted in the depths of amber night
That hold the hollows of the lily-pool –
  Our own dear lily-pool!

And does she gaze into the lily-pool
  As one that is enchanted?
Or does she try the cause to find
  How the reflection's slanted,
That sleeps within the lily-pool?
  Or does she take it all for granted
With the sweet natural logic of her kind?
  The lazy logic of the lily-pool,
  Our own bright, innocent, stupid lily-pool!

She knows that it is nice – our lily-pool:
  She likes the water-rings around her knees;
  She likes the shadow of the trees,
That droop above the lily-pool;
  She likes to scatter with a silly sneeze
The long-legged flies that skim the lily pool –
The peaceful-sleeping, baby lily-pool.

So may I look upon the lily-pool,
  Nor ever in the slightest care
  Why I am there;
Why upon land and sea
Is ever stamped the inevitable me;
But rather say with that most gentle fool –
'How pleasant is this lily-pool!
How nice and cool!
Be off, you long-legged flies! O what a spree!
To drive the flies from off the lily-pool!
From off this most sufficient, absolute lily-pool!'
                              T. E. Brown.

EPITAPH ON A HARE

HERE lies, whom hound did ne'er pursue,
  Nor swifter greyhound follow,
Whose foot ne'er tainted morning dew,
  Nor ear heard huntsman's hollo;

Old Tiney, surliest of his kind,
  Who, nursed with tender care,
And to domestic bounds confined,
  Was still a wild Jack-hare.

Through duly from my hand he took
  His pittance every night,
He did it with a jealous look,
  And when he could, would bite.

His diet was of wheaten bread,
  And milk, and oats, and straw,
Thistles, or lettuces instead,
  With sand to scour his maw.

On twigs of hawthorn he regaled,
  On pippins' russet peel;
And, when his juicy salads fail'd,
  Sliced carrot pleased him well.

A Turkey carpet was his lawn,
  Whereon he loved to bound,
To skip and gambol like a fawn,
  And swing his rump around.

His frisking was at evening hours,
  For then he lost his fear;
But most before approaching showers,
  Or when a storm drew near.

Eight years and five round-rolling moons
  He thus saw steal away,
Dozing out all his idle noons,
  And every night at play.

I kept him for his humour's sake,
  For he would oft beguile
My heart of thoughts that made it ache,
  And force me to a smile.

THE ZOO

But now, beneath this walnut-shade
   He finds his long last home,
And waits, in snug concealment laid,
   Till gentler Puss shall come.

He, still more aged, feels the shocks
   From which no care can save,
And partner once of Tiney's box,
   Must soon partake his grave.
                 William Cowper.

THE LINNET

T H E Baby Linnet
Is not so big as a minute,
Yet the worms it devours
Are longer than hours;
It can eat and eat and eat.
This must be because of the neat
Way in which the parents Linnet
Pack things in it.   *Marie de L. Welch.*

THE IBIS

T H E Ibis
Is born believing that his tribe is
Sacred upon the Nile;
Whereas, for a long while,
It must decidedly has not
Been too sacred to be shot,
Though it remains sacred enough
To stuff.
Parents hasten to describe this
Danger to the infant Ibis.
                 Marie de L. Welch.

THE SPARROW

T H E viewpoint of the Sparrow
Is arrogant and narrow,
He *knows* that he excels.
He is selfishly obsessed;
He would not give an ostrich best.
His children leave the shells
Puffed to their very marrows
With pride at being Sparrows.
                 Marie de L. Welch.

237

THE HORSE

I KNOW two things about the horse
And one of them is rather coarse.

Naomi Royde-Smith.

THE RABBIT

THE rabbit has a charming face:
Its private life is a disgrace.
I really dare not name to you
The awful things that rabbits do;
Things that your paper never prints –
You only mention them in hints.
They have such lost, degraded souls
No wonder they inhabit holes;
When such depravity is found
It only can live underground.

Anon.: 20th Cent.

THE KINGFISHER

IT was the Rainbow gave thee birth,
And left thee all her lovely hues;
And, as her mother's name was Tears,
So runs it in thy blood to choose
For haunts the lonely pools, and keep
In company with trees that weep.

Go you and, with such glorious hues,
Live with proud Peacocks in green parks;
On lawns as smooth as shining glass,
Let every feather show its marks;
Get thee on boughs and clap thy wings
Before the windows of proud kings.

Nay, lovely Bird, thou art not vain;
Thou hast no proud ambitious mind;
I also love a quiet place
That's green, away from all mankind;
A lonely pool, and let a tree
Sigh with her bosom over me.

W. H. Davies.

238

JENNY WREN

HER sight is short, she comes quite near;
A foot to me's a mile to her;
And she is known as Jenny Wren,
The smallest bird in England. When
I heard that little bird at first,
Methought her frame would surely burst
With earnest song. Oft had I seen
Her running under leaves so green,
Or in the grass when fresh and wet,
As though her wings she would forget.
And, seeing this, I said to her –
'My pretty runner, you prefer
To be a thing to run unheard
Through leaves and grass, and not a bird!'
'Twas then she burst, to prove me wrong,
Into a sudden storm of song;
So very loud and earnest, I
Feared she would break her heart and die.
'Nay, nay,' I laughed, 'be you no thing
To run unheard, sweet scold, but sing!
O I could hear your voice near me,
Above the din in that oak tree,
When almost all the twigs on top
Had starlings chattering without stop.'

W. H. Davies.

Blackbird

VESPERS

O BLACKBIRD, what a boy you are!
How you do go it!
Blowing your bugle to that one sweet star –
How you do blow it!
And does she hear you, blackbird boy, so far?
Or is it wasted breath?
'Good Lord! she is so bright
To-night!'
The blackbird saith.   *T. E. Brown.*

THE OCTOBER REDBREAST

AUTUMN is weary, halt, and old;
    Ah, but she owns the song of joy!
Her colours fade, her woods are cold.
    Her singing-bird's a boy, a boy.

239

THE ZOO

In lovely Spring the birds were bent
   On nests, on use, on love, forsooth!
Grown-up were they. This boy's content,
   For his is liberty, his is youth.

The musical stripling sings for play
   Taking no thought, and virgin-glad.
For duty sang those mates in May.
   This singing-bird's a lad, a lad.

                    Alice Meynell.

THE EAGLE

H E clasps the crag with crooked hands;
Close to the sun in lonely lands,
Ringed with the azure world, he stands.

The wrinkled sea beneath him crawls;
He watches from his mountain walls,
And like a thunderbolt he falls.

                    Alfred Tennyson.

COCK-CROW

O U T of the wood of thoughts that grows by night
To be cut down by the sharp ax of light,–
Out of the night, two cocks together crow,
Cleaving the darkness with a silver blow:
And bright before my eyes twin trumpeters stand,
Heralds of splendour, one at either hand,
Each facing each as in a coat of arms: –
The milkers lace their boots up at the farm.

                    Edward Thomas.

¶

I H A V E a gentyl cock
   crowyth me day
he doth me rysyn erly
   my matyns for to say

I have a gentyl cock
   comyn he is of gret
his comb is of red coral
   his tayl is of jet

240

THE ZOO

I have a gentyl cock
   comyn he is of kynde
his comb is of red squirrel
   his tayl is of inde

his legges arn of azour
   so gentyl and so smale
his spores arn of silver quyt
   into the wortewale [root]

his eynyn arn of cristal
   lokyn al in amber
and every nyht he perchyth him
   in myn ladyis chamber.

Anonymous.

THE GRASSHOPPER

O THOU that swing'st upon the waving hair
   Of some well-fillèd oaten beard,
Drunk every night with a delicious tear
   Dropt thee from Heaven, where thou wert rear'd!

The joys of earth and air are thine entire,
   That with thy feet and wings dost hop and fly;
And when thy poppy works, thou dost retire
   To thy carved acorn-bed to lie.

Up with the day, the Sun thou welcom'st then,
   Sport'st in the gilt plaits of his beams.
And all these merry days mak'st merry men,
   Thyself, and melancholy streams.

Richard Lovelace.

THE ANT

FORBEAR, thou great good husband, little ant;
   A little respite from thy flood of sweat!
Thou, thine own horse and cart, under this plant,
   Thy spacious tent, fan thy prodigious heat;
Down with thy double load of that one grain!
It is a granarie for all thy train.

Cease, large example of wise thrift, awhile
   (For thy example is become our law),
And teach thy frowns a seasonable smile:
   So Cato sometimes the nak'd Florals saw.
And thou, almighty foe, lay by thy sting,
Whilst thy unpay'd musicians, crickets, sing.

241

Lucasta, she that holy makes the day,
  And 'stills new life in fields of feuillemort,
Hath back restor'd their verdure with one ray,
  And with her eye bid all to play and sport,
Ant, to work still! age will thee truant call;
And to save now, th'art worse than prodigal.

Austere and cynick! not one hour t'allow,
  To lose with pleasure, what thou got'st with pain;
But drive on sacred festivals thy plow,
  Tearing high-ways with thy o'er-chargèd wain;
Not all thy life-time one poor minute live,
And thy o'er-labour'd bulk with mirth relieve?

Look up then, miserable ant, and spie
  Thy fatal foes, for breaking of their law,
Hov'ring above thee: Madam *Margaret Pie:*
  And her fierce servant, meagre Sir *John Daw:*
Thy self and storehouse now they do store up,
And thy whole harvest too within their crop.

Thus we unthrifty thrive within earth's tomb
  For some more rav'nous and ambitious jaw:
The grain in th' ant's, the ant in the pie's womb,
  The pie in th' hawk's, the hawk i' th' eagle's maw.
So scattering to hoard 'gainst a long day,
Thinking to save all, we cast all away.

                                   Richard Lovelace.

ODE TO THE MOSQUITO

VOCIFEROUS Culicids! From what vast
  Ancestral arthropod were you derived
That hovered through a dim Silurian past
  Or in some dank primeval forest thrived?
Perhaps you pestered some huge dinosaur
  And purged his Mesozoic dreams of joy;
    Or made a flapping pterodactyl screech
And hastily flap more,
  In swift remonstrance at your kisses coy
    Impressed in some soft spot he could not reach.

Æons have passed. We meet you once again!
  Though shrunk in size, your sins are still as great –
Reduplicated punctures fraught with pain;
  Your hideous hum – a haunting hymn of hate.

THE ZOO

O hedonists, whose hectic lives but wake
  For aliment and love, you little know
    That fever-germs within you laugh and leap
Until their nuclei shake!
    And yet you think to mock us! Have it so
      Your young are at our mercy: Oil is cheap.
                          Gilbert Brooke.

THE FLY

H O W large unto the tiny fly
Must little things appear! –
A rosebud like a feather-bed,
Its prickle like a spear;

A dewdrop like a looking-glass;
A hair like golden wire;
The smallest grain of mustard-seed
As fierce as coals of fire;

A loaf of bread, a lofty hill;
A wasp, a cruel leopard;
And specks of salt as bright to see
As lambkins to a shepherd.
                          Walter De la Mare.

FLYING CROOKED

T H E butterfly, the cabbage white,
(His honest idiocy of flight)
Will never now, it is too late,
Master the art of flying straight,
Yet has – who knows so well as I ? –
A just sense of how not to fly:
He lurches here and here by guess
And God and hope and hopelessness.
Even the aerobatic swift
Has not his flying-crooked gift.
                          Robert Graves.

Flea

HARLOT'S CATCH

O N C E on a time I used to be
The Patriarch Abraham's pet Flea,
Over his heart he nourished me,
      Hip, hop !

Often he thrust his hairy phiz
And most remarkable proboscis
Into his breast for conferences,
Hip, hip, hip! Hop, hop!

Quoth Abraham, 'Full well I wot
I labour, wife, but you do not.
How shall I get a son, old trot?'
Hip, hop!
Snapped Sarah, 'La! – take my advice:
Go ask that Flea you find so nice,
Do what he bids and don't think twice.'
Hip, hip, hip! Hop, hop!

'Come, Little Comrade, what do you bid?'
Said I, 'I marked, while you two chid,
One who kept a smile half hid.'
Hip, hop!
Then Abraham, 'What? why? When? who?'
And I, 'I'll tell, if what you do
And where you go, your Flea may too.'
Hip, hip, hip! Hop, hop!

'Come, Little Friend, proceed, proceed;
My case is very hard indeed –'
Chirped I, 'Abe, did you never heed,
Hip, hop!
How softly Hagar's eyelids sink
When by your bed she pours your drink?' . . .
The Patriarch gave a mighty wink,
Hip, hip, hip! Hop, hop!

Then 'Ha-ha-ha! and Ho-ho-ho!
Bravo, my Little Friend, bravo!
Hop-skip-and-jump and away-we-go!'
Hip, hop!
All night in Paradise I dwelt,
How dainty sweet each arbour smelled,
The things I saw! The things I felt!
Hip, hip, hip! Hop, hop!

Robert Nichols.

SONNET TO A MONKEY

O LIVELY, O most charming pug,
Thy graceful air, and heavenly mug;
The beauties of his mind do shine,

THE ZOO

And every bit is shaped and fine.
Your teeth are whiter than the snow,
You're a great buck, you're a great beau;
Your eyes are of so nice a shape,
More like a Christian's than an ape;
Your cheek is like the rose's blume,
Your hair is like the raven's plume;
His nose's cast is of the Roman,
He is a very pretty woman.
I could not get a rhyme for Roman,
So was obliged to call him woman.

Marjorie Fleming (obit 1811, ætat: 8).

Man

HYMN TO MOLOCH

O THOU who didst furnish
The fowls of the air
With loverly feathers
For leydies to wear
Receive this Petition
For blessin and aid,
From the principal Ouses
Engaged in the Trade.

The trouble's as follows:
A white livered Scum,
What if they was choked
'Twould be better for some,
S'been pokin about an
Creatin a fuss
An talkin too loud to be
Ealthy for us.

Thou'lt ardly believe
Ow damn friendly they are,
They say there's a time
In the future not far
When birds worth good money'll
Waste by the ton
An the Trade can look perishin
Pleased to look on.

With best lines in Paradies
Equal to what
Is fetchin a pony
A time in the at,

245

THE ZOO

An ospreys an ummins
An other choice goods
Wastefully oppin
About in the woods.

They're kiddin the papers,
An callin us names,
Not Yorkshire ones neither,
That's one of their games,
They've others as pleasin
An soakin with spite,
An it don't make us appy,
Ow can it do, quite!

We thank thee most earty
For mercies to date,
The Olesales is pickin
Nice profits per crate,
Reports from the Retails
Is pleasin to read
We certainly thank thee
Most earty indeed.

Vouchsafe, then, to muzzle
These meddlesome swine,
An learn em to andle goods
More in their line,
Be faithful, be foxy
Till peril is past,
An plant thy strong sword
In their livers at last.

Ralph Hodgson.

MAN AND BEAST

I AM less patient than this horse
And it is fleeter far than I.
Its hair is silky, mine is coarse;
Grasses have shaped that larger eye,
While to feed me live things must die.

The birds make little darts in air,
And fishes little darts in water,
Old sheep a silver glory share,
Peacocks are peacocks everywhere . . .
Man lies awake, planning the slaughter.

246

THE ZOO

What woman has this old cat's graces?
What boy can sing as the thrush sings?
For me, I'd rather not run races
With dragon-flies, nor thread the mazes
Of a smooth lawn with ants and things.

Yet horse and sheep tread leaf and stem
And bud and flower beneath their feet;
They sniff at Stars-of-Bethlehem
And buttercups are food to them,
No more than bitter food or sweet.

I, to whom air and waves are sealed,
I yet possess the human part.
O better beasts, you now must yield!
I name the cool stars of the field,
I have the flowers of heaven by heart.

Francis Meynell.

◆◆

ALL CREATURES THAT ON
EARTH DO DWELL

A dewdrop like a looking-glass. A hair like golden wire.

Great things are done when men and mountains meet;
This is not done by jostling in the street.

Blake.

◆◆

All Creatures that on Earth do Dwell

'A dewdrop like a looking-glass; A hair like golden wire'

SUPPOSE we go walking in the English countryside. Its pleasing pattern lies all about us: woods, meadows, valleys, hills. We are aware of the flowers in the hedgerows, the butterflies fluttering about them, the birds in the trees, the crops and beasts in the farmers' fields, the slow-meandering river, the close-cropped Downland, dotted with sheep and quarries, which rises out of the vale. We accept the pattern unquestioningly, in the same way that we accept the ubiquitous summer hum of countless tiny atomies; it is simply part of our background. Nevertheless it will be fun to ask and answer some questions, to try to project our sight *behind* the familiar landscape, into its origins and its history, and to consider how it came about: how geological factors sculpted it, how weather and climate shaped its contours, how living things painted the pattern upon it, and how the most ingenious, adaptable and (so far) the most powerful of these organisms made out of the wilderness his garden and his playground.

You and I are specimens of that organism: so we had better begin with a moment's reflection upon our own place in the order of things.

Homo sapiens, despite the fact that he is the lord of the earth or at any rate the only creature capable of rationalising a belief that he is so, nevertheless is a newcomer and parvenu. The scientists' best guess is that life has existed on this planet for some 500 million years; Man has strutted here at most for one million, the greater part of which he has spent as a humble competitor with the beasts for a precarious livelihood. The period of his mastery and dominion is measured in mere centuries. It is rather less than a hundred years since he began to understand his own relationship to the innumerable creatures, ranging from the Protozoa consisting of a single cell to the Atlantosaurus 80 feet long, which preceded him upon the earth.

The remains of these creatures, which he has named and classified, are found in the rocks which form the outer crust of the planet. If you take a hammer and chisel to almost any quarry you can break open their sarcophagus, which is older by hundreds of million years than Tutankhamen's. They died in the lakes, seas and swamps of long ago, and the silt or sediment entombed them where they lay. Some rocks, such as chalk, are composed almost entirely of the tiny shells of marine molluscs; others of fish-scales and bones; others of coral; while the seams of coal represent petrified forests and petrified swamps.

These 'sedimentary' rocks were deposited in layers, of mud, of limestone, of sand or gravel; so we are able to 'date' them by their organic remains, which a Victorian geologist pleasantly described as the footprints of time. For instance, the earliest rocks of all contain the prototypes of Life – shrimplike creatures, marine worms, Trilobites (resembling our King Crabs) and so on; later come the molluscs, the fishes, the first birds, the great lizards; and so the cavalcade marches on, to mouse and mammoth and at last to man.

From this record Darwin and others drew the conclusion that all existing and extinct creatures were manifestations of a continuous process of evolution. This evolution did not, of course, proceed in a straight line; it was more in the nature of a series of experimental gropings and questings, sometimes in this direction, sometimes in that, sometimes parallel, sometimes divergent. All the experiments did not succeed. The reptiles made two attempts to fly. The first attempt, conducted by the Pterodactyl, was remarkably similar to man's earliest efforts; it involved a launch from a high place and a glide or flutter to a lower one. It failed, so Pterodactyl paid the usual penalty for failure and ceased to be. The next attempt, by Archaeopteryx, was based on sounder principles and resulted in the birds.

Here and there nature's gropings seem to have run parallel and reached different conclusions which nevertheless have something in common: for example the social communities in an anthill or a beehive, and the social communities in the crowded cities of man.

But it is misleading to use the word 'conclusion' in connexion with the processes of evolution; for their pattern is one of ceaseless trial-and-error and continual change. Change is the necessary consequence of the unrelenting struggle in which living things have been engaged ever since life began: the struggle of each different organism to adapt itself to the ever-changing environment. It may have taken a million years to modify a leg-muscle for faster running to escape a new foe or to catch a new prey; ten million perhaps to amend the operation of a digestive system to assimilate a new food; twenty million perhaps to get rid of a no-longer-necessary appendage, such as a tail! No matter, *if the amendment was made in time*. If it wasn't made in time, the creature concerned was thrown on the scrap-heap to which the signpost reads Extinct.

Such is the struggle for survival which has been going on ever since life began. *How* it began nobody knows, nor can confidently speculate.

THE SCULPTING OF THE SCENE

THE SCIENTISTS would perhaps have developed a Theory of Evolution a little earlier if the successive rock-formations existed in the form of a vast Neapolitan ice, layer upon layer each neatly superimposed in the order of their antiquity. The sedimentary rocks would of course look like that if earth's history had been a less turbulent one: if the heavings and convulsions, explosions and earthquakes, had not torn apart the strata, folded them, upended them, and here and there even turned them upside down. It is supposed that since the beginning of life there were three major earth-movements, widely separated in time and involving areas equivalent to continents. We cannot easily imagine them, for the earthquakes of today are but 'the final murmurs of a great storm' (Professor Dudley Stamp). Those birth-pangs of Alps, Himalayas and Andes may each have continued for centuries. They threw up continents out of oceans; redistributed the seas on the face of the earth; and sent earth-waves running round the world like giant ripples.

Such a ripple determined roughly the shape of that gently-rolling Down which lies before us as we set off upon our walk in the country.

Its contours make for easy walking. This is generally the case where the rock beneath is of the 'sedimentary' kind, fairly soft and easily weathered. But there is another kind of rock. Into the fissures and folds caused by the surface-splitting flowed lava, molten and plastic minerals, the 'magma' of which the bowels of the earth are composed. Cooling, it formed the igneous (fire-wrought) and volcanic rocks, which are generally hard and uncompromising, good for climbers, bad for fossil-hunters (for if any living things were engulfed in the molten flow the heat has utterly destroyed them). You will find such rocks as these in the West Highlands, in the Lake District, in the Pennines, in Ireland and Wales, and here and there (as at Malvern) rising unexpectedly out of a plain. Being so hard, they are necessarily rugged; the rain, ice and snow of long geological ages have failed to rub smooth their jagged outcrops and sharp peaks.

But upon the landscape as a whole the physical forces which we lump together as 'weather' have acted powerfully to modify and amend the results of the ancient cataclysms. Expansion and contraction, due to heat and cold, have caused mountains to 'peel' and split. The sandpapering action of moraines and glaciers has worn away the sides of the valleys. Rock-falls and silting have dammed rivers to create lakes. The polar ice has advanced and retreated, each time leaving behind it an altered scene. Seas have flowed in and out of the low-lying areas: estuaries have silted up, islands have emerged. Everywhere the watercourses have carved their hieroglyphs great and small.

Most of these processes are still going on. Mountains are being denuded, rocks laid down, and fossils formed, including those of our skeletal selves. But the contemporary eye is not equipped to record happenings so gradual. The geologist's understanding of time requires to be somewhat godlike: he must think of a million years as a very short space indeed. 'A thousand ages in Thy sight Is like an evening gone.'

THE LIVING THINGS

ALL THE TIME, while earth-movements and climate-changes have been going on, life has pullulated, evolving a series of organisms infinitely various in shape and function, 'multiplex of wing and eye', furred, feathered, scaly, armoured, creeping, floating, swimming, flying, creatures of soil, sea and air – the mind boggles at their diversity.

254

Now the influences which *shaped* the landscape also determined what kinds of creatures should inhabit it: soil, rainfall, temperature, altitude and many other factors dictated the pattern of life in any given place. For instance, if we compare the sheep-cropped Downland, which we glanced at earlier, with our memories of similar hill-country in, say, Devon, Surrey or Scotland, we may wonder why no heather grows upon it. This is because heather likes an acid or peaty soil, and cannot grow on limestone, which is alkaline. In consequence our Downs will show us no heather-loving insects or birds. All living things exist in a complex relationship not only to their environment but to each other. They are competitors for food, space, water, air, sun; they are preyed upon or predatory, or parasites one of another; interacting, interdependent. Biologists use the term ecology for the study of these fascinating relationships. It is a comparatively new science, covering a huge field which we have only just begun to explore; but we cannot look at any country scene without being aware of the interacting relationships and seeing some of the effects of them.

For example, an extremely small organism, the virus which produces myxomatosis, has nearly wiped out the rabbit-population in many parts of England. The grass grows more freely in the absence of the rabbits; so the farmers can feed more sheep. They can also grow corn crops or vegetables in some places where it was too risky to plant them before; and thus, perhaps, the whole aspect of the landscape is changed. So much for the effects which we can *see*. But there must be other effects which we are as yet unaware of: the creatures which prey upon rabbits (foxes, badgers, buzzards) will be compelled to seek other food. They will prey upon other animals or birds, and possibly in time may seriously reduce the numbers, or even threaten the existence, of some species to which the rabbit stood in no direct relationship at all.

There is a very rare and lovely butterfly, the Large Blue, which exists in precarious colonies here and there in two or three English counties. The caterpillar feeds on wild thyme; but when autumn comes it falls to the ground and is picked up by ants, which carry it into their anthills not, as you might suppose, for the purpose of devouring it but to keep it alive as a source of some sticky sweet secretion which the ants love. For this reason they cherish their captive, feeding it

255

upon their own offspring, the tiny ant-grubs which are less precious to them than the stuff which they 'milk' from the caterpillars. In the spring the caterpillars crawl forth, turn into chrysalises, and ultimately hatch out as Large Blue butterflies. The butterfly therefore requires for its continued existence (a) the wild thyme and (b) the ant, to be present in conjunction; its caterpillar could not survive the English winter without the shelter of the anthill. Here is a very intricate relationship not of predator and prey but of mutual benefactors. It is called symbiosis. The butterfly, however, *is* the victim of a predator – Man with his butterfly-net; for it is now so rare that single specimens fetch 5s each. The farmer with his ploughs and his tractors also threatens its existence, destroying both thyme and anthills. So the Large Blue, which has become too specialized to adapt itself to changing circumstances, may shortly join upon the scrapheap the millions of failures labelled Extinct.

There is yet another relationship, of parasite to host:

Big fleas have little fleas upon their backs to bite 'em.

And little fleas have lesser fleas and so ad infinitum.

The 'wiser' parasites do not destroy their hosts: the louse which sucks the blood impartially of man and of man's foe the rat does little harm to either unless it happens to be infected with another and deadlier parasite, the bacillus of typhus. The Ichneumon fly allows its victims to live for just so long as it has use for them. It lays its eggs under the skin of the Cabbage Butterfly, the grubs hatch out and feed upon the caterpillar's tissues but do it no mortal harm until they are ready to vacate its dying body. Were it not for Ichneumons, Man would probably have found it impossible to grow cabbages; at any rate until he discovered DDT, which is another story.

Two parasites working in association are at present altering the appearance of much of the English landscape: the fungus which causes elm-disease, and the bark-boring beetle which carries the spores of the fungus from tree to tree. In the course of time the elms become rotten and unsafe; the gales bring them down or they are felled by the landowners. In many parts they were the only tall hedgerow trees, and their disappearance makes the country look very bare. One misses, too, the clamour of the rookeries in March. Possibly the passing of the great elms may result here and there in a local reduction in the rook-population: and fewer rooks may also mean more wireworms and less corn, for ecological changes have chain-reactions of which we cannot easily predict the end.

Our stretch of Downland, dotted with quarries and sheep, provides perhaps the best example of a long chain of cause-and-effect. The limestone in the quarries is composed of tiny grains rather like fish-eggs and consequently called Oolite; it also contains the calcified remains of the creatures that swam in the seas 200 million years ago. Now this stone crumbles at the surface, where it is exposed to the action of the weather, into a reddish-brown soil which countrymen call foxes' mould because it is often seen piled up outside the earths of foxes. A particular kind of grass, called Fescue, grows best upon this porous, limey soil, and Fescue happens to provide excellent grazing for sheep. When the great wool-boom occurred in the 14th and 15th centuries huge flocks were pastured on the Downs. Stone-walls were built to keep them apart and later, when the wool-growers and wool-staplers had made great fortunes, the craft of the quarryman was employed to build the fine manor-houses and the great churches of Cotswold.

They have a saying in those parts, that 'the sheep built the churches'. But we can go back farther than the sheep and see the churches as the end-result of a chain of circumstance which started with the little creatures swimming or floating in the Mesozoic sea:

Marine creatures – limestone – foxes' mould – fescue grass – sheep – rich men –

and so to the handiwork of the servants of the rich men, the noble square towers which lord it over 'the hundred little towns of stone Which nestle in the western wold'.

LANDSCAPE, then, is the product of circumstance: of geological happenings, historical accidents, and of the inter-action of all the warring, struggling, fiercely competing organ-isms which at any moment make up the sum total of Life. But, as we remarked at the beginning, there is one organism which by its ingenuity and its predominance exerts a greater influence upon its environment than any other. That creature is Man; and the time has come to consider those aspects of the country scene which have resulted from the toil of his hands and the cunning of his mind.

257

THE GREEN AND PLEASANT LAND AND
HOW IT CAME TO BE SO

How blessed is he, who leads a country life
Unvex'd with cares, and void of strife!

Dryden.

A fool sees not the same tree that a wise man sees.

Blake.

A flowery, green, bird-singing land.

W. H. Davies.

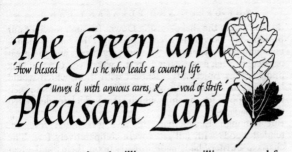

the Green and
Pleasant Land

'How blessed is he who leads a country life
Unvex'd with anxious cares, & void of Strife'

OF BRITAIN'S 56 million acres 45 million are used for
agriculture; one third of these are under the plough. The uncultivated areas, the 'highlands' and rough heaths, lie mainly
to the west of a line drawn from the mouth of the Tees to the
mouth of the Exe, which roughly divides the country into
two halves. To the east of that line cultivation is practically
continuous; pastoral England is really an immense garden.
So in fact is a large part of the temperate and a small part
of the tropic world. The landscape-gardener is Man. His
necessities chiefly, to a lesser degree his sports and pastimes,
and his aesthetic appreciation least of all, have dictated the
design. In his self-appointed task he has been sometimes
helped, sometimes hindered, by a host of his fellow-
inhabitants of the planet: viruses, bacilli, plants, trees, insects, birds and beasts.

Possibly he has been hindered more than helped. There is a
tale told of a country vicar who was congratulating one of his
parishioners upon the tidiness and fertility of his little plot,
recently reclaimed from a patch of waste-land. Next Sunday
was Harvest Festival: 'We must go to church and thank God
for these fruits of His bountiful earth.' 'Yes indeed,' replied
the gardener dutifully, 'but you ought to have seen what this
here piece was like when the Almighty had it on his own.'

THE WILDERNESS THAT WAS

IN SUCH a condition was the greater part of Britain during
Shakespeare's lifetime: when Michael Drayton surveyed it
in his long topographical poem *Poly-Olbion*. Pastoral settle-
ments were scattered here and there, mainly in the neighbourhood of the towns; but these were not 'farms' as we
know them.

Probably the only areas which looked much the same as they

261

do today were the sheep-raising Downs (though much of our present-day Downland is corn-growing); the rugged mountains and rough heaths of the north and west; and the great oak-woods such as the New Forest – where you can still look upon scenes practically identical with those which would have met the eye of a shipwright in, say, 1580, as he searched for stern-posts for the ships which eight years later destroyed the Armada.

But although Elizabethan England was much forested, tended woods with tall trees were comparatively few. The charcoal-burners had made inroads upon them; and great tracts of the country were covered with tangled scrub composed of hawthorn, small birches, brambles and stunted, crooked oaks. This was the 'woodland waste'; and you may imagine it as resembling that 'part of a Heath with a Hovel' in *King Lear* which was Edgar's home: '*Through the sharp hawthorn blows the cold wind.*' The lower grounds consisted of bog, malarial fen and rushy marsh; for the rivers which we now confine in deep narrow courses ran much shallower, and spilled over a wider area, often dividing into separate rivulets. In winter and early spring the silted channels could not carry away the mass of water that poured down from the hills, and the floods spread far and wide. Even in the places unaffected by flooding the lack of drainage caused rainwater to lie for months. These areas became reed-beds, impenetrable as jungles except by the fowler with his punt; you can see what they looked like at Wicken in Cambridgeshire, which is now preserved as a sanctuary for the disappearing fauna and flora of the Fens.

Nowadays we think of the 'unspoilt countryside' as something idyllic: it was not considered so in Shakespeare's day. Blasted heaths, bogs, and the nearly-impassable roads through the forest were regarded with dismay, and travellers were pitied whose paths lay among them. The lord's demesne, with its safety and its orderliness and a good high wall enclosing it, was the kind of 'country' that was most admired; and the well-tilled fields of peasant-farmers came a good second. When Shakespeare in *Henry the Fifth* described the war-wasted fields of France he found no loveliness in the 'fallow leas' which

> The darnel, hemlock and rank fumitory
> Doth root upon,

and it was always Man's handiwork, not Nature's, which seemed beautiful to him:

> The even mead, which erst brought sweetly forth
> The freckled cowslip, burnet and green clover,
> Wanting the scythe, all uncorrected, rank,
> Conceives by idleness; and nothing teems
> But hateful docks, rough thistles, kecksies, burs,
> Losing both beauty and utility.

Those lines describe precisely the condition to which the land returns if even for a season the husbandmen cease to till it or to graze it with their beasts. Within two or three seasons the scrub encroaches upon it and, as the drains become blocked, the marsh-vegetation begins to claim the low-lying areas. If husbandry suddenly ceased in Britain, Nature would win back her wilderness in less than ten years: woodland waste on the higher ground, reeds and bogs in the parts which lie in flood's way. Such is the pattern of 'unspoilt Nature' in temperate climates; and it does not make a green and pleasant land.

THE COLOURED COUNTIES

FOR CONTRAST, let us now look about us at the modern scene – at that stretch of pleasant, pastoral and gently undulating countryside somewhere in the heart of England which we chose for our leisurely walk on a summer's day. Within it, Nature is expelled, whenever necessary, not with a fork only but with a tractor-drawn plough, a bulldozer, a rotary cultivator or a poison spray; and we take good care that she does not come back again.

The underlying theme, the *motif* of the landscape is the green-brown-yellow of 'mixed' farming: smallish fields growing a rotation of crops, divided by hedges chiefly of hawthorn. But England is a hotch-potch of scenery as it is of soil, and often within a few miles the pattern of the fields changes half a dozen times: from arable to meadowland, from orchards, say, to hopyards, from market-gardens to Downs. Scattered here and there in between the cultivations are the relics of a previous landscape: some left-over fragments of that England of the squires which was not wholly agricultural. For instance there are parks with isolated trees and ornamental shrubberies of rhododendrons, woods laid out for the convenience of a Master of Foxhounds, avenues

I

planted perhaps to celebrate an heir's coming-of-age, spinneys situated so as to please a lordling's eye or to conceal from his windows the distasteful sight of human habitation other than his own. There are also occasional furzey commons and village greens which somehow survived the Acts of Enclosure. There are osier-beds, willow-fringed pools, disused canals, slow-running rivers in the vale and swifter trout-streams in the hills. Railways with their flowery cuttings and embankments, old lanes and newer motor-roads, criss-cross the land. There are villages built of stone, brick, flint, half-timber-and-thatch; churchyards with their grave chestnuts and yews, churches with towers or spires, farmsteads, byres, barns, oasthouses, rickyards, cottages . . .

The sum of all these familiar things makes up the pattern which we know as the English Countryside. We are so used to it that we are apt to forget it is a very recent pattern; even the patchwork of the fields has existed for less than two centuries. The oldest man-made features in our landscape are probably the churches; a few are Saxon, many are Norman, but the majority were built later than 1400. We shall be hard put to it to find many traces of man's presence on the scene before the time of William the Conqueror. Here and there ancient burial places are marked by barrows and tumuli; here and there as at Stonehenge the old altars still stand. There are the White Horses on the Downs, and the enormous Long Man at Cerne Abbas, a naked giant 200 feet high brandishing a club. These are much more than mere scrawls on the green turf and the white chalk; they are man's first signature upon the scene. It was a primitive scene, in which he lived precariously among wild beasts, devils and gods; he put his bold mark upon it in affirmation that it was his. The White Horse at Wantage is nearly 400 feet long, and you can see it for 15 miles. It is thought to have been set there by Alfred the Great to commemorate his victory over the Danes. More than a thousand years later his countrymen, being threatened by another invasion, were put to some trouble and expense to cover it up lest it serve as a landmark for their airborne foes.

Fortifications, both Roman and British, have left a few scratches on some of our hilltops; some sections of Hadrian's Wall and Offa's Dyke remain. There are also the great military roads of the Romans, which run like steel rulers across the country: Ermine Street, Akeman Street, the three Watling Streets, the Fosse Way. They look straight on the spot but not on the map – for they were sighted line by line from one hilltop to another. Sometimes two gangs working in opposite directions failed to make good their meeting-place, and there was a kink in the road – a kink which remains in the modern motor-road that we have built on top of it.

In places these Roman roads have disappeared, under the plough or in woodland; but even so you can often trace their course from the air. Flying over them, you see what a hovering eagle might have seen, in the time of the Emperor Claudius! To a small extent they have had a share in the shaping of our modern landscape; not only do they form part of our road system, but they have determined the siting of some of our towns. It is doubtful if Cirencester would stand where it does today if the Fosse Way and the Akeman Street hadn't happened to intersect at a spot which the Romans called Corinium.

But for the most part, the marks which man's handiwork left upon the landscape in Roman, Saxon, and even Norman times were scattered, few and faint except in the neighbourhood of the towns. The 'country' remained under nature's stern dominion; and we scarcely began even to challenge that dominion until the Middle Ages had gone by.

THREE BAGS FULL

THE FIRST effective weapon which man employed in his battle with nature was not his spade, his axe, or even his wooden plough, but his domesticated herbivorous animals. The grazing of cattle, horses and especially sheep won more acres from the wasteland than all his digging and ploughing. So the first great change which came over certain parts of England in the 15th and 16th centuries was due to the wool boom which occurred when the exiled Huguenots taught their first English pupils the arts of weaving. The flocks grazing on the uplands cropped close the rank grasses and fertilized the thin chalky soil: furze, bracken and scrub retreated before them. The shepherds began to build their drystone walls, getting their stone from the handy outcrops or hewing it from quarries. These stone walls gave to the landscape of our Downs a distinctive character which hasn't changed much since 1500; probably many of them follow the

265

same course today over the hills' broad shoulders as they did then. The craftsmen in stone were ready at hand when (as we have seen) the wool-merchants grew rich and sought to spend their new wealth on the lovely and lasting things. So the bare hills blossomed during those two centuries which were England's spring: the tall churches sprang up, the manor-houses four-square to all the winds that blew; the little grey villages huddled about them. If you stand on Cotswold now your view will be much the same as that which William Grevel, *flos mercantorum*, looked upon as he watched the sheep grazing in his huge pastures (about the time when Chaucer was writing *The Canterbury Tales*) and followed with his eye the straggling line of the stone-walls to the great tower of his own proud church at Chipping Campden.

WHEN ADAM DELVED

E X C E P T where the sheep flourished, farming continued to be localised, scattered and on a primitive scale.

During the Middle Ages the Black Death had decimated the rural population, and it took a century to recover from that disaster. Thereafter the recurring plague, typhus and the enormous infant mortality, kept down the numbers to about 4 million, which was the total when Elizabeth I came to the throne.

(Here are some more examples of very small organisms producing a large effect upon their environment. The virus that caused the Black Death, the bacilli of Bubonic plague and typhus, the louse that carried the latter, the black rat that carried both, caused the deaths of so many peasants that there were not enough left to cultivate even the small acreage which they had won from the waste; and some of this land slipped back into its weedy anarchy.)

During the next two centuries the population increased; but agricultural methods remained primitive, communications and transport were appallingly difficult, and even the main roads were often impassable in winter; so the face of England did not change much except in a few places where the multiplying peasants were able to steal back a piece of good land from the waste, or a prosperous landowner with plenty of labour at his disposal decided to increase the area of his demesne. In the 17th and early 18th centuries the process of bringing land under cultivation went on very slowly in relation to the increase in population; it was a gradual erosion, a nibble here, a nibble there, and much less extensive than the deforestation caused earlier by the charcoal-burners. There was no radical change in the practice of farming. When at last it did happen it was sudden, thorough-going and complete, and it transformed in about 80 years the whole aspect of England.

TRANSFORMATION SCENE

E V E N as late as 1700 the proportion of arable land was very small in relation to the pasture. Sheep grazed the Downs, as we have seen, and the river meadows, enriched by winter flooding, provided summer grazing for cattle as well as hay; the woodland afforded acorns and beech-nuts for swine. The arable, mostly in the neighbourhood of villages, consisted generally of three largish unfenced fields cultivated in parallel strips. Each season one of these fields would be sown with wheat or rye; another with oats, barley, beans or peas; the third remained fallow, providing a triennial rotation of crops.

Here and there in England still you can see traces of this open field cultivation in the curved ridges or 'lands' which run lengthwise down some of our pastures. When you walk across a field which has a surface resembling a series of waves, you can be pretty sure that this was one of the pieces of arable.

The peasant-farmers did not hold adjacent strips, but separate ones in different parts of each field, so that every individual had his share both of the good and the less good land. The strips were divided by baulks or unploughed strips of green turf; these are the 'ridges' which you see to-day. There were no fences or hedges. Consequently there had to be common agreement about how the land should be used; for of course animals could not be turned into any part of the field until the last crop had been gathered in. There was therefore little natural manuring, and drainage was to say the least of it chancy, since any strip-owner by negligence or malice might block the outfall of his neighbours' ditches. Now towards the end of the 17th century, when the rise in population increased the demand for produce, the strip-owners began to find an advantage in cultivating all their strips together. There was less waste (for the baulks could be

267

ploughed and cultivated) and when each man's land was fenced he was free to use his piece in whatever fashion best profited him. So the separate strips were exchanged for adjoining ones (doubtless after some hard bargaining) and the first hedges appeared. The cultivated part of the landscape – still a very small proportion – began to take on the patchwork appearance which gives the countryside its character today. What had been essentially a feudal landscape (though continuing long past feudal times) became suddenly a capitalist landscape; and each little patch, differing from its neighbours in size and shape, became an expression of the individuality of the little capitalist who cultivated it.

At first the process was slow and the changes local; but here and there between 1680 and 1750 there began to emerge a shape and pattern which we should have recognised as a sort of blueprint of the modern English scene. The 'parallel' landscape was broken up, and became a higgledy-piggledy one; not only were the big open fields divided into rectangles and even triangles, but a new diversity entered into the farmers' methods and their choice of crops. In 1724 turnips were first grown in the fields as winter-feed for cattle; clover suddenly came into favour for the same purpose. The fresh green of the turnip leaves, the warm reddish-purple of the clover and vetches, alternated with the rusty yellow of the ripening corn as it does in England today. The land lost its sameness, and the 'coloured counties' became a fact.

During the next 70 years the pace of these changes quickened, as diehard farmers and diehard landlords faded from the scene. Evolution became revolution. Early in the 18th century Jethro Tull invented his new plough and the first effective seed-drill. Lord Townshend, nicknamed 'Turnip', introduced the Four Course system of cultivation which substituted for the year of fallow a crop of turnips and so increased the productivity of the land by a third. Meanwhile Bakewell of Leicestershire began his campaign for the improvement of the English flocks and herds. He bred for uniformity, quick maturing, and good meaty joints, and created the first modern breed of sheep, the Leicester. The brothers Collins on Tees-side followed suit with cattle, and by careful selection established the breed of Shorthorns. A

268

great landlord, Coke of Holkham in Norfolk, demonstrated how to reclaim a sandy waste by heavy manuring and by planting shelter-belts of trees. (His trees still stand at Holkham, his living memorial.) An ingenious fellow called Small, who was not a farmer, turned his attention to the old-fashioned plough and invented a vastly improved one.

It has been said that Tull produced the bread and Bakewell produced the meat which made it possible for Britain to become an industrial country. In fact these lively-minded and far-seeing countrymen not only changed the whole aspect of rural England but created the conditions which resulted in the dark satanic mills, the slag-heaps and the pit-heads of the Industrial Revolution.

The immediate effect of their inventions and improvements was to treble or quadruple the productivity of any given piece of land. In theory Britain could already support a large population; in practice the cultivated land was not available. But as food prices rose it became worth while for the first time to bring into cultivation the waste and the marshes, where large-scale drainage now proceeded apace. The commons and the open fields were enclosed, and the peasant-farmers, who could not afford the new machines, were mostly dispossessed and became labourers upon what had been their own land.

For those who lived through it the transformation of England must have been astonishing indeed; no scenic change has ever happened so quickly. Within a man's lifetime most of the fens and much of the woodland disappeared, the countryside became criss-crossed with a myriad hedges, the new multi-coloured crops filled the new arable fields, barns and byres, hayricks and straw-ricks grew up like mushrooms where none had been before, and for the first time in English history fat cattle and sheep went to Christmas market down the muddy lanes. The services of Peter Piper with his peck of pickled pepper were no longer required; for it had ceased to be necessary to kill off in autumn the stock which was not needed for breeding and to salt and spice the meat so that it would keep until the spring.

The revolution, of course, brought prosperity to a few but misery and poverty to many more. The Acts of Enclosure which ruined the peasant farmers made petty squires enormously rich. A lampooner wrote:

The law locks up the man or woman
Who steals the goose from off the common,
But leaves the greater villain loose
Who steals the common from the goose.

Here and there, as a direct consequence of the Enclosures,
whole villages ceased to be. Oliver Goldsmith in 1770, com-
plaining that 'all the bloomy flush of life is fled', wrote of a
Deserted Village:

But a poor peasantry, their country's pride,
When once destroy'd, can never be supplied . . .

and he went on to praise the pleasures of the frugal country
life which, he imagined, the simple peasant had enjoyed
before:

For him light labour spread her wholesome store,
Just gave what life requir'd, but gave no more;
His best companions, innocence and health;
And his best riches, ignorance of wealth.

If this were so, he could be ignorant of wealth no longer. He
could see all round him how rascals thrived, greedy men
prospered, little tyrants became great tyrants, while poor and
honest men went down. The history of the English countryside during those 70 hectic years is one of cut-throat competition resulting in the survival of the fittest – or perhaps
the most acquisitive. It is a tale of neighbours' squabbles,
endless litigation, and plain rapine: an unlovely turmoil out
of which emerged the lovely pattern of pastoral England.

THE LEGACY OF LEISURED FOLK

H U S B A N D R Y was the main though not the only cause of
the transformation. When the huge task of feeding 10
million people instead of 4 million had been achieved with
the aid of new inventions and new ways, some other factors
came into play which helped to shape the modern countryside. The most important of these were rich men and sport.
Both the Agricultural and Industrial Revolutions threw up
nouveau riche classes, some of whom invested their quickly-
earned money in great estates. These new landed gentry
were very much richer than the old squires and even the old
nobility had been. (It was the view of the Meltonians about
1820 that a man could 'jog along all right on ten thousand a
year'.) They possessed the large extravagance which comes
with easy money and those of them that were not entirely

preoccupied with horseflesh have left their mark upon the land in the form of great country houses, elaborately laid-out gardens, stables, kennels, weird hilltop 'follies,' spacious parks and so on. They introduced from abroad ornamental trees and shrubs, some of which (such as rhododendrons and certain conifers) have flourished and multiplied. The laying out of parks, with appropriate vistas, mazes, lakes, woodland walks, spinneys and copses was an expensive hobby which has left us a legacy of great loveliness: and when we consider the relation of man to his environment it is amusing to reflect that we owe many delightful clumps of trees to the fact that some arrogant squire couldn't abide the spectacle of his up-start neighbour's new and pretentious dwelling glimpsed across the intervening fields.

The ecology of rich men makes a fascinating study; it is deeply involved with sport. Foxhunters, for example, require largish scattered coverts, good galloping country in between, jumpable but difficult fences, adequate gates, and the absence of barbed wire. Pheasant-shooters must have woods also, but they tend them differently, cutting rides in certain places and using wire-netting for fencing, which foxhunters abhor. They try to arrange the whole lay-out of the coverts in such a fashion that the birds can be driven high over the guns. (There was a lord who conceived the strange desire to drop a pheasant, shot from his favourite stand, upon his own greenhouses at the other side of the valley. He achieved this feat in the end, but it involved planting a completely new covert at the top of the hill to make the pheasants fly high enough!)

Grouse-shooters need very large moorlands upon which they burn the heather from time to time in accordance with a carefully worked-out plan. Deerstalkers demand the preservation in their natural state of the almost tree-less 'forests' of Scotland; and so on.

It happens that much of the beauty of the countryside is a direct consequence of the activities of these thoughtless and rather selfish individuals. We are indebted to a few thousand country squires and to their love of guns, dogs and horses for most of our loveliest woodlands, for the preservation of moors, for the fine 'bullfinch' sloe-hedges of the Shires, and for the rides and bridle-paths which make it so easy for a walker to go where he will in the country. Other kinds of

271

sportsmen have given us race-courses and golf-courses, – and the golfers at any rate have saved thousands of acres of cliff-top, heath and warren from haphazard 'development' by the jerry-builder. The cricket-field, too, has its place in the country scene; and when cricket is played on village greens we see a reflection of those Acts of Enclosure, for the greens were often pieces of grassland given to the villages in compensation for the expropriated 'strips'. Cricketers, incidentally, exert another influence upon the landscape, where willows are grown commercially for the purpose of making cricket-bats.

Even fishermen have left their marks upon the scene, for the monks made stew-ponds for their carp, and in recent years salmon-anglers have built weirs and salmon-ladders, and trout-anglers have dammed or diverted small streams, cut waterweeds and reedbeds and trimmed the growth on the banks.

WATERWAYS AND WATERWORKS

ON THE WHOLE the pattern of our rivers and streams is less artificial than that of the land. The great rivers, Humber and Tweed, Thames and Severn, run much the same courses as they did 500 years ago; Shakespeare's Avon goes down from Stratford through the Vale of Evesham by the same winding way which he knew well. But dredging, better drainage, locks, weirs and flood-gates enable us to control the flow, so that there is less winter flooding and the rivers hold a good head of water even in dry seasons. At Stratford and most of the other 'fords' you must cross by the bridge or swim; the river is ten or twelve feet deep where once it was possible to drive a wagon across it in summer-time.

If we have not greatly changed the old waterways, we have at any rate contrived some new ones. The canals by which, until a few years ago, a barge could travel right across England from east to west or north to south provide a curious man-made landscape of their own, utterly different from the landscape of natural streams and rivers. Their low banks are treeless, but have been colonised by the loosestrife and the willowherb which in places form two parallel purple hedges between which the canal runs as straight as a Roman road. There are no pools or rapids; but here and there the unruffled water is gently lifted over a gradient by a series of

272

locks like the steps of a ladder. All the way the towpath goes beside it, like a footpath beside a main road.

These canals were important means of communication before the railways superseded them. A few are still in use; but many have fallen into disrepair, they are choked with weeds, banks are falling in, the locks are broken, and you feel, when you come upon them unexpectedly, as if you had found the remains of an old lost civilization – which indeed they are.

The engineers who work with water found a bigger job to do long before their canals ceased to be profitable. The population of the great growing cities demanded not only food from the fields but water from the lakes and rivers. There was rarely enough in the neighbourhood of the cities; so the mountain watersheds must provide it. Thus, to ensure the water supply of Birmingham the engineers blasted away part of a hillside in Wales, built great dams, inundated a valley, obliterated some farms and made at Rhayader a chain of lakes lying between steep hills covered with conifers: a Swiss landscape rather than a British one. Glen Affric in Scotland has been dammed to provide the electrical power for towns hundreds of miles away; other huge schemes are in progress. So industrial man's necessities work changes upon the landscape not only where he lives and labours but on the high hills and bleak moorlands to which even the Agricultural Revolution brought no change.

THE EFFECT OF COMMUNICATIONS

I N D U S T R Y demanded, as well as food, water and (later) electric power, a network of roads and railways between the cities. MacAdam, Telford, Stevenson played their parts as architects of the modern scene. As each innovation occurred there were sober and thoughtful people who prophesied that it would destroy the countryside. When Mr MacAdam's new roads, about 1800, caused a revolution in travel which enabled the London to Edinburgh mail-coach to do the journey in 62 hours instead of 82, heads were shaken over the possible effects of the fumes of tar. When the railways began to stretch out their tentacles the early Victorians visualised a landscape intersected by steel rods along which the engines snorted between blackened fields. Horses would bolt, cattle stampede, crops would be set on fire. The later Victorians, smelling their first whiff of petrol, predicted that the very

273

herbs of the roadside would droop and wither and the hedges die on account of it. None of these catastrophes happened; and this is worth remembering when we look gloomily into the future and see certain destruction of many a lovely scene. The man-made landscape inevitably changes as man's habits change; but the changes are not always as destructive as we fear. The railways did not spread soot over the fields, the petrol-fumes did not kill the roadside grass; the new pylons that spider the Downs do not, as many predicted, ruin their loveliness. The eye grows used to them, they become a part of the pattern like the railways and the roads.

There are gains as well as losses. The railways have their own characteristic fauna and flora; what child has not been tempted into trespassing past the black noticeboard with its forty-shilling warning because of a summer spectacle of poppies and harebells, brimstones and blue butterflies, upon a gorse-dotted embankment beside the line? As for the roads, wherever one runs across country two hedges accompany it. Out of the hedges grow up trees; along the hedge-roots spring up flowers. Some wise and public-spirited authorities plant saplings along the verges, or shrubs in the grassy ribbons between the traffic-lanes. Where this happens, we probably gain more than we lose.

THE EVER-CHANGING SCENE

ONE THING is certain: that we cannot arrest the process of change however much we may wish to do so. For while man holds his dominion over it, landscape is but a reflection of his changing ways. It mirrors his science and his sociology, his customs, sports, economy, his evolutions and revolutions. Every piece of scenery has a tale to tell about these changes. We have seen, for instance, how the stone-walls are related to the economics of sheep-breeding in the 15th century, how an avenue of chestnuts may be the legacy of a man who grew rich out of the East India Company, how the hedges are hieroglyphs which explain the Acts of Enclosure, how a spacious park fallen into ruin may be a consequence of the rising surtax during the 1930's.

The story is not ended; and if we now take a look about us at the countryside as it is today we shall see that new changes are taking place and history is still being written upon the farms and the fields.

━━━

THE FIELDS AND THE BEASTS
THEREOF

We are assured that the compassion of Heaven will not
be wanting to them.

This is the farmer sowing his corn,
That kept the cock that crowed in the morn.
Nursery Rhyme.

A painted meadow, or a purling stream.
Joseph Addison.

━━━

HARVEST

from 'The Land' by V. Sackville-West.

An English cornfield in full harvesting
Is English as the Bible, though no more
(These clanking times) the gleaners following
The reapers by their rhythm rapt
Plunder the gavels for their little store;
Or the sickle cut the poppies and the corn,
Save when the crop is tangled by a gale,
Beaten by rain, twisted like murdered hair:
Then comes the sickle to its old avail
Crook'd as the young moon in her narrowest horn,
And steals in the poor broken tangle, where
Straightforward knives are parried, and the apt
Inventiveness of man shall not prevail.
Then to the simplest shapes of his first craft,
– Livelihood wrested from the earth that bore,
Cradled, and coffined him,– man shall repair;
Shapes copied from the sky, with cutting edge;
Natural shapes, to meet the natural hitch
Of hindering weather, the permanent enemy;
Then, with the noonscape, underneath the hedge,
His fingers blistered by the rubbing haft,
His shoulders propped by hedge, his feet in ditch,
The random reaper drains his pint of ale.

Look to your stooking, for full many a field
Of hearty grain and straw runs half to waste
Through heedless stooking, and the proper yield
Leaves half its measure to the rook and daw.
But if you'd have full grain and ripened straw,
After a week of drying fit to cart,
Stooker, take up a sheaf in either hand,
Between the ears and band,
And swing them clear, and bring the butts apart
Sharply to ground, ears sloping to a peak,
(Ten sheaves for Kent) clashing together, braced,
So that the little ridge be thatched and sleek,
Firm to the wind, secure to rain and hail,
That winnower and that flail,
Those thieves of harvest, pilfering what they can
In last-hour larceny from rival man.
For nature gives, and nature takes again;
Therefore be eager of her liberal hours;
To drought succeeds the flood, to calm the gale,
And winter's frost lays low the summer's flowers.

277

Therefore, you harvesters, before the rain
Trample your crop with roguish feet,
Wring what you may, and if too fast and fleet
Even the summer sun describe his arc
Leaving you with your shocks but half-way set,
Be prouder than the punctual rigid clerk,
And stickle not to labour after dark,
For you take nature's orders, he the clock's.
The cooler night shall spare your noonday sweat;
The breeze shall whisper in the rustling shocks;
The moon above the thorn
Rise harvest-tawny on the stubble shorn,
And in the bending lines of girls and men
Some snatch of song be born.
Lovers shall find their magic then,
And jolly farmers wink at privilege;
Only the moon shall look behind the hedge,
Confederate of youth;
Only the moon shall hear the whispered pledge,
Great lyric liar, to a lovelier truth
Transcending, setting purport free,
And touching all things with her alchemy.

the Fields, and the Beasts thereof

'We are assured that the compassion of Heaven will not be wanting to them'

KEY: *a* Water Vole; *b* Fox; *c* Otter; *d* Grey Squirrel; *e* Brown Rat; *f* Wild Cat; *g* Fallow Deer; *h* Stoat; *i* Badger; *j* Hedgehog. The drawings are not to scale.

THE ENGLISH HEDGE

B E F O R E we look over the hedge at the growing crops and the grazing beasts let us glance for a moment at the hedge itself.

It is really a narrow strip of the natural 'forest floor' of England adapted to man's needs. Hedges grow best in those parts of the country which were originally clothed with the 'woodland waste' (and to which, if husbandmen ceased to toil, the 'woodland waste' would swiftly return). In the places which were bare, or covered with very light scrub, we have to use some other means to divide our fields – stonewalls, for instance, if the quarries are handy. But in most of pastoral England the hedge is the cheapest form of fencing. You do not need to plant it; you have only to prevent the beasts from grazing in the place where you want it to grow. Then up springs the hawthorn and the other sturdy and indestructible plants and shrubs which grow in association with it; the ungrazed, uncultivated strip goes back to its natural state, and within ten years your rough and ready hedge is ten feet tall.

However, the farmer generally improves on nature's version by 'laying' his hedges. The stems of the bushes are 'nicked' and bent over horizontally, all facing in the same direction *along* the hedge, and then are woven between upright stakes

279

driven in at intervals. This makes the hedge stronger. It is done as a rule every three or four years. The hedges of good farmers are also trimmed every season, which gives them a sturdier growth. Nowadays this job is often done by an ingenious machine which moves parallel with the hedge and chops off the top with rotating knives. A disadvantage of the machine is that it may not spare a likely sapling here and there, as good hedge-cutters generally do, and its use may mean that in a score of years there will be very little hedge-row timber.

The main constituent of most hedges is hawthorn, which of all our native trees loves best the English soil. In some places, notably Leicestershire, it is replaced by the sloe or black-thorn, which makes those great 'black' hedges that test the courage of hunting men. ('How on earth do you manage to jump them?' asked an awe-stricken visitor to the Shires about 1820. 'We throw our hearts over first and then we follow as best we can.')

Mixed with the hawthorn and the sloe there are generally at least a dozen other shrubs and climbers which have woven themselves into the homogeneous whole: within a few score yards, sometimes, you will find elm, elder, bird-cherry, ash, spindle, sycamore, sallow, willow, dog-rose, privet, way-faring-tree, honeysuckle, bryony both black and white, bramble, dewberry, and old man's beard. These diverse components paint the hedge a different colour as each season goes by: orange-pink of sallow twigs in the early spring, wine-purple of elm, then the fresh green of the crinkly hawthorn-leaves, sprinkled snow of blackthorn-flowers, curded cream of the may, shell-pink dog-rose in high summer, red autumnal leaves of sycamore, scarlet berries of bryony, purplish-black of elder, pink of spindle – and then when winter comes the fluffy grey-white of the old man's beard.

The hedge, in fact, probably contributes more loveliness to the English scene than any other single feature; what a dull sameness the landscape must have had before the Acts of Enclosure!

But there are fewer hedges in England than there were only a dozen years ago; very soon there may be fewer still. The increase in market-gardening and arable farming generally is partly responsible for this; there is no need for a fence to protect the wheat from the brussels sprouts adjacent to it, and where there is intensive cultivation hedges are wasteful of land. Another cause is the invention of electrified fencing. A single strand of wire, carrying enough current to give a harmless electric shock, can keep a whole herd of hungry cattle from a patch of luscious-looking kale. The advantage to the farmer is that his wire fence is *moveable*. He can change every season, or if he likes every day, the shape and pattern of his fields. He can let his cows into any part of his kale-patch, and bar them from the rest; so that they eat it bit by bit as they need it and do not trample and spoil the whole field. Moreover, because the electrified fence is moved so frequently there is no risk that the thorn and the thistle, those native daemons of the English soil, will spring up beneath it, creating an unwanted hedge – which happens whenever a permanent wire fence prevents the beasts from grazing along the line of the wire.

It is possible that in a few years' time electrified fencing may completely alter the appearance of the land; and that the pastoral scene (coming full circle, as it were) may look much the same as it did when peasant-farmers cultivated the 'open field' three or four hundred years ago. Here and there, in the great market-gardening areas around Evesham or Wisbech, you can see what is conceivably the shape of things to come; for the hedges have already disappeared. For the most part, however, the effect of electric fencing is local and confined to the bigger farms; and the lovely patchwork of farming England remains.

THE PATTERN OF THE FIELDS

THIS patchwork pattern is always changing. The large trends of commerce change it: our economics, our emergencies. During world wars we plough up the grassland to grow corn and potatoes; in slumps, when the price of wheat falls steeply, the arable land is turned back to grass.

But there is also an annual change in the pattern of any given farm, due to the Rotation of Crops.

Different crops 'rob the soil' of different constituents. (For example, cereals use up a lot of nitrogen, peas and beans use hardly any). So if the same crop is grown on the same patch year after year the soil becomes poor in the particular plant-food which the crop needs most. Also the pests which

281

are specific to that crop flourish and multiply. Therefore the farmer arranges his cropping-plan so that each year for at least four successive years every arable field grows a different crop. The usual 'four-course system' runs like this:

Wheat – Turnips – Barley – Clover and Grass.

But there is no hard-and-fast rule so long as the chosen system of cropping does not, as the farmers put it, 'take the heart out of the land'. The kind of soil, its texture and its thickness, even the weather, may cause a variation in the plan; and some farmers adopt six or seven year rotations such as 'oats – beans – wheat – roots – barley – grass'.

THE YEAR'S WORK

THE ROTATION of crops also enables the farmer to make the best use of his labour. A year's work in the arable fields may go something like this, but it varies considerably from one district to another and there is no set pattern for the whole country:

January and February:	Carting muck; ploughing
March:	Sowing oats and barley
April:	Planting potatoes and spring wheat
May:	Sowing turnips and swedes
June:	Singling roots: hoeing and other summer cultivation
July:	Haymaking
August:	Corn harvest
September:	Corn harvest and potato lifting
October:	Potato lifting and ploughing
November:	Root lifting and sowing winter wheat
December:	Ploughing and carting muck once again.

That is a fair sample, and it takes no account (for instance) of sugar-beet, nor of silage-making which is now becoming common on many farms throughout the summer.

You must not suppose, however, that these are the farmer's only jobs. His stock must be fed and tended, his cows milked, his machinery kept in order. He must buy and sell, either at market or privately. And his other major tasks include hedgetrimming and laying, ditching, draining, spreading artificial fertilisers or lime, spraying crops and fruit trees, fruit picking and so on. He must be handy with at least ten different sorts of tools and a dozen more or less complicated mechanical implements. He must be a rough carpenter, motor-mechanic, wheelwright, blacksmith, and a bit of a meteorologist, chemist, botanist and biologist as well.

THE CROPS IN THE FIELDS

U N T I L about 1700 the only important farm crops grown in Britain were cereals, beans, peas, and of course, hay. Lord Townshend, whom we mentioned earlier, added turnips to the rotation, and later William Cobbett sang the praises of swedes with as much enthusiasm as that with which he cursed what he called 'the ever-damned potato'. Despite him potatoes (which had long been a staple crop in Ireland) took their place upon the English farms wherever the land suited them; and during the next 100 years a variety of crops unfamiliar to Englishmen painted the fields as many-coloured as Joseph's coat. Unless you are country-bred you can hardly expect to recognise them all; for even a country-man, unless he looked very carefully, would not easily tell the difference between winter wheat and winter oats pricking the brown fields in spring. Here are some notes, however, which may serve as a rough guide:

Root-crops include turnips, swedes and mangolds, sugar and fodder beet, and kohlrabi. You can tell swedes from turnips because the former have a reddish-purple tinge in the stems and leaves. Turnip leaves are rougher and much less glossy-looking than those of fodder beet, and of mangolds (a culti-vated variety of the wild sea-beet) which are also called mangel-wurzels, a bucolic-sounding name which, however, comes from the German and means 'root of scarcity'. All these roots provide winter feed for stock; they are often stored in clamps which look like long barrows. When the clamps are first opened the young blanched shoots are astonishingly lovely; they caught the eye of the poet Edward Thomas who promptly wrote his poem 'Swedes':

> They have let in the sun
> To the white and gold and purple of curled fronds
> Unsunned. It is a sight more tender-gorgeous
> Than when, in the Valley of the Tomb of Kings,
> A boy crawls down into a Pharaoh's tomb
> And, first of Christian men, beholds the mummy,
> God and monkey, chariot and throne and vase,
> Blue pottery, alabaster and gold . . .

283

Sugar-beet is sent to the factories as soon as the permits arrive after it has been lifted and any time between October and January. Only the tops are fed to the cattle and sheep. As you see it growing in the field you cannot, at a glance, distinguish it from either fodder-beet or mangolds. Kohlrabi is grown only locally, chiefly in Suffolk and Essex. It is a cabbage-like plant with a large white fleshy swelling (erroneously called the root) at the base of the stem. This is the part which is eaten by cattle and sometimes, we think misguidedly, by human beings.

Forage-crops are generally fed to stock in their fresh green state. They include cabbage and kale (like a giant cabbage with crinkly leaves), clover (red or white), lucerne (purple-flowered, grown chiefly on limey land in the south east, fed to milking-cows), vetches, sainfoin (rose-red flowers, chiefly fed to sheep), rape (belongs to the cabbage family, has glaucous smooth leaves like a swede, its seeds are rich in oil), and mustard (bright yellow cruciferous flowers). Mustard is often fed to stock but is also used for 'green manuring' – that is to say it is grown simply for the purpose of ploughing it back into the land to increase the content of humus. It grows so fast that it can be put in as an 'extra' between a normal rotation; such crops are called *catch-crops*.

Potatoes are grown chiefly for human consumption; only the small ones are used for stock-feed. Almost everybody can recognise a growing crop of potatoes, moulded up into 'ridges', but if you present a friend with a single potato-flower, divorced as it were from its context, he is quite likely to pronounce, after careful consideration, that 'it is probably an exotic nightshade, grown in a greenhouse'. Few people ever really *look* at a potato flower. It is as pretty as many a garden favourite, and is in fact a nightshade, closely related to the Deadly one and also to the tomato. Its berries are said to be poisonous.

Field peas when grown by themselves nowadays are generally for canning or drying; but they form part of some mixed crops which are used for stock-feed, e.g. peas, vetches, oats and beans grown together, which combination in Scotland is called by the pleasant name of Mashlum and in England Dredge Corn.

Beans, called Horse Beans to distinguish them from the garden variety, advertise themselves by the sweet smell of their flowers and the perpetual murmur of bees among them. They are fed to stock, especially to working horses, milch cows and pigs; horses eat the bean straw and it is also used for litter. As a farm crop, beans are less grown than formerly; they were excellent fuel for horses, but are no use in the tanks of tractors.

Grain-crops, the most important next to grass, include wheat, oats, barley and rye. Wheat has an ear of largish grains without long 'whiskers' and goes rust-red, almost the colour of a marmalade cat, when it is really ripe. Barley varies very much in the colour of the grain but the 'whiskers' will always identify it; a field ready for cutting ripples like a cat's fur when it is purring. The best grains are bought by the brewers for malting, and make our beer and whisky. The least breeze causes the barley to sigh in a fashion quite different from the swishing sound made by oats, which bear their separate seeds on branched panicles (like quaker-grass) and are ash-blonde when ripe. Rye has a seed-head, or ear, rather like wheat, but slenderer, longer, and more compressed. It is grown very little in Britain, mainly on the sandy soils in the east.

THE CORN HARVEST

U N T I L well into the 19th century corn was cut by hand with scythes or sickles and the harvest was a long toil that rarely finished before October. In 1826 a Scottish minister, of all people, invented the first reaping machine, which was the ancestor of the modern binder. Even the binder looks antiquated today, an Emmet-like contrivance, with its revolving wooden bars somewhat reminiscent of a waterwheel, and its place is being taken by the combine harvester, which threshes and bags the corn as it cuts it.

When the combine is at work there are no sheaves thrown out behind the machine to be stacked by hand into the lovely 'stooks' which used to stand in the field until they were dry enough for ricking. The combine moves steadily over the field like some great juggernaut, devouring all. We miss the stooks which used to delight the eye when their long shadows fell across the golden stubble in the evening and the pigeons fluttered about them, taking their tithe of the corn; but the combine enormously speeds up the business of harvesting, and is capable of cutting corn beaten down by rain and wind, which otherwise would have to be gathered in the ancient way, with a scythe. We still see the binder at work here and there, for it can reap when the corn is too wet to be threshed in the combine; also the combine is too expensive a machine for very small farmers.

The corn-rick (which was generally a round one) is disappearing as the combines become more numerous. Thus each new invention has its effect upon the agricultural scene, – and also, incidentally, upon the population of animals and birds. The harvest-mouse, our tiniest mammal, which weighs less than half an ounce and can climb up a corn-stalk without bending it, was common enough in the days when men harvested by hand; but the binder and the combine reap its little nest with the corn, and it is now extinct in all but a few of our eastern counties. The corncrake, whose insistent sawing used to match the sound of the whetstones rubbing the reapers' scythes, has become a rare bird for the same reason. The partridge, on the other hand, probably benefits from the introduction of combines; for these machines leave a longer stubble than the binder did, providing the partridges with good cover.

CHEMICAL WARFARE IN THE FIELDS

BUT it is our chemical inventions, rather than our mechanical ones, which affect the fauna and flora most. Nowadays most farmers spray their crops at various stages of their growth, against pests, fungi or virus diseases, and also to destroy the weeds which grow among them. The invention of DDT put into man's hands a weapon with which any trifling rebellion of the insects could be instantly quelled; probably without DDT and other insecticides we could not grow enough food to support the increasing world-population of mankind. Hormone weed-killers, which kill certain plants by over-stimulating their growth, gave us a similar weapon against the weeds. It is roughly selective, acting chiefly on broad-leaved plants upon which the spray can settle, and hardly at all upon narrow-leaved upright plants such as cereals and grasses. Thus for the first time the farmer can kill the weeds in his cornfield without killing the corn. The thistles, nettles, docks and tares which compete with the corn for plant-food and sunlight disappear almost as if a magician had waved his wand; the poppies which used to stain the oatfields blood-red are vanishing from the scene.

We have, however, possessed these very deadly weapons for a very short time; and their long-term effects are uncertain. For instance, if we kill the caterpillars of the cabbage butterfly with DDT in the autumn, their parasites, the grubs of the Ichneumon fly which live within them, will certainly share their doom; a fresh immigration of cabbage butterflies from the continent next year may produce a plague of caterpillars in the absence of the parasite which normally controls them. Likewise the sprays which kill aphis or 'blight' deal impartially with the ladybirds which live upon aphis. Among the weeds which we destroy in the cornfields are numerous 'host-plants' of beneficent insects; pests may multiply if these insects which prey upon them become rare. Grain-eating birds, which live mainly upon weed-seeds, may alter their habits in the absence of their natural food; they may be compelled to feed upon *our* grain. Insect-eating birds, many of which are killed by the chemical sprays, may become too few to control this pest or that one.

These are *risks* only; and we must beware of prophesying woe to those who 'interfere with the balance of nature' because 'the balance of nature' is a meaningless phrase. What we really imply by it is the arrangement which best suits ourselves; for every operation upon the farm interferes with 'Nature' to a certain extent and if 'Nature' is left to herself in England the land returns, as we have seen, to light forest and scrub. So when the farmer sprays his crops to get a larger yield the small incalculable risk of inconvenient long-term consequences is certainly justified. When County Councils spray the grass verges and roadside hedgerows simply to save the wages of a few roadmen it is a different matter. A 'weed' has been defined as 'a plant growing in the wrong place'; and the beautiful plants of the roadsides cannot be described as weeds. The hormone blackens and withers not only the thistle and the nettle, but the delicate lacy hedge-parsley, the stichwort with its sprig-muslin petals, the sweet violet, the exquisite meadow cranesbill. It may indeed extinguish forever a few rarities which have their last refuge by the sides of the roads; replacing them with the tidy suburban sameness of lawn-like turf.

The roadman with his scythe cuts the herbage from time to time, but does not permanently destroy the plants. It will be sad if the destructive sprayer takes his place; for the beauty

287

of our roadsides has an imponderable value, and cannot be measured in terms of a halfpenny Rate. Incidentally the roadman, nowadays, is generally an oldish man who uses a scythe with the graceful ease which he learned in his youth-from his father, perhaps, who would go into the hayfields at four o'clock in the morning and cut his acre of grass before dusk fell.

THE HAY HARVEST

FOR HAY was mown by hand, here and there, within the memory of old men. The mowers would start at the first light, when the dew was on the grass and the scythe cut clean; they would break off when the sun rose high, eat their bait and drink their cider, sleep a little, and start again in the cool of the evening; from six o'clock, say, they would work till dark. Each man's scythe was his personal, cherished possession, upon which his livelihood partly depended: he would not lend it to another man, nor dream of using it to cut rough bents or thistles, for which he would use an old, discarded blade. When haymaking was over he would hang it in a tree; the dews would rust it; but the rust would enable him to get a better edge on it, when the corn harvest came round. The scythe, the rake and the pitchfork, all very ancient tools, were the only instruments of haymaking up till the last quarter of the 19th century, when they gave place to the mowing-machine, the horse-rake, and the tedder, a machine which kicks up the swathe of hay behind it and turns it over, leaving it loose so that the wind can dry it. Later came other inventions, such as the haysweep which collected up the hay and the elevator which lifted it on to the rick. Haymaking was speeded up, but the pattern of haymaking was unchanged. The hay was still cut in swathes when it was 'ripe' (i.e. ready to seed), the sun and the summer air dried it, and it was ricked as soon as it was ready. The hay harvest was still a job needing plenty of labour; the fields were populous with the men in their broad straw hats, the women in their floppy white ones, the arms and faces of all burned brick-red by the sun.

But the modern fashion does away with this busy scene. As a rule nowadays the hay is baled by a machine as soon as possible after it is cut. You can see the bales lying about in the fields, some oblong, some cylindrical, according to the kind of machine which the farmer uses. Later the tractor with the big trailer goes round and picks them up; and they are stored until they are needed, generally in a Dutch barn.

Many farmers do not make hay at all. Either they cut their grass when it is still very young and fresh, to make silage; or (on very big farms) they feed the grass into a grass-dryer, whence it emerges in the form of powder or pellets. The grass-dryer costs several thousand pounds; so the silo is more general. It is a simple pit (occasionally a tower) in which the grass is packed tight when green and mixed with molasses. The resulting silage provides the milking-cows with a much richer winter feed than hay. Incidentally as you walk through the country your nose will possibly tell you when you are in the neighbourhood of a silo. If it is not very well made it gives off a sourly unpleasant smell.

These more profitable ways of using grass may soon cause haymaking to be a thing of the past. Silage also cuts out the climatic risks of haymaking. The hayrick may disappear, as the loaded wain, so beloved of landscape painters, has gone into limbo already. Perhaps our grandchildren, as they glance at old paintings some 20 years hence, will point at the hayricks and the wagons and ask: 'What are those funny things?' Film-producers on location, trying to recapture Ye Olde Englysshe Scene, may build rickyards at colossal expense out of plastics in order to convey 'the atmosphere of the period'.

MEADOW AND PASTURE

A WORD about grassland. To the townsman, and indeed to many countrymen, all green fields look more or less alike. The farmer's eye sees differences in the type of pasture and the kind of herbage which composes it. There is the rough grazing of the uplands; there is the permanent pasture, some of it unploughed for many years; there are water-meadows which are artificially flooded each season; and there are the 'leys' in which grass is sown just as cereals or turnips are sown, as part of a rotation. The 'leys' remain under grass for one, two, three or more years; and are then ploughed up again to grow a different crop. They have one great advantage over permanent pasture; we can choose what kind of grass-mixture we shall grow, and can provide for a long grazing season. There are hundreds of species of grasses, and many varieties of each species artificially produced at the plant-breeding establishments; so the modern 'ley' contains a mixture of the sorts most suited to a particular soil, climate and purpose (e.g. silage, grazing, hay). It contains as well as grasses other nutritious plants, such as wild white clover and the pretty blue chicory, which makes available to cattle certain 'trace-elements' which they need for their well-being. So even the meadows, nowadays, have little to do with 'Nature', but are the product of highly-specialised scientific research, a far cry indeed from the green fields which Falstaff babbled of.

THE BEASTS OF THE FIELDS

I F Y O U chance to come across an old print of a Champion Ram or a Prizewinning Fat Cow you will stare in astonishment at a weird and wonderful creature utterly unlike the animals you see on the farms today. The artist was not at fault; for within the last two hundred years we have learned to mould the very beasts we feed on to match our changing whims. When the consumer demands a smaller joint or a leaner joint, a richer milk or a greater quantity of milk, our farmers do their best to breed the kind of animal which meets the demand; and nowadays our knowledge of genetics enables them to do so within a very few years. Selective breeding is a process similar to natural evolution, but with Man standing in the place of God, the Life Force, or what you will.

You would think that breeding to match the consumer's needs would lead to standardisation: and that we should achieve, perhaps, a People's Milch Cow or a Common Man's Lamb. We have done nothing so totalitarian; for certain kinds of beasts seem to suit certain soils, climates and conditions of farming, and some which thrive in their native county turn out to be bad doers elsewhere. The Danes have gone to great trouble to produce a pig which represents the common denominator of their needs; the Irish are trying to do so, and have made it illegal to possess any other than the 'Government pig'. But in Britain we still breed 13 different kinds (not counting crosses) which perhaps express the individualism of our farmers as well as demonstrating the diversity of conditions under which they farm.

Pigs

Most of the pig breeds are quite easy to recognise. The

290

SADDLEBACKS are black with a white 'saddle' across their shoulders which runs down to their forelegs. The GLOSTER OLD SPOT is white with black spots. The TAMWORTH is sandy with a fine coat, and claims descent from the original Wild Boar of Britain. The MIDDLE WHITE is a pork pig, trimmer and smaller than the baconers, with a somewhat squashed-in and pug-like face; its ancestors came from China. THE BERKSHIRE is like a black version of the Middle White. The LARGE BLACK and the LARGE WHITE are as their names imply. A favourite cross is between white and black, which produces 'blues', the white pigs with blue-grey mottlings.

A female pig is called a gilt or hilt or yilt until she has had her first litter (i.e. farrowed); thereafter she is a sow. A good litter is ten or twelve. A pleasing phrase in a book designed to help novice pig farmers runs 'See that your sow is equipped with at least twelve teats'– suggestive of a visit to the spares shop for supplying any deficiency . . . A sow suckling her piglets (which arrange themselves neatly in two layers) is a pleasing sight. Not until all the piglets have found their places, each with a teat, will she let her milk down. Then, all squealing ceasing, the sow's talkative grunts and the suck-suck of the piglets combine to make a very satisfactory sound. Sows are in general gentle creatures. They like to be talked to. A sow who has her belly rubbed will almost always respond by slowly rolling on her side, emitting pleasurable grunts. Very occasionally a sow will become fierce at farrowing. It should be remembered that it is not a good idea to turn your back on a near-by boar.

Sheep

Sheep breeds are much more difficult; you can divide them roughly into Shortwools and Longwools, White-faced and Black-faced. The kinds you are most likely to see during your country walks are:

S H O R T W O O L S : *Southdown* (white woolly faces); *Oxford* (grey-brown faces with a woolly topknot); *Dorset* (horned, with pink noses); *Suffolk* (black faces and black feet, no wool on either; *Hampshire* (woolly faces, black noses and black round the eyes, woolly legs).

L O N G W O O L S : *Leicester* (white-faced); *Lincoln* (white-faced, much larger than Leicester); *Wensleydale* (black-faced).

MOUNTAINY SHEEP: smaller and lighter in build than most of the other breeds. *Welsh Mountain* have slightly-tanned faces and legs, and the rams are horned; *Scotch Blackface* are shaggy and both sexes are horned; *Cheviots* (pronounced with a long 'e') are white-faced with a longish coat of very white and lustrous wool, which is the raw material of Scotch Tweed.

Tegs are yearling sheep; teg-wool is the wool of the first shearing. Gelded rams are called wethers. Ewes in lamb are described by countrymen as being in yean; lambing is yeaning.

Cattle

Cattle can be divided into those bred for beef, those bred for milk, and those which are 'dual-purpose'. The beef sorts include:

HEREFORD, white faced, fierce-looking (though in fact they are exceptionally gentle) with somewhat downward-curving horns. They have thick coats of rich red which match the red Hereford soil; rather curly hair, especially on the forehead. They were originally used as draught-oxen.

SUSSEX, deep red with wide spreading horns and very short hair.

GALLOWAY, black, hornless, rather shaggy, very short legged; bred mainly in Scotland.

ABERDEEN ANGUS, black, hornless but smaller and smoother coated than the Galloway.

WEST HIGHLAND, very shaggy with huge spreading horns; variously coloured, red, dun, yellow, cream, black and brindle. The closest breed to the original wild cattle of Britain and now confined to the north west of Scotland and the Outer Isles.

The following kinds are bred mainly for milk:

AYRSHIRE, dapple, red, brown or black with irregular white patches; udder rather flat and not at all pendulous; long up-turned sickle shaped horns. Certainly the most delightful breed from the aesthetic point of view.

BRITISH FRIESIAN, black and white in patches; short horns. Gives the highest yield of milk but not of the best quality. There are also Friesian steers.

JERSEY, yellow-fawn to silver-grey, very small with a

292

rather deer-like look. Forward curved horns. Its milk is richer in butter fat than that of any other breed.

GUERNSEY, bigger than the Jersey. Variously coloured, dun, fawn or reddish-fawn often with white patches.

KERRY, an Irish breed of black with very thin upward curving horns.

The dual-purpose cattle, which produce good quality beef and also plenty of milk include:

DAIRY SHORTHORNS, largish cattle with flesh-coloured muzzles, short coats of red, white or roan, and short straight horizontal horns. There are also Beef Shorthorns.

RED POLL, brown-red, hornless.

There are some other very local breeds e.g. LINCOLN RED, WELSH BLACK, and DEXTER which are the smallest cattle of all; a Dexter cow is not much taller than a Great Dane.

Cattle which normally bear horns are often 'de-horned' to prevent them from injuring each other. A young cow remains a heifer until after her second calving. A bullock is a gelded male. A steer is a fat bullock. It generally takes 30 months to produce a fat beast from a calf – which is why beef can never be a cheap commodity.

Bulls are often docile but no countryman would care to cross a field where a strange bull was at large. There is no panacea against bulls except to run faster than they do. A lady in a red coat is in no special peril since bulls in common with all mammals except apes and man are colour blind; any rag, and not only a red one, will provoke them.

MARKET GARDENS AND ORCHARDS

THERE ARE a few places in rural England where you can walk for miles without seeing any beasts of the field save perhaps a working horse or two. These are the areas given over entirely to market gardening. The gardens present a higgledy-piggledy landscape, quite unlike the bold pattern of the farms; it is a landscape dictated by short-term expediency rather than long-term planning, for if the farmer is a strategist the market-gardener is a tactician, matching his crops and cultivations to swiftly-changing conditions. It doesn't matter very much if the corn-harvest is a fortnight late; but if a crop of radishes comes a fortnight late and misses the 'early trade' it may be more profitable to plough them back into the ground than to pull them for market. Supply and demand fluctuate from day to day, depending on weather conditions, imports, the public's whim. The cost of growing market-garden produce is high; much more labour, much more fertiliser, is used per acre than on the farm. Rewards and penalties are greater too. A single lucky crop may bring in £250 an acre; but there are proportionately more bankrupts among market-gardeners than among farmers.

The scenery of market-gardening is dreary and dull. Sprouts, parsnips, spring onions, carrots, cabbages, cauliflowers, lettuces do not decorate the landscape as farm crops do. But here and there are patches of warm colour: red pickling cabbage glowing in a glint of sunshine on a winter's day, kidneybeans in flower – an orange-scarlet furnace – gillyflowers grown for bunching in the spring, sweet williams in high summer. Where asparagus is grown there is a transformation in July and another in September. The growers cease to cut their 'grass' in late June, and let the fern grow tall. Its feathery greenness delights the eye; but as it fades to tawny it takes on an autumnal splendour and a large patch of it just before it is cut down looks almost like a field on fire.

Many market-gardeners grow soft fruit as well as vegetables, and often the gardening areas merge into orchard-country where the chief crops are apples, pears, cherries and plums. This is so in Kent and in Worcestershire, where the orchards are set amid the sprout-fields and the bleak landscape blossoms suddenly in the spring. The plum-blossom comes first (the end of March to the middle of April, its climax often coinciding happily with Eastertide). Unless the season is very late it comes on the bare black boughs, and is like a lace curtain drawn across the orchard-land. The pear and the cherry come in together.

> Loveliest of trees, the cherry now
> Is hung with bloom along the bough,

wrote Housman; but of pear and cherry who shall say which is the lovelier or set either above the apple; shell-pink when fully open, rose-pink when in bud? Incidentally the most free-flowering apple-trees are the cider sorts, which produce hard sour bellyaching apples; and the loveliest pear-trees, tall snowy pyramids in April, are not the kinds with aristo-

294

cratic names (such as Williams Bon-Chretien and Doyenne du Comice) but the ones which bear little rough perry pears. The demand for home-made cider and perry seemes to be declining; and every year a few more of the old beautiful orchards are cut down.

Frost in May is the fruit-grower's ever-present fear. It is the invisible slayer that creeps among the branches at dead of night and blackens the hearts of the blossom or the tiny green berries of the setting fruit. Frost tends to 'flow' down-hill and gather in the valleys and the sheltered places, just as water would do; so nowadays the orchards are planted on the exposed slopes of hills rather than in the hollows. You will notice that the trees are planted in parallel rows in line with the slope of the land, to give good 'air drainage' when the frost flows between them. Even peaches will grow well in the open in England on a southward facing slope if they are clear of the frost-pockets.

There is not much defence against frost; but some growers build bonfires around their orchards and light those on the windward side on nights when frost is expected. The smoke forms a sort of protective canopy and sometimes the fruit is saved. Oil-burning orchard-heaters are also used in places sheltered from the wind.

By June, in England, the risk is past; and the growers, as they put it, 'feel safe to get their ladders mended', ready for picking time. In most fruit districts cherry picking comes first, beginning in mid-June. The plum harvest comes next, beginning with the Early Prolifics, which are small sloe-like purple plums; the yellow egg plums follow, and are mostly picked green for stewing or jam-making; then come the big purple eating plums, such as Czar, Victoria, Monarch – in that order. Cherry-picking may go on into early August in some parts, running on into the pear and apple time. Beauty of Bath and the bright scarlet Worcester Pearmains are the earliest apples; Blenheims are not picked till October; and the old-fashioned russets will cling to the trees long after they are bare and last till next spring, staying sound though their skins are as brown and wrinkled as an old countryman's face.

The names of apples roll splendidly round the tongue: Duke of Devonshire, Lord Lambourne, Newton Wonder, King o' the Pippins, Laxton Superb, Cox's Orange Pippin. But by

K

contrast there are some humble and as it were cottager's kinds, as Annie Elizabeth, so named after the two daughters of the man who first produced it.

HOPS

THERE is one more crop of local importance, though it is only grown on a large scale in four of our counties: Kent and Hampshire, Hereford and Worcester. Its harvest is the merriest of all; and the hopfields (gardens as they are called in Kent, yards in Herefordshire) have at that season a somewhat Bacchanalian air, for the beautiful leaves of the hops are very like those of the grape and the green bines that drape the poles and the strings make a frieze like that on a Grecian vase. The word 'bine' is only a local variant of 'vine'.

The landscape of hopfields has a derelict appearance for eight months of the year, when the poles alone are seen in the bare fields; but the other four months make up for all. The hops begin to run up the strings in early May – in an anticlockwise direction, which is contrary to the way of most vegetable climbers – and they grow on the average 2 inches in 24 hours, reaching $14\frac{1}{2}$ feet by mid-June. They are ripe and ready by the first week in September, when the hordes of hop-pickers arrive in the districts where they are grown: cockneys and gypsies in Kent, Welsh and Black-country folk as well as gypsies in Hereford. The picking lasts for 3 or 4 weeks. Whole families, with their children, spend their holidays in this way and are paid at piece rates, so much a 'bushel' though the bushel-basket which measures it varies in size from district to district or even from farm to farm. Each family or group of pickers is allotted an area to pick in which must be cleared before they move elsewhere. This is called a 'drift' in Kent, a 'house' in Hereford. Hop-growing has its own quaint vocabulary. The special hoe used in the early cultivations is called a kerf. The yellow resinous dust that is found in the hop-flowers and gives them their distinctive smell is called the Gold. The two most popular sorts of hop are named respectively Bramblings and Fuggles.

On many of the bigger hop-farms nowadays picking is done by machine. Although the machine is complicated and very expensive, it saves a great deal of labour and avoids difficulty with education regulations; and in a few years, alas, the hop-picking holiday may be a thing of the past.

Hops, by the way, do *not* make beer stronger. Their only purpose is to give it a bitter flavour. Ground ivy was used for this purpose before hops were introduced into England, about the middle of the 16th century. According to an old rhyme

> Turkey, carp, hops, pickerill and beer
> Came into England all in a year.

THE WOODLANDS

WE HAVE wandered leisurely through the farmers' fields and glanced at the domestic beasts and crops which occupy about 85 in every 100 acres of Britain. The remaining 15 is accounted for by urban areas, aerodromes, uncultivated mountainsides, and woods. There are more than 3 million acres of woodland. Much of this is owned by the Forestry Commission, which pursues a policy of planting the 'marginal land', which is unsuited to agriculture, with quick-growing softwoods; 92% of all its plantings consist of various conifers, firs, larches and pines. These new woods look somewhat alien in our countryside; 'natural' forest of Britain is a mixture of hardwoods, mainly oak, beech, elm, birch and ash. Savernake, Sherwood, Dean and the New Forest were the famous woodlands of England, and not much is left of Savernake, only a fragment of Sherwood. The Forest of Dean and the New Forest are 'Royal' Forests, in the charge of the Commission, which has indulged its passion for planting conifers here and there. For the most part, however, the oaks remain; and as we walk among them we can imagine ourselves in the ancient Greenwood of England. We owe the New Forest to a king's inordinate addiction to sport. William the Conqueror is said to have 'loved the red deer as if he were their father'. He made for the deer a sanctuary, and for himself a hunting ground, of nearly 100,000 acres upon the thin and hungry soil of Hampshire; and that county would look very different today but for the accident that a ruthless, hard-swearing, hard-riding Norman loved his deer, his horses and his hounds much better than he loved his conquered people. Although modern forestry has altered the appearance of a good deal of it, you will still find there groves of oak and holly where the dark shadows of the trees have scarcely shifted, and where the sunlight has not fallen on the leaf-mould beneath, since Domesday.

297

'Greenwood' was the poets' word; 'Black Wood' might have been more fitting, for in the Middle Ages the Forests were dark and savage places hedged about by dark and savage laws. Certainly they were playgrounds for kings (though the game was sometimes a grim one, as Rufus discovered) but they were by no means playgrounds for the kings' subjects. Unless a man had business there he was wise to shun the Forest lest he lose his right hand for the crime of shooting an arrow with it, or his eyes for the sin of looking covetously at the fat hinds. 'Hunting in Forest, Chases, and suchlike priviledged places of pleasure', wrote Manwood in his *Forest Laws* (1598) 'is only for Kings, Princes, and great worthy personages, and not for mean men of mean calling or ambition'. Despite the ghastly penalties, there seems to have been a good deal of poaching, and presumably a black market in deer-flesh was not unknown; for there is a proverb in Latin which was common in the Middle Ages: *Non est inquirendum unde venit venison.*

In Shakespeare's *As You Like It* we find the sunlight breaking into the black wood at last; the fear of the deep woods is lifted, perhaps because Man as well as the sunlight was beginning to break into them. There must have been a great deal of felling during the reign of Elizabeth and much more during the fifty years after her death; John Evelyn in his *Sylva* (1664) complained of the ruin of the woods in England. Since then there has been a steady erosion which has left us a few islands of old woodland widely scattered in various parts of the country. None is so large as the New Forest, and none gives you such a good idea of the kind of scenery among which the wolf and the wild boar roamed, even as late as 1500.

The great oakwoods are rich in fauna and flora: you will find in the New Forest, for example, most of our 71 sorts of butterflies, including the great Purple Emperor which sails high among the treetops yet deigns to descend to the ground now and then to settle on carrion, which it loves. You will find more representatives of our 2218 different sorts of moths than in any other area of the same size. You will find three species of deer, most of our other mammals. (We still possess 75 kinds, having made extinct during historical times only 5, the wolf, the wild boar, the brown bear, the beaver and the reindeer.) You may even come across creatures weird and wonderful, for instance an adder with belly of beautiful porcelain blue; the great naturalist W. H. Hudson found such a one basking upon a Forest heath.

Flowers, ferns and all sort of vegetation flourish between the oaks; beechwoods in contrast are barren, for their wide-spreading branches keep out the light. It is only in the glades and open spaces that the bluebells grow, and the foxglove, which is surely the typical flower of the oakwoods, is hardly ever seen among the beech. The beech (like the box) is really a tree of the chalk; and where it grows well it forms still and lovely woods of soft green shade, in which few birds twitter, and which have a quiet cathedral air. The botanist, finding little to interest him under the trees, will do well to hunt along the edges of the wood; the chalk-loving flowers include some of the quaintest and most local of our orchids, the Musk, Frog, Wasp and Bee, and the rarest of all, the Red Helleborine of the Cotswolds.

Flowers, incidentally, provide the best indication of the kind of soil in any particular area; wherever you find the foxglove, the ling, the whortleberry, the rhododendron you may be sure you are not on chalk. But wherever the Traveller's Joy or Old Man's Beard drapes the hedgerows, you will know that you are back on the limestone, for in common with about a dozen other plants (the Bloody Cranesbill and the Kidney Vetch are the best known) it will not grow anywhere else.

Many of our woods are 'mixed': they contain oak, birch, hazel, sycamore, alder and aspen growing naturally together. When from time to time such woods are felled, the stumps are left in the ground to sprout again and form new woodland in a few years' time. This is called 'natural regeneration', and the new growth is described as coppice.

Now and then, in the course of our wanderings, we may come across a small patch of woodland, perhaps on the slope of a hill, which consists of old birch trees, rather widely scattered, hawthorns, occasional hollies, and stunted, crooked oaks. These oaks, when the winter gales have ripped the leaves off them, seem to hold out gnarled arms in gesticulation to the sky. We have a sense of something primitive, druidical; for this is a fragment of the ancient, original scrub. By chance it has survived the encroachment of man. His plough has never ripped open the soil, his axe has never been wielded here. All around us, north, south, east and west, is spread out the garden that man has made; but we have come full-circle, and where we stand is the woodland waste, that once was England.

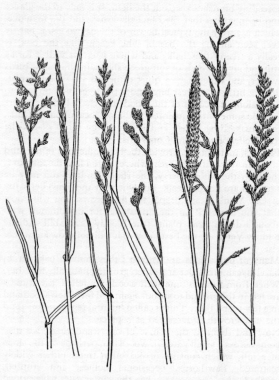

Left to right : Annual Meadow Grass; Couch Grass; Italian Rye Grass; Cocksfoot; Timothy; Meadow Fescue; Crested Dogtail.

A KALENDAR OF WILD FLOWERS

To see a World in a Grain of Sand
And Heaven in a Wild Flower.
William Blake.

A wilderness of sweets.

Milton.

In the green grass she loves to lie
And there with her fair aspect tames
The wilder flowers, and gives them names.
Andrew Marvell.

No season is dead. In January look for small weeds already flowering, and remember that a weed can be regarded as a flower out of place. GROUNDSEL (1) introduces gold to the year, SHEPHERD'S PURSE (2) has both flowers and seeds, and you will find the first tiny white stars of CHICKWEED (3). This is the main flowering time for CHRISTMAS ROSES (4), though in shelter they may have bloomed earlier. You will find WINTER HELIOTROPE (5) in an old garden and often outside it. YEW (6) and BOX (7) will stiffen a winter posy.

Though most of the dry stems are battered now and berries eaten, save for black IVY berries (8), long grasses still droop gracefully in the lanes. But the best prize is in a cleared patch of copse, for there you will find a few short-stemmed PRIMROSES (9). Pick HAZEL catkins (10) now, and they will soon treble their length and be spilling gold dust in a warm room.

February is often the worst month of winter; but if we use the poet's eye we shall see Spring as the infant that 'flutters sudden 'neath the breast of Earth A month before the birth'. First of the CROCUSES (1) is the orange; then comes the purple, then the white. There are drifts of SNOWDROPS (2); ACONITES (3) pushing up with the frills of their necks; GORSE (4) on the common, smelling almost warm and summery, and little BARREN STRAWBERRY (5) in the short grass. In the woods DOG'S MERCURY (6) is flowering and HONEYSUCKLE (7) is putting out the first leaves of the year. On chalky soil you will find SPURGE LAUREL (8) on a shady bank, shiny green and poisonous, and very rarely, you will find its sweet smelling cousin, DAPHNE (9). Towards the end of the month FERNS (10) uncoil and DAFFODILS come spearing up – look for one carrying a leaf on its point 'stabbing winter at a blow' (11).

DAISIES (1) are out, 'smell-less yet most quaint'. Let them have first place on the page as on the lawn, where soon they will be beheaded. March is golden: KINGCUPS (2) by the pond; COLTSFOOT (3) along the roadside, and glistening LESSER CELANDINE (4) in the ditch. In the garden daffodils bend stiffly in March winds and, if you know where to look, you will find WILD DAFFODILS (5) in the copse. We may have 'blackthorn winter' this month when the BLACKTHORN (6) is snowy, and dry frozen ground – but remember 'a peck of March dust is worth a king's ransom'. GREEN HELLEBORE (7), wild relation of the Christmas rose, is rare, but you may find it in a chalk wood of the South. Watch the trees: the ALDER (8) hangs down purple catkins, the POPLAR (9) red ones, and the ELMS (10), their twigs rosetted with small flowers, wear the pink-purple bloom of a ripe peach.

APRIL

April is the great month in the weald. Spring is in the hazel copses, a green mist in the branches, soon to settle as clouds of new leaves. Walk delicately between cushions of primroses and constellations of ANEMONES (1). You will find the EARLY PURPLE ORCHIS (2) with spotted leaves; LADY'S SMOCKS (3) silver-white in the shade, but pinker where the sun can reach them; and DOG VIOLETS (4) and GROUND IVY (5), both purple-blue. There may be a patch of WILD GARLIC (6) but walk round it, for if it is bruised its onion smell will drown the better scents of spring. Watch for delicate WOOD SORREL (7) in a bed of moss, with its veined white flowers and the young leaves neatly folded down on their pink stems like a shut parasol. PERIWINKLE (8) likes a half-shady bank, and the brittle STITCHWORT (9) stars a sunny one. At the fringe of the wood look up for WILD CHERRY blossom (10), and shell pink CRAB APPLE (11) buds.

MAY

May is pink and blue and gold, with YELLOW ARCHANGEL (1) for her herald: BLUEBELLS (2) in the woods; magenta CAMPION (3) in the clearings; BUGLE (4) with its blue flowers and shiny bronze leaves, and YELLOW PIMPERNEL (5). You may chance on WOODRUFF (6), one of the Bedstraws, with white waxen flowers and leaves arranged in ruffs round the stem. The GREATER CELANDINE (7), no connexion of the Lesser but really a poppy, is the only common flower with yellow juice and because of that property it was, redundantly, used in treating jaundice. You will find it growing on a bank usually near a farm or village. A field pond may be shining white with WATER CROWFOOT (8), a buttercup, which gets the best of two worlds with sturdy leaves above and trailing thread-like leaves below the water. Notice small GERMANDER SPEEDWELL (9) under the hedge, with flowers of heavenly blue. Best of all, the COWSLIPS (10) are out.

In June hay rises to its flood, almost submerging the rose-embroidered hedgerows. It is the high month for daisies and buttercups and cloves, for grasses dusty with pollen as mauve as the FIELD SCABIOUS (1). But climb up past the hay, up the edge of the plough – you may find HEARTSEASE (2) in passing – to the open down, and lie on a warm turf. There you will smell THYME (3) and, head near the ground, look down the purple veined throat of EYEBRIGHT (4) and watch butterflies on the pink stars of CENTAURY (5). The ROCK ROSES (6) will be out, their petals like crumpled yellow silk, and MILKWORT (7) crimson and blue. Perhaps you will find a BEE ORCHIS (8) or CLUSTERED BELLFLOWER (9). Certainly there will be BUGLOSS (10), royal blue and scratchy, very hard to pick, and wine red SALAD BURNET (11). As you descend to the valley again through a dim hanging wood search for HERB PARIS (12) – one day you will find it.

In July, be proud, and walk nose in air for the scent of lime blossom. Wander by a fen river or chalk stream and you will find PURPLE LOOSESTRIFE (1) spearing up through the meadow-sweet. Look for handsome ARROWHEAD (2); FLOWERING RUSH (3); MIMULUS (4) cool and juicy with its feet in the water; little CREEPING JENNY (5) and water FORGET-ME-NOT (6) between the rushes on the edge of the bank. Or if the water meadows are too hot, lie in the shade at the edge of the wood and eat WILD STRAWBERRIES (7) under a bower of HONEYSUCKLE (8)

But if you cannot go to the country at all, picnic on a bomb-site near St Paul's before they are all built over. There among the willowherb and ragwort you will find EVENING PRIM-ROSES (9), and BINDWEED (10) with fragile snowy trumpets, using rusty wire for trellis. Next month the willowherb fluff will be blowing between the buses.

August is the month for the harvest flowers, though with cleaner seed much beauty has been exchanged for more bread. Cornfields seldom harbour POPPIES (1) now, nor blue cornflowers. The wine red CORNCOCKLE (2), once so common, is becoming rare. Look along the roadsides for WHITE CAMPION (3); golden spires of TOADFLAX (4); for great-mullein, grey Goliath of the hedgerow, and its smaller purple-eyed cousin, DARK MULLEIN (5). On the moors listen to bees in BELL HEATHER (6). Eat BILBERRIES (7) while you look for a small parasite, LESSER DODDER (8), wound on a furze bush like a pink cocoon. Squelch through a brown bog to seek GRASS OF PARNASSUS (9); pink BOG PIMPERNEL (10), and insect catching SUNDEW (11). A fly settling on a sundew leaf is caught in the sticky hairs, and the leaf curls over and digests it. In wiry turf there grow slender ST JOHN'S WORT (12) and blue HAREBELLS (13) that rustle if you shake them.

310

If you go to the sea in September and walk above the tide-rim you may find growing among dusty pebbles and dry seaweed and litter a golden horned SEA POPPY (1) – it has been flowering all summer and now its horns are long – and SEA HOLLY (2), which is really a thistle, all the colours of sea on a cloudy day. In crevices of cliff rocks SAMPHIRE (3) grows right down to high-water mark. It is a seaside relation of the parsleys with aromatic fleshy leaves. On the cliff edge itself are the last few flowers of THRIFT (4) and white SEA CAMPION (5) which had their gay season in June. In a marsh behind dunes you may come on patches of shrubby BOG MYRTLE (6) which smells sweet as you run your fingers through it. Up on the short grass of flanking headlands look for the little white orchis of September, the twisting LADY'S TRESSES (7). SEA LAVENDER (8) and PRICKLY SALTWORT (9) belong to the mud flats of the East coast.

October is the month of chestnut harvest. Who does not
stoop for a CONKER (1)? SWEET CHESTNUTS (2) should be
gathered too, and roasted if possible in a log fire.

The colour of the year is changing: scarlet, unseen in spring,
rare in summer, is becoming the focal point of the hedge's
colour scheme. The WOODY NIGHTSHADE berries (3) are shiny
red and squashy, and SPINDLEBERRIES (4) have split to show
the orange seed inside the bright pink cases. Unnoticeable
in spring, Spindle is now the glory of any chalk lane. Look
for WILD HOP (5) decorating the hedges; PELLITORY (6)
growing between the stones of an old wall, and neat white
SNEEZEWORT (7), last to bloom in the year's succession.
The STINKING IRIS (8), growing on the edge of woods in a
limestone district, had dully greyish-mauve flowers, but
now its fat seed-cases have split into three parts, each showing a double row of brilliant orange seeds that will last
through the winter in your room.

Squirrels must hurry, and we too, for the last of the hedge-row harvest. As you peer in the bushes to see if just one hazel nut has been left, look under the yellow leaves for spring catkins, packed tight for winter storms. You may find a few BEECH NUTS (1), but only every five or seven years is there a heavy crop of beech mast. Nuts may be scarce, but as birds have no storage arrangements there are plenty of berries still: scarlet HIPS (2) and claret HAWS (3), which will serve for jelly, but only in dolls' quantities, PRIVET berries (4), like old-fashioned packets of black headed pins, and ELDER-BERRIES (5) hanging in heavy clusters. HONEYSUCKLE berries (6) are rose-red and glassy, the berries of BRYONY (7) red and orange and yellow, and bitter black SLOES (8) are ripe. It is a very red and black and gold month. Trails of BLACKBERRY (9) make a good if scratchy decoration. Frothing over nearly every lane is OLD MAN'S BEARD (10). Another name for this wild clematis is Traveller's Joy.

313

A bunch picked in December has line, not colour, and is a prickly and fragile load. Seek HOGWEED (1) stripped like a scarecrow's umbrella, and bleached NIPPLEWORT (2), SELF-HEAL (3), still neat, and KNAPWEED's ragged cups (4). PLAN-TAIN (5) is as erect as ever and WOODSAGE (6) keeps its summer curve. These will make a brown etching on your mantelshelf and their shadows will double your design. You may find TEASEL (7) towering over some rough patch, with spines as fierce as when they protected the tiny mauve flowers from insects' feet in July – the 'Fullers' Teasel', once used to raise nap on cloth. Stretch for a bunch of ASH seeds (8) and pick up a blown-down twig from the high SCOTS PINE (9). Though the beech trees are bare, the HEDGE BEECH (10) still has leaves to rustle, and OAK leaves (11) cling curled as if carved by Grinling Gibbons. Do not forget the Christmas-pudding HOLLY (12), and perhaps you can claim a sprig of MISTLETOE (13) from an old cottage apple tree.

314

BIRD SONG AT MORNING

Yes, I will spend the livelong day
With nature in this month of May;
And sit beneath the trees, and share
My bread with birds whose homes are there.
W. H. Davies.

Crave the tuneful nightingale to help you
    with her lay,
The ousel and the throstlecock, chief music
    of our May.

Michael Drayton.

To hear the lark begin his flight
And singing startle the dull night.
Milton.

Thou was not born for death, immortal
    Bird!
No hungry generations tread thee down;
The voice I hear this passing night was
    heard
In ancient days by emperor and clown:
Perhaps the self-same song that found a
    path
Through the sad heart of Ruth, when sick
    for home,
She stood in tears amid the alien corn;
    The same that oft-times hath
Charm'd magic casements, opening on the
    foam
Of perilous seas, in faery lands forlorn.
Keats.

Bird engravings by Bewick (1753-1828)

Bird Song at Morning

".. And sit beneath the trees, and share
My bread with birds whose homes are there" PB

> *... that al the wode rong*
> *So sodainly, that, as it were a sot,*
> *I stood astonied ...*
> *   ... until late and long*
> *Ne wist I in what place I was, ne where;*
> *The birdes song was more convenient,*
> *Than mete or drink, or any other thing.*
>   *Anonymous, 15th Century.*

The following pages are designed for the unfledged student
of birds. By the week-end's end, perhaps, he will be a fully
fledged Birdwatcher. No longer can birds be safely and conveniently lumped together as small brown birds, large black
birds and seagulls; no longer can a glib literary allusion to
'the sea-blue bird of March' or 'a small hot bird' be accepted in lieu of ornithological exactitude. For this is an age
of specialisation, and anyone who looks at a bird today calls
himself a Birdwatcher and must submit to all the rigours of
that dedicated life, whether he watch for reasons of aesthetic
appreciation, scientific enquiry, artistic endeavour, or merely
from curiosity.

Bird-watching, advised a famous Field-Marshal, is the ideal
hobby for all young officers. He probably had in mind the
encouragement of some of those qualities desirable in both
military and ornithological operations: the quick eye, the
scientific assessment of the field, patience, and a passionate
belief that the end justifies the means, that the ten-mile walk
into the east wind, the scaling of the unscalable cliff, the
crawl on hands and knees over wet mud, are worthwhile for

317

the sight of one small bird disappearing into an impenetrable
bramble bush.

A hundred and thirty million years ago the chase would not
have been so arduous. The blundering flight of *Archaeopteryx*, with his toothy jaws and claw-tipped fingers and long
pointed tail, would have been easy to identify. Even among
the rapidly changing forms of avifauna in the Eocene
period, from sixty to forty million years ago, it would not
have been difficult to pick out the huge head and tiny wings
and large arched beak of 7-foot *Diatryma*. But with 8,500
species of birds in the world today – and over 450 of them
on the British list – the Birdwatcher has a life's work before
him.

How shall he begin, in a brief week-end?

HOW TO WATCH BIRDS

First, he must equip himself with the right tools. Of these,
the essentials are field-glasses, a library, and a note-book. Re-
finements such as hides and cameras can be added later as he
becomes more proficient.

FIELD-GLASSES. This is the only really expensive
item of the Birdwatcher's equipment, and it will pay him to
get the best he can afford, for a good pair of field-glasses will
last a life-time. Ross, Barr and Stroud, Kershaw, Zeiss, and
Leitz are the best makers. As well as price, consideration
must be given to magnification, field of vision, illumination,
weight and durability.

For bird-watching, a magnification of not less than 6 and not
more than 9 is desirable. (The sign 6 x on a pair of field-
glasses means that the object is magnified 6 times.) With a
higher magnification, the field of vision is smaller and it is
more difficult to follow a quickly moving bird. The higher
powered glasses are also heavier, and they magnify the shake
of one's hands as well as the size of the image. Only people
with steady hands and strong eyes and the ability to support
a millstone round the neck should use 10 or 12-power glasses.
On the other hand, if the glasses are very light, as in the case
of those made of some of the new light-weight alloys, durability will be sacrificed.

Some binoculars have a centre focusing screw, and others
have independent focusing of each eyepiece. Although the

former is slightly heavier it is to be preferred, as it can be quickly altered with one hand.

Many of the modern field-glasses are made with 'coated' lenses, which provide a more brightly illuminated image. They are especially useful in a poor light.

To sum up: the best field-glasses for a Birdwatcher will be 6 to 9 magnification; they will have the widest possible field; they will have coated lenses, central focusing, and will be both light and strong.

Such an expensive toy must be properly cared for. The lens should be carefully wiped after use with a soft silk handkerchief or cleaning tissue. If the strap suspending the glasses is too long, they will swing out against fences and rocks as the wearer bends over or climbs up and will become chipped and dented. The strap should be shortened to avoid damage – and this will also take some of the strain from the neck and will make it easier to raise the glasses quickly to the eyes. It is also advisable to cover the glasses in some way when they are not in the case, either by protecting the eyepieces from rain by a piece of leather or rubber fitted over them, or by tucking the glasses into the jacket.

LIBRARY. This will also depend to some extent on the size of the Birdwatcher's purse. The library could be extended indefinitely. The most essential requirement, however, will be a good field-guide – one that will go into the pocket. The best of all guides is *A Field Guide to the Birds of Britain and Europe* by Roger Peterson, Guy Mountfort and P. A. D. Hollom. Then, even if he cannot afford it, the serious Birdwatcher will never be satisfied until he has acquired the 5-volume *Handbook of British Birds*, an avian *Who's Who, Kelly's* and *Debrett* combined: it contains everything of importance that is known about every bird on the British list. If he does not have the *Handbook* he will probably substitute *The Birds of the British Isles* (3 volumes) by Coward. Books to guide him in the art and science of birdwatching should include James Fisher's *Watching Birds*, and, if he can get hold of it, *A Guide to Bird Watching* by Joseph Hickey (published in U.S.A.). And he would be well advised to listen again and again to the recordings of *Songs of British Birds* by Ludwig Koch until he has them by heart.

NOTEBOOK. For whatever reason birds are watched, notes should be taken of the observations made. Even if the

Birdwatcher has no other motive than the enjoyment of a delightful hobby, he will want to recall the details of exciting and memorable moments. A small notebook should always be carried in the pocket, and observations should be jotted down in this on the spot. Details should be as full as possible: the kind and number of birds seen, where they were seen, their behaviour, particulars of the light and weather, and so on. Sketches should be made whenever an identification is in doubt. These rough notes should be written up at home as soon as possible, while the experience is still fresh in the memory.

The permanent record can take various forms. The sentimental beginner will probably confide his emotions to a rather colourful diary: 'A dainty little bird watched me with bright eyes from the branch of an oak tree. It made a pretty picture against the young April green. Could it have been a willow warbler? The sad little song reminded me . . .' But with practice his style will tauten, his observations will expand, and he will become altogether more scientific. He will probably abandon the diary in favour of a card-index system or a large loose-leaf notebook, either of which will allow for indefinite expansion. The arrangement will be a matter of the Birdwatcher's temperament and his own particular interests, but each species should have a separate heading, with others for Song, Behaviour, Plumage, Nests, and so on, and there should be plenty of cross-references. Very soon our Birdwatcher, if he is worth the salt he has attempted to sprinkle on the tail of many a rare bird, will be writing to the press – and then his Notebook will be indispensible.

WHAT TO WATCH FOR

Now that the Birdwatcher is fully equipped, the really difficult part of the business begins. How will he recognise a bird when he sees it? He has his field guide – but birds do not always sit still enough for comparison with the coloured plate. He must learn what to look for.

There goes a bird! It is flying across a meadow, too far off for us to see clearly the details of its plumage. What size is it? It seems to be larger than a sparrow, smaller than a blackbird. How does it fly? Its flight is undulating, in long curves. It might be a finch of some sort: undulating flight is an identifying field mark of most finches, our guide book tells us. Or it might be a lark. It is unlikely to be a warbler, so far from the trees – and anyway the flight is too strong, the bird too large. It cannot be a starling, whose flight is swift and straight. Now the bird is down on the ground. It is against the sun, so still we cannot see its markings. But we can make out that the bill is long and slender, not short and stout as it would be on a seed-eating finch. Nor is the bird hopping on the ground, as a finch would; nor walking with the slightly waddling gait of a lark. It is running, with an occasional little hop into the air after an insect. And now that we can see the long tail wagging up and down as it runs, we know for certain that it is a wagtail. The tail is not long enough for a grey wagtail: it will probably be either yellow or pied, and when we get closer to the bird we can make out the black and white patterning of a pied wagtail.

These, then, are some of the questions the Birdwatcher must ask himself. What size is it – as big as a dodo, or smaller than a humming-bird? What shape is it – thick or thin, long or short? What is the shape of its beak, its wings, its tail? How does it behave? Does it walk or hop or run or climb trees or bury its head in the sand? How does it fly – with a straight or undulating flight, rapid or slow or flap-flap-glide? Does it hover or dive or soar or wade? Is it alone or is it in a flock? Has it got a kind face, or does it look rather predatory? What colour is it? What are its distinguishing field marks? Has it wing-bars? White in the tail, or on the rump? An eye-stripe? Where is it found? Every bird has its own niche, and is unlikely to be found out of it, except on migration. A wood warbler will not be found in a ploughed field, and it is no good looking for a sky lark in a wood. When is it found? Some birds will be summer migrants: others will be seen only in winter.

WHERE TO WATCH

In his selection of terrain, the week-end Birdwatcher may have to confine himself to his own home ground. If he is free of ties, however, he can choose to spend his week-ends in a wide variety of localities, in each of which he will find a different group of birds. He can also extend his hobby by visiting one of the Field Study Centres, where bird-watching courses are held several times a year under the direction of experienced ornithologists. Then, as his interest grows with knowledge, he will be able to stay at some of the bird observatories round the coast of Britain at which the study of migration is carried on.

Wherever he may be, the Birdwatcher will find scope for his activities. He may live 'in the highlands, in the country places'; by meres or moors or marshes, or in the middle of a turnip field; in a cottage in a wood or a mansion on a hill. Whichever way his path lies, there will be birds on either side of it. There will be warblers in the woodlands and waders on the mud-flats; finches in the stubble and hawks on the hills and titmice at the milk-bottles on his doorstep. Even a city, if he cannot escape from it, can be an excellent place for watching birds, in the parks and public gardens, at the reservoirs and along the rivers. There can be few keener pleasures for the city-dweller than to watch a pair of blackbirds building a nest against a drain-pipe oblivious of the clamour of the crowded street below; or to follow the daily movements of a kestrel that owns the bombed church at the end of his square; or to lie awake in the dark and suddenly to recognise the lonely call of a golden plover high above the city on its migratory passage. Many large towns possess a Natural History Society or similar group which organises bird-watching walks and trips at week-ends.

But the best place for the beginner to learn his birds is undoubtedly in his own garden. (And those who prefer to do their bird-watching with a minimum of effort can manage quite well from a deck-chair on the lawn or an arm-chair at the window.) Here he can watch the story of his birds unfold from month to month, and here he can even combine his hobbies, and dig for birds. There is much that a good bird-gardener can do, by planting the right fruit- and seed-bearing shrubs and plants in the right places, to attract to the garden birds that would otherwise pass it by. The berried lure of hawthorn, mountain ash, cotoneaster and elder will prove irresistible. If possible a corner of the garden should be devoted to weeds and allowed to run to seed, and the more thistles there are the more goldfinches there will be. Cover is important, too, both for nesting purposes and for protection from the wind and sun and from natural predators. Beech, privet, yew and holly afford good cover. If the garden is large enough to contain a wild patch of brambles, briars and

322

bracken, this will bring in warblers. Well-placed nesting boxes will provide homes for birds that normally nest in holes, such as tits, nuthatches and even woodpeckers – and also for the sparrows and starlings who will try to 'gate-crash' on them; and a roofed-over tray sort of affair will often appeal to robins, spotted flycatchers, blackbirds and thrushes as a nest-support. The provision of water in the garden is very important, both for drinking and bathing, and if there is no pool or pond a bird-bath should be provided. Dripping water is a great attraction to warblers. And of course there will be a bird table in every Birdwatcher's garden. Set with breadcrumbs, suet, nuts, seeds, berries and scraps from the human table, it will be an excellent place for observing birds. Here at close range the details of their plumage and behaviour can be studied during the lean days of winter, so that when the seasons of courtship and nesting and migration follow in their cycle, the Birdwatcher's eye is already 'in'. Here, too, in his own melodious plot he can familiarise himself with many of the best songs, and this branch of birding can often – especially on Sunday mornings – be most successfully conducted from his bed.

The following pages give a brief description of some of the birds the week-end Birdwatcher is likely to find in his own garden.

HOUSE-SPARROW, Philip Sparrow, Spug or Roo-Doo. Length, 5¾ inches.

Because it is present in every garden in Britain, the sparrow heads the list of garden birds, but it is very far from being first in the affections of either gardener or bird-lover. Wherever man goes, the sparrow follows – but there is no disguising the fact that he makes use of us in the most impudent manner and gives nothing in return. He takes over our houses, eats our food, disturbs our sleep with his noisy quarreling, and delights in the wanton destruction of our peas and crocuses; but he refuses to make friends and remains aloof and suspicious. The sparrow is always bustling about, hopping perkily or in fussy flight, but a good deal of his activity appears to be entirely aimless. This is evident even in the ardour of courtship, when several males will hop jauntily round a female indulging in every form of noisy display and then, apparently losing interest, will all suddenly fly off together. The sparrow's incessant two-syllabled chirp of *phillip* earned him the old nickname of 'Philip Sparrow'. The male has a brown back streaked with black, a dark grey

crown to his head with chestnut nape, a black throat and greyish-white underparts. A country cock sparrow, free of the grime that camouflages his city brother, is a handsome bird; but his hen, brown above and dingy white below, is undeniably dowdy. The nest, which is an untidy mess of straw and rubbish thickly lined with feathers, is merely a lining to a cavity when it is built under the eaves or stuffed into a hole in the wall or in ivy or a drainpipe; but when no house is available and a tree site is used, the nest is domed with a side entrance. The eggs are 'spickled and spackled' with black, brown or grey on a white ground: they vary both in colour and size.

ROBIN, Redbreast or Ruddock. Length, 5¾ inches.

There are certain birds which show a preference for the society of man and take advantage of his curious activities to make their habitations in the neighbourhood of his own. Of these the robin is the most intimate. The reason for the universal recognition of the robin in England is not merely his friendship for or indifference to the presence of man, but also his strong personality. It is his original departure from the timidity characteristic of the race of small birds which

endears him to us and invites us to woo him – especially with the irresistible bait of the meal-worm – to familiarities we can achieve with no other species. In defence of his territory he is exceedingly pugnacious towards his own kind. His alarm note is as explosive as his nature, and sounds like the tocking of a grandfather clock. The song follows no set pattern, being at once ringing, exultant and full of timbre, but at the same time a kind of musing recitative with a sad and beautiful undersong.

The robin's flight is low and somewhat jerky, and he does not fly far without alighting. On the ground he progresses in swift long hops, pausing occasionally to draw himself up with almost military precision. He is easily recognised by his challenging red breast above white underparts. The rest of his spruce form is olive brown. Young robins have spotted breasts up to the first moult and so deceive the uninitiated into thinking them a different species. There is no difference

325

in the sexes' colouring. A roughish nest of dead leaves, grass and moss interwoven with hair and a few feathers is built pretty well anywhere and in anything from a tin kettle to an orthodox hole in a tree or bank. Five to six eggs, white in ground colour with freckles of light red, are laid in it.

BLACKBIRD, Ousel, or Amsel. Length, 10 inches.

The blackbird possesses an emotional quality quite different from that of the robin, being full of fears, suspicions and nervous reactions. He is almost as conspicuous about human dwelling-places, but never reposes in man the same degree of confidence. His loud chuck of alarm is a sign of his volatile and unstable temperament; anger, rufflement, uneasy protest change in a moment to the most taking airs of gallantry to his brown mate. His movements, too, are typical of his character. In the air, over a short distance, his flight is weak and wavering, though he seems to gather courage and

326

strength over a longer distance; and on the ground, where
he proceeds by hopping and running as a thrush does, he
makes a great show of jerking his tail and wings in a nervous
and excitable manner. When the blackbird begins to sing in
February his low fluting is unrivalled for its pure and mellow tone, and is delivered with a leisureliness which draws out
the full value of each note.

The brown female has not the distinction of the ebony male
with his golden dagger of a bill. She builds very early, and
her shack is an untidy affair of grasses, roots, and herbs,
lined with finer grasses and mud-plastered within. The eggs
are four to six in number, greeny blue in colour, smeared
with light brown.

MISTLE-THRUSH or Stormcock. Length, 10½ inches.

SONG THRUSH, Mavis or Throstle. Length, 9 inches.

Temperamentally there is much kinship between thrush and
blackbird; but the thrush's song is far less moving in musical
quality than the blackbird's, being at once more powerful
and more strident – so much so that at close quarters it can
be very harsh. The melancholy tenderness of the blackbird's
flute is quite absent. If one may express it in human terms,
the thrush's song seems to represent unreflecting joy and the
blackbird's the fulfilment of experience. No singer lives more
in his song, for he will persist in repeating, from a bold and
commanding perch, old phrases and experimenting with new
ones for hours at a stretch and in all months of temperate
weather.

On the ground the thrush will run or hop a little way, then
stand still, his head cocked to one side, as though he were
listening to secret movements within the earth. In reality,
however, he turns his head the better to detect the worms or
insects on the surface. Snails are a favourite food, and a
snail-stone will be found in most gardens, surrounded by the
splintered shells of the victims who have been battered to
pieces. The thrush's flight is direct and swift, with a rapid
wing movement. The nest, which may be found in any imaginable site, is unlike the blackbird's in the use of small twigs
and moss and of a final smooth lining of rotten wood for the
interior. The eggs, usually four to five in number, and laid
two or three times during the season, are of a fine blue tinged
with green and stippled with black spots. Both sexes are
alike.

A predilection for mistletoe berries gave the Mistle-thrush
this name; but his other name of Stormcock is even more ex-
pressive, for that is how most people remember him – a bold,
conspicuous figure blowing his bugle of a song from the bare
topmost boughs across a wintry sky. The loud notes of his
ringing challenge have a blackbird-like quality, but the force-
ful manner of their delivery helps to disguise the fact that his
short phrases are really rather monotonous and repetitive.
His call note is a harsh and grating chatter.

On the ground the mistle-thrush behaves very like a song
thrush, but in flight his action is stronger, with a distinctive
long closure of the wings, and he flies higher. In appearance
he is easily distinguished from his relative: he is much larger
and greyer, and the spots on his breast are bigger and bolder.
In fact, he is a bolder bird in every way, quarrelsome and in-

tolerant of competition, and fearlessly aggressive in defence
of his large grassy nest, which is usually conspicuously sited
in the bare fork of a tall tree. The eggs are cream or greenish
white blotched with brown and mauve.

DUNNOCK, Hedge-Sparrow, Shuffle-Wing, Creepie,
Darby or Hatcher. Length, 5¾ inches.

The dunnock, as he is now officially called, is more familiar
to many as the hedge-sparrow, though he comes of a family
entirely unrelated to the house-sparrow – that of the Accen-
tors, who, as the name implies, are concerned with singing.
And sing he does, more or less all the year round, a bright,
jingling, high-pitched little song which sounds remarkably
like *weeso, sissi-weeso, sissi-weeso, sissi-weeso.* His call note is a
monotonous shrill 'peep'. The dunnock is not exactly secre-

tive, but he very often passes unnoticed as he creeps and shuffles about unobtrusively among fallen leaves and under hedges. He always seems to be busy, in a quiet way, and minding his own business. When he flies it is on rapid, purposeful wings, and he never goes far.

His nest is what you would expect of him – or, rather, of her, as it is built by the hen alone – an efficient job of woven grass, moss and roots, neatly lined with hair or wool. It is usually placed in a thick hedge or shrubbery, or in a faggot stack. The main consideration seems to be that the site should be private and impenetrable. The eggs are of a very lovely shade of clear deep blue. The sexes are alike: dark brown back finely streaked with black, slaty grey head and neck and slaty grey beneath. The fine pointed beak, hallmark of an insect eater, is enough to distinguish the dunnock from the house-sparrow with his short thick seed-eater's beak.

BLUE TIT, Tom Tit, Blue-Cap, Billy-Biter, or Nun. Length, 4½ inches.

GREAT TIT, Saw-Finch, Saw-Sharpener, Black-Capped
Lolly, or Sit-ye-Down. Length, 5½ inches.

The titmouse forces his minute presence upon our attention
not only because of his slightly supercilious fearlessness of
man, his intense vitality and handsome colouring, but from
the eccentricity of his ways. There is no other bird in the calendar who so far succeeds in defying the humdrum in movement, performing an endless variety of unnatural postures on
branch or twig with such topsy-turvy agility that only the
most patient observer is able to record the sight of a titmouse motionless on his perch. In winter, for there is a
roaming and gregarious but not definitely a migratory im-
pulse through the dark days, fat or coconut will bring him
within arm's length.

The blue tit is perhaps the most familiar in the garden and
is certainly the most endearing of this troupe of acrobats. He
possesses a spring song of a very bright and limpid trill
which has been compared to a musical escape of water. As
few as five eggs and as many as twenty (pure white with
spots and freckles of vandyke brown) may be laid in a convenient cavity of a wall or tree or stump or letter-box, into
which the cock bird helps the hen to bundle a surprising
quantity of moss and dry grass, with wool, hair and feathers
for the lining. The bird himself is richly and strikingly
coloured with a blue crown rimmed with white, and his
cheeks are patterned with the same chequer, while a fainter
blue is suffused into the wings and tail. The back is olive-
green, and the under-parts are yellow crossed by yet another
dark blue line.

The great tit is the largest of the common tits. He can immediately be distinguished from his relatives by the broad
black band which cuts down the centre of his sulphur-
yellow breast. His head and neck are glossily blue-black with
white cheeks. His back is olive-green and the wings and tail
are blue-grey. He shares with the other tits a number of
similar call notes, of which his own repertoire is the most

331

extensive, but his song is individual and distinctive – a metallic and rasping 'saw-sharpening' of *teacher, teacher, teacher*. The siting and construction of the nest and the number and colour of the eggs are very similar to the blue tit's, but the eggs are larger. Both species will hiss with anger if disturbed on the nest. Both species, also, move in the same manner: on the ground, with a jerkey hop, and in the air, by swift and undulating, though rather laboured, flight from tree to tree.

The COAL-TIT and MARSH-TIT, though more confined to solitary places, will often be seen in the larger gardens, the former particularly on conifers. Both have black heads and white cheeks, but the coal-tit is distinguished by a large white patch on the nape of the neck. A family party of tiny pussy-faced LONG-TAILED TITS may also pass through the garden, apparently utterly oblivious of the presence of man, however close.

CHAFFINCH, Spink, Shilfa, Scobbey, Skelly, or Shel-Apple. Length, 6½ inches.

The chaffinch frequents human habitations more closely than any other bird except the house-sparrow, and so is seldom noticed as he really is, a bird of lustrous and even gaudy plumage, suiting the rollick of his song and his mettlesome disposition. His jovial rattle is one of the most copious and familiar set songs between February and June, and its first tentative rendering is one of the earliest signs of spring. His flight conforms to the undulating finch type, but is less volatile than the goldfinch's or the linnet's, though more buoyant than that of the hawfinch or bunting. On the wing he delivers a sibilant double note not unlike the pied wagtail's, and his alarm cry is a sharp *ping*. He prefers the ground more than all other finches, except brambling and house-sparrow, and in winter joins the mixed companies of roaming flocks in the fields.

The nest, which is built entirely by the much drabber female, is fashioned perfectly, felted without of mosses, lichens, grasses, wool and other very soft substances deftly woven. It is compacted with cobwebs and lined with hair, feathers, and the down of plants. Four to six rather variable eggs, pale

Two 8ᵛᴱᴿ Higher

bluish green or reddish brown in ground colour with streaks and freckles of black or purplish brown, are laid twice in a season. The forehead of the male is black and the rest of his crown and nape a greyish sea-blue, with chestnut pinkily diluted on the cheeks, while the same blend of pink, deepening to reddish brown, suffuses the under-parts which fade into white. The rump is green, the back a warm chestnut, while two bands of white on the brown wings make a conspicuous recognition mark.

Other finches of the garden are the GREENFINCH, with a toy golden sword strapped to his side and constant twittering talk; the stocky BULLFINCH, despoiler of orchard buds, with his tender pipe, velvety black head and wonderful rose-madder breast; the GOLDFINCH 'pausing upon his yellow flutterings'; and the rarer, bulky HAWFINCH, very shy and very handsomely plumaged, with an adze-like bill.

WREN, Stumpy, Jenny Wren, Titty Todger, Tit Meg, or Stag. Length, 3½ inches.

The wren is as individual a bird as the robin, and his haunts

333

are much the same, except that the wren's distribution is a little more extensive. You will see a wren creeping mouse-like among the stalks from your window, and you will see the same movements, the same upcocked tail, and hear the same

blast of song from the undergrowth of the wildest and most desolate moor, cliff or forest. The quaintness of the wren comes from his exceeding small size and secret elusive ways in contrast with his vigorous and brave personality. The latter shows itself in his song, a bright clear gush of notes hastening to a trill and wonderfully heartening on grey winter mornings, for the wren is almost as abundant a singer as the robin or thrush. It is delivered with extraordinary virility and indifference to the presence of an observer. His excitement note resembles the ticking of a clock sharply anxious to be much faster than other clocks, and when he flies his blunt wings whirr like clockwork, which is all too soon unwound. No bird is so much at home in the densest maze of undergrowth, threading the labyrinth with a dexterity rivalling the most cunning movements of any small mammal, and emerging upon a free spray to sing his song.

334

The wren's energy is also vented in building more nests than are ever used, while the regular nest, wedged into holes or crevices in houses or faggots or other odd litter, or woven in bush-tangle, ivy, rock-shelter or heather, is larger than that of birds twice his strength. The external structure is domed of moss, dead leaves, lichens or grasses, which usually match the surroundings, though hardly with intent, since wrens' nests are often so conspicuous; and the snuggery within is warm with moss, hair and feathers. From four to nine, or occasionally even thirteen, eggs are laid twice in a season, of white lightly and ruddily splashed, The plumage is a warm rufous above, a greyer brown below, and barred and mottled with a pale streak through the eye.

PIED WAGTAIL, Water Wagtail, Trotty Wagtail, Polly-Wash-Dish or Devil's Bird. Length, 7½ inches, including the long tail.

The pied wagtail is a duodecimo edition of the magpie, both in the variegated black and white (greyer in winter) of his plumage and the inconsequence of his ways. The term 'water' wagtail is far too narrow, for he is as happy on the lawn or in the farmyard as he is by pond or stream. He is also particularly fond of hawking flies on the sun-warmed roof of

335

the house. The pied wagtail is never in the same posture for a minute at a time. He trips nimbly to and fro, whirrs round upon himself, leaps into the air after an insect, goes tittering across the grass so swiftly that the movements of his feet are lost, stops dead and then bounds off into a dipping switch-back flight with a double note of *tschizzik* and *tzi-wirrp*.

The nest of the pied wagtail is a hole packed with welded grass-roots, leaves and other material lined with hair, wool and feathers. He will build it in almost any imaginable site, in a bank, against a wall, among rocks, under a clod, at the roots of a tree, between railway sleepers, in an old nest of the magpie. The eggs, four to six in number, are correspondingly variable and capricious in colouring, the more normal having a bluish white background streaked and flecked with greys and browns. Some of the birds migrate in winter. The sexes are more or less alike in plumage.

SPOTTED FLYCATCHER, Post-Bird, Egypt Bird, Old Man, Beam-Bird, Cobweb, or Bee-Bird. Length, 5½ inches.

The spotted flycatcher, who, in May, is almost the last of the summer visitors to arrive, is nothing much to look at. His back is ashy-brown, his brown head streaked with darker brown, his whitish breast streaked lightly – an unremarkable effect. His behaviour, however, is so distinctive that he can be recognised immediately. He sits, bolt upright, silent, absorbed, perched like a little monument on a bare branch, post, or fence before some open space. Here he appears almost indifferent to his surroundings; but in reality nothing is escaping that bright eye, and at the chosen moment he will sally out to seize some passing insect in mid-air, twisting and turning in aerial pursuit before he takes it with an audible snap. He seldom misses.

Spotted flycatchers prefer a solid support for their nest in the vicinity of buildings, on the ledge of a window, on a beam, in a hole, or in a climbing shrub or trellis against a wall. They will also build in the old nest of another bird. They are wise to choose some solid foundation, for their own nest is a flimsy affair, loosely constructed of trailing grass, moss and cobwebs. The eggs are bluish white, spotted and blotched with red. The sexes are alike.

WILLOW WARBLER, Willow Wren, Willow-Biter, Peggy Whitethroat, Banty-Jug, Tom Thumb, Willie Muftie, Sallypecker, Pettichaps or Grass Mumruffin. Length, 4¼ inches.

A slender, graceful, greenish-yellow little bird, glimpsed momentarily among the boughs unfolding their spring buds, will be one of the three 'leaf warblers'. They are easily confused: the CHIFF-CHAFF is usually slightly browner than the willow-warbler, and has black legs, while those of the willow-warbler are light brown. The WOOD-WARBLER is brighter and yellower than the other two, and has much longer wings: he is, moreover, a bird of the woods and is unlikely to be seen in a garden. But all of them keep closely to the trees, and only occasionally is their jerky, flitting flight visible as they pass from one tree to another. Sometimes they will make an aerial pounce on a passing insect, or hover to investigate the under-surface of the leaves. The best way to distinguish between the chiff-chaff and the

337

willow-warbler is by their song. The *chiff-chaff-chaff-chaff-chiff-chiff-chaff-chaff* of the former is unmistakable; and so will soon be the song of the willow-warbler to anyone with half an ear. It is a tender, lyrical, simple song and has a dying fall, so sweet, so sad, that even in its beginning one is reminded of its end. The chiff-chaff is the earliest of these summer visitors from Africa, arriving in March, but the willow-warbler's song is not normally heard until the middle of April. The nest of the willow-warbler is usually built on the ground among grass, at the foot of a tree or by a path or hedgerow. Moss, grasses, stalks and dead leaves are neatly interwoven to form a domed nest with a side entrance and a cosy lining of feathers. The eggs are white blotched with red. There are several other warblers whose joyous recognition of mate and kingdom gladden any garden. The BLACKCAP'S is one of the loveliest songs, a rich, liquid jet of melody. The tone resembles the blackbird's, but the utterance is very rapid and much more confident. The song will probably be heard from the depths of some dense shrubbery at the bottom of the garden. The black cap of the male and the rich chestnut cap of the hen bird will distinguish them at sight

338

from other warblers. The song of the GARDEN WARB-
LER is very like that of the blackcap, but more breathless and
not so rich in tone; and the bird himself is not unlike a plump
blackcap without the cap. The WHITETHROAT, unlike
the other warblers, will often go out of his way to advertise
his presence: he is a great scold at any passer-by. The
boundary hedge will be the place to look for him. From here
he may suddenly shoot into the air, to descend with open
wings in song – a brisk, cheerful but often rather unmelo-
dious song of varying quality. The NIGHTINGALE is
not properly a bird of the garden, but a large garden with a
thick copse and plenty of tangled undergrowth on the out-
skirts could easily harbour a nightingale.

SWALLOW. Length, 7½ inches.

HOUSE MARTIN, Easing Swallow or Martlet. Length,
5 inches.
The swallow leads a double life, his own and a symbolic one
in human imagination. Not the voices of all the warblers that
announce the spring can evoke its presence and banish winter
so surely as the sight of the first swallow. His habits are so
universally known as to need no description, but the song,
delivered in full air or from a gable, stump, telegraph wire,
or coign of vantage, is, though a very abundant music, less
familiar. When the swallow sings from a perch, he will

339

often conclude his warm, warbling stave by rattling the mandibles in a self-appreciative clap.

The first swallows arrive on our coasts towards the end of March, but the first clutch of from four to six white eggs, freckled with reddish brown and grey, is rarely laid before early May, though the nesting season may continue until October. The beam or joist of a barn is a favourite site, and the saucer of mud is lined with grass and feathers. Old hats, shrimp-pots on shelves, and even boughs of trees may also become homes for the swallow.

He is a far more brilliantly coloured bird than the house-martin, wearing a many-coloured dress of steel-blue above with a rich chestnut on the throat and forehead, a band of blue across the chest, buff underparts and a greenish gloss on the wings and tail.

The easiest way to tell a house-martin from a swallow when they are in flight is by the conspicuous white rump of the house-martin. His underparts are also white, and his back, wings and tail are black – but these details are not so noticeable in the air. Another identifying mark is the tail, which is short and forked and lacks the streamers of the swallow. It is the house-martin which builds the enclosed mud nest under the eaves of the house, but it is extraordinary how many people refer to this familiar spectacle as a swallow's nest. Both sexes assist in its construction, but work is often interrupted for a playful interchange of billing at the edge of the muddy cup or to quarrel with a sparrow who may be attempting to take over the unfinished nest for his own use. House-martins are sociable birds and often nest together in considerable numbers. The eggs, usually four or five, are white. The first clutch is not laid until early June, but it is often followed by another two, and sometimes the last late nestlings are left to starve while the parents gather for their return flight to Africa.

STARLING, Stare, Sterlin, Chepster or Jacob. Length, $8\frac{1}{2}$ inches.

The starling, a bird belonging everywhere, and especially to buildings, presents on first acquaintance a rough-and-ready manner and hobbledehoy appearance. Only at close view and in the spring can his iridescent coat be seen, the feathers of a beaten-out metallic gleam throwing a lustre of black, purple,

blue and green reflections changing colour at different angles
and in striking tone with the lemon yellow of his bill. In
autumn the tipping of the feathers with buff and white dulls
their brilliance. His morning and evening song, time-keeper
of the dawning and failing light, for all its hotch-potch of
melodious and instrumental sound, its squealings, whistl-
ings, chatterings, clickings, smackings and bubblings, for all
its casual mimicries, has a very beautiful and moving effect,
especially when uttered in chorus. The autumn flocking of
the starling is one of the seven wonders of Britain. Along
well-defined lines, starting sometimes from as far as thirty
miles from their roost, thousands, and in favourable places

341

hundreds of thousands, of birds converge in swift, direct flight and perform as one bird a number of rapidly changing figures on rapid triangular wings. Then as the dusk thickens they fall like hail upon trees or buildings or reed and osier beds and burst into a shrill massive chanting.

On the ground the starling walks with bustling, jerky gait, and often runs. The nest is built in a cavity in a tree, cliff, water-spout, chimney, haystack, ruin, barn, quarry or spire, and is a mere litter of straw, twigs and grass, lined with soft substances. The eggs are pale blue and from four to seven in number. The female is more spotted than the male.

CUCKOO, or Gowk. Length, 13 inches.

This famed and enigmatic bird looks on the wing something like a disconsolate hawk, and his flight, though powerful, is at times uncertain in direction and unsteady in poise. Poetic associations have invested the male cuckoo with a symbolic

342

romance as the messenger of spring, on account of the soft flute-like major third of his call, first heard on his arrival in mid-April. But scientific interest centres in the female, who diverges from avian custom in her promiscuous mating and in her habit of depositing her eggs in the nests of pipits, wagtails, robins, dunnocks and various warblers, at the same time removing one of the eggs from the chosen nest in her bill. The nestling, a very ill-conditioned young oaf, has an irritant surface to the hollow of the back which enables it to pitch the other inmates out of the nest on to the ground, where they perish.

The 'song' of the male cuckoo needs no description: the female employs a bubbling cry rather like water poured out of the neck of a bottle, and a strange howling note. Occasionally one bird will use both calls. On the ground the cuckoo is a clumsy, waddling walker. Both sexes are very greedy and irritable. Five or six eggs are laid at intervals of several days between each egg, and though these are often similar in size and colouring to those of the species victimized, there is no evidence that the cuckoo deliberately chooses a clutch to match the eggs she lays. Even more curious than the behaviour of the cuckoo is the apparent willingness of the foster-parents to play the role assigned to them without a hitch. It has been suggested that the young cuckoo has a mesmeric power in its voice. Another point of interest is that the old birds depart for Africa a month or six weeks earlier than the young.

The sexes are alike in their handsome plumage, bluish-grey above, lighter on the neck and breast and darker on the wings and tail, whitish on the underparts with dark transverse bars. The long, rounded tail is spotted and tipped with white. The feet are yellow and the inside of the mouth is orange.

GREEN WOODPECKER, Yaffle, Rain-Bird, Woodall, Woodspite, High-Hoe, Hew-Hole, or Pick-a-Tree. Length, 12½ inches.

It is difficult to believe in the green woodpecker as an English bird, what with his bold tropical colouring, so foreign to the subdued tones of our landscape, his piercing cry, his oddly demoniac appearance, and his superlative animation. The green woodpecker, digging his trunk-dwelling, will be heard

over the length and breadth of the land, and his movements seem to match that blithe laugh which, for those who love him, makes him the bird of liberty.

This indeed is true in fact as well as impression, for the yaffle displays his independence by being one day a bird of the woodlands, flying in huge drooping loops and crests among the pillars of the trees to seek his food from their bark and branches; and the next a bird of the open spaces, getting his livelihood entirely from ants' nests on the ground. As an instance of this change of habit, due in part to the increasing scarcity of old timber, the green woodpecker is heard nowadays in open parkland and the margins of meadow and woodland as much as in deep woods, and often he is to be seen in gardens, where he will sit bolt upright on the lawn, stooping to plunge his dagger of a beak up to the hilt again and again into the ground in his fanatical quest for ants.

344

The nest is hammered out of a trunk that has begun to decay, though it often gives no visible sign of it. Chips of wood are laid on the floor of the hole as a bedding, and five to seven polished oval white eggs are laid upon them. The bird's colours are disposed in an abrupt and sharply contrasted manner. His face is black, his crown, moustaches and back of the head are crimson, his rump is bright yellow, his wings have the outer webs barred black and white, his back is olive green, and his underparts run to green with an infusion of yellow. The sexes are alike, except that the female lacks the crimson in the moustachial stripe.

BARN OWL, Billy Wix, Cherubim, Gilly Howlet, Oolert or Jenny Owl. Length, $13\frac{1}{2}$ inches.

Many misconceptions of the nature and behaviour of birds have originated in the poetic imagination. Just as the nightingale has been inescapably branded as the broken hearted lover who sings only at night, so has the owl come to symbolise death and disaster and the darker side of witchcraft. A bird that passes invisibly on silent wings and wakes the sleeping world with an unearthly voice must expect to be misunderstood to some extent by the ignorant populace; but the poets have certainly made matters worse by referring to him as 'the rude bird of hate', the 'gibbering', 'baleful', 'deadlie', 'ghastly owle', the 'bird of omen dark and foul'. Even the most desperate need of a rhyme cannot excuse that last epithet.

Of the three common species, the one most likely to be seen from the garden is the barn owl, which has a partiality for the vicinity of human habitations. As dusk softens the outline of landscape, his pale and ghostly form will materialise suddenly in silent wavering flight like some enormous nocturnal butterfly. It is his habit to quarter the ground systematically, flying some ten to twenty feet above it, in search of the rats, mice, voles, and shrews on which he feeds. He will also take small birds, particularly house-sparrows, from the ivy where they roost. He is indeed a useful ally to the farmer, who in former days recognised this when he built a barn by always leaving for the owl an opening high in the barn wall.

The barn owl's voice, a weirdly horrible shriek, together with the loud hissing and snoring noises with which he finds it necessary to express his feelings, do not prepare one for the beauty of his person. He is the loveliest of owls, with his flat white heart-shaped face and large black eyes, his satin-white underparts and orange-buff back spotted with grey and white. The barn owl makes no nest, but will lay four to seven matt white eggs on a layer of dry pellets (of the un-digested bones and fur which are regurgitated by all owls), among the rafters of a house, or in a barn or belfry, or a church tower or dovecote or in any ruined or unoccupied building. The eggs are laid at intervals of several days but are incubated from the start, so that a nest will contain young of varying ages and sometimes eggs at the same time.

The T A W N Y O W L , although mainly a bird of the woods, is also often heard in the garden. Heard, but seldom seen, for he is a thoroughly nocturnal species. His melodious *hoo-hoo-*

hoo . . . oo . . . hoooooooooooo is the familiar hoot which many
people wrongly attribute to any and every owl. The L I T T L E
O W L is much more a bird of agricultural country, and can
sometimes be seen during the day sitting on a post or fence
or telegraph wire.

' W E E K - E N D I N G '   B I R D S

Apart from the common and not-so-common birds which
can be expected in their own habitual environments, there is
always the tantalising possibility for a Birdwatcher of spotting a distinguished casual visitor from the Continent, from
Greenland or Iceland or even from America. These transient,
'week-ending' birds, some of them drifting with unfavour-
able winds, or perhaps deficient in that magnetic sense of
direction which guides a migratory bird from one latitude to
another, turn up from time to time in any and every corner
of the country. Their appearance marks the red-letter days
of the Birdwatcher's calendar. The following are a few of the
more conspicuous among them.

H O O P O E or Dung Bird. Length, 11 inches: slightly larger
than a mistle-thrush.

This spectacular bird – which possesses the splendid Latin
name of *Upupa epops epops* – is one of the most regular
'week-enders' from the Continent and has visited most parts
of the British Isles at some time or other, even in winter. In
fact, several times he has stayed on to nest in the southern
counties, and he would undoubtedly become one of the
regular British breeding birds if allowed to do so. But the
Hoopoe is tame to the point of stupidity and an easy prey to
the man with a gun. His plumage is pinkish cinnamon
brown, with boldly barred black and white wings, and a
striking crest tipped with black which, when erected, gives
the bird the appearance of a Red Indian brave. His diet consists of the larvæ of insects, worms, woodlice, ants and
beetles, and he is often seen probing for these with his long
curved bill on lawns and manure heaps.

This exploratory operation, carried out with the head bob-
bing up and down in a rather portentous way, accounts perhaps for the superstitious awe in which 'The Doctor Bird'
was held by the Arabs. They believed that it possessed remarkable medical qualities and also that it had the power of

347

water-divining. Its head was once in great demand as a charm and in the practice of witchcraft.

BEE-EATER or Gnat Snapper. Length, 11 inches: slightly larger than a mistle-thrush.

The bee-eater summers in southern Europe and winters in Africa, and it is hard to understand what attraction an English summer could hold for such a bird. But he is obviously of a wandering and adventurous disposition, for he has appeared at irregular intervals in all the south and east coast counties, usually in small parties. When the weather is fine he spends much time on the wing hawking for insects, and often perches on telegraph wires. This is one of the most gorgeously attired of our 'week-enders': the back is a rich chestnut-brown and yellow, the tail and wings and underparts are metallic green and blue, the throat is brilliant yellow. The middle tail feathers project well beyond the others, and this feature makes the bird easy to identify in flight. The beak is long and curved. The bee-eater really does eat bees, and he will even perch outside a hive and eat the bees as they emerge.

GOLDEN ORIOLE or Golden Thrush. Length, 9½ inches: midway between a blackbird and a song thrush.

This dazzling visitor is more often heard than seen, though once seen the male oriole is easily recognised and is not easily forgotten. But he is of a shy and exceedingly secretive disposition, and were it not for his unmistakable loud clear musical call (which sounds rather like *We'll owe it you*), his week-ends would often pass undetected in the depths of his aroboreal hotel. The oriole is essentially a bird of the trees, and is seldom seen in the open or on the ground. The male is brilliantly yellow, with black wings and a black tail patterned in yellow; the hen bird is greener, and might be confused with a green woodpecker. The oriole usually visits England in the spring, coming from the Continent. Very occasionally he stays to nest. He is usually seen in parks, old gardens, woods and copses. He eats mainly insects in spring, taking cockchafers, grasshoppers, humble-bees and spiders; but in autumn he is a great fruit-eater, and enjoys mulberries, grapes, figs and every sort of berry.

GREAT GREY SHRIKE, Great Butcher-Bird, Murdering Pie, or Mattagess. Length, 9½ inches: midway between a blackbird and a song thrush.

In contrast to the exotic appearance of the last three visitors, the great grey shrike strikes a somewhat sinister note, with his grey head and back, black and white wings and tail, whitish breast and bold black eye-patch. But this lonely butcher-bird is, nevertheless, a conspicuous and easily identified figure as he stands sentinel on his watch tower of telegraph-wire or tree-top, waiting to pounce on a meal of other bird, mouse or insect. The shrike perches upright, rather like a hawk; and, again hawk-like, hovers over his selected prey before the final pounce. And like all shrikes, the great grey uses a larder of thorn-twig or barb of wire-railing on which to impale and dismember his victim; and often the rapacious bird kills and suspends more than he can use, leaving the bodies to decay. The great grey shrike is an inhabitant of northern and eastern Europe and visits Britain regularly, usually in autumn and winter.

SNOWY OWL. Length, 21-26 inches: slightly larger than a buzzard.

On the rare occasions when a snowy owl souths to Britain from his Arctic home it would be difficult not to notice such a large and conspicuous stranger, for the almost white plumage which camouflages his activities in Greenland, Northern Scandinavia and North Russia, in this country renders him visible, literally, a mile off. He is, moreover, a bird of open country, and hunts by day. He usually perches on the ground, preferably on a rock or log, and seldom on anything higher than twenty feet. He is seen most often in the north of Scotland and the Scottish islands, but has also been reported from a number of English counties. The snowy owl arrives here for a long 'week-end' when food in the Arctic is scarce. His diet while in Britain consists of rabbits, mice, insects and small birds. In the far north he is said also to be an experienced fisherman.

OSPREY, Fish Hawk or Mullett Hawk. Length, 20-23 inches: about the same as a herring gull.

'And the Lord spake unto Moses and to Aaron, saying unto them, Speak unto the children of Israel, saying . . . these are they which ye shall have in abomination among the fowls; they shall not be eaten, they are an abomination.' The unfortunate osprey was third on this list of nineteen prohibited birds.

It was not for this reason, however, that he was exterminated as a British resident (the last Scottish eyrie was deserted in 1911), but because jealous fishermen and game preservers grudged his fishy diet, and eager gunners finished him off as he grew more scarce. Now the osprey is a rare but regular 'week-ender' from Scandinavia to the coastal and inland waters of most parts of England and Scotland. The fish hawk is a handsome bird: dark brown above, except for the white head, slightly crested, with a conspicuous black cheek stripe; and snowy white beneath, with dusky breast-band. The wings are narrow, long and angled. When fishing, the osprey sails about thirty feet above the water, frequently hovering like a kestrel before plunging, feet first, on to his prey. The captive fish – trout, bream, perch, roach, carp or grey mullet – is then carried, head foremost in the talons.

BIRDS IN COMPANIES

A sege of herons and bitterns.

A herd of swans, cranes and curlews.

A dopping of sheldrakes.

A spring of teals.

A covert of coots.

A gaggle of geese.

A skein of geese (flying).

A bevy of quails.

A covey of partridges.

A congregation of plovers.

A walk (or wisp) of snipe.

A fall of woodcocks.

A murmuration of starlings.

An exaltation of larks.

A watch of nightingales.

A badelynge of ducks.

A sord (or sute) of mallards.

A muster of peacocks.

A flight of doves and swallows.

A building of rooks.

A brood of hens.

A host of sparrows.

A nye of pheasants.

A cast of hawks.

A plump of wildfowl.

A desert of lapwings.

A company of widgeon.

A chattering of choughs.

BEASTS ALSO IN COMPANIES

A pride of lions.

A lepe of leopards.

A herd of harts, bucks and all sorts of deer.

A bevy of roes.

A sloth of bears.

A singular of boars.

A sownder of wild swine.

A dryft of tame swine.

A route of wolves.

A harras of horses.

A rag of colts.

A stud of mares.

A pace of asses.

A baren of mules.

A flock of sheep.

A tribe of goats.

A sculk of foxes.

A cete of badgers.

A richesse of martens.

A fesynes of ferrets.

A huske (or down) of hares.

A dule of turtle.

A nest of rabbits.

A clowder of cats.

A kendel of young cats.

A shrewdness of apes.

A labour of moles.

A mute of hounds.

A cowardice of curs.

A drove of kine.

351

STARSHINE AT NIGHT

The pride of the height, the clear firmament, the beauty of heaven, with his
glorious shew.

Ecclesiasticus.

Night of South winds – night of the few
large stars!

Walt Whitman.

I stood and stared; the sky was lit,
The sky was stars all over it,
I stood, I knew not why,
Without a wish, without a will,
I stood upon that silent hill
And stared into the sky until
My eyes were blind with stars and still
I stared into the sky.

Ralph Hodgson.

the pride of the height, the clear firmament,

starshine at Night

ISTI MIRANT STELLA

the beauty of heaven, with his glorious shew.

THE EARTH AND THE MOON

The Earth is grilled by the Sun like a joint on a spit. It returns round and round on its axis, one complete turn taking a time of 24 hours. It is this rotation of the Earth that causes the procession of night and day. It is daytime when we are turned towards the Sun and it is night when we are turned away from the Sun.

In addition to this spinning motion, the Earth also moves along a more or less circular path around the Sun. It takes a year to make a complete circuit of this path and it is this second motion that causes the seasons of the year. Our yearly trip around the Sun also causes the stars that we see in the night sky to change with the seasons. (See star maps on pages 360-367.)

The distance from the Sun to the Earth is about 93,000,000 miles, a vast distance compared with the size of the Earth itself, which is a mere 8,000 miles or so in diameter – or, what comes to the same thing, when viewed on an astronomical scale the Earth is a very tiny body.

We do not travel our yearly journey around the Sun alone. Always accompanying us is our faithful satellite, the Moon. The Moon is another very tiny body, about a quarter of the dimensions of the Earth. Although it is so small the Moon appears a notable object in the night sky because it is very near to us, a mere quarter of a million miles away. The Sun and the Moon appear to the eye to be of about the same size, but this is because the Sun is nearly four hundred times farther away.

In addition to sharing the Earth's motion around the Sun, the Moon possesses a motion of its own, one that takes it

355

round and round the Earth. The Moon completes one circuit of this path in 27⅓ days, which is known as the lunar month. Now because of this monthly motion, the Moon sometimes lies on the sunward side of the Earth, and at other times it lies on the lee side. In the latter case we see the Moon in the night sky and in the former case we see it in the day time. During each lunar month there is a point at which the Moon lies in practically the same direction as the Sun. This is the time of new Moon. There is also a time, about a fortnight later, when the Moon lies in nearly the opposite direction from the Sun. This is the time of full Moon.

The Moon shines because it reflects sunlight, not because it emits light of its own. The well-known phases of the Moon are a property of the reflected sunlight. For a week before and after it is 'new' the Moon is seen as a crescent. For a week before and after full Moon it is seen in its gibbous phases.

The Moon is dotted with largish dark nearly circular patches, patches that are 500 miles or so in diameter. These it is that produce the well-known 'Man in the Moon' appearance. At one time they were thought to be oceans and were given rather fanciful names: *Mare Crisium*, the Sea of Crises; *Mare Tranquillitatis*, the Sea of Tranquillity; *Mare Humorum*, the Sea of Mists; and so on. But we know that they are not oceans for there is no water at all on the Moon. Future travellers to the Moon will have to take their drinks with them.

Being so near to us, the Moon is well situated for telescopic study. Indeed, astronomers can detect objects on the lunar surface that are no larger than St. Paul's Cathedral. Photographs show that the whole surface is pitted with craters large and small. These are thought to be a product of the impact of chunks of material that once struck the Moon. They are the relics of an age-old celestial bombardment, a bombardment that was probably associated with the process in which the Moon itself was formed. The Earth must have suffered a similar, or even a greater, bombardment, but the terrestrial scars have long since disappeared through the erosive action of wind and water. As we have already remarked, there is no water on the Moon, and there is no atmosphere either. Because of this the Moon suffers another sort of bombardment, a bombardment of ultra-violet light

356

and X-rays from the Sun, a bombardment against which we are protected by the shielding action of our atmosphere. This second bombardment must cause the surface rocks of the Moon to be powdered and it seems very likely that for this reason the lunar surface is very dusty.

The lack of an atmosphere produces extremes of temperature on the Moon. At midday on the lunar equator your blood would boil. At night time the temperature falls to about – 250°F. and you would be frozen solid. It seems that those people who wish to visit the Moon can be dubbed, appropriately from every point of view, lunatics.

THE PLANETS

Besides the Earth there are eight other planets, five of which can be seen with the unaided eye. Like the Earth the other planets all move around the Sun and they also move along paths that are very nearly circular. Not only this, but the paths all lie in more or less the same plane; that is to say, the whole solar system can be fitted very nearly into one plane. This plane intersects the sky in a line – a line on which all the Planets and the Sun and the Moon lie. You can often see the Moon and two or three Planets in the night sky and indeed you will find that they do lie on a common line.

The four planets nearest the Sun are all small. They are made mainly of rock and iron, and in their order of distance from the Sun they are Mercury, Venus, the Earth and Mars.

MERCURY is the smallest of the planets, not very much larger than the Moon. Because it is so close to the Sun it can only be seen just after sunset or just before sunrise and even then it is a very fleeting object, as indeed its name implies. Yet if you are fortunate, and the conditions are just right, and you know just when and where to look, it is not difficult to see.

There is no procession of night and day on Mercury; one half of the planet lies in perpetual day and the other half lies in perpetual night. If you want to consign someone to Hell, send him to Mercury. It doesn't matter whether you want the hot Hell of the Mediterranean and near-Eastern religions, or the cold Hell of the Nordic peoples, Mercury has got them both.

VENUS, the next planet, is practically a twin sister of the Earth, although as befits a sister she is a little smaller than

357

the Earth. Venus wraps herself perpetually in a mantle of white cloud. No one has ever seen through to the underlying surface of the planet. The nature of the clouds of Venus is an astronomical mystery. They do not seem to be made of water like the clouds of our own atmosphere.

M A R S is the first planet beyond the Earth, and is reckoned the only planet except the Earth on which it might be possible for life to exist. From time to time greenish markings appear on Mars and it is a matter for speculation whether they arise from the growth of plants. Some astronomers think that they do.

The next four planets differ enormously from the four inner planets. They are much bigger and they are made of quite different materials. They seem to contain very little rock and iron but great quantities of water, ammonia, methane and possibly neon, while Jupiter and Saturn, but not Uranus and Neptune, contain enormous quantities of hydrogen. These are all planets highly hostile to life.

J U P I T E R is the largest of all the planets and like both Venus and Mars it is a notable object when seen in the night sky. It has twelve satellites that move around it. S A T U R N , the next planet in order of size, has nine satellites and is, in addition, surrounded by a beautiful system of rings composed, it is thought, of fine particles of ice.

U R A N U S and N E P T U N E are considerably smaller than Saturn but are still very much larger than the Earth. Because of their great distance from the Sun, they cannot be seen with the unaided eye. Beyond them lies the last planet of the solar system, the little Pluto. P L U T O is not a member of the family of great planets. It is small like the four inner ones. Indeed it is thought by some astronomers to be no more than a satellite that at one time succeeded in escaping from the influence of Neptune.

When seen through a telescope the two largest planets, Jupiter and Saturn, are easily the most striking. They show wonderful variations of colour. Jupiter is rich in reds and browns with an occasional olive green. Saturn has a brilliant yellowish zone near the equator and darkish caps of a greenish hue at its poles. Uranus shows red, orange and green tints, but Uranus is too far away and appears too small to be really impressive even when seen in a large telescope. Neptune also is too small to be really noteworthy. It appears as a small green object, rather like a little shrunken apple.

Of the four inner planets Venus appears a dazzling white, Mars derives its name from its pronouncedly red colour, while we can only guess at what the Earth must look like. Probably the Earth is the jewel of the solar system with an amazing variety of colour: white from the clouds; light green from growing crops; darker greens from the forests; reds, browns and yellows from the deserts; the flashing white of the polar ice caps, and the sombre dark tones of the oceans, except perhaps where here and there a brilliant flash of sunlight happens to be reflected from the surface of the water. When seen from afar off, the delicate rich colouring of the Earth must be in a truly strange contrast with the dull sterile surface of the Moon.

To get an idea of relative sizes in the solar system, imagine the Sun to be the size of a football. Then Mercury would be a speck of dust some 15 yards away from the Sun, Venus would be another speck 25 yards away; the Earth 35 yards away, Mars 55 yards away; Jupiter would be a little pea about 190 yards away; Saturn 350 yards; Uranus about 700 yards; Neptune over 1,000 yards; and Pluto very nearly a mile. There is plenty of space inside the solar system.

THE CONSTELLATIONS

We lie inside a vast aggregate of stars. Most of them are so far away that you can't see them at all with the naked eye. It is only the very nearest of the stars that show up at all notably. There is nothing special about the way that they are distributed over the sky. This was not understood by the astrologers of the ancient world, who sought to relate the stars to human experience. Attempts were made to associate groups of stars with animals and people. The stars in one patch of the sky became Draco, the dragon; another became Leo, the lion; Pisces, the fish; Ursa Major, the great bear; Orion, the hunter; Andromeda, after the heroine of ancient legend; and other such picturesque names. These imaginary associations became known as the constellations. They are still retained as appellations in modern astronomy in spite of their complete lack of physical significance, because it is often convenient to have a rough and ready way of referring to various parts of the sky.

M
359

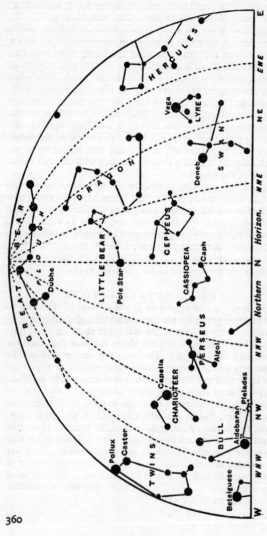

Position correct for April 7 at 11 p.m. and for four minutes earlier on each succeeding night.

360

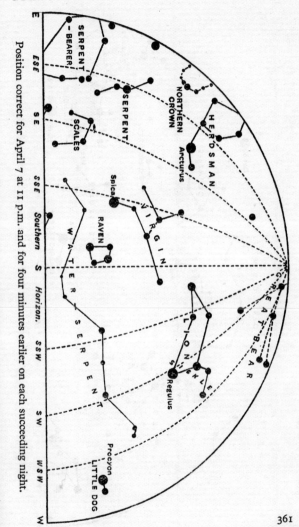

Position correct for April 7 at 11 p.m. and for four minutes earlier on each succeeding night.

E
ESE
SE
SSE
Southern
S
Horizon.
SSW
SW
WSW
W

SERPENT-BEARER
SERPENT
SCALES
NORTHERN CROWN
HERDSMAN
Arcturus
Spica
VIRGIN
RAVEN
WATER SERPENT
LION
SICKLE
Regulus
GREAT BEAR
Procyon
LITTLE DOG

361

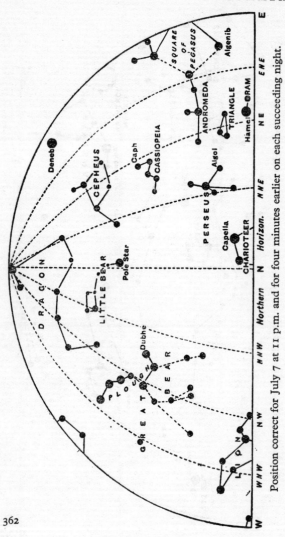

SUMMER

Position correct for July 7 at 11 p.m. and for four minutes earlier on each succeeding night.

362

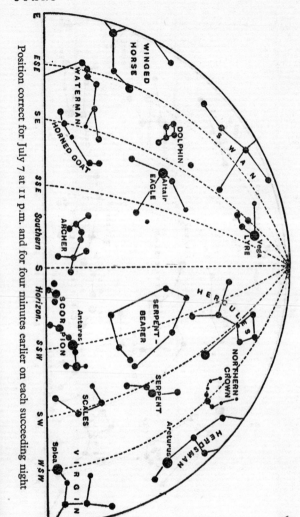

Position correct for July 7 at 11 p.m. and for four minutes earlier on each succeeding night

E
ESE
SE
SSE
Southern S
Horizon. SSW
SW
WSW
W

WINGED HORSE
WATERMAN
HORNED GOAT
DOLPHIN
EAGLE Altair
SWAN
LYRE Vega
ARCHER
HERCULES
SERPENT-BEARER
SCORPION Antares
NORTHERN CROWN
SERPENT
SCALES
Arcturus
HERDSMAN
VIRGIN
Spica

363

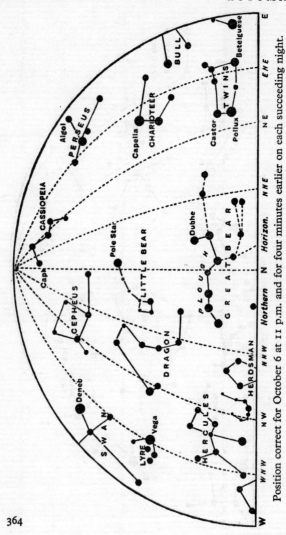

Position correct for October 6 at 11 p.m. and for four minutes earlier on each succeeding night.

364

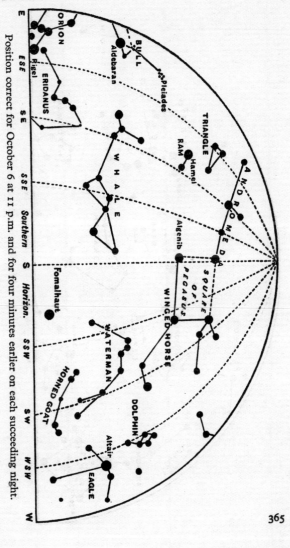

Position correct for October 6 at 11 p.m. and for four minutes earlier on each succeeding night.

365

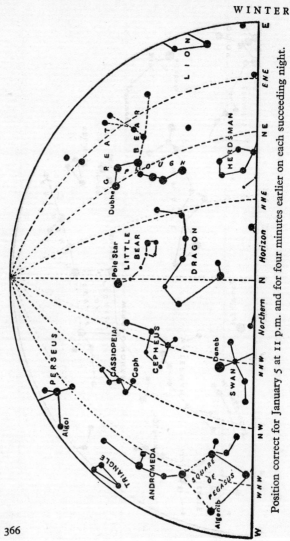

WINTER

Position correct for January 5 at 11 p.m. and for four minutes earlier on each succeeding night.

366

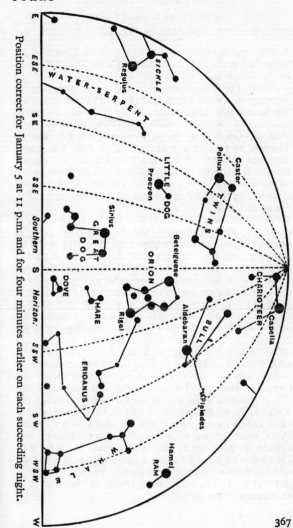

Position correct for January 5 at 11 p.m. and for four minutes earlier on each succeeding night.

E

ESE

SE

WATER-SERPENT

SSE

Regulus

SICKLE

Castor

Pollux

LITTLE DOG

TWINS

Precyon

Sirius

GREAT DOG

Betelguese

Southern

ORION

S

Horizon:

DOVE

Rigel

HARE

Aldebaran

CHARIOTEER

Capella

SSW

BULL

ERIDANUS

Pleiades

SW

Hamel

WSW

WHALE

RAM

W

367

NIGHT SKY IN SPRING
(*See* Map, pp. 360, 361)

At this time of year URSA MAJOR or the Plough or the
Great Bear or the Dipper or Charles's Wain (or the Waggon,
as the Babylonians called this constellation) shines right
overhead. The arrangement of its seven bright stars suggests
the shape of a ploughshare, and the countryman knows the
minute one close to the central of the three which form its
handle, as 'Jack by the middle horse.' The two stars which
bind the Great Bear on its north-western side are the
'Pointers' to STELLA POLARIS, the Pole Star, which
forms the nether tip of URSA MINOR's tail. Though the
Persians said of this, the most constant among the stars and
the pivot of their whole population, that 'it held all the constellations by the hand', it is, to our eyes, the least impressive
among its fellows.

To the south-east of the Great Bear lies the constellation of
BOÖTES, the 'Keeper of the Bear', whose glory is
ARCTURUS, the seventh brightest star in all the sky. The
glittering semi-circle to the east of Arcturus is CORONA
BOREALIS – the Northern Crown, and another brilliance
to the west of Arcturus and south-west of the Great Bear
is REGULUS, the southernmost luminary of the constel-
lation of LEO. Yet another star of the first magnitude is
VEGA, the fourth brightest in the heavens, gleaming blue
in the constellation of LYRA and almost directly east of the
Pole Star. South of the Great Bear, beyond Leo, is the con-
stellation VIRGO, conspicuous only for the star SPICA,
while LIBRA, a little to the east, lacks any dominant stars.
Not so subdued are CASTOR AND POLLUX, the
Gemini or Heavenly Twins of a religion far older than the
Greek, gleaming to the west of the Great Bear. Beyond the
Twins to the south-west is CANIS MINOR, containing
PROCYON as its pride, the eighth brightest among the stars.
Other constellations visible near the north-eastern and
western horizons are in the order named – CYGNUS,
ANDROMEDA, CASSIOPEIA – the great W stretched
world-beyond-worlds across the sky – PERSEUS, AURIGA
and TAURUS. The Milky Way, low in the heavens, is at
its dimmest in the spring.

THE SUMMER SKY
(*See* Map, pp. 362, 363)

V E G A is the guiding star in the summer sky and shines almost directly overhead. But the splendour of the firmament in mid-year is the Milky Way, now flowing across the middle of the heavenly vault from north to south. The constellation of C Y G N U S , a little to the north-east of Vega, marks the point where the starry river splits into two great streams. In the cleft of the northern stream is the constellation of A Q U I L A , dominated by A L T A I R , the eleventh brightest star. The course of the Milky Way flows on south-westward to the constellation of S C O R P I O , near the horizon, with its sickle-shaped row of stars and A N T A R E S , glowing red, to form the eastern beacon. C A S S I O P E I A lies in the north-eastern reach of the Milky Way between two stars of the first magnitude – C A P E L L A in Auriga and D E N E B in Cygnus – to the north and south of it. Nearer to the north-eastern horizon are P E R S E U S and A N D R O M E D A . A R C T U R U S , being nearer to the zenith, is at its greatest brilliance in the summer sky. Between Lyra and the Corona Borealis, which have shifted their spring positions from E.N.E. to S.S.W., lies the constellation of H E R C U L E S .

THE AUTUMN SKY
(*See* Map, pp. 364, 365)

The square constellation of P E G A S U S , almost overhead, is a convenient landmark for observing the autumn sky. In its north-eastern corner is the Great Nebula of A N D R O - M E D A , just visible to the eye. By now the Milky Way has made an immense curve across the sky-world until it lies almost due west and east, with Cassiopeia as its central constellation a little to the north of the zenith. The most prominent stars of the autumn sky are Vega, Alpha Cygni or Deneb, and Capella, south-east of which are the P L E I A D E S . Below the Pleiades flames the great star A L D E B A R A N , the eye of T A U R U S the Bull. Now for the first time in the year the constellation of O R I O N , with S I R I U S , the brightest star in all heaven, comes into view low above the southern horizon,

369

THE WINTER SKY
(*See* Map, pp. 366, 367)

CAPELLA, the golden star in Auriga, is near the zenith of the winter sky and the Milky Way has swung round to its fourth quarterly position spanning the heavens from north to south and separating the Gemini, Procyon, Lyra and the Great and Little Bears from Canis Major, Orion, Taurus Andromeda and Perseus.

The constellation of Taurus with its fiery red Aldebaran hangs from a branch of the V-shaped cluster of the HYADES (neighbours of the Pleiades), in which the brightest is ALCYONE, once thought to be the central star of the universe. ORION, with its jewelled belt, is the chiefest **glory** of the winter sky. Hanging in the south, a tremendous question mark thrown out upon so vast a canvas, this 'burning rhetoric' across the heavens has stirred the awe of countless generations of watchers.

East of Orion is Canis Major, containing SIRIUS, the first heavenly light to draw the speculations of the human mind and fix the divisions of the calendar.

STARS, GALAXIES, AND THE UNIVERSE

The number of stars that you can separately distinguish with the unaided eye is surprisingly few, only two or three thousand. Yet with even a small telescope millions of stars can be seen and with a large telescope the number rises to many thousands of millions. The naked-eye stars are found all over the sky. In contrast, the great multitude of telescopic stars are confined to a special strip of the sky – they are found along the Milky Way. It is indeed just the combined light from a huge number of very faint stars – too faint to be seen separately by eye only, that makes the Milky Way appear as a bright band across the sky. Few sights are so impressive as this vast glowing arch seen on a clear moonless night. Unlike the conjuring trick that loses interest as soon as we know how it is done, the night sky actually gains in its impressive qualities (and perhaps even in its romantic qualities) from a knowledge of what it is that we are looking at. We are looking at nothing less than the stage on which the Universe acts out its play.

Some important settings of the stage can be guessed from a casual glance at the sky: for instance, that we live inside a disc-shaped collection of stars. Imagine two dinner plates placed rim to rim so as to enclose a lens-like space between them and imagine that in this space there are a hundred thousand million stars, one of them being our Sun. Then you will have some idea of what the Milky Way is and of why the great majority of stars are found in the band of the Milky Way. When we look at the Milky Way we are looking along the dinner plates; when we look at parts of the sky distant from the Milky Way we are looking outside and away from the plates. To make this a little clearer think of a plate covered by grains of rice and suppose that you are a tiny microcosm attached to one of the grains – as we are attached to the Sun. Then if you look along the plate you will see a multitude of rice, but if you look away from the plate you will see only a few neighbouring grains. This is just the situation with the stars. The ones that we see outside the Milky Way are close neighbours: that is why so many of them seem very bright, because they are comparatively close to us. But when we look along the Milky Way we see a multitude of stars, appearing faint for the most part because they are very much farther away.

371

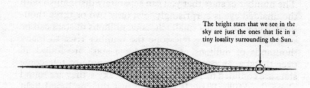

A schematic representation of our Galaxy seen on edge. The shaded area is the space between our dinner plates. It contains about 100,000,000,000 stars

A few words now about distances. Astronomical distances are so vast that it is inconvenient to measure them in miles. Instead the length of the path travelled by light in a year may be used as a distance indicator. Thus it takes light about 60,000 years to travel right across the Milky Way. In each second of time light travels 186,000 miles, so that in 60,000 years the length of its path becomes about 400,000,000,000,-000,000 miles. This is the size that our dinner plates must have.

The Milky Way is usually referred to as our Galaxy, or as *the* Galaxy. The Sun is one of a hundred thousand million stars that make up the Galaxy. Together with its attendant planets (the Earth being one of them) it lies far out from the centre, almost near the edge of the Galaxy. It moves around the centre along a roughly circular path, much as the Earth moves along a roughly circular path around the Sun itself. But whereas the Earth takes only a year to move around the Sun, the Sun (plus planets) takes some 200 million years to move around the centre of the Galaxy. Since the Sun was born about 4,000 million years ago it has done only about 20 trips around the Galaxy. In contrast, since the Earth was born it has done some 3,000 million trips around the Sun. Recently important differences have been discovered between the stars in the central regions of the Galaxy and stars like the Sun that lie away out from the centre. The latter are called Type I stars and the former Type II stars. The great majority of the naked-eye stars are Type I stars, as indeed are most of the stars of the Milky Way that you can distinguish with binoculars or with a small telescope. It needs a large

372

telescope to pick up the vast number of Type II stars located in the central regions of the Galaxy.

As the common run of stars go, the Sun is quite a bright specimen. But it is not by any means the most outstanding member of the stellar company. With increasing rarity, stars are found ten thousand, a hundred thousand, times brighter than the Sun, and the brightest star known is about a million times more luminous than the Sun. Such giants (as they are called) all belong to the Type I group. They are all exceptionally young stars, in some cases no more than a few million years old. In contrast, the Type II stars are all old stars, perhaps some 5 or 6 thousand million years old.

Gas is required to make stars. Stars originate as condensations within great gas clouds that lie along the band of the Milky Way. Since young stars are ones that have condensed recently, it is clear that young stars will be found only in the vicinity of gas clouds, and since most of the gas of the Galaxy is confined to its outer parts – little gas is present in the central regions – this explains why the very bright giants are always situated in the outer regions, never in the centre of the Galaxy. It also explains why only old stars are to be found near the centre.

A notable cloud of gas in which star formation is apparently going on at the present time can just be detected with the naked eye. It appears as a slight fuzziness in the 'sword' of Orion. The gas of this cloud is heated by stars inside it and is thereby set aglow. It is this glow that you see.

Recent observational work on the formation of stars inside gas clouds like the Orion cloud makes it seem likely that the Type I stars are not born singly, one at a time, but in groups. Showers of several hundred stars are formed simultaneously. For the most part the showers are self-dispersive. That is to say, the stars of a particular shower usually spread out from the region of their origin and separate away from each other. But there are exceptions to the general rule.

Occasionally a shower of stars stays together as a cluster instead of dispersing. The Pleiades, a well-known and notable group that you can easily see for yourself, is one such cluster. These remarks apply to the Type I stars. Since the Type II stars are old stars, born long ago, it is not possible to determine the conditions of their birth quite so readily. But it seems likely that the Type II stars also originated in showers

373

– not in showers of a few hundreds at a time, however, but in showers of many thousands of millions at a time. The Type II stars must have been born in a truly gigantic star-making cataclysm.

The degree of compression required to produce a star is very great indeed. A cloud such as the one in Orion probably averages about 1,000 atoms to a cubic centimetre. The material of the Sun averages rather more than 1,000,000,000,000,000, 000,000,000 atoms to the cubic centimetre. Evidently then an enormous condensation of gas must take place in the process of star formation. We require a cloud that is initially very large, perhaps some 10,000,000,000,000 miles in diameter, to shrink down to a diameter of about a million miles, the density within the cloud rising meanwhile to an enormous degree.

Not only does the density rise during the process of star formation but the temperature inside the shrinking cloud rises very considerably too. Eventually temperatures in excess of ten million degrees are attained. A crucially important process is then set up. In the central regions of the cloud the hydrogen of the original gas begins to be very slowly changed into helium. Energy is released by this conversion. Ultimately when the internal temperature has risen high enough, the energy production becomes sufficient to balance the energy that constantly streams out of the cloud and which is radiated away into space from its surface. When this stage of balance is reached the shrinkage of the cloud stops and the birth of the star is complete.

The conversion of hydrogen into helium takes place by nuclear reactions. A star is a gigantic nuclear reactor. Nuclear energy is indeed a corner-stone in the structure of the Universe.

It may be wondered what happens inside a star once all the hydrogen of the inner regions has become converted into helium. While this is a problem that scarcely concerns the Sun – since the Sun has not yet by any means exhausted its inner hydrogen – it is a matter that does concern some stars, particularly stars of great intrinsic brightness, the giants. What happens is that exhaustion of hydrogen leads to a further shrinkage of the innermost parts of the star. This further shrinkage leads to increasing temperatures that eventually become high enough for nuclear energy to be generated from the hitherto inert helium. The helium then becomes largely converted into carbon, oxygen and neon. This happens at a temperature of about a hundred million degrees.

Once the helium becomes exhausted there is a further shrinkage phase that again leads to rising temperatures, causing carbon, oxygen and neon to be changed into sodium, magnesium, aluminium, silicon, phosphorus, sulphur, chlorine, argon, potassium and calcium. This happens at temperatures between five hundred million and two thousand million degrees. At still higher temperatures the material changes mainly into iron, but appreciable quantities of chromium, manganese, cobalt, nickel, copper and zinc are also produced. Deep inside the stars the dreams of the alchemists are completely realised.

When temperatures above five thousand million degrees arise, stars explode with unprecedented violence – the explosion of one star being equivalent to the simultaneous explosion of some 1,000,000,000,000,000,000,000,000,000 hydrogen bombs. The explosions are generated by an instability that develops in the nuclear reactions. Such exploding stars are observed to happen. They are called supernovae.

It is now generally believed that hydrogen is the only primaeval material and that all other elements are produced by nuclear transmutations inside these very hot stars, stars that distribute their contents into space by gigantic supernova explosions. Apparently the iron of the cutlery that we feed ourselves with was once cooked in a star to temperatures of thousands of million degrees. So was the material of the Earth and much of the materials of our own bodies.

We have referred to our Galaxy as a vast plate-shaped aggregate of stars. It was at one time thought that the Galaxy lies alone in space with nothing outside it. This old view is now known to be utterly wrong. Space is populated with other similar great aggregates of stars. With large modern telescopes more than 100,000,000 of these 'galaxies' can be detected. For the most part the galaxies are grouped in clusters. Some clusters are small, containing only two or three main members, while other clusters contain upwards of a thousand large galaxies. Our Galaxy belongs to a small cluster, the so-called 'Local' Group. The Local Group contains two monsters. One is our Galaxy and the other is a galaxy that can be seen by the naked eye, if you know just where to look for it, in the constellation of Andromeda. It shows up as a fairly extensive faint blur of light – faint because it is at the enormous distance of 1,500,000 light years (1 light year = 5,880,000,000,000 miles) away from us. Even so it lies within the Local Group.

The largest modern telescopes can detect galaxies out to a fantastic distance of some 2,000,000,000 light years. The outcome of a telescopic survey of a truly gigantic region of space is easily described – the contents of one bit of space are very like the contents of another bit. The galaxies that inhabit our particular neighbourhood seem very similar to the galaxies that populate the depths of space.

Just as stars are condensations that form within the gas clouds within a galaxy, so the galaxies themselves, and the clusters of galaxies, seem as if they must be condensations that formed within a supergalactic cloud. And since the galaxies are spread through space it seems that the supergalactic cloud from which they formed must also have occupied all space. It must have been (or must still be!) a veritable universal cloud.

To explain how such a universal cloud came into existence is perhaps the most difficult problem in astronomy. Some scientists believe that the whole Universe 'began' about 5 thousand million years ago, and that the universal cloud came into existence at the moment of the origin of the Universe itself. Other scientists reject such a 'beginning' of the Universe. They believe that matter is originating in space all the time – that the universal cloud is constantly being augmented by new matter.

At first sight this latter idea might seem open to the objection that as time goes on space would become more and more crowded with material. This would certainly be the case if the Universe were static, but it is known from astronomical observations that the Universe is not static. The distances between the clusters of galaxies (but not the distances within a cluster) are constantly increasing in a uniform sort of way. That is to say, the speed with which two clusters separate is in direct ratio to the distance between them.

Now if matter were not originating continuously in space this expansion of the Universe would lead to space becoming less and less occupied with matter. Thus we have the following situation: the continuous origin of matter tends to fill space while the expansion tends to empty. it. Might it not be that one effect just balances the other? According to the theories that have recently been developed such an exact balancing does indeed take place. Nor does this turn out to be a fortuitous circumstance but a deep-rooted consequence arising from the expansion being *caused* by the origin of matter. Expansion must keep step with the rate of origin – if by some magic the rate of origin were doubled the rate of expansion would also have to double. In short, the origin of matter apparently forces the Universe to expand at just such a rate that the average density of the material in space remains constant.

This conclusion carries with it an interesting philosophical implication; for if the average density of matter does not change with time, the large-scale features of the Universe will also remain unaltered. This does not mean that individual galaxies will not change – they will. It means that an observer at a random point in space who happened to sleep – not like Rip Van Winkle for a mere twenty years, but for, let us say, ten thousand million years – would not notice much change when he awoke. He would certainly notice changes in the nearby galaxies but he would find it difficult to detect much change in the aspects of comparatively distant galaxies.

The philosophical upshot is that, if the bulk features of the Universe have always been the same as they are now, the necessity for supposing that the Universe came into being at a definite epoch in the past disappears. There is no reason to suppose that the Universe as a whole ever had an origin. An individual aggregation of matter, whether a galaxy or a star or a man must have a definite origin, but we need no longer suppose that there was once a time before which the Universe did not exist and after which it did. Time does not lie outside the Universe.

ROUNDS AND SONGS

Everyone suddenly burst out singing.
Siegfried Sassoon.

Wednesday 23 March (1763). I breakfasted
with Lord Eglinton, who was very good to
me. He said nobody liked me better than he
did. He begun and taught me to sing
catches, of which he was very fond. He gave
me much encouragement, and said that
there were not five people in the whole
Catch Club who had a better ear than I
have.

Boswell.

Come; and come strong,
To the conspiracy of our spacious song.
Richard Crashaw.

Rounds

'Everyone suddenly burst out singing'

SOPHOCLES

Three voices.

by Dr Hayes.

Wind, gentle e — vergreen, to form a shade, A-
round the tomb where So - pho - cles is laid;

Sweet i — vy, bend thy boughs and in-ter-twine With
blush — ing ro - ses and the clust' - ring vine.

Thus shall thy last - ing leaves with beauty hung, Prove
grace - ful em — blems of the lays he sung.

HEY, HO, TO THE GREENWOOD

Canon for three voices.   *by William Byrd.*

Hey, ho --- to the green-wood now let us go, sing

Hey -- ho --- to the green-

Hey -- ho -

heave and ho, And there shall we find both buck and

wood now let us go, sing heave and ho, And there shall we

-- to the green-wood now let us go, sing heave and

doe, sing heave and ho, The hart and

find both bu - ck and doe, sing heave and

ho, And there shall we find both buck and

hind & the little pret - - ty roe, sing heave and ho,

ho, The hart & hind & the little pret - ty roe, sing heave

doe, sing heave and ho, the hart & hind & the little pret-

Hey ho — to the green - wood now

and ho Hey ho, —

— ty roe, sing heave and ho.

GO TO JOAN GLOVER

Four voices.

Go to Joan Glover and tell her I love her, And

at the mid of the morn I will come to her.

MAUDIT SOIS TU, CARILLONNEUR

Five voices.

1. Mau - dit sois tu, ca - ril - lon - neur,

2. Que Dieu cré - a pour mon mal - heur.

3. Dès le point du jour à la cloch' il s'ac - cro - che,

4. Et le soir en - cor' ca - ril - lon - ne plus fort

5. Quand son - ne - ra - t-on la mort du son - neur?

LET'S HAVE A PEAL

Eight voices.

1. Let's *2.* have a *3.* peal for John Cook's *4.* soul. *5.* For he was a ve — ry *6.* hon - est man, *7.* an hon - est *8.* man.

WELL RUNG, TOM

Four voices.

1. Well rung, Tom, boy, well rung, Tom!

2. Ding, dong, cuckoo, well rung, Tom! The

3. owl and the cuckoo, the fool and the song.

4. Well sung, cuc - koo! well rung, Tom!

CALCUTTA

Three voices.

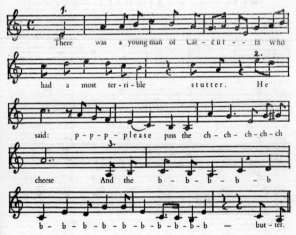

1. There was a young man of Cal - cut - ta who

had a most ter - ri - ble stutter. He

2. said: p - p - p - please pass the ch - ch - ch - ch - ch

3. cheese And the b - b - b - b - b

b - b - b - b - b - b - b - b - b — but - ter.

THE OLD DOG

Three voices.

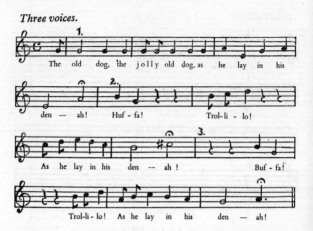

The old dog, the jolly old dog, as he lay in his den — ah! Huf-fa! Trol-li-lo!

As he lay in his den -- ah! Buf-fa!

Trol-li-lo! As he lay in his den — ah!

HEY, HO, WHAT SHALL I SAY?

Nine voices.

Hey, ho! what shall I say? A rogue hath sto-len my purse a — way; It was gone ere I wist, On-ly now it is miss'd; Hey trolly lol-ly lol — lo! Come a-gain ho!

'FIE, NAY, PRITHEE JOHN'

Three voices.   by *Purcell.*

1. 'Fie, nay, pri-thee John, Do not quarrel, man, Let's be mer-ry and drink a — bout.

2. 'You're a rogue, you cheat-ed me, I'll prove be — fore this com — pan — y, I caren't a far-thing, Sir, for all you are so stout.'

3. 'Sir, you lie; I scorn your word or a — ny man that wears a sword, For all your huff, who cares a damn, and who cares for you?

GREAT BIG CLOCKS

Three voices.   *by Karl Karow.*

DONA NOBIS PACEM

Three voices.

VIVA LA MUSICA

Three voices.   *by Praetorius.*

Vi — va, vi — va la Mu — si — ca! Vi — va,

vi — va la Mu — si — ca! Vi — va la Mu — si — ca!

SIGNOR ABBATE

Three voices.   *by Ludwig van Beethoven.*

Signor Ab — ba — te, io so — no, io so — no, io

so — no am — ma — la — to. San — to — Pad — re,

vien' — e da — te mi la be — ne — di — zi

o — ne, la be — ne — di — zi — o — ne.

Hol' Sie der Teu — fel wenn Sie nicht kom — men, Hol' Sie der

Teu — fel wenn Sie nicht kom — men! Hol' Sie der Teu — fel.

SANCTUS

Five voices.   *by Clemens non Papa.*

San — — — ctus, san — — ctus, san — — — — — ctus, San — — ctus

AMARYLLIS

Three voices.

A – dieu sweet A – ma – ryl – lis, For since to part your will is, A – dieu, sweet A — ma — ryl — lis

O, woe – ful — ti — ding,

There is for me no bi — — ding.

Yet once a – gain ere that I part from thee, A — ma – ryl — lis, sweet A – dieu!

JOLLY SHEPHERD

Three voices.

1. Jol - ly shep - herd and up - on a hill as he sate. So loud he blew his lit - tle horn and kept right well his gate.

2. Ear - ly in the morn - ing, late of an even - ing, So loud - ly blew that lit — tle boy so mer - ri - ly pi — ping.

3. Ter - li ter - lo ter - li ter - lo ter - li ter - lo ter - lee ter - li ter - lo ter - li ter - lo ter - li ter - lo ter — lee

GOD SAVE THE KING

Six voices.

God save the King, long live the King.

May the King live, may the King live for

e — ver and e-ver. A — — men.

SLAVES TO THE WORLD

Three voices. *by E. Nelham.*

Slaves to the world should be tossed in a blan—ket

If I might have my will,

Like to the wheel that turn—eth round So

fast on yon-der hill, And fall——eth

down a—gain and down a—gain, The

ground it touch un—til.

GREAT TOM

Three voices.

by Henry Lawes.

Great Tom is cast, and Christ Church bells ring

1, 2, 3, 4, 5, 6, and Tom comes last.,

MUSING

Four voices.

tone Mus — ing, mus — ing, mus — ing, mine

own self all a — lone, I heard a maid, I

heard a maid, I heard a maid mak-

ing great moan, With sobs and sighs and

man — y a griev — ous groan, Wail — ing

wail — ing her love in sad and piteous

393

HOT MUTTON PIES, HOT

Three voices.

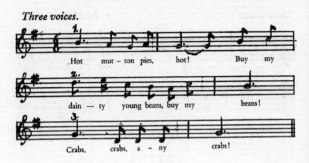

Hot mut-ton pies, hot! Buy my

dain—ty young beans, buy my beans!

Crabs, crabs, a-ny crabs!

SHE WEEPETH SORE IN THE NIGHT

Four voices.   *by William Lawes.*

She weep-eth sore in the night, And her

tears are on her cheeks;— Her priests sigh

—and her vir-gins are af-flict-ed and a-mong

all her lov-ers she—hath—none to comfort her.

NON NOBIS DOMINE

Canon for three voices.   *by William Byrd.*

Non no-bis Do-mi-ne non no — bis; sed

Non no-bis Do-mi-ne, non no — bis;

Non no-bis Do-mi-ne, non

no-mi-ni tu — o da glo-ri-am; sed no-mi-ni

sed no-mi-ni tu — o da glo-ri-am; sed

no — bis; sed no-mi-ni tu — o da glo-ri-

tu — o da glo-ri-am. Non no-bis Do-mi-

no-mi-ni tu — o da glo-ri-am. Non no-bis

-am; sed no-mi-ni tu — o da glo-ri-am.

SUMER IS ICUMEN IN

Three or four voices and two basses.

Sum-er is i—cu-men in—— Lhu-de sing cuc-
cu Grow-eth sed, And blow-eth med, And
spring'th the wd-e nu. Sing cuc——cu.
Aw—e blet-eth af—ter lomb, Lhouth af—ter cal—ve
cu, Bul—luc ster-teth Buck-e vert—eth,
Mu—rie sing cu-cu, cu——cu,—cuc-cu, Wel
sing—es thu cu-cu Ne——swik thu na-ver nu;

These four bars are repeated ad infinitum by two male voices:

cuc—cu, cuc—cu, cuc——cu, cuc—cu—

* *The second, third and fourth voices enter in turn at this point.*

396

THE NIGHTINGALE

Three voices.

The night - in - gale, the mer - ry night - in - gale, She sweet — ly sits and sings, and sings. The pret - ty nim - ble doe doth trip it to and fro; The wild horse kicks and flings and flings; The cuck — oo she doth fly from tree to tree, And mer - ri '- ly through the woods 'Cuckoo, cuckoo!' rings.

AND THE SWAN SANG

Four voices.

And the swan sang te — re — li — o - te — re — li — o, te — re — li — o.

O ABSALOM

Three voices.   *by Henry Lawes.*

O 'Ab - sa - lom, O Absa-lom my son, my son,

Ab - sa - lom! O Ab - sa - lom, my son, my son,

O Ab - sa - lom, my son, my son, would God I had died, would

God I had died, would God I had died for thee!

SCHLAF UND TOD

Four voices.   *by Haydn.*

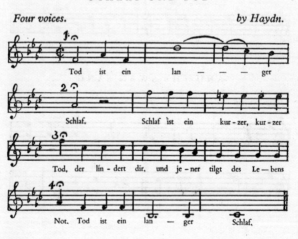

Tod ist ein lan — — — ger

Schlaf. Schlaf ist ein kur - zer, kur - zer

Tod, der lin - dert dir, und je - ner tilgt des Le — bens

Not. Tod ist ein lan — ger Schlaf.

398

MIRANDA'S ROUND

Four voices.

Why shouldn't my goose sing as well as thy goose
When I paid for my goose twice as much as thine.

TURN AMARILLIS

Three voices.   *by T. Hilton.*

Turn A — ma — ril — lis to thy swain, Thy
Da — mon bids thee back a — gain.
There is a pret-ty, pret-ty, pret-ty gar-den nigh, Where
— A- pol -lo, where A- pol -lo can — not spy.
There we'll sit and while we may,
Sing to our pipes a round — e — lay.

GLIDE ALONG

Three voices.

Glide a — long my bonny bon—ny boat, While on the tide we gent—ly float We chant to the deep sea's mel—low note Glide a— long my bon—ny bon — ny boat.

ABENDLIED

Four voices.

Ru — het von des Ta — ges Müh'

Es wird A — bend wer — den.

Lass die Sorg' bis Mor — gen früh

Gott be — wacht die Erd — en.

ROSE, ROSE, ROSE

Four voices.

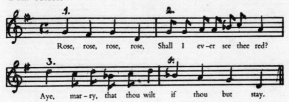

Rose, rose, rose, rose, Shall I ev-er see thee red?

Aye, mar-ry, that thou wilt if thou but stay.

AMEN

Two voices.

Al-le-lu-ja, Al-le-lu-ja, A - - - men, A - - - men.

Chorus, in march time.

The ani-mals came in two by two, *Vive la com-pagnie* the
centipede with the kangaroo, *Vive la compagnie!*
One more river, and that's the river of Jordan,
One more river, There's one more river to cross.

The animals came in three by three,
　　Vive la compagnie.
The elephant on the back of the flea,
　　—*Vive la compagnie.*
　　　　One more river, etc.

The animals came in four by four, etc.

The camel, he got stuck in the door.

Some were dead and some were alive.

The monkey he was up to his tricks.

Some went to Hell, and some went to Heaven.

The worm was early, the bird was late.

Some had water and some had wine.

If you want any more you must sing it again.

EN PASSANT PAR LA LORRAINE

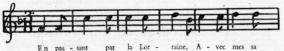

En pas - sant par la Lor - raine, A - vec mes sa

(Chorus.)

bots, En pas - sant par la Lor - rain - e A - vec

(Solo.)

mes sa - bots, Ren - con - trai trois cap - i -

tain - es, A - vec mes sabots, Don - dain - e

Oh! Oh! Oh! A - vec mes sa - bots.

(Chorus.)

Ren - con - trai trois ca - pi - tai - nes, A - vec

mes sa - bots, Don - dai - ne, Oh! Oh! Oh!

A - vec mes sa - bots.

Rencontrai trois capitaines, Avec mes sabots,
(Repeat chorus.)

Ils m'ont appelé vilaine, Avec mes sabots,
Dondaine, Oh! Oh! Oh! Avec mes sabots.
(Repeat chorus.)

Ils m'ont appelé vilaine, Avec mes sabots,
Je ne suis pas si vilaine, Avec, etc.

Je ne suis pas si vilaine, etc.
Puisque le fils du roi m'aime, etc.

Puisque le fils du roi m'aime,
Il m'a donné pour étrenne.

Il m'a donné pour étrenne,
Un bouquet de marjolaine.

Un bouquet de marjolaine,
S'il fleurit, je serai reine.

S'il fleurit, je serai reine,
S'il y meurt je perds ma peine.

AUPRÈS DE MA BLONDE

Chorus, in march time.

Dans les jardins d'mon pè — re Les li-las sont flu-ris, — — — Dans les jardins d'mon pè - re Les li-las sont fleu - ris —— Tous les oi-seaux du mon - de Vien'nt y faire leaurs nids — Au - près de ma blon — de, Qu'il fait bon, fait bon, fait bon, Au - -près de ma blon - de, Qu'il fait bon dor - mi - - —

        Tous les oiseaux du monde }
        Vien'nt y faire leurs nids   } Repeat.
        La caill', la tourterelle   }
        Et la joli' perdrix – Auprès de ma blonde, etc.

N.B. – The two new lines in each verse are sung twice at the beginning of the following verse.

        La caill', etc., etc.
        Et ma joli' colombe
        Qui chante jour et nuit.

Qui chante pour les filles
Qui n'ont pas de mari.

Pour moi ne chante guère
Car j'en ai un joli.

Dites-nous donc la belle,
Ou donc est votr' mari.

Il est dans la Hollande
Les Hollandais l'ont pris.

Que donneriez-vous belle,
Pour avoir votre ami ?

Je donnerais Versailles,
Paris et Saint Denis.

Les tours de Notre Dame,
Et l'clocher d'mon pays.

Et ma joli' colombe,
Pour avoir mon mari.

AND WHEN I DIE

Slowly and with much pathos.

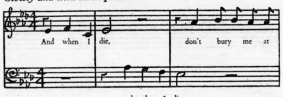

And when I die, don't bury me at

and when I die,

all, Just pickle my bones

Don't bury me at all, Just pickle my

in al - co hol ; Put a bottle o'

bones in al - co - hol ;

booze At my head and my

Put a bottle o' booze

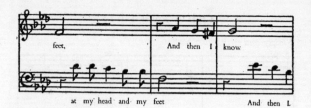

feet,   And then I know

at my head and my feet   And then I

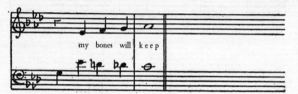

my bones will keep

k n o w my bones will k e e p

O, ME TATERS

In chorus.

O, me ta-ters and me 'ot fried fish; You can 'ave a little

if you wish, You can 'ave it on a plate or on a dish, or

in a lit-tle bit o' pa - - - per!

x

408

COME, LANDLORD,
FILL THE FLOWING BOWL

Bibulously, in chorus.

Come land - lord, fill the flowing bowl, Un -
til it doth run ov - er. Come, land - lord, fill the
flowing bowl un - til it doth run ov - - er.
For to - night we'll merry, merry be, For to-night, we'll
merry, merry be For - to - night we'll
merry, merry be, to - mor - row we'll be so - - ber

The man who drinketh small beer,
   And goes to bed quite sober,
Fades as the leaves do fade,
   That drop off in October.
    For to-night, etc.

The man who drinketh strong beer,
   And goes to bed quite mellow,
Lives as he aught to live,
   And dies a jolly good fellow.
    For to-night, etc.

But he who drinks just what he likes
 And getteth half-seas over,
Will live until he dies perhaps,
 And then lie down in clover.
  For to-night, etc.

The man who kisses a pretty girl,
 And goes and tells his mother,
Ought to have his lips cut off,
 And never kiss another.
  For to-night, etc.

I'LL STICK TO THE SHIP

Chorus, in waltz time.

I'll stick to the ship, boys, You save your
lives, I've no one to love me, You've
sweet - hearts and wives— You take to the boats, boys
Trust - ing , in Heav'n a - bove—— While I go
down in the an - gry deep with the ship I love.

It is probable that the hero of this tragical ballad had time to compose more verses before his ship went down. If they are known to the reader let them be added here.

ETON BOYS

In chorus, with feeling and a nasal Cockney intonation.

E - ton boys, Eton boys, boys of the good old

school, Eton boys, Eton boys, what

cheers for the red, white and blue

Some makes for fame others for shame, while

others with life plays the fool; But bring

life what it may, We're all proud to say, We're

boys of the old E - ton Sch - ool.

MRS DYER, THE BABY FARMER

Indignantly.

The old baby far-mer 'as been exe-cuted, It's quite time' she was put out of the way. She was a bad wo-man, it is not dis-puted, Not a word in her fa-vour can an-y-one say.

Chorus

The old baby farmer, the wretched Mrs Dyer,
    At *the* Old Bailey her wages is paid.
In times long ago we'd ha' made a big fyer
    And roasted so nicely that wicked old jade.

It seems rather hard to run down a woman,
    But this one was hardly a woman at all;
To get a fine livin' in a way so unhuman,
    Crossin' (carousing ?) in luxury on poor girls'
      downfall,
    Chorus.

Poor girls who fall from the straight path of virtue,
    What *could* they do with a child in their arms ?
The fault they committed they could not undo,
    So the baby was sent to the cruel baby farms.
    Chorus.

412

To all these sad crimes there must be an ending,
  Secrets like these for ever can't last.
Say as you like there is no defending
  The 'orrible tales we have heard in the past.
  Chorus.

What did she think as she stood on the gallows,
  Poor little victims in front of her eyes?
Her heart if she 'ad one must have been callous,
  The rope round her neck – how quickly time flies!
  Chorus.

Down through the trap-door quickly disappearing,
  The old baby farmer to eternity 'ome.
The sound of her own death bell she was 'earing.
  Maybe she was sent to the cruel baby farm.
  Chorus.

ALLELUIA, I'M A BUM

Very noisily, in chorus.

A la-dy came out when I knocked at the
door: 'You'll get no-thing here, for I've
seen you be-fore.' Al-le lu-ia, I'm a
bum, bum, Al-le-lu-ia, bum a-gain, Al-le
lu-ia give us a hand-out to re-vive us a-gain

'Oh why don't you work as the other fellows do?'
'How the hell can I work when there's no work to do?'
        Alleluia, etc.

'Oh why don't you pray for your daily bread?'
'If that's all I did I would damn soon be dead.'
        Alleluia, etc.

'Oh I love my boss, he's a good friend of mine,
And that's why I am starving out on the bread line.'
        Alleluia, etc.

N.B. – A 'bum' is a migratory worker. This is a popular I.W.W. or 'wobbly' song.

414

MISS BAILEY

Fast but sad.
(Solo.)

A captain bold in Hali - fax that dwelt in country

quar - ters De - ceived a maid who hanged herself one

morning in her gar - ters, His wicked conscience

smited him, he lost his stomach dai-ly, He

took to drinking turpentine and thought upon Miss

(Chorus.)

Bai - - ley, O, Miss Bailey, un - fortunate Miss

Bai - - ley, O, Miss Bailey, un - fortunate Miss

Bailey.

WEIGHTS AND WEATHERS

But all sorts of things and weather
Must be taken in together,
To make up a year
And a sphere.

R. W. Emerson.

When two Englishmen meet, their first talk
is of the weather.

Samuel Johnson.

In Spring I have counted one hundred and
thirty-six different kinds of weather inside
of four-and-twenty hours.

Mark Twain.

'After sharpest shoures,'quoth Pees, 'most
    sheene is the sonne;
Ys no weder warmer than after watery
    cloudes'.

William Langland.

'Tis very warm weather when one's in bed.
Jonathan Swift.

For he, by geometric scale,
Could take the size of pots of ale; . . .
And wisely tell what hour o' th' day
The clock doth strike, by algebra.
Samuel Butler, 1612-1680.

The bearings of this observation lays in the
application on it.

Charles Dickens.

'Write that down,' the King said to the jury,
and the jury eagerly wrote down all three
dates on their slates, and then added them
up, and reduced the answer to shillings and
pence.

Lewis Carroll.

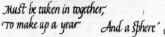

'But all sorts of things and weather
Must be taken in together,
To make up a year And a Sphere'

WEIGHTS

RULE OF THUMB

It is sometimes convenient to be able to measure by rule of thumb – literally. The following figures are those for that elusive character 'the average man':

Span of thumb and index finger	7 inches
Span of thumb and little finger	9 inches
Nail joint of index finger	1 inch
Wrist to elbow	10 inches

The average size of a shod male foot is nearer 11 inches than a foot.

WEIGHTS AND MEASURES FROM COINS

Five pennies in a row measure just over 6 inches.
One halfpenny measures 1 inch.
One sixpence measures $\frac{3}{4}$ of an inch.

1 halfpenny and a threepenny piece	$\frac{1}{4}$ oz
2 halfpennies and a farthing	$\frac{1}{2}$ oz
3 pennies	1 oz

KITCHEN MEASURES
Liquids

1 teacupful	$\frac{1}{4}$ pint
1 breakfast-cupful	$\frac{1}{2}$ pint
1 tumbler	$\frac{1}{2}$ pint

WEIGHTS AND WEATHERS

LINEAR MEASURES

7·92 inches	=	1 link
12 inches	=	1 foot
3 feet	=	1 yard
5½ yards	=	1 rod, pole or perch
4 poles	=	1 chain
10 chains	=	1 furlong
8 furlongs	=	1 mile
1,760 yards	=	1 mile
5,280 feet	=	1 mile
100 links	=	1 chain
6 feet	=	1 fathom
100 fathoms	=	1 cable length
6,080 feet	=	1 nautical mile
1 nautical mile	=	1·15152 land miles
4 inches	=	1 hand
9 inches	=	1 span
5 feet	=	1 pace

A GEOGRAPHICAL MILE is the length of one minute of Latitude. As the earth is a spheroid, the length of a minute increases from 6,046 feet at the Equator to 6,108 feet at the Poles. The length of the geographical mile is held to be 6,076·8 feet (2,025·6 yards).

THE LEGAL MILE in the British Empire and the United States is 1,760 yards, but in Scotland and Ireland, on the Continent and in Scandinavia the 'mile' is very variable. For instance, the Scottish mile is 1,976·5 yards; the Irish 2,240 yards and the Swedish 11,000 yards.

A CRICKET PITCH is 22 yards (1 chain) between the stumps.

A LAWN TENNIS COURT is 78 × 36 feet (double) and 78 × 27 feet (single).

SQUARE MEASURES

144 sq. inches	=	1 sq. foot
9 sq. feet	=	1 sq. yard
30¼ sq. yards	=	1 sq. rod, pole or perch
40 sq. rods	=	1 rood
4 roods	=	1 acre

4,840 sq. yards	= 1 acre
10 sq. chains	= 1 acre
640 acres	= 1 sq. mile
3,097,600 sq. yards	= 1 sq. mile

CUBIC MEASURES

| 1,728 cu. inches | = 1 cu. foot |
| 27 cu. feet | = 1 cu. yard |

MEASURES OF CAPACITY

60 minims	= 1 fluid dram (drachm)
8 fluid drams	= 1 fluid ounce
5 fluid ounces	= 1 gill
4 gills (20 ozs.)	= 1 pint
2 pints	= 1 quart
4 quarts	= 1 Imperial gallon
2 gallons	= 1 peck
4 pecks (8 gallons)	= 1 bushel
8 bushels	= 1 quarter

WEIGHTS (AVOIRDUPOIS)

437½ grains*	= 1 ounce
16 drams	= 1 ounce
7,000 grains*	= 1 pound
16 ounces	= 1 pound
14 pounds	= 1 stone
28 pounds	= 1 quarter
112 pounds	= 1 hundredweight
4 quarters	= 1 hundredweight
20 hundredweights	= 1 ton

* The grain is the same whether it is avoirdupois, troy or apothecaries' weight.

MISCELLANEOUS MEASURES

Bag of cement = 112 lb. = 1¼ cu. ft.
Barony of land = 4,000 acres
Barrel of apples = 120 – 140 lb.
    beef = 200 lb.
    beer = 36 gallons
    butter = 224 lb.
    herring = 500 herrings
    potatoes = 200 lb.

Billion = a million millions in U.K. and Germany
a thousand millions in U.S.A. and France

Bolt of canvas = 42 yards

Bottle of wine or spirits = 26⅔ fluid ounces. A bottle of whisky produces in England 32 singles, or tots; in Scotland, 26 singles.

Bushel of barley = 56 lb.
flour = 56 lb.
maize = 60 lb.
oats = 42 lb.
rye = 60 lb.
wheat = 63 lb.

Carat = 3 grains

Cartload = 45 cu. ft.

Chaldron = 4½ quarters

Cental = 100 lb

Clove of cheese = 8 lb.

Chest of tea = 84 lb.

Coil of rope = 112 fathoms

Coomb = 4 bushels

Digit = 0·91 inches

Ell, English = 45 inches
Scottish = 37·06 inches

Gill, Imperial = ¼ pint
North and West England = ½ pint

Jeroboam = 4 bottles

Knot = 1·15 m.p.h.

Last = 10 quarters

Load of bricks = 500
flour = 240 lb.
hay and straw = 36 trusses

Magnum = 2 bottles

Noggin = ¼ pint

Peck of flour = 14 lb.

Pint, Imperial = 0·125 gallon
Scottish = 0·376 „
Glasgow = 0·5 „

Pottle = 2 quarts

Puncheon of beer = 72 gallons
brandy = 120 gallons
wine = 84 gallons

Quintal = 100 kg. = 220 lb.

Ream of writing paper = 20 quires = 480 sheets
Rehoboam = 6 bottles
Roll of butter = 24 ounces
Sack of barley = 224 lb.
     coals = 224 lb.
     flour = 280 lb.
     oats = 168 lb.
     potatoes = 168 lb.
     wheat = 252 lb.
Stack of timber = 108 cu. ft.
Stone of cheese = 16 lb. (U.K.)
     „ = 24 lb. (Scotland)
Strike = 2 bushels
Truss of hay, old = 56 lb.
     hay, new (till 1 Sept.) = 60 lb.
     straw = 36 lb.
Wey (or Load) = 5 quarters
Windle of wheat = 220 lb.
Yard of land = 30 acres
1 gallon of milk = 10·3 lb.
1 ton of barley produces approximately 105 proof gallons of whisky.
100 average sized cigarettes contain about $3\frac{1}{2}$ oz. of tobacco
1000 „ „ „ „ „ 2·2 lb. „ „
1000 medium size cigars „ „ 8·8 lb. „ „
1 cu. ft. of water = $6\frac{1}{4}$ gallons = $62\frac{1}{2}$ lb.
1 inch of rainfall = 22,622 gallons per acre = 101 tons.
The circumference of a circle is 3·14 times its diameter.

SPEED
Miles per hour

Antelope	55 – 60
Cheetah	70
Dog	38
Emu	40
Hare	45
Horse	44
Man	24 (running, during 100 yds.)
Pigeon	67
Rabbit	35
Swift	200
Woman	20 (running)

o

Feet per hour

Snail	1·916
Worm	10·5

2 miles per hour = about 3 feet per second

CONCRETE MIX

FOR FLOORS, PAVEMENTS, WALLS, PITS, STEPS AND PATHS

1 bucket Portland Cement (loose), 2 buckets sand (damp), 3 buckets coarse aggregate (not larger than $\frac{3}{4}''$) mixed together with $\frac{1}{2}$ to $\frac{3}{4}$ of a bucket of water.

CROP YIELDS

For Great Britain the ten-year average, 1941-1950, was, per acre: wheat, 19·5 cwt.; barley, 18·2 cwt.; oats, 16·8 cwt.; meadow hay, 19·8 cwt.; clover, lucerne and seeds hay, 28·4 cwt.; potatoes, 7 tons; mangolds, 20 tons; turnips and swedes, 14·6 tons; sugar beet (washed and topped), 9·5 tons.

LIVESTOCK

PUBERTY AND BREEDING AGE

The age at which puberty is reached is roughly:

Bitch	7 to 10 months
Cat	8 to 12 months
Ewe	8 to 12 months
Gilt (Pig)	4 to 5 months
Goat	8 to 12 months
Heifer	12 to 18 months
Mare	12 to 24 months

The age at which breeding starts is roughly:

Gilts	7 to 9 months
Heifers	18 months
Mares	in their third year

The seasons at which Oestrum Periods ('heat') occur are: *Mare* – February to July; *Goat* – autumn; *Ewe* – autumn; *Cow, Sow, Ass, Bitch* and *Cat* – all the year round.

424

WEIGHTS AND WEATHERS
PERIOD OF GESTATION AND INCUBATION

Days:	Shortest period	Usual period	Longest period
Ass	365	380	391
Bitch	55	60	68
Cat	48	50	56
Cow	240	283	321
Duck	28	30	32
Elephant	—	600	—
Ewe	146	151	161
Ferret	—	45	—
Giraffe	—	430	—
Goat	150	156	163
Goose	27	30	33
Guinea fowl	—	26	—
Guineapig	62	64	66
Hen	19	21	24
Mare	322	340	419
Pigeon	16	18	20
Rabbit	20	28	35
Sow	109	115	143
Turkey	24	26	30
Woman	252	266	280

WATER REQUIREMENTS

Cow in Milk: approximately 1 gallon a day for each 1 cwt. liveweight and at least 2 gallons for each gallon of milk produced. For washing down, cleaning utensils, etc. about 15 gallons.

Bullock or Dry Cow:	10 gallons a day
Horses on Pasture :	6 ,, ,, ,,
Pigs (fattening) :	3 ,, ,, ,,
Sheep :	1½ ,, ,, ,,

GRAZING

In terms of grazing requirements 1 calf = 2 sheep; 1 heifer or store beast = 4 to 5 sheep; 1 cow = 1 fattening bullock = 1 horse = 10 geese = 6 sheep.

WEIGHTS AND WEATHERS
FOR THE TRAVELLER ABROAD

KILOMETRE
A quick way of converting kilometres into miles (8 km. = 5 m.) is to divide by two and add a quarter of the result. *Example:* 100 km. = 50 + 12½ = 62½ miles. Or, rougher but readier, bring the number of kilometres up to the nearest ten, knock off the nought, and multiply by 6. *Example:* call 67 km. 70, and then multiply 7 by 6 = 42 miles.

LITRES
When buying petrol remember that 10 litres make 2·2 gallons. When buying oil (or milk) use the following table:

Litres	Pints
1	1¾
2	3½
3	5
4	7

AMERICAN AND IMPERIAL MEASURES
U.S.A. gills, pints and gallons are one-fifth less than Imperial gills, pints and gallons. In the United States there are 16 fluid ounces to a liquid pint.

METRES
If you are tempted by lengths of material in the market place, remember that a metre is a little longer than a yard. You can afford to ignore the difference till you get up to 5 yards, for which the equivalent is 4½ metres. If you want 6 yards, buy 5½ metres. The width of material is 39 inches instead of 36. There are 1094 yards in a kilometre.

KILOGRAMS
When buying by weight remember that a kilogram is 2⅕ lbs. (1016 kilograms in a ton). Half a kilo is called a livre and for all practical purposes can be regarded as the equivalent of a lb. In France some commodities will be marked at so much a 100 grs. (grammes), in Italy at so much an etto. This is a trifle less than ¼ lb.

426

TYRE PRESSURES

18 lb. sq. in.	1·26 kg. sq. c.m.
20 ,, ,, ,,	1·40 ,, ,, ,,
22 ,, ,, ,,	1·54 ,, ,, ,,
24 ,, ,, ,,	1·68 ,, ,, ,,
26 ,, ,, ,,	1·82 ,, ,, ,,
28 ,, ,, ,,	1·96 ,, ,, ,,
30 ,, ,, ,,	2·10 ,, ,, ,,

CENTIGRADE AND FAHRENHEIT

For cold spells, heat waves, or illness:

°Centigrade	°Fahrenheit	
−10	14	(or 18 degrees of frost)
− 5	23	(or 9 degrees of frost)
0	32	
5	41	
10	50	
15	59	
20	68	
25	77	
30	86	
35	95	
37	98·6	
38	100.4	
39	102.2	
40	104	

To convert °Fahrenheit to °Centigrade: subtract 32, multiply by 5, and divide by 9.

GR.

A prescription written in England will use grains (gr.) as a measure. If you have this prescription made up by a small chemist abroad he may interpret this as grammes. One gramme is 15·4 grains – and you may be heavily, perhaps disastrously, over-dosed. It has happened.

PERPETUAL KALENDAR
TO FIND THE WEEK DAY OF ANY DATE IN THE CHRISTIAN ERA

Add together the following numbers:

1. The number of the year.
2. The quotient (omitting fractions) after dividing the number of the year by 4.

427

3.* Six times the number of completed centuries.
4.* The quotient (omitting fractions) after dividing the number of completed centuries by 4.
5. The Index number of the month from Table I.
6. The number of the day of the month.

Then divide the total by 7: the remainder will give the day of the week according to Table II.

* For dates expressed in Old Style (in Great Britain before 14th September 1752, in France before 20th December 1582) omit steps 3 and 4 and simply add 5 in all cases.

Table I				Table II	
Month	Index No.	Month	Index No.	Remainder	Day of Week
January	0	May	1	1	Sunday
January		June	4	2	Monday
(in leap year)	6	July	6		
February	3	August	2	3	Tuesday
February		September	5	4	Wednesday
(in leap year)	2	October	0	5	Thursday
March	3	November	3	6	Friday
April	6	December	5	0	Saturday

Note. A year is leap in OLD STYLE if its number is exactly divisible by 4. In NEW STYLE it is leap if its number is divisible by 4, unless its number ends in 00, in which case it is only leap if the preceding figures form a number divisible by 4 exactly (e.g. 1600 and 2000 are leap years; 1800 and 1900 are common years).

Example. What is the day of the week of 1st January 1956?

1. Number of the year   1956
2. Quotient after division by 4 489
3. Number of completed centuries is 19. 6×19 .. 114
4. Quotient after dividing 19 by 4   4
5. Index No. for January (from Table I)   .. 6
6. Day of the month 1

$$\text{Total} \quad 7)\overline{2570}$$
$$\text{Divide by 7} \quad 367$$
$$\text{Remainder} \quad .. \quad 1$$

From Table II the day of the week is Sunday.

428

TO FIND THE DATE OF EASTER SUNDAY
IN ANY YEAR OF THE CHRISTIAN ERA

Divide the number of the year by 4 and call the remainder: a

Divide the number of the year by 7 and call the remainder: b

Divide the number of the year by 19 and call the remainder: c

Divide 19c + P by 30 and call the remainder: d

Divide 2a + 4b + 6d + Q by 7 and call the remainder: e

where P and Q are quantities to be determined by the method given below.

Then d + e is equal to the number of days that Easter Sunday falls after March 22nd.

Thus if d + e is equal to less than 9 Easter Day is March (22 + d + e)th, and if d + e is greater than 9 Easter Day is April (d + e — 9)th.

Special Cases:

(1) If d + e = 35, Easter Day falls on April 19th (*not* on April 26th).

(2) If d + e = 34, and if also d = 28 and c is less than 10, Easter Day falls on April 18th (*not* on April 25th).

Determination of P and Q:

For OLD STYLE these are constants: P = 15, Q = 6.

For NEW STYLE they are constant for a century at a time.

Thus for 1700–1799: P = 23, Q = 3.

Thus for 1800–1899: P = 23, Q = 4.

Thus for 1900–1999: P = 24, Q = 5.

Thus for 2000–2099: P = 24, Q = 5.

To determine P and Q for any given century:

Call the hundreds' figure of the year   K

Divide K by 4 and call the quotient (excluding fractions)   L

Divide K − 17 by 25 and call the quotient (excluding fractions)   M

Divide K − M by 3 and call the quotient (excluding fractions)   N

Divide 15 + K − L − N by 30 and the remainder will be   P

Divide 4 + K − L by 7 and the remainder will be   Q

N.B. Until the year 4200, M = 0.

Example. On what day does Easter fall in 1956?

(For 1900 to 1999, P = 24 Q = 5)

Remainder after dividing 1956 by 4	0	= a
Remainder after dividing 1956 by 7	3	= b
Remainder after dividing 1956 by 19	18	= c

Then $19 \times 18 + 24 = 366$

Remainder after dividing 366 by 30 $6 = d$

Then $2 \times 0 + 4 \times 3 + 6 \times 6 + 5 = 53$

Remainder after dividing 53 by 7 $4 = e$

Then $d + e = 10$

Therefore Easter Sunday is April $(10 - 9)$ *i.e.* April 1st.

✦✦✦✦✦✦✦✦✦✦✦✦✦✦✦✦✦✦✦✦✦✦✦✦✦✦✦✦✦✦✦✦✦✦

WEATHERS

BE not so anxious, friend,
  About to-morrow's weather;
Whether our sports it may commend,
  And the fair morn
Deserve the tribute of the cheerful horn;
    Or drizzly wet
    Compel us sit
Around the fire together,
    Both Whigs and Tories,
    And ply the glass,
    Or, time to pass,
Hum tunes, or tell old stories.

Think, whatsoe'er shall hap,
  That by to-morrow night,
When we are laid in sleep's soft lap,
    'Twill be the same,
Whether of hounds, or Trojan tales we dream.
    Pursue the thought,
    As sure you ought,
  'Twill set all cares to right;
  For such the case is
    When life is past,
    And we, at last,
Lie down *in gremio pacis.*   *Anon (1735).*

THE WEATHER: METEOROLOGICAL

Whoso hath but a mouth
Shall ne'er in England suffer drought.

Before making an irrevocable decision to spend the week-end out of doors it is advisable to obtain the latest weather fore-

430

casts. Forecasts are given in the newspapers and by the B.B.C., but the most accurate information about the state of the weather in various parts of the British Isles, the Continent and the Eastern Atlantic, and also the latest weather forecasts, may be obtained by calling one of the Meteorological Offices listed below, which are open daily from 9 am to 5 pm Mondays to Fridays, and from 9 am to 1 pm on Saturdays, or the London Office, telephone number HOLborn 3434 (asking for 'Forecast Office') where the service is available at any time of the day or night, including Sundays. The only charge made is for the call to the Meteorological Office. By naming the particular area in which one is interested and the activities – walking, camping, sailing, gliding, etc. – one intends to pursue, a detailed forecast may be obtained and discussed with the forecaster himself.

The Meteorological Offices and their telephone numbers (other than London) are: Abingdon (288, Ext. 121, 209); Aldergrove (Antrim 2202, Ext. 125, 126, 127); Bawtry (363-7, Ext. 111, 45); Eastleigh (Southampton) (Eastleigh 8722-8-9, Ext. 10); Gloucester (24465-7, Ext. 109, 113); Mildenhall (Newmarket 3151, Ext. 15, 25 and Mildenhall 2281-2); Pitreavie (Inverkeithing 264-7, Ext. 118, 119); Plymouth (Plymstock 2224, Ext. 108, 109); Preston (4602, Ext. 20); Renfrew (2352, Ext. 21, 23); Shawbury (351); Speke (Liverpool) (Garston 1240, Ext. 21, 22, and Garston 2437); Upavon (7-8, Ext. 8, 9); Watnall (Nottingham 45731, Ext. 230, 231).

Everybody knows that the atmosphere is constantly in a state of flux, partly because the earth goes round, and partly because water (*e.g.* seas and lakes) is always either condensing or evaporating owing to the action of the sun's rays. As a result of this changeability, the atmospheric pressure on the earth varies with place and time; this is shown in the weather charts made by meteorologists. They have discovered a variety of tricks performed by the atmosphere, each of which has a specific bearing on the weather in the locality in which it is performed. The star turn, so to speak, is the pattern formed by an area of low pressure or the familiar *depression* which is indicated by a series of closed curves, roughly circular, with greater and greater pressure from the centre outwards. These curved lines are called *isobars*. They perform a function similar to the contour lines on a geographical map

431

where successive height levels are indicated, while in the weather chart all places with the same pressure lie on the same isobar. Much of the variety of our weather arises from the interaction of two air masses with different temperatures and moisture content and its worst features occur near to their boundary. The location of these boundaries helps us to find where the weather is at its worst. In the depression we have a warm damp air mass moving anticlockwise round the centre of low pressure and at the same time ascending above colder air ahead of it. This ascending air gives rise to the cloud and rain, or in winter, the snow. The forward edge of this warm air is marked on the weather chart by a line with small solid hemispheres above it, ●●●●●●●● and it is called a warm front. However, the inflow of this warm damp air into the depression is in turn being gradually cut off by the arrival of a colder air mass from higher latitudes. The forward edge of this colder air is also marked on the weather chart by another line with small solid triangles, ▲▲▲▲▲ and it is called a cold front. In time the faster travelling cold front catches up with the warm front and this joint boundary is called an occlusion. This is shown on the weather chart by a line with a combination of the warm and cold front symbols, ▲▲●▲●. Maxim: avoid areas where these fronts are shown, unless it is forecast that they will move away. For the habit of these meteorological 'patterns' is to move about, to become more extensive and more vigorous in the earlier stages of their life and to contract and become less vigorous in the later stages.

Here we arrive at a second point of interest to the chart-reader. Namely, the wider apart the lines of equal pressure (isobars) in a low pressure or a high pressure area, the less strong the wind.

Winds tend to blow along the isobars, with a slight deviation inwards towards lower pressure in the depression, but outwards in high pressure areas. They are marked on the chart by an arrow which is flying with the wind while the speed (in miles per hour) is inserted in a small circle at the head of the arrow.

Areas of high pressure are the precise opposite of low pressure; they consist of a central area of high pressure with surrounding isobars showing less and less pressure outwards from the centre. The weather is more often fine and warm in

432

summer, while it may be fine and cold, with sharp frost or fog at night in winter.

In some cases the direction and rate of travel of a depression or anticyclone and its intensification or weakening can be estimated with accuracy but on other occasions a considerable element of doubt exists. Their movements are at least partially governed by the movement of air in the higher levels of the atmosphere. This has been the subject of much more intensive study since the early 1940's as much more information about the temperature, moisture content and wind speed and direction at these levels became available. Some experienced map-reader may say that according to his experience of sequences, he expects such and such a change to take place consequent upon what he observes. Therefore, if such a one forecasts that a given atmospheric 'pattern' will move in such and such a direction at such and such a pace, trailing sun, wind, or rain in its wake, it is not incumbent on anyone to believe him, but it is more than probable that his experience will stand the test of events. The experience of sequences is however only one guide, for two similar 'patterns' may not follow such a rule because of different conditions in the upper atmosphere.

The map-maker gives the general character of the weather by the following conventional signs:

b — blue sky
bc — half clouded
c — cloudy
o — overcast
f — fog
d — drizzle
h — hail
m — mist
r — rain
s — snow
tlr — thunderstorm
p — showers

Isobars are drawn for every four millibars and the values in millibars and inches are indicated against each isobar.

A typical weather chart has been reproduced. The warm front extends from northeast Ireland across northern England to Holland with rain falling ahead of it over the whole of north Ireland, north England and south and east

433

Scotland. Behind the warm front there are higher temperatures and some rain or drizzle is indicated. The cold front extends from north to southeast Ireland and has nearly reached the Scilly Isles. Behind it the air is colder and the weather is showery with no doubt broken clouds and some sunshine. The occlusion is shown lying from the centre of the depression to northwest Ireland.

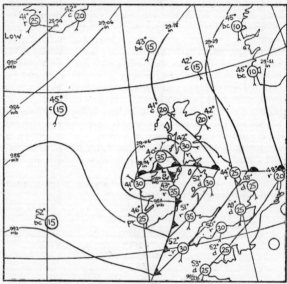

The BEAUFORT SCALE (named after Admiral Sir Francis Beaufort who devised it in 1806) is also used in communicating weather conditions. It is a numerical scale, each number representing a certain strength or velocity of wind from calm to hurricane.

Scale No.	Wind Force	M.p.h.
0	Calm	0
1	Light air	1–3
2	Slight breeze	4–7
3	Gentle breeze	8–12
4	Moderate breeze	13–18

Scale No.	Wind Force	M.p.h.
5	Fresh breeze	19–24
6	Strong breeze	25–31
7	High wind	32–38
8	Gale	39–46
9	Strong gale	47–54
10	Whole gale	55–63
11	Storm	64–75
12	Hurricane	over 75

THE WEATHER: MYTHOLOGICAL
with some Meteorological asides.

To supplement the instruments of science, there is the traditional wisdom of the countryside.

❡

When the wind is in the East
'Tis neither good for man nor beast:
When the wind is in the North
The skilful fisher goes not forth:
When the wind is in the South
It blows the bait in the fishes' mouth:
When the wind is in the West
Then it is the very best.

❡

Between one and two.
See what the day will do.

❡

Rain before seven,
Fine before eleven.

True. Continuous rain seldom lasts more than five hours over most of England.

❡

A green Christmas makes a fat churchyard.

Untrue. The death rate is higher in a cold winter.

435

¶

Candlemas Day ! Candlemas Day !
Half our fire and half our hay.

True. Half the winter is over on February 2 and we should
have half our fuel and winter feed still in store.

¶

Better late spring and bear than early blossom and blast.

¶

February, fill dyke;
March, lick it out.

This is an exhortation, not a description of what necessarily
happens.

¶

A peck of March dust is worth a king's ransom.

¶

So many fogs in March you see,
So many frosts in May will be.

Often fulfilled. In London there are four foggy mornings in
an average March and four nights of ground frost in an
average May.

¶

If the oak be out before the ash
The summer will be but a splash:
If the ash be out before the oak
The summer will be all a soak.

BUCHAN

There are generally some warm days at the end of March or
beginning of April which bring the blackthorn into bloom
and which are followed by a cold period called the Blackthorn Winter. The Blackthorn Winter sometimes occurs on
April 11 to 14, and it then coincides with 'Buchan's second
cold period'.

436

In 1867 Alexander Buchan, the Secretary of the Scottish Meteorological Society, came to the conclusion that there was a tendency towards the occurrence of cold and warm weather in Scotland at certain specified times of year. Four of these periods were already recognised under other names in the weather lore of Europe. In 1928 Buchan's name became a household word in England when the Bill to fix Easter on the Sunday following the second Saturday in April came before Parliament. This meant that Easter would fall some time between April 9 and 15, and therefore probably during Buchan's 'second cold period', or the Blackthorn Winter. In 1929, the following year, the weather exactly followed Buchan's pattern.

§

May 11, 12 and 13. A period of unseasonably cold weather, known as the Festival of the Three Ice Men, being the feast days of St Mamertus, St Pancras and St Servatius.

May 9 to 14. Buchan's third cold period.

§

> *St Swithin's Day, if ye do rain,*
> *For forty days it will remain;*
> *St Swithin's Day, an' ye be fair,*
> *For forty days 'twill rain nae mair.*

This would be slightly truer if reversed. Records taken in London over the last fifty years, and averaged, show that when July 15 is dry, seventeen of the following forty days are wet (total rainfall 3¼ inches), while after a wet July 15 sixteen of the following forty days are wet (total rainfall 2½ inches). N.B. Swithin or Swithun, Bishop of Winchester, died in 862. His body was buried at his own request outside the church 'in a vile and unworthy place, under the drop of the eaves, where the sweet rain of heaven might fall upon his grave'. A century later it was decided to move his remains into the interior of the church on July 15; the saint arranged for a forty-day deluge which persuaded the monks to abandon the project.

§

September 15 is fine six years out of seven.

437

Records show that the odds against rain falling in London are greater in mid-September than at any other time of year. The odds are rather more than six to one on September 15 being dry.

¶

October 18. The Feast of St Luke. 'St Luke's Little Summer.'

There is often a spell of fine dry weather at this time.

¶

October 28, the Feast of SS. Simon and Jude, is proverbially wet.

Records show that the last week of October is the wettest of the year in Southern England.

¶

November 11. The Feast of St Martin. 'St Martin's Summer.'

On a cold November 11, circa 380, Martin, Bishop of Tours, gave half his cloak to a poor man. God set the sun shining warmly till the bishop could get himself a new cloak and it has been fine at this time of year ever since.

¶

Mackerel skies and mares' tails
Make great ships carry low sails.

¶

The Equinoctial Gales.

Records do not show any special tendency to windy weather around March 21 or September 21.

¶

How the Red Indians foretold wet weather: 'When the locks of the Navajos turn damp in the scalp-house, surely it will rain.'

In England, seaweed may be substituted for scalps.

¶

If on a dull and threatening summer morning there is a break of blue in the clouds large enough to make a Dutchman's jacket or a pair of sailor's trousers, the day will turn out fine.

438

True. If rain is at hand, breaks in a sheet of cloud usually reveal another layer of cloud higher up. A single sheet of cloud is usually burned off by the summer sun before noon.

¶

The belief that solar or lunar haloes presage wet weather has been tested, and proves true in December and January four times out of five, and over the year as a whole seven times out of ten.

¶

Red at night is the shepherd's delight.
Red in the morning is the shepherd's warning.

A red sunrise: if the red disappears as the sun rises, it will be fine. If the red spreads to the West, or is echoed there, it will be wet.

A red sunset: localised red, disappearing with the sun, is a sign of rain. Red spreading to the East, or echoed there, is a sign of fine weather.

(Batting's Lore.)

GAMES

If you can't volley, wear velvet socks.
S. Potter.

'Play!'– *Any Umpire.*

Life's too short for Chess.
Henry James Byron.

The player on the other side is hidden from us. We know that his play is always fair, just, and patient.
Thomas Henry Huxley.

I cannot play alone.
Felicia Dorothy Hemans.

Sport that wrinkled Care derides,
And Laughter holding both his sides.
Milton.

Games

'If you can't volley, wear velvet socks'

INDOOR GAMES

UP-JENKYNS!

Everybody knows *Up-Jenkyns*, but here are a few finer points. Orders can only be legally obeyed when given by one of the Captains; and if the team which is hiding the Sixpence obeys any other order, it loses. The 'In' team, which is hiding the coin, must put up its hands the instant the opposing Captain calls 'Up-Jenkyns!' but he ought to allow them at least five seconds before he calls. He can keep their hands in the air as long as he likes, for examination purposes; the 'Down' calls are 'Down Jenkyns' (hands can be put down as players please); 'Smash-ums!' (hands must be crashed down on the table); 'Crawlers!' (hands placed quietly on the table, and fingers quietly undone till the hands lie flat); 'Open Windows' (hands must lie on the table with all the fingers, but not the thumbs, apart); and 'Lobster-Pots' (finger-tips only to rest on the table, and fingers to be held at an angle to the palm). In lifting the hands, only the Captain's order must be obeyed; but he should allow free and fair consultation to his own side first. Scores can be played for, by the number of separate 'wins', or the show of hands on the table when the Sixpence is discovered. *Before* the game starts, all rings and spurs to be removed. *After* the game, let the provider of the sixpence see that he gets it back!

TISHY-TOSHY

An early version of the game is said to have taught Bosanquet the googly. You need a table (rectangular, the largest possible) and a tennis-ball. Two players stand at opposite ends,

443

and throw the ball to each other in turn; the Server may roll, bounce or full pitch the ball, but it must not drop off the sides of the table (only off the ends) and must only leave the table between imaginary parallel lines continuing the sides of the table. The Receiver may not put his hands over the table, or touch it with his hands or any part of his person. If he does so, or if he fails to catch the ball, the Server scores one point. If the Receiver catches the ball lawfully, neither scores. But the Receiver scores a point if the Server sends the ball off the sides of the table. Game is for any number of points agreed upon – say five. The very expert can make a rule to use one hand only, or to bar catches made against the body. Remember always that this is a game of skill, not of strength; and the ball must never be thrown at all fast.

THE ANIMAL AND STICK GAME

Two sides sit face to face, without a Referee. Each Captain has a stick. A member of one side calls the name of any animal, bird, fish or insect, beginning with A, and his Captain instantly begins to count 10 aloud (not *too* fast), thumping the floor with his stick at each count. Before he reaches 10, some member of the opposing side must retaliate with another creature beginning with A, on which the second Captain begins to count and thump, while the first side thinks of a new beast. Captains are allowed to call like the rest; but if two members of a side call out different names together, the opposing side may instantly bag the second name given. When one team wins, because the other has run out of A's, it may choose a member of the losing team and add him to their number. The second bout begins with B, and the game continues through the alphabet, until all of one side has been absorbed by the other. No penalty is incurred for Fake Names of animals, and if, when stumped for an N, you *can* bring off 'Nicaragua' unchallenged, you may; but on the whole these should not be indulged in too often, and, once disproved, the Opposing Captain takes up the count where the bluff interrupted it.

This game can also be played more quietly with pencils and paper.

CHARADES

are too well-known to be described – but do you *bring in* the syllable or merely *suggest* it? and if you *suggest* it, are you vocal or dumb? And do you ransack the dressing-up cupboard or merely the pegs in the hall?

DRAWING CLUMPS

Two equally-matched sides go into separate rooms, each supplied either with blackboard, duster and chalk, or plenty of paper and a pencil. A Master of Ceremonies stands at a point equidistant from the two rooms armed with an already-carefully-prepared list of objects or drawable abstractions. This is a team race. At the word 'Go' each side sends its youngest to the middle-man who whispers a word such as 'milk' or 'earth' and this has to be conveyed by drawing (no sound must be uttered) to the rest of the side who never for one moment stop guessing at what the shapes suggest. When the correct word has been hit on the next member of the team dashes from the room to get *his* word from the middle-man, and so on through the team.

By the time it is the turn of the older members concepts such as 'emigration' or 'depression' can be given, while teenagers can usually cope with 'the last straw' or 'Savonarola'. No cheating allowed: only the exact word as given by the Master of Ceremonies, not one that approximates to it, must be accepted by the drawer however desperate and frustrated he feels, and he must remember that if one approach to his subject fails to get results, he must try another – e.g. if the word is 'patience' and a monument has proved ineffectual, he must see if he is more successful with cards. He must never stop drawing – trying new angles of approach – just as the guessers must never stop guessing.

ACTING CLUMPS

Two evenly-balanced teams go into separate rooms. A. team prepares written slips of paper for each member (considered individually) of B. team, and *vice versa*. The writing on the slips is a word or phrase capable of being acted or anyway conveyed to the rest of the team by means of actions *only* – no props. For the young, advertisements ('prevents that sinking feeling'), proverbs, and book titles serve well (*Invitation to the Waltz, Murder in the Cathedral* are, for example, gifts – though the latter tends to be indistinguishable from *Death comes for the Archbishop*); a degree more difficult would be *The Odyssey, Measure for Measure, Brideshead Revisited*. For the older or more practised members of

445

the team quite arbitrary phrases such as 'a late night' or 'worth his salt' serve.

Now, when the slips have been carefully prepared both teams congregate in one room so that all can share the fun. They sit opposite each other and the slips are distributed and, of course, kept *strictly secret* by the recipients. Each member of A. team has now to act his word or phrase in turn to his own side, while B. team, all-knowing, looks on; and, as in Drawing Clumps, A. team never ceases to guess. When these guesses are warm the actor encourages the guessers with come-hither gestures, when cold he repudiates them with go-hence ones. No word whatever must be spoken by the actor, though different lines of approach can, naturally, be attempted. Then it is the turn of B. team, while the A.s watch benignly.

If the phrase on the slip of paper has one key or actable or give-away word, that can be acted first – in this manner: the victim – for he is no less – shows how many words his 'phrase' is by holding up the same number of fingers, and again on his fingers he shows which word – the 2nd or 5th or whatever – he is going to act first, as being the most revealing. Further aids: if the phrase is a book-title he indicates that it is so by scrutinising the palms of his hands, if a play by striking a dramatic pose, if a film by turning an imaginary handle at eye-level.

HANGING

One member of the company is picked out and told that he is deemed guilty of murder and will be hanged at the end of five (or ten) minutes unless he can prove himself innocent. All the rest of the company are *omniscient* witnesses and have to answer any question he puts to them. He questions them in turn, and is acquitted if he can find any contradiction or flat inconsistency in their story. The wildest improbabilities are allowable, and are to be encouraged, in their answers, but witnesses cannot abrogate the laws of nature, though they may play tricks with artificial human ones. E.g. You may make the criminal travel by a non-existent train, but if you make him arrive at his destination before he started, he is acquitted.

ALIBI

A variant is Alibi. Two people are accused of being involved in a murder at a given time and place. They plan their water-

446

tight alibi in another room and are called, singly, into court. The rest of the company, in this case prosecuting, fire questions at the defendants in turn and if their alibi does not tally they are guilty. N.B. They are not allowed to 'forget' what they were wearing or whether it was raining or what the bill came to.

A word about 'going out of the room'. It is inevitable that in some of these games two people, or a side, have to leave the comfortable room with a fire to hatch their plots elsewhere, hence it is desirable to have another centre of warmth and refreshment so that the 'outs' are as cosy as the 'ins'.

WHO ARE THEY?

Two go outside and decide who they'll be, and return to hold a conversation in front of the others, always talking in character, but of course not mentioning their names. When they are guessed, two others go out. It's a very good opportunity for bringing nice people together who would have liked to meet, but can't: Hobbs and Medusa, or Dempsey and Little Nell.

HURDLES

This is a talking game, good for meal-times if the company is ill-assorted. One player, A., thinks of an object and the others have to guess what it is by asking questions in the manner of Clumps or Twenty Questions. The elaboration lies in this, that the others have to cross a hurdle before they can ask a 'business' question, i.e. a question concerning the nature of A.'s object, and to do this they must pose a general knowledge question that stumps A.

Let us suppose A.'s object is a Rustic Seat. He tells the company that it begins with R. and the general knowledge questions then put to him have to concern objects beginning with R. Example: Q. 'Are you a cow?' A. 'No, I'm not a Red Poll.' Q. 'Are you a Pope?' A. is unable to reply with an R. and must thus submit to a 'business' question about his object. Then the questioners begin again battering at their hurdles. Q. 'Are you a composer?' A. 'No, I'm not Ravel,' etc., etc.,

DOG AND BONE

A game for two. You and your opponent face each other, backs to opposite walls. Midway between you on the floor is put a handkerchief. At the word 'go' you both approach the

447

handkerchief. Your object is to get back to *either* wall, his or yours, with the handkerchief without being touched by your opponent, (2 points); or by a pretended pick-up to induce your opponent to touch you when you have *not* got the handkerchief (1 point); or to touch your opponent while he is carrying the handkerchief home (1 point). Game is five points. Note that if a player has once touched the handkerchief he cannot drop it but must try to get to the wall with it. 'Home' on either wall should not be more than about 4 feet broad, and should be clearly defined by some unbreakable objects.

PENCIL AND PAPER GAMES

CONSEQUENCES

Consequences is well known to all, but

BOOK REVIEWS

is better for a round or two. It's played like Consequences, but first you invent the Title of a Book – say 'Crimson Nights'– turn down, and pass on; on the paper you receive you write a sub-title, say 'Or 366 Ways of Cooking Lentils'; round three is the Author's name, real or imaginary; round four a brief extract from the book, poetry or prose; round five another extract (for contrast); six, extract from a review of the book; seven, name of Journal the review comes from; eight, extract from another review (contrast again!); nine, and last, name of Journal.

THE WORD AND QUESTION GAME

Each player takes two slips of paper and writes a question on one and a word on the other. The slips are pooled and everyone draws a word and a question. (Or all may be given the same problem.) The object then is to write a poem, answering or treating of the question and introducing the word. The time-limit is a quarter of an hour.

Here is an example by Sir Walter Raleigh:

Question: Who rang the bell?

Word: Life.

> Life rang the bell to call the people in;
> The play was played by Folly, Pride and Sin;
> Old Age, with fingers trembling and uncertain,
> Turned off the gas, and Death let down the curtain.

Maybe you won't write as good a morality as this, or any morality at all; but that doesn't invalidate the game.

QUALITIES

At the end of the book there is a list of qualities. The subject has to give himself marks for each quality and then pass the book on to the rest in turn to mark him. When all have finished with him, he may read out the verdicts and if you like even work out his average for each quality. After all, he'll have his revenge later.

PERSONAL ANALOGIES

You write the names of those present perpendicularly down your paper, and each in turn chooses a subject – a Colour, Food, Drink, Street, Material, etc.– which are written horizontally across the top. Then everybody sets to and writes against each person's name the nearest analogy he can think of in the different subjects. They're read out afterwards, and no one need explain *why* he thinks you are Scarlet or Putty-Coloured, or like Suet-Pudding or Pêche Melba, or Bond Street or the City Road. It's a good way of paying compliments *and* paying off old scores.

CATEGORIES

A four-letter word is chosen, let us say G N A T , and written in capitals downwards. Each player then provides a 'category' – English musicians, Roman emperors, hot-house flowers, beverages (*G*rappa, *N*escafé, *A*sti, *T*okay), anything – and each player has to write down four of each category beginning with the initial letter provided. Easy, perhaps, but no one ever obtains full marks. Naturally the category each player gives is one in which he himself will shine – at least he will have all four filled in *there* . . . A time limit of course.

TELEGRAMS

Each player writes a given twelve-letter word downwards in capitals on a slip of paper – let us suggest C H I M N E Y - P I E C E . A subject is set, a recipient (known to everyone) is selected, and a telegram has to be drafted, the words beginning with the initial letters provided. The theme of the telegram can be a public one (e.g. *C*hurchill *H*as *I*nfluenza *M*alenkov *N*euralgia *E*den *Y*ellow-fever *P*lease *I*nform *E*isenhower (signed) *C*onference *E*xecutive). The first two and last two letters *may* be used to designate recipient and sender. Among a family or group of friends the private telegram gives better results – sent to an absent aunt, a distraught

449

publisher or an expected guest telling something of the circumstances that await him. A time limit must be set.

FIVE-LETTER CROSSWORDS

Draw a square of five lines by five, giving the *cadre* for a
five-letter crossword puzzle with no blacks. Each player
suggests a letter in turn and all have to fit it in somewhere,
the aim being to make as many five-letter words as possible.
Scoring: 10 points for five-letter words, 5 for four-letter
words and 2 for three-letter words. Two-letter words score
nothing. This game can be played by two or by any number
up to five; though, naturally, the more players there are, the
less likely each is to get certainly the letter he needs, i.e. his
own choice.

THREE-ADJECTIVE PORTRAITS

Each player writes the name of the present company, excluding himself, along the top of a sizeable piece of paper. He
then, within a prescribed time limit, writes three adjectives
to describe each person – bold broad strokes like a charcoal
sketch, instantly suggestive and significant (adjectives of
character rather than of appearance). When the time is up
each player in turn reads his list and the others guess to
which person the adjectives refer. At the end each player
adds up his total of correct guesses and the one with the
highest score wins.

GALLOWS

This is a game for two people – stranded in a pub in the rain
or waiting on a deserted railway station. One of them writes
a line of poetry with dashes representing letters and strokes
between the words: he also draws a picture of a gallows (the
old-fashioned kind). The other asks for various letters of the
alphabet to be filled in in any one place where they occur,
but if they don't occur at all then one of the six basic portions
of his anatomy is suspended from the rope. His aim is to
avoid being totally hanged before he has guessed the
quotation.

SOME OUTDOOR GAMES

THE ROOF GAME

is played by two persons with a discarded tennis ball and a
sloping roof. The ideal roof is 30 feet long, slopes at an angle
of 90°, ends 8 feet from the ground and has a perfectly

clear space in front of it. Each player in turn serves one ball from any position in this run-way and at any speed. The ball must roll or bounce off the roof within its length. The receiver must catch the ball before it touches the ground. If he does so, neither scores; if he fails, the server scores one point. In either event the service passes. The receiver scores one point if the server fails to reach the roof or throws it so that it falls beyond the end of the roof, or throws the ball over the roof. In the latter event he must fetch it, as well as lose a point. A game is five points. No feints are legitimate, but one need not look in the direction in which one is throwing. A player may throw the moment he has received, to catch the receiver out of position. Given the right roof it is a great game, almost as sweaty as Squash. A long roof should be smooth. But even on a short and tiley shed the game can be fast and the loser furious.

A chimney is a hazard: a ball may be served against it with such force as frequently to elude the receiver; but if the server misses it he risks the penalties for throwing over the roof. This game can be played as a foursome.

HUMAN POLO

The biggest men are the ponies, and the girls or lighter weights mount them pick-a-back, hold on with one hand and use walking-sticks to drive a tennis-ball through goals at opposite ends of a lawn or tennis-court. Holding opponents with the hands is not allowed, nor kicking (of man or ball), but bumping, boring and hooking sticks are all part of the game. A player may remount; but may not play from the ground. Numbers to a side according to the size of lawn.

THREE STEPS

This game was invented by Harry Farjeon.

The players scatter themselves about the lawn and its surroundings (but the kitchen garden should be out of bounds) each placing himself at a distance of at least three large paces from his nearest neighbour.

The Master of Ceremonies, with the name of each player on a separate slip in his hand, now goes round the lawn in his best hush-hush manner, passing a slip to each player. The name on the slip is that player's prey, to be caught with slow calculated cunning; but that player, or A., is, at the same time, someone else's prey.

When the distribution of slips has taken place the Master of Ceremonies reads out the names of the players one by one and *each in turn* takes three steps. Feints and dissimulation are of the essence of this game. A. catches his victim by touching him *without* falling over; B. is then out of the game and gives his slip to A. with the name of the player that A. is now after. When only two players are left in the game, each intent to catch the other first, the nicest judgments have to be made concerning very short or very long steps. N.B. The longest step must always be a *walking* step – no leaps and no drawing up of the foot and starting again.

N.B. It tends to spoil the game, or anyway it is disappointing to the parties concerned, if, by the second or third round when a certain amount of handing-on of slips has taken place, two players turn out to be after each other. This can be avoided if the Master of Ceremonies distributes the names according to some secret order or sequence.

FRENCH AND ENGLISH
or
PRISONERS' BASE

This game cannot be played without a sizeable lawn.

Two well-matched sides are picked up or arranged, one half of the lawn being the camp or territory of the A.s, the other of the B.s. A given number of treasures (old shoes, red handkerchiefs and so on) are spaced along the base line of each camp, and the aim of the game is to seize the enemy's treasure. Yet if you are caught on the enemy's ground you are a prisoner and have to join the treasure on the base line until you are rescued, i.e. touched, by one of your side. Once a treasure or a rescued prisoner is in your bag (and each sortie across the enemy lines can only achieve *one* prize) you can make the return journey to your own territory unmolested. Players usually make their own subsidiary rules as the game (after all it *is* only a game) progresses. But where there are young it is better to allow the charge across the base line of the enemy camp to bring immunity and not the actual picking-up of a treasure or touching a prisoner; this can then be done at leisure while gaining breath and applying the dock leaves. N.B. It can spoil the fun if each side places a grown-up with a sadistic streak as 'goalie' guarding the treasure, for it paralyses the free movement of the game.

452

ON FOOD AND DRINK

It snewed in his hous of mete and drinke.
Chaucer.

And cooks recorded frames of mind
In sad and subtle chops.
G. K. Chesterton.

I told him . . . that we ate when we were not
hungry, and drank without the provocation
of thirst.
Swift.

it snewéd in his hous of mete and drinke

On Food & Drink

The faculty the Stomach has of communicating the impressions made by the various substances that are put into it, is such, that it seems more like a nervous expansion from the Brain than a mere receptacle for Food.

Dr Waterhouse's *Lecture on Health*, 1823.

NOTABLE AND AMUSING FOOD

Week-end cookery should be either very quick, a good meal produced in half an hour, or very slow, put on before you go out. However witty the talk, however shady the garden, however original the cottage and its furnishings, it won't be by these things alone that your week-ends will be judged for repetition, but also by the food you offer.

Serve unusual dishes that will be remembered and spoken of. Settle on a speciality and learn it up, be it the art of devilling, of making pancakes, of serving hors-d'oeuvres, or of compounding a salad. Get an unusual, not a humdrum, cookery book and practise a few dishes between week-ends. Never let any dish be dull. Your guests eat with their eyes as well as with their palates and noses.

Week-end food can be divided into four parts: food which you take out with you ready to eat; food which you cook out-of-doors; dishes which, prepared before setting out, are left to cook slowly in readiness for your return; and dishes which can be prepared very rapidly when you come home.

PICNIC FOOD : READY TO EAT

Although sandwiches are often the mainstay of a picnic there are many ways of ringing the changes. Take screw-topped

P

jars filled with cold kedgeree, fish mousse, or soused her-
rings. A jar filled with potato salad will go well with any kind
of cold meat, poultry or game which can be taken tinned or
previously home-cooked and carved, wrapped in greaseproof
paper and put in a container. (Flat hinge-lidded 'sandwich'
tins can be bought very cheaply and are ideal for this purpose.) Or take tins of tunny fish, goose pâté, sardines; or
stuffed eggs, with the halves put together again and wrapped
in lettuce leaves to keep them moist. If you are a good pastry
hand, pastry cases filled with savoury mixtures are well
worth the extra effort. Cold omelettes are an excellent picnic
dish. Salami and other ready-to-eat sausages, a choice of
cheeses and fruit in addition to the main dish make it certain
that there will be enough for even the most epicurean and the
hungriest.

A green salad can travel in its own bowl if it is washed and
dried in advance. The dressing must be in a separate jar. If
the weather is hot, pack cos lettuces in a tin with a very little
water. The lettuce will remain crisp and a jar of butter and a
small plastic bottle of milk placed between the leaves will stay
cool and fresh. Unbuttered French rolls, French bread, water
biscuits or crisp-breads can then be taken in addition or as an
alternative to thin brown bread and butter, which should be
wrapped in a damp cloth.

For sandwiches themselves, bread is easier to cut and digest
if it is a day old – much nicer if it is new. If rolls are preferred
they must be fresh, or they can be crisped by sprinkling them
with water and heating them for a few minutes on a baking
sheet in a very hot oven. Finger out the soft middles, so that
you have two empty 'boats' for your filling. You might also
consider using brioches, poppy-seed rolls and scones instead
of bread; and malt and raisin bread make good sweet sandwiches.

Prepare the butter in advance by creaming it with a per-
forated spoon in a warm bowl. Half a cup (a quarter pound)
of creamed butter will spread a 2lb loaf (about 45 slices). Mustard, horseradish cream, vegetable extract, mayonnaise,
curry sauce, chopped chives or parsley can be added to the
butter according to the filling.

Use a palette knife for spreading, butter the inner sides of
both slices of the bread, and when filling sandwiches with
meat remember that several plies of thin shavings are far, far

better than thick slices. Remember that if you are using fat meat the butter should be reduced or eliminated. Salted meat and fish fillings are improved by a drop of lemon juice (a drop means a drop, no more), chopped pickles or capers. To keep sandwiches fresh wrap them in aluminium foil, or failing that, in waxed or greaseproof paper.

To make a Sandwich Loaf cut off the ends of a French loaf, scoop out the crumb, brush the inside with melted butter, and pack with any fairly solid sandwich mixture. Alternatively, stuff a number of rolls in the same way, one for each member of the party.

SANDWICH FILLINGS

Cream cheese and grated walnuts or chopped olives or, creamed with paprika, with sliced tomatoes.

Flaked fish mixed with a thick shrimp sauce.

Finely-chopped cooked liver and crisp bacon.

Tunny fish with lemon juice, grated onion and parsley.

Kipper fillets with mustard butter (if the fillets are marinated instead of cooked they make an excellent substitute for costly smoked salmon).

Chopped egg with chutney or 'Gentleman's Relish' or Worcester sauce.

Eggs fried in oil (oil being the only cooked fat that is nice cold) until the yolks are almost hard.

Minced ham and anchovy.

Peanut butter and grated onion, or chopped olives, or chopped pickle.

Flaked buckling with lemon juice and plenty of pepper.

Minced corned beef and mustard butter.

Chopped crisp bacon and peanut butter.

Sardines and tomato sauce; or sardines mashed to a paste with an equal quantity of sieved egg yolk seasoned with salt, cayenne pepper, a drop of lemon juice and moistened with olive oil.

English Cheddar, Cheshire or cottage cheese with slivers of green peppers or chopped tinned pimiento.

Any kind of cold meat, game or poultry – and try mixing thin shavings of different kinds of meat.

Chopped dates, cheese and nuts.

Honey and fresh mint.

Honey and banana (with lemon juice added).

Devonshire cream and strawberry jam.

457

MEALS COOKED OUT-OF-DOORS

The Barbecue is a means of cooking meat on a spit or grid over direct heat, with or without a special highly seasoned sauce. The trick is to get a red-hot, almost smokeless fire, lay the meat on the grid and grill it, turning when necessary. Steaks, chops or sausages can be cooked in this way; or you can make Shish Kebabs, one of each of the following being arranged on long skewers, one for each member of the party: loin of lamb in inch-thick cubes, chipolata sausages, small mushrooms, squares of onion, small pieces of bacon, a bay leaf and quarters of tomato or slices of red pepper. These ingredients are improved if they are taken to the picnic covered with a pile of chopped raw onion. Lay the loaded skewers on the grid for about ten minutes; turn them over and cook for another ten minutes.

If a frying pan is available, and there are not more than four people in the party, Minute steak is your best bet, the thin steaks being fried for one minute on each side in a mixture of butter and Worcester sauce. Bananas baked in their skins are a delicious substitute for green vegetables.

Stews and soups can be re-heated over a picnic fire if you have a solid grid over the fire or a suitable pot with a clamp-on lid.

Frankfurters and toasted marshmallows are the easiest of all picnic food. The only cooking implements needed are long skewers or forks or strong green twigs.

THE OYSTER BAKE

If you have a sea-shore, seaweed, a piece of sail cloth, oysters, and hours to spare you can make a Memorable Meal (but notice that this is a neutral term).

The sea-shore is the natural place for the oyster bake. Begin the preparations several hours before the time set for the meal and make a circle of flat stones 2′ to 4′ in diameter and in this circle build a hot fire of wood. When this has burned for two to three hours, rake out the fire and on the bed of ashes arrange a layer of fresh seaweed, and then your oysters in their shells, potatoes in their skins or corn on the cob. Cover with a thick layer of seaweed and then with a piece of sailcloth, fastening down the edges with stones. Leave for two to three hours and then rake out the food.

THE DUCK AND THE HARE

If you are camping, and tomorrow's meal has to be thought of as well as today's, then be sure to have in sequence a hare and a duck. Today's hare, jugged, will have (you must see that it has) a quantity of thick gravy left over. In this gravy simmer your cut-up duck on the next day. You will have, simply and inexpensively, a Canard Rouennais that the Tour d'Argent itself would be proud of.

DISHES TO COME HOME TO

Dishes to come home to are either prepared the day before and re-heated, or are dishes which have been cooking slowly while you were out. Dishes which are improved by having been made the day before are: Curry, Hungarian Goulash, Chicken Paprika, Oxtail with haricot beans, Irish Stew, Lancashire Hot-pot, Baked Beans, Mushrooms in Sour Cream, Red Cabbage with chestnuts, and Veal Matelote.

BAKED BEANS

Empty two large tins of baked beans into a large fireproof dish. Stir in two tablespoonfuls of treacle, 1 small onion, 1 teaspoonful of made mustard, a pinch of soda bicarbonate. Lay 6 slices of streaky bacon on top and cook in a very slow oven for 2 hours. When ready to eat, re-heat and place under grill to crisp the bacon.

MUSHROOMS IN SOUR CREAM

Wash one pound of mushrooms, and cut a sliver off the end of the stems, but do not peel. Then slice each mushroom down through the stalk. Heat three tablespoonfuls of butter in a frying pan, add a thin layer of mushrooms, being careful not to overcrowd them or to stir them roughly (this lets the juice escape). When they are delicately brown, remove them and do another layer, adding more butter if necessary. When the last layer has been removed from the pan, mix two table-spoonfuls of flour with the remaining fat and cook, stirring continuously; then add one-and-a-half cups of milk to make a smooth sauce. Put the mushrooms back into this sauce, add half-a-cup of sour cream (a little yoghourt mixed with cream and allowed to stand will make an excellent sour cream), salt and freshly-ground pepper to taste. Cook over a low flame for about 5 minutes. This can be stored for days in the refrigerator, and can be used in a number of ways. It can be served

plain on toast, or as a sauce over gently fried slices of ham on
buttered toast. It also makes an excellent casserole.

For the casserole, open a tin of lobster, crab, or boned
chicken, or take shelled prawns or shrimps, or bits of left-
over fowl of any sort, and arrange them, together with one
hard-boiled egg for each person, sliced lengthwise, in a
shallow oven-dish. Cover with mushrooms in sour cream
and heat in a moderate oven.

RED CABBAGE WITH CHESTNUTS

Melt an ounce of fat, preferably dripping, in a heavy
saucepan. Add about a pound of shredded red cabbage, a
large onion, sliced, 1 large apple, sliced, 2 tablespoonfuls of
stock (or water), 1 tablespoonful of wine vinegar (or red
wine), 1 heaped dessertspoonful of brown sugar, 2 teaspoonfuls of salt, and several turns of the pepper mill. Cover with
a tightly fitting lid and cook gently for about 40 minutes,
shaking the pan occasionally to prevent sticking.

The chestnuts are cooked separately, and added to the cabbage when it is re-heated. Cut crosses in the end of each
chestnut, then cook them for 15 to 20 minutes in boiling
water. Take them out of the water one at a time and remove
their skins with a sharp knife while they are still very hot.
Just before serving the cabbage, sauté the chestnuts in butter
and surround the dish of cabbage with them.

VEAL MATELOTE

Cut 2 lbs of stewing veal into small cubes, removing the
bones. Brown these gently in pork or chicken fat, and then
put them into a saucepan. Fry in the same fat six sliced
onions and about 6 diced carrots. When they are gently
browned add them to the meat. Then fry a quarter pound of
mushrooms in the same fat, and put them aside (or use a tin
of mushrooms baked in butter). Add 1½ ozs of flour to the
frying pan and cook it slowly with the fat, adding gradually
½ pint of boiling water and ½ pint of red wine. Boil this for
10 minutes, stirring continuously, and pour over the meat
and vegetables. Season with salt and several turns of the
pepper mill, add a little thyme and 1 bayleaf, and simmer for
1½ hours, putting the mushrooms in for the last half-hour.
Serve with shell-shaped pasta.

CHICKEN IN WINE

Cut a young tender chicken in serving pieces, rub with salt

and pepper and roll in flour. Brown in butter, and add 10 small onions or shallots and 8 slices of bacon, diced. Cover and cook for 15 minutes. Now add a tin of mushrooms, a glass of wine, ½ bay leaf, ½ teaspoon minced parsley and ¼ teaspoon each of thyme and marjoram, salt and pepper. Cook for a further 30 minutes.

RISOTTO MILANESE

Clean one large cupful of Patna rice by rubbing in a tea cloth – no, don't wash in water – then fry in 2 tablespoonfuls of butter with 2 finely chopped onions for 5 minutes. Add 1 pint of chicken bouillon, boiling, 4 tablespoonfuls wine, 2 table-spoonfuls tomato puree, a pinch of saffron, salt and pepper. Cook covered for 20 minutes; then mix in 2 tablespoonfuls of butter and serve with plenty of grated cheese.

ROASTS

Of all week-end dishes the easiest to prepare is the roast, especially if you have one of the new covered self-basting roasting pans. Very little advance preparation is needed, and there is nothing to do while it cooks in the oven beyond occasional basting if you use an ordinary roasting pan.

For a change from the usual mint sauce, lamb is delicious when larded, sparingly, with slivers of garlic (not more than one clove of garlic for a leg or shoulder of lamb) before roasting. Pan-roasted potatoes cut lengthways or potatoes baked in their jackets are the obvious accompaniment.

Carrots can also be cooked at the same time in the oven and take about 45 minutes to cook if sliced very fine lengthwise (this brings out the best flavour). Put them in a covered casserole with a good lump of butter and about ½ cup of water and salt and pepper to taste.

Incidentally, any batter or dough (whether it be for Yorkshire pudding or scones) should be mixed in advance. If it has no leavening it can be completely mixed and ready to put in the oven or frying pan. If it is made with leavening (other than yeast which does not take to this treatment) the dry and wet ingredients can be mixed and the two bowlfuls combined when wanted. The important thing to remember is that baking powder and soda bicarbonate must stay dry until you are ready to cook them.

461

QUICK DISHES
TO MAKE AT HOME-COMING

GRILLS

Of all forms of cookery that allow you to get a meal ready after you come in and before your guests' appetites ruin their tempers, grilling or frying is the best: cutlets, chops, steaks, lambs' kidneys or fish. Meat should first be placed very close to the heat to seal the juice, then moved to a cooler spot (or the gas turned lower) and cooked four minutes or so on each side, according to thickness. Salt only when on the dish.

Food is given an unusual taste before grilling by being marinated, that is, steeped in a mixture of oil and vinegar to which herbs have been added. Steep for some hours.

Well-grilled steak dished with watercress and potatoes fried in deep fat is excellent. But next time try putting on top of your steak or fish a pat of savoury butter. For this, work the butter with a spoon, season with pepper, and work in parsley chopped as finely as may be, or anchovy pulp: pounded anchovies and sieved capers.

OMELETTES

The secret of making the best omelettes is to withdraw the white of one egg for every six eggs used, and not to beat the eggs but to mix them gently. Omelettes containing minced ham, potatoes, pimientos, mushrooms, spinach are easy to improvise, and the 'Spanish' omelette, which contains a mixture of vegetables (onion is a 'must') and a little chopped ham, makes a delicious change. This omelette is left flat; not folded over.

SCRAMBLED EGGS

With mushrooms and/or kidneys which have just been fried in butter.

HOT SANDWICHES

Cut bread slices, butter them and fill with one or a mixture of these fillings: bacon, tomato and cheese; chopped onion, egg and red pepper; cream cheese, watercress and salad dressing; cinnamon powder in ham paste; bacon, lettuce and mayonnaise; chopped apple with nut and lettuce. These sandwiches may be either buttered all over the outside or dipped in a batter made by stirring one beaten egg into half a pint of milk. They are then fried until they are a golden colour on both sides.

SAVOURY PANCAKES

The day before you plan to eat this dish (1) Cook a large finnan haddock in milk and, removing skin and bone, flake the fish. (Keep the stock, skin and bones to make an excellent soup for another meal.) (2) Make a batter with 4 ozs flour, 2 eggs, 1 tablespoonful of olive oil and ½ pint of milk. Keep it in a cool place – in the refrigerator if you have one. The pancakes will be the thinner.

The following day when you come home, melt 1 oz butter, stir in the fish, add pepper and 2 oz cream. Fry the pancakes, keeping them very thin. Stuff and serve very hot.

A good filling can also be made with the remains of a goulash or pieces of left-over game or poultry mixed with some Mushrooms in Sour Cream (see p. 459) or any other thick and savoury sauce.

CORNED BEEF HASH

Grate 3 onions and add to the contents of a tin of corned beef with ½ lb of diced cooked potatoes (held over from the previous day), some Worcester sauce and horseradish sauce. Heat some butter in a frying pan and put in the hash mixture. When heated through, turn out in the shape of a flat cake into a fireproof dish. Brown under the grill and serve with tomato sauce.

CONSOMMÉ WITH POACHED EGG

Take 2 pints of consommé (see p. 465) and bring to the boil. Slice 2 French rolls, butter the rounds, then brown in the oven. Poach 4 eggs in the boiling consommé, removing each one when cooked to a soup tureen in which you have already placed the French rolls. Pour the soup gently over and serve with grated cheese.

VEAL WITH MUSHROOMS

Take 4 veal cutlets, white and tender; trim them and fry in butter. When they are brown, put them in the oven to continue cooking, and pour stock over the meat, repeating at intervals until the veal is well cooked. Remove the cutlets to a hot dish, brown a little flour in butter and add to the gravy in the dish. Allow this to thicken over a low heat, stirring all the time; then add a tin of mushrooms and a large glass of sherry and heat again. Pour the sauce over the veal and serve hot.

463

EGGS IN RAMEKINS

Butter some ramekin dishes and two-thirds fill with flaked salmon or smoked haddock and cooked rice. Break an egg into each, season and stand in a covered pan of boiling water until the eggs are set. Add a teaspoonful of cream to each with salt and pepper and drop of Tabasco sauce. Put under the grill for a minute or two before serving.

SALADS

Green salads may be made of many plants other than lettuce. Chicory, dandelion leaves, sorrel and white cabbage, for instance. They should be perfectly clean and perfectly dry. For drying, use a wire basket, whirling it at arm's length – out-of-doors. The best dressing for green salads is French dressing which can be made in large quantities and stored in a jar in a refrigerator for weeks. When it is needed all you have to do is to shake the jar thoroughly. A good recipe is 4 oz. olive oil, 2 oz. *white wine* vinegar, 1 dessertspoonful of sugar, 1 teaspoonful salt, ½ teaspoonful dry mustard, ten or more twists of the pepper grinder, and a garlic clove which should be removed once the dressing has been very thoroughly shaken and tasted. An alternative is to rub the salad bowl with half a clove of garlic.

Waldorf salad is made of equal parts of raw cooking apple and raw celery, sliced, disposed on a bed of lettuce, liberally garnished with half-walnuts, and dressed with mayonnaise. Orange and lettuce; grapefruit and lettuce; shrimp and lettuce; watercress and creamed cheese with nuts, are quite as easy to mix as lettuce and beetroot, and much more fun.

Try Huile d'Arachides instead of olive oil. It is a great deal cheaper and very nearly as good for salad dressings and for cooking. For cooking it is infinitely better than lard or margarine and for some dishes part oil, part butter makes an excellent mixture. (Beef, pork or poultry dripping is always good to use for frying or roasting, but never use mutton dripping.)

A passable mayonnaise can be made by adding oil and a little cream to a reputable bottled mayonnaise. (Heinz is the best.)

TINNED AND PACKAGED FOODS

Use tinned foods, but disguise them. No one should ever suspect that they are tinned. All tinned foods are improved by

464

additions during the heating up. (Never follow the directions
on the tin for heating up; it takes longer than applying direct
heat to the contents; all but the most agile burn their fingers
and spot their clothes when opening a heated tin.)

SOUP

Remember that Campbell's and Heinz's Tomato soups are
not the only good tinned soups. There are also creams of
mushroom, of asparagus, of pea, of chicken, of onion
and (if you are lucky enough to find it) Shippam's excellent hare soup. Tinned soups may be made more interesting as well as disguised as to origin, which has its own advantage, by mixing cream of chicken and cream of mushroom;
cream of chicken and cream of onion; cream of pea and
cream of chicken – and others as fancy dictates.
There are also three good brands of packet soups: Knorr
(onion and pea are admirable but some others are too
glutinous); Batchelor's (particularly the chicken noodle); and
Maggi.
Clear soups (Knorr make excellent chicken and beef con-
sommés) are improved by a tablespoonful of sherry or white
wine. Likewise tomato and spinach soups are improved by
the addition of a little thick cream just before serving; celery
and cauliflower soup are improved by the addition of an egg
beaten in a cup of milk (this is true of most cream soups).
Use the water in which vegetables have been cooked to vary
and extend tinned soups. And do not forget the virtues of
grated parmesan with any clear soup.

FISH

If you are not eating it cold, tinned fish should be wrapped
in buttered paper and heated in a covered frying-pan; or
cooked in crumbs and cheese; or served with a good lemon or
anchovy sauce; or poached in white wine or broth and served
with shrimps, mixed gherkins, chipped olives, minced onion
or anchovy paste.

MEAT

To re-cook tinned meat place it on a bed of finely shredded
vegetables, top with fried minced onion, pour gravy over,
bring to the boil, then simmer, adding herbs, currant jelly,
or a touch of lemon. Spiced sausages renew the youth of a
tinned stew to be served on a bed of rice or macaroni.

465

VEGETABLES AND FRUIT

Tinned sweet corn should be heated with additional butter, salt, pepper and sugar. Tinned peas should be drained, washed very thoroughly and treated like sweet corn, with the addition of a sprig of mint. Don't use processed ones, and don't use those bright with artificial colouring and over-flavoured with mint essence. Tinned spinach, branch or purée; celery and, for those who have donkey-tastes, tinned carrots (which are delicious sliced very thinly and sautéd in butter) are useful stand-bys. Avoid cut-up asparagus and artichoke hearts. Both are expensive, and neither are worth eating.

Frozen vegetables, and fruit, are quick and easy, and, though not as good as fresh ones, they are far better than most tinned ones, and allow you to have out-of-season foods at a reasonable price. But don't keep them once they are defrosted – and remember that even a refrigerator is not cold enough to prevent them defrosting.

QUICK SWEETS

The French fashion of fruit and cake served after the cheese may well replace elaborate puddings. But if you are drinking wine and serving pudding, again follow the French fashion and serve the cheese before the pudding and your wine will not be sour on the palate.

Fresh fruit alone with some white wine and sugar, or with junket, is an ideal sweet. Failing that, have a plentiful stock of tinned fruits, to serve as they are or in jelly form. Buy packets of jellies in preference to gelatin by the ounce, even though their flavours are usually unpleasant; they are surer in use and you can superimpose a real fruit flavour by adding fruit juice instead of water. For fruit jelly, add berries or any fruit cut in slices. For a sponge jelly, whisk white of egg into the jelly just before it begins to set. For a wine jelly: 1 packet of lemon jelly, a wine glass of orange juice, a wine glass of sherry (or Marsala, or Madeira) and boiling water to make a total of 1 pint of liquid.

When Sir Thomas B., that wise and gracious man – he has the best collection of Hocks in England and the best private collection of Dürer prints in Europe – was, very young, at his first party, leaning against the wall, nervously fingering his tie, there came to him an obviously assured Man-of-the-World. 'Your

466

first party ? I thought so. I am going to tell you something which will stand you in good stead for the whole of your life. If they serve wine-jelly, and they probably will, help yourself to the knobs. They always make the damn things upside down and all the wine runs into the knobs.'

Tinned cherries, muscats, green figs, loganberries are as nice as peaches, pineapple, and pears and less hackneyed. Don't buy the most expensive form of peaches: the cheaper kinds are packed riper. Don't buy pineapple chunks. Only sliced pineapple eliminates the wood-like core of the fruit. Hawaiian brands are the best.

ZAMBAGLIONE

This is a memorable sweet. For four helpings: 4 eggs, 4 tablespoons sugar, 8 tablespoons Marsala, ¼ teaspoon vanilla essence. Combine all ingredients in the top of a double boiler, place over hot water and beat constantly until frothy, smooth and thick. Remember that a Zambaglione boiled is a Zambaglione spoiled, but do not be disheartened if it separates: it does not look as nice, and it should not be so – but it will still taste delicious. When it is thick, empty into warmed glasses (to be eaten hot) or turn it into a dish and go on beating it until it is cold.

PRESERVED GINGER (or DATES with their stones taken out) with whipped cream.

APPLE FLUFF

Beat 2 tablespoonfuls of castor sugar into 1 stiffly beaten egg white and fold into a small tinful of apple sauce with ¼ teaspoonful of nutmeg, a few drops of lemon juice and a little grated lemon rind. Top with whipped cream.

JAMAICA JUNKET

Add 1 tablespoonful of treacle, instead of the usual sugar, to a pint of warm milk, and make the junket as usual. When set, cover the junket with 2 tablespoonfuls of Jamaica rum. Serve with cream.

MELON WITH LIQUEUR

Remove the top of a ripe melon, scoop out the seeds and pour in a glass of any favourite liqueur or white vermouth. Chill for several hours.

HONEYED PINEAPPLE

Fry slices of fresh or tinned pineapple with honey over a very low heat. A little Marsala can be added before serving.

RASPBERRIES IN WINE

Use fresh raspberries, or if they are not in season, defrost a packet of frozen raspberries slowly. Add a glassful of red wine.

APPLE MUESLI

Grate an unpeeled apple for each person, stir in 1 heaped tablespoonful rolled oats to each apple and add enough cream or top milk to make a moist mixture. Add any of the following: soaked sultanas, chopped dates, grated nuts, chopped ginger. Serve in individual glasses.

BANANA WHIP

Mash two bananas for each person. Add the juice and grated rind of ½ lemon for each 4 bananas, and sugar to taste. It is fine and unrich like this. But you can also mix it with an equal quantity of cream. (The lemon makes a Jamaica taste like a Canary.)

MERINGUES

The shells can be made in advance and kept for several days. Serve with whipped cream, or chestnut purée and whipped cream.

BAKED EGG CUSTARD WITH CARAMEL SAUCE

The custard can be made in advance and the sauce keeps almost indefinitely. For the custard, take 6 eggs, beat them slightly, add ½ cup of sugar and ¼ teaspoon of salt. Heat 1 pint of milk and pour it gradually on to the eggs and sugar, stirring all the time. Strain the mixture into a greased dish and stand this in a baking pan with hot water halfway up the sides of the dish, and bake in a moderate oven (350°) until firm (when an inserted knife comes out clean). While baking you must take care that the water around the moulds does not boil or the custard will whey.

To make *Caramel Sauce* take 1 lb. of lump sugar. Put 9 lumps in a heavy pan and burn them. Add 2 tablespoonfuls of boiling water, the rest of the sugar and another 2 tablespoonfuls of hot water and let it boil until it thickens. This will take about half-an-hour but there will be enough sauce for several custards. Store in a screw-top jar. Do not place in the refrigerator. This sauce is also delicious served with junket.

COFFEE

Coffee, as used on the Continent, serves the double purpose of an agreeable tonic and an exhilarating beverage, without the unpleasant effects of wine.

Coffee, as drunk in England, debilitates the Stomach, and produces a slight nausea. In Italy it is made strong from the best Coffee, and is poured out hot and transparent.

In England it is usually made from bad Coffee, served out tepid and muddy, and drowned in a deluge of water, and sometimes deserves the title given it in 'the Petition against Coffee', 4to, 1674, page 4, 'a base, black, thick, nasty, bitter, stinking Puddle Water'.

from *The Cook's Oracle* by
William Kitchiner, M.D. 1838.

But coffee need not be 'Puddle water'. There is no difficulty in making good, strong, aromatic, stimulating coffee. How is it done?

First, remember a few basic facts about coffee. There are oils in the coffee bean and they provide the aroma and flavour. They are partly released in the roasting and more so in the grinding. They are volatile. Therefore, freshly roasted beans, ground just before use, will make the best coffee. Use vacuum-packed coffee as a stand-by only: you pay for the pack and you lose much of the aroma. (If it has chicory in it, it is not to be tolerated even as a stand-by. It is said that when Bismarck was in a Paris hotel he ordered the waiter to bring him six cups of an infusion of chicory. Six were brought and he ordered a dozen. They were brought and he ordered two dozen. The waiter came back trembling with only twenty-three cups: 'Alas, Excellency, there is no more chicory.' 'Ah', said Bismarck, '*now* bring me a cup of coffee.') Coffee beans stored in an air-tight container should keep 10 to 14 days; ground coffee from 2 days (if finely ground) to 4 days (if medium or coarsely ground). The days are reckoned from the date of roasting or grinding, *not* the day of purchase. Therefore, the grocer who gets a delivery once a week or once a fortnight may not be much use to you. If you can, grind your beans shortly before you use them. It is not arduous and it is well worth the trouble. Electric grinders are now available, and many of the hand-operated coffee-mills are efficient; or perhaps you are lucky enough to have a Kenwood Liquidiser: this will deal with coffee beans as promptly as it will pulverise vegetables and fruit.

Next, what coffee should you buy? Go to a good coffee-merchant, tell him what coffee-making appliance you use and take a small quantity of the blend and roast he recommends. (As coffee is nowadays sold in the form of blends only, there is no point in asking for one particular kind – Santos, Costa Rica, etc.) If what your merchant has sold you is not to your liking, try another blend, or another roast, or another merchant; and don't despair: there is a blend and a roast for every palate. Here is, however, a tip which we can give you. If you have had a cup of coffee which you particularly enjoyed, it will in all probability have been made from a blend which was highly roasted (commonly called continental roast) and which contained a fair quantity of mocha.

There are many methods of coffee-making, and there is a confusing choice of coffee-making appliances in the shops. The least good, and perhaps the most generally used, is the so-called percolator which is so made that water circulates through the coffee continuously at boiling point, thus stewing and spoiling the coffee. If you use one of these pots, do consider buying one of the simple Italian coffee-makers which range in price from half-a-guinea for the smallest *Napolitana* to several guineas for the larger sizes of the *Vesuviana*, *Columbia* and other makes. They are very economical in use; they are quick – and they are virtually unbreakable.

But if you want your week-end guests to exclaim after dinner 'this indeed is different, this is cream of coffee, nay elixir of coffee . . . liqueur of coffee', then you must buy the small domestic *Espresso* machine. And by this we mean the one true Espresso machine called *Gaggia* and not the many other machines, admirable though some of them are, to which their manufacturers have chosen to attach the label 'Expresso' (with an 'x', not 'Espresso'). The Gaggia is interesting to handle, it looks good, but it is without doubt expensive. If you cannot afford one now and if you really care for superlative coffee, start saving immediately. You will not regret it. And meantime practise your palate at the Espresso bars.

DRINK

For hard drinkers, whisky, gin and the vermouths; for soft drinkers, tea, coffee and ginger-beer are the standard refreshments supplied at the village pub. But imagination and bold experiment can break this monotony with many happy improvisations.

'Ginandit' is the weary walker's counsel of despair. Any enterprising week-end pub, or cottage, will possess ingredients from which one or other of the following may be compounded:

COCKTAILS

EAST INDIAN: Equal parts of French vermouth and sherry, with a dash of orange bitters.

WEST INDIAN: Two parts rum to one part fresh lime or lemon juice, with some sugar dissolved in it, or failing this, 'Kia-ora' lemon crush (not squash) or Rose's lime juice.

HAWAIIAN: Four parts gin, two parts orange juice and one part curaçao (or any other of the orange liqueurs).

SIDE-CAR: Equal parts of fresh lemon juice (no alternative), cointreau (or one of the orange liqueurs) and brandy.

SATAN'S WHISKER (*straight*): Of Italian vermouth, French vermouth, gin and orange juice, two parts each; of Grand Marnier one part; orange bitters.

Ditto (*curled*): For the Grand Marnier substitute an equal quantity of orange curaçao.

JOHN WOOD: Italian vermouth, four parts; Irish whisky and lemon juice, two parts each; Kummel, one part; Angostura bitters.

MR. SUTTON'S GIN-BLIND (*to be drunk with discretion*): Six parts gin, three parts curaçao, two parts brandy and a dash of orange bitters.

NOTE ON THE USE OF BITTERS: When cocktails are mixed in bulk, any bitters should be introduced in the proportion of one half to one teaspoonful per pint. In more intimate drinking, delicacy of flavour and economy of material are secured by rinsing each glass with bitters, which are then returned to the bottle, while the glass is filled with a mixture from which bitters have been omitted. If possible, ALL COCKTAILS should stand on ice for at least half an hour before shaking and taking. If you cannot wait so long,

471

you must adulterate your mixture with ice. A large jug, and an egg-whisk (or even a fork) efficiently replace the shaker. The glasses should be as cold as possible before the cocktail is poured out.

ICED DRINKS

GINGER-BEER: (*a*) with gin and lemon or lime juice, preferably fresh but, if need be, bottled; (*b*) (for sweet-tooths) with cointreau and orange juice. (There is no bottled substitute for orange juice, but the orange Crushes taste much better than the old Squashes—tho' they don't keep as well.

Strong, cold black COFFEE with a wineglassful of brandy to a quart and some ice.

For people who can bear to be seen drinking it: Equal parts of GIN and CREME DE MENTHE, with plenty of cracked ice.

JOHN COLLINS: The juice of two oranges and one lemon with an equal measure of gin, some soda water and ice.

BAVARIAN CUP: Mix a small wineglassful of cherry brandy (or plain brandy) with a bottle of white wine, and add crushed strawberries and ice *ad lib.*

CIDER CUP: Three large bottles of sparkling cider, a pint of old Marsala, a little sugar, a lot of lemon rind, two bottles of soda water and maraschino or brandy quant: suff:

RAJAH'S PEG: A claret glass of old brandy in a pint of dry champagne.

MINT JULEP: Pack a tumbler as tightly as possible with alternate layers of finely cracked ice and sprigs of mint, freshly picked and bruised; fill the interstices with whisky (rye if available, otherwise Irish or, if need be, Scotch). This tastes as good as it smells. It is drunk by degrees, as it melts, and through a straw.

CASSIS (black-currant syrup made in France) is obtainable in Soho, and when mixed with French vermouth, soda-water and ice, makes a delicious 'soft' drink. If you can afford the veritable liqueur cassis, it is not 'soft'. If you cannot shop in Soho, Ribena is a good alternative to Cassis syrup.

COLD TEA should be made as follows: Steep the leaves in *cold water* (the same proportion as you use when boiling) for 12 hours and then strain.

HOT DRINKS

T E A with rum, lemon juice and a shaving of lemon peel.

M U L L E D C L A R E T (1) *For Boys:* Warm (but do not boil) the wine with nutmeg, cinnamon, cloves, sugar and lemon rind. (2) *For Men:* Ditto, adding dry port one part to six of claret. (3) *For Heroes:* As for boys, adding one part port to three parts claret and as much old brandy as you think the company can stand.

R U M P U N C H : one part rum, one part whisky and two parts (or a trifle less) water, heated with sugar, cinnamon, nutmeg, cloves and dried orange and lemon peel.

H A N D Y P U N C H : to two bottles of whisky and one of rum, add an equal quantity of water. Heat these with a little nutmeg and cinnamon, the juice of two lemons and sugar to taste. When it is very hot, set it alight with a red-hot poker and, after a moment's admiration, blow out the flames.

R E D C U R R A N T T E A is a good hot 'soft' drink. It is made by pouring boiling water on plenty of red currant jelly and adding a squeeze of lemon juice. Black currant jam will make B L A C K C U R R A N T T E A .

FOR THE WEEK-END STORE CUPBOARD

Salt, black pepper (*ground and corns*), mustard
Curry powder (*Indian*)
Paprika
Garlic salt
Onion salt
White or Red Wine Vinegar
Anchovy Sauce
Italian tomato purée and sugo (*they can be bought in Soho and in special shops*)
Chestnut purée
Rennet
Garlic
Spices and Herbs (*as good a collection as you can make; these can rarely be bought in the country and it is very annoying to have to change the menu for the want of one of them*)
Gentleman's Relish (*this can be used as a ready-made anchovy-butter*)
Tinned and packeted soups and bouillon cubes
Pimiento (*small tins*)
Olives

Liver pâté (*Danish*)
Tinned Mushrooms baked in butter
Sardines in varieties
Anchovies
Tunny fish
Parmesan cheese
Tinned sweet corn
Frankfurter sausages
Corned beef
Rice
Packets of long Italian spaghetti and other Italian pasta
Packets of Jelly
Tinned Fruit
Orange Crush
Lemon Squash

FOOD AND DRINK

W H Y has our poetry eschewed
The rapture and response of food?
What hymns are sung, what praises said
For home-made miracles of bread?
Since what we love has always found
Expression in enduring sound,
Music and verse should be competing
To match the transient joy of eating.
There should be present in our songs
As many tastes as there are tongues;
There should be humbly celebrated
One passion that is never sated.
Let us begin it with the first
Distinction of a conscious thirst
When the collusion of the vine
Uplifted water into wine.

Let us give thanks before we turn
To other things of less concern
For all the poetry of the table:
Clams that parade their silent fable
Lobsters that have a rock for stable
Red-faced tomatoes ample as
A countryman's full-bosomed lass;
Plain-spoken turnips; honest beets;
The carnal gusto of red meats;
The insipidity of lamb;
The wood-fire pungence of smoked ham;
Young veal that's smooth as natural silk;
The lavish motherliness of milk;

474

Parsley and lemon-butter that add
Spring sweetness unto river shad;
Thin flakes of halibut and cod,
Pickerel, flounder, snapper, scrod,
And every fish whose veins may be
Charged with the secrets of the sea;
Sweet-sour carp, beloved by Jews;
Pot-luck simplicity of stews;
Crabs, juiciest of Nature's jokes;
The deep reserve of artichokes;
Mushrooms, whose taste is texture, loath
To tell of their mysterious growth;
Quick, mealy comfort glowing in
A baked potato's crackled skin;
The morning promise, hailed by man,
Of bacon crisping in the pan;
The sage compound of *Hasenpfeffer*
With dumplings born of flour and zephyr;
Spinach whose spirit is the soil;
Anchovies glorified in oil;
The slow-gold nectar maples yield;
Pale honey tasting of the field
Where every clover is Hymettus;
The cooling sanity of lettuce
And every other herbal green
Whose touch is calm, whose heart is clean;
Succulent bean-sprouts, bamboo-shoots;
The sapid catalogue of fruits:
Plebeian apple, caustic grape,
Quinces that have no gift for shape,
Dull plums that mind their own affairs,
Incurably bland and blunted pears,
Fantastic passion-fruit, frank lemons
With acid tongues as sharp as women's,
Exotic loquats, sly persimmons,
White currants, amber-fleshed sultanas,
(Miniature and sweetened mannas)
Expansive peaches, suave bananas,
Oranges ripening in crates,
Tight-bodied figs, sun-wrinkled dates,
Melons that have their own vagaries;
The bright astringency of berries;
Crepe-satin luxury of cream;
Wedding-cake that fulfils the dream;
Pepper, whose satire stings and cuts;
Raw liberality of nuts;
Sauces of complex mysteries;
Proverbial parsnips; muscular cheese;

Innocent eggs that scorn disguises;
Languid molasses; burning spices
In kitchen-oracles to Isis;
Thick sauerkraut's fat-bellied savour;
Anything with a chocolate flavour;
Large generosity of pies;
Hot puddings bursting to surprise;
The smug monotony of rice;
Raisins that doze in cinnamon buns;
Kentucky biscuits, Scottish scones;
Falstaffian tarts that mock the chaste
Rose-elegance of almond-paste;
Venison steaks that smack of cloisters;
Goose-liver for the soul that roisters;
Reticent prawn; Lucullan oysters;
Sausages, fragrant link on link;
The vast ambrosias of drink:
Tea, that domestic mandarin;
Bucolic cider; loose-lipped gin;
Coffee, extract of common sense,
Purgative of the night's pretense;
Cocoa's prim nursery; the male
Companionship of crusty ale;
Cognac as oily as a ferret;
The faintly iron thrust of claret;
Episcopal port, aged and austere;
Rebellious must of grape; the clear,
Bluff confraternity of beer –

All these are good, all are a part
Of man's imperative needs that start
Not in the palate but the heart.
Thus fat and fibre, root and leaf
Become quick fuel and slow grief.
These, through the chemistry of blood,
Sustain his hungering manhood,
Fulfilling passion, ripening pain,
Steel in his bone, fire at his brain . . .
So until man abjures the meats
Terrestrial and impermanent sweets,
Growing beyond the things he eats,
Let us be thankful for the good
Beauty and benison of food,
Let us join chiming vowel with vowel
To rhapsodize fish, flesh and fowl,
And let us thank God in our songs
There are as many tastes as tongues.

Louis Untermeyer.

ARCHITECTURE

Architectooralooral.

Dickens.

When we build, let us think that we build
for ever.

Ruskin.

They dreamt not of a perishable home
Who thus could build.

Wordsworth.

What is a church ? – Our honest sexton tells,
'Tis a tall building with a tower and bells.

Crabbe.

Nor till the hours of light return
All we have built do we discern.

Matthew Arnold.

Architecture

'Architectooralooral'

KEY: *a* and *b* 15th century hand-axes; *c* small paring-knife; *d* stonesetter's trowel (15th cent.); *e* carpenter's gouge; *f* fine chisel for wood; *g* moulding-template; *h* Cotswold tile-pick; *i* Cotswold tiler's hammer; *j* Cotswold tiler's pegging-knife; *k* Cotswold waller's hand-hammer; *l* Elm mallet; *m* hammer for use with cup-headed carving-chisel; *n* cup-headed chisel; *o* punch, to reduce stone in a series of parallel furrows; *p* claw-tool, used in sequence to the punch; *q* pitching-tool, for coarsely reducing surface of stone.

The kinds of building one happens upon most often in country walks, and on week-end visits, are farms and manor houses and parish churches, with an occasional ruined Abbey or Great House by way of grandeur and diversity. For this reason the first place in these short notes will be given to the more modest kinds of architecture. These have a special fascination in that, being built by local contractors of local material, they vary in character with every district; for example, the brick or timber houses and flint churches of the Eastern Counties, where stone was an expensive luxury imported by water-carriage from a distance, and by contrast the Cotswolds where almost every kind of building is in stone. Mention of the Cotswolds brings in another interesting aspect of country building: the filtering down into the country of new architectural fashions from London and the big towns, so that one can often find charming simplified variations of smart London architectural features in the attempts of the local builders to keep up-to-date. The Cotswold builders, from among whom came most of the great contractors who executed the masonry of St. Paul's Cathedral, showed the

479

effect of this training under the eye of Sir Christopher Wren in the astonishingly accomplished series of early Georgian houses to be found in almost all the villages of that district. Other local styles are the extravagant timber work of Tudor and Stuart times in Lancashire and Cheshire and the Welsh Border counties, the timber in combination with tile and brick of Surrey, Sussex and Kent, the splendid Georgian brickwork of Buckinghamshire with its extraordinarily high proportion of darker burnt bricks, and the luscious golden stone work of the Ham Hill quarries which is to be found all over Dorset and South Somerset, and, finally, the work of all the good stone-building counties stretching diagonally across England from Somerset, through the Cotswolds, Oxfordshire, Northants, Rutland to Lincolnshire. In all these local styles the determining factor is in the main the materials used in construction, though political and economic conditions appear in some places as the Peel towers of the Scottish border, where defence was a primary consideration, or the Oast Houses of Kent.

The Georgian architecture of America, called by its owners colonial, though it continued long after the War of Independence, comes intermediate between a regional or local school and a small national school such as that of Ireland or Scotland. There is good Georgian brick building in America, but the most remarkable feature of this group to English eyes is the weather-boarded work. This is found in England, in Surrey especially (there are good examples in Dorking), but in America houses of a size and dignity that would have demanded stone or stucco in England were carried out in weather-boarding. (The 'Cape Cod House', rather in favour in America for a week-ending style, resembles the simpler and sturdier form of Georgian cottage. Its charms are rather those of atmosphere than architecture.) The great majority of old farm-houses are either Tudor or Stuart, that is, late mediæval, for the Middle Ages lingered on in the country till the eighteenth century almost, or what we may call classical, that is, Georgian and early nineteenth century. The typical late mediæval house is as illustrated overleaf.

The part between the Porch and the Upper end chambers (sometimes called Parlour and Solar above) was in the earliest examples, that is, before Edward VI (1550 about), all one room open from the ground to the roof – the 'baronial '

hall in fact – but in the second half of the sixteenth century
a floor was often inserted in older houses, providing a big
upstairs sitting-room in the roof part of the old hall, and
leaving the hall itself as rather a low-ceilinged, unimposing
room below. This making of a big sitting-room upstairs was
the origin of the grand staircase in larger houses: in the
Middle Ages proper staircases are rarely of much importance. This division of the hall into two storeys is the only
important change in medium-sized house design from
Plantagenet times down to Cromwell. Various details do
alter, however, and can serve as closer indications of date.
The barge-boards on gables, for example:

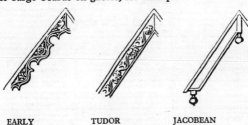

EARLY   TUDOR   JACOBEAN

Windows, too, are a good rough guide to date:

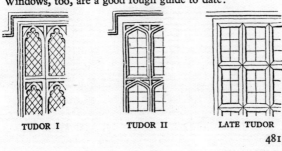

TUDOR I   TUDOR II   LATE TUDOR

481

Most of these examples have been taken from timber-built houses, but the main forms are the same all over the country. The Great Houses of Mediæval and Tudor times follow the same general plan, but in these cases the Upper and Lower end chambers have grown into long wings which are returned to form a court like those of the Colleges of Oxford and Cambridge. Often a second court was formed in front of the house proper out of ranges of farm buildings. These courts were entered through gate-houses over which were sets of rooms, in some cases important enough to be a little annexe to the house.

Simpler examples of gate-houses had a timber top storey on a brick or stone gate.

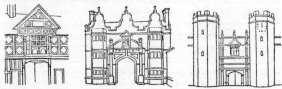

But in Tudor times brick gate-houses with octagonal turrets became popular. They were bright with gilding and diaper patterns, and generally picturesque, and there is a smack of knightly chivalry about them that pleased an age of realistic politicians playing at romance. This taste for pageantry, colouring and a flavour of chivalry in architecture is the first 'art' fashion that can be recognized in England. Beside the fondness for gate-houses and turrets and gay colouring, all symptoms of this first fashionable taste, there are the Tudor chimneys, of which a few examples below.

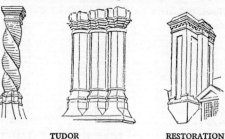

TUDOR   RESTORATION

In the later sixteenth century the 'chivalrous' taste is seen rapidly giving place to a 'classical', not real classic in the sense of Roman archæologists or even true Italian Renaissance, but a sort of barbarised version of the Italian derived from copybooks printed and engraved in Belgium or Germany. In grand houses the decorative work was often actually done by Flemish and German workmen. Below are instances of typical Flemish ornament in English buildings.

This thoroughly over-decorated Flemish type of architecture was the last word in fashion at the time of Shakespeare, but as the seventeenth century proceeds the influence of Holland

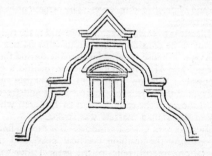

began to supersede that of Belgium and a bolder, rather less rich and less over-ripe manner began to prevail. The type of

483

gable shown is found chiefly in the South-East of England, and is definitely Dutch in origin. It is a sort of halfway house between the pure barbarity of James I architecture and the complete Classicism that came in with the Restoration.

The Restoration and William-and-Mary to Queen Anne type of country house is rightly celebrated for the way in which it is able to combine classical restraint with geniality. The typical house of the time takes this form:

The roof and chimneys are marked features of the design, and a sure indication of this period is the heavy ornamental cornice and wide-spreading eaves. The ornament to doors is bold and rich.

As the Classic movement became more and more rigid, large roofs came to be considered barbarous (that is, not Italian) and this type of house became fashionable during the reigns of George I and II. The roof is hidden behind a parapet. (See opposite.) Window frames in Classic houses vary considerably and there is even more variety and freedom of invention shown in the country than in London, where the tyranny of the Italian masters was strong.

The earliest form of Classic window – it is rare to find it unaltered – retains the mullion (vertical post) and transom (horizontal crosspiece), relics of the great Tudor windows, but the window opening has taken on its classic shape.

When sash windows were introduced – the first recorded is

in the sixteen-eighties – many of these early Classic windows were adapted and lost their mullion and transom. The early Georgian sash windows have very thick glazing bars, and are often placed flush with the surrounding brickwork. As the

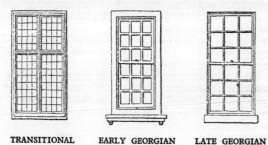

TRANSITIONAL   EARLY GEORGIAN   LATE GEORGIAN

eighteenth century went on, however, the tendency was to make the glazing bars more and more thin and elegant, and by the time of George III (1790) they began to assume the thickness we are accustomed to. Many delightful varieties of window were made by local firms during the eighteenth century, as the 'Siamese Twin' and the Venetian.

The latter became fashionable with London architects after the return of Lord Burlington (after whom Burlington House is named) from his Italian tour in George I's time, but they do not appear much in country districts till the seventeen thirties and forties. All these types of window are often to be seen inserted into earlier buildings. There is hardly space

485

here to do more than mention the extraordinary variety of types of bow-window, often richly decorated, and of ornamental doorways. It is often possible to recognize the work of one local firm in the windows and doors of a district.

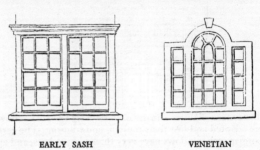

EARLY SASH   VENETIAN

Towards the end of the eighteenth century and in the first quarter of the nineteenth (Regency and George IV), a new type of country house appears.

It is long and low and has a roof of very flat pitch and very far-overhanging eaves. The roof is very often of slate. It is generally severely plain as regards stonework – when it is of brick it is often stuccoed and painted – and the chief ornamental feature often takes the form of a balcony or verandah or porch – sometimes all three – of cast-iron treillage of geometrical design. These are the counterparts of the houses in

Bloomsbury and Phillimore Terrace in London. Cheltenham and Brighton were largely built in this style, and there are many charming examples in South Devon. It prevails in

486

the older seaside resorts such as Sidmouth, which came into fashion after George III was ordered sea bathing for his health. There are a great many pleasant country rectories built in this style.

Of the great houses of the Georgian period the most striking feature is the pillared portico. The earlier Georgian mansions tend to be designed on the scheme of a big four-square central block connected by low passage wings often with arcades or columns to wing pavilions.

In the latter part of the eighteenth century the wings and the connecting arcades tend to disappear, leaving nothing but a grand square box. The Portico, however, remains the symbol of grandeur to the end. A curious by-product of the 'Great House' architecture of the Regency and George IV periods is to be found in the gamekeepers' cottages and lodges of the time.

They are the result of the theory of 'picturesque beauty' –or 'sketchable bits'– that prevailed at that time. Remembering how our great aunts were taught to sketch, and forgetting the

Q

works of Gainsborough and Constable, we are apt to scoff at the Picturesque Theory. But our own crazy pavements hardly establish our right to do so. These lodges and cottages anticipate the Babel of styles which characterizes the reign of Queen Victoria.

Most people's interest in church architecture, and on country holidays it is generally parish churches that are met with, is confined to spotting the date. But again, spotting the local building character and assessing the good purpose to which it has been put is a considerable improvement on the merely chronological game. Of course, church architecture takes us back so far in time, to the twelfth and eleventh centuries even, with their echoes of the arts of the heroic age of the Vikings and the early Christian East, that the question of dates so romantically remote overwhelms all other interest: moreover, these survivals from such very early times are hardly plentiful enough for comparison to establish local building schools. Date spotting is best done by mouldings:

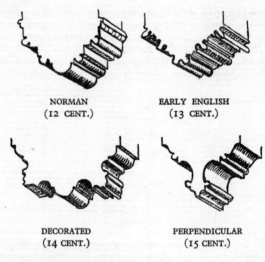

NORMAN
(12 CENT.)

EARLY ENGLISH
(13 CENT.)

DECORATED
(14 CENT.)

PERPENDICULAR
(15 CENT.)

or less safely by windows:

488

12 CENT.   13 CENT.   14 CENT.   15 CENT.

Windows are not so safe because they were often altered to give more light and more room for a display of stained glass, and one often finds windows of the last phase (called in the guide-books Perpendicular or Perp.) inserted in earlier buildings. There are, of course, plenty of other indications of date, for example, the character of the ornament, changing from the primitive barbaric splendour of the twelfth century through gradual stages of refinement to the immensely varied, slightly sentimental, naturalistic ornament of the end of the thirteenth and beginning of the fourteenth centuries, and finally to the standardized decorations of the last phase with its frequent use of heraldry and endlessly repeated angels. In the earlier phases of Mediæval architecture experts can date by mouldings to within very few years, but in this last phase, which had begun to establish itself by about 1375, one can hardly be certain without external evidence to within 50 or even 100 years. But it is in this phase that we can see the local varieties of church building most clearly, for in the period 1350-1550 England enjoyed such an unparalleled commercial prosperity that parish churches were rebuilt and done up all over the country, very often, as in Somerset, the Cotswolds and East Anglia, to mention only three outstanding cases, on the proceeds of the woollen industry. The money for all this rebuilding came from the parishioners themselves, and was therefore spent on the naves of the churches or on the western towers, parts of the church fabric for which the parish as a whole was responsible, as against the chancel, which was often appropriated with the living to some richly endowed institution, monastic or other. The institution, having many such livings appropriated to it, regarded the care of the chancel of any one of its parish churches merely as a business liability and did not care to

489

spend more money on it than was absolutely necessary, hence chancels were often patched up from generation to generation, and often contain the oldest surviving parts of the church. The picture of Lavenham Church makes this point very clearly. The chancel with its old-fashioned high-pointed roof can be seen standing out among the flat roofs of the later parts of the building, the nave to the west of it, and the private chapels of rich parishioners on each side of it. In this matter of roofs the flatter pitch gradually tended to supersede the steeper, probably because it was found that the lead sheets were inclined to sag with the heat on a high-pitch roof. Often one can see the line of the older high-pitch roof quite clearly marked on the face of a tower.

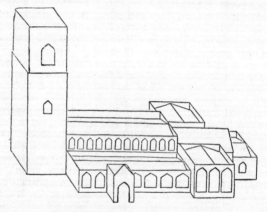

ISOMETRIC VIEW OF LAVENHAM CHURCH

The churches we have mentioned so far have western towers. The true cross plan, with a central tower, is to be found at all dates, but is more popular in earlier times, and is related to the Abbey church plan of the great period of monastic building – the twelfth century. Abbey ruins are chiefly of interest to those who week-end in Yorkshire, where there are a number of celebrated examples. For date-spotting the rules are the same with Abbeys as with parish churches, except that one should rely on mouldings rather than on window forms, as windows are apt to be altered to meet the increasing desire for more light. On the whole Abbey buildings tend to belong to the earlier periods, for men gradually began to prefer to rebuild their own parish church as something more individual to themselves instead of leaving their money to be swallowed up in the already vast endowments of a monastery. Unless there are special circumstances, a disastrous fire, or a sudden access of wealth from unexpected sources, to occasion the rebuilding of an Abbey church, the later monastic buildings are inclined to be of a domestic character, a gate-house as often as not. While speaking of Abbey ruins and gate-houses, a word should be said of castles. The earliest form often met with has a keep which in some cases is filled up with living-rooms, and even a chapel, but the more usual form relies on its immensely strong outer walls and towers. Within these was a house for the lord, planned like the ordinary mediæval house we have illustrated, and there may be, as often as not, a strong tower on a mound as a place of last resort in time of siege.

Church furniture, stalls, screens, fonts and so forth, are a special sideline; not to mention sculptured tombs. Most surviving church woodwork is either fifteenth or sixteenth century or Victorian imitation, the latter unhappily predominating. But it is always exciting to find odd bits of James or Charles I or Georgian church furniture. It has often been said that this kind of woodwork, the three-decker pulpits and the high-panelled pews, is too domestic and not churchy enough. This is an accident of survival. More church woodwork has survived from the Middle Ages than domestic, and more domestic Jacobean and Georgian than ecclesiastical. In both cases the style was the same for houses and churches. It was not till last century that a special style became associated with religion and nothing else.

ABOUT PUBS

Next to the house and (if he is devout, a hypocrite or an antiquarian) the church, the English week-ender goes more often into the pub than into any other kind of building. It is therefore worth his while to notice pub architecture and the deeply rooted traditions it possesses; the more so because these are rapidly being confused, and are even in danger of

THE INTERIOR OF THE COUNTRY PUB REFLECTS ITS ORIGINS IN THE FARMHOUSE KITCHEN

A STONE-BUILT PUB: TUDOR WITH LATER ADDITIONS

A WAYSIDE PUB: EARLY VICTORIAN IN PLAIN BRICK AND TILE

A VILLAGE PUB IN ROMANTIC VICTORIAN GOTHIC STYLE

493

being exterminated, by the modernization schemes of well-meaning brewers, by losses due to age and obsolescence and by changes in social habits – such as, for instance, the introduction into pubs of women, the juke-box and the television set.

Do not let these words suggest, however, that the devotee of pub architecture should look back to past times in the belief that the good old ways are always the most desirable. In that direction lies the cult of the phony-antique, a disease to which the pub has always been specially prone. Who does not know plenty of 'olde hostelries' crammed with improbable black oak beams, hung with horse-brasses and lit through leaded, bottle-glass windows, installed by brewers and landlords who imagine that to have been visited by Elizabeth Tudor or described by Charles Dickens (or to look as if they might have been one or the other – or even both) are the only attributes a successful pub requires?

A pub, on the contrary, has a vital social function which it can perform only if it keeps up with the times. The sense in which it must also remain true to tradition is that – inside at any rate – it must conserve those qualities that have always made people feel at home in pubs. Although for obvious reasons these are more likely to be found in old, mellowed pubs than in new, they have nothing to do with the survival or imitation of period styles. They can equally well be evoked by modern means and materials – so long as the main objectives are not lost sight of. These are: warmth and cheerfulness and a sense of seclusion, to which should be added a capacity to lift people a little out of themselves.

Warmth and cheerfulness are chiefly given by the colours used – especially those of grained and polished woods – and by low varnished ceilings; also by the glitter of glasses and bottles, which at the same time helps to create the required effect of heightened reality. Seclusion is given by the subdivision of the interior into smallish rooms, and of these into bays and screened-off corners, which besides enabling crowds to separate into groups, creates a sense of something intriguing round the corner – a surprising number of pubs, it will be noticed, have L-shaped rooms.

Such are the traditional ingredients of the sympathetic pub interior, ancient and modern. Yet how much havoc has been wrought – and still is – on charming, homely pubs all over

494

the country by the introduction, in their place, in the name of modernization, of cold, hard 'easy-to-clean' materials like stainless steel and plastics, of cream paint and scumbled plaster and tasteful lounge furniture, and above all by the growing practice of merging the small, separate bars into one, to crowd in more people at peak hours or to placate the licensing magistrates' passion for supervision? The conversion of a sequence of cosy bars into one cheerless public hall has been further encouraged by the arrival of television. The traditional means by which the proper pub atmosphere is achieved – rich colours, sympathetic materials and intricacy of plan – can best be studied, of course, in the town pub, where the woodwork is elaborated into the form of mahogany curlicues, where the colours of the paintwork are supplemented by red velvet upholstery, and the glitter of bottles and glasses by multiple mirrors in which every movement is reflected and engraved glass screens that enhance, by partly disclosing, the mystery of what lies next door. But this gin-palace style of interior decoration, though it has influenced pubs everywhere, is a thing of its own which belongs strictly to the era when the town pub was changing its character from that of a house where drink was consumed at leisure to that of a shop where it was sold over the counter in an atmosphere of somewhat hectic sociability.

The village or country pub retains a more relaxed domestic character; indeed the arrangement of its various rooms still reflects the way it gradually evolved out of the ale-house kitchen in which it had its beginnings. This was simply the kitchen of a roadside cottage or farmhouse in which the owner sold refreshments to passers-by. It had its brew-house at the back, across the yard, but as time went on a corner of the kitchen was screened off to hold an evening's supply of beer and save repeated journeys outside. This was the origin of the tap-room, which later became a servery and was eventually provided with a serving-counter or bar, the name *tap-room* being transferred to the public room as a whole – which afterwards happened to the name *bar*. Meanwhile as the kitchen became crowded, the landlord had begun to invite favoured callers – the gentry or his own special cronies – into his private parlour, which itself was taken over in due course as part of the pub, the landlord retreating to some inner sanctum. Arrangements were then made to serve this parlour direct, usually by transferring the servery to a more central part of the house, and it became the bar-parlour. Later the landlord's inner parlour was invaded in turn and became the private bar, and his living-quarters were confined to the upper floor.

So evolved the sequence of rooms that make up the pub as we know it, served in part from a bar (which in the town pub grew into a wide shop-counter, a feature that did not appear in the country pub till well into the nineteenth century) and in part through hatches from the service area. The interior of the town pub is dominated by the bar and its elaborate bar-furniture (or 'wagon', as the range of shelving behind it is called); not so the country pub, where the word parlour is not a misnomer and the main public bar often still retains the

A GEORGIAN MARKET-TOWN PUB, WITH CHARACTERISTIC
LARGE BAY-WINDOW

style of furniture – scrubbed tables, high-backed settles and seats built into the wide fireplace – that it has inherited from the farmhouse kitchen.

The story of the exterior is much the same. Country and village pubs differ but little architecturally from cottages and farmhouses of their period and locality: Jacobean, Georgian or Victorian; brick, stone or plaster. The best examples, however, are distinguished from their domestic prototypes by a kind of unconscious heightening of every effect: gables are more pointed, barge-boards more elaborately carved, bay-windows (a speciality of pubs) more pronounced. Oddity of any kind is emphasized, giving the building a subtly un-inhibited flavour, so that whether it be a hedgerow ale-house,

ODDITY OF CHARACTER AND PROPORTION IS FOUND IN
MANY PUBS

the house where farmers gather on market-day, the social centre of the village or a remote inn catering for the casual wayfarer or the seasonal fisherman, it does not require the hanging sign, the seats outside the door or the brewer's house-mark on the wall to proclaim its purpose.

497

FIRST AID

Some of your hurts you have cured,
    And the sharpest you still have survived,
But what torments of grief you endured
    From evils which never arrived!
                    Emerson.

'Tis his great happiness that he is distempered, thereby to have an opportunity of experiencing the efficacy and sweetness of the remedies which you have so judiciously propounded. I approve 'em all.
                    Congreve.

First Aid

Some of your hurts you have cured,
And the sharpest you still have survived,
But what torments of grief you endured
From evils which never arrived!"

In general: Minor Accidents p. 502 to p. 505;
Major Accidents p. 505 to p. 508.

DEFINITIONS

ACETIC ACID: vinegar slightly diluted with water. Neutralises alkalines.

BICARBONATE OF SODA SOLUTION: one teaspoonful to half a pint of water. Neutralises acids.

EMETICS: (1) Salt and water: two tablespoonfuls in a tumbler of lukewarm water. *Or* (2) Mustard and water: two teaspoonfuls in a tumbler of water.

FOMENTATION: a dressing which is applied hot and damp. The moisture is retained by placing a piece of oiled

501

silk or greaseproof paper immediately over the dressing. The heat is retained by placing a piece of cotton wool over the oiled silk or paper, and the whole is kept in place with a bandage.

SALINE SOLUTION: NORMAL: dissolve one teaspoonful of salt in a pint of water.

SALINE SOLUTION: QUADRUPLE: dissolve four teaspoonfuls of salt in a pint of water.

TOURNIQUET: can be improvised by tying a scarf or large handkerchief around the limb, between the injury and the heart. A stick should be tied in the knot, and twisted until the tourniquet is really tight. It should then be fixed in such a way that it cannot become loose. The patient must have a large letter T marked on his forehead, and the time at which the tourniquet was applied. The tourniquet must be loosened for a few moments every fifteen minutes. A tourniquet is better not placed on the bare skin.

TREATMENTS

According to the nature of your mishap, and your diligence in following these prescriptions, they may save your life, render your misfortune more tolerable, cancel it, or prevent it. Those small accidents which may be treated without professional assistance are dealt with first. There follows a very brief summary of what to do while waiting for the doctor or ambulance in the case of more serious accidents.

¶ MINOR ACCIDENTS

BLISTERS ON THE FEET

Prevent these by (1) bathing the feet with methylated spirit and then dusting them with talcum powder daily for several weeks before a walking week-end; (2) wearing woollen socks, soaped at toe and heel, and ball of foot.

If after these precautions blisters nevertheless occur treat by (1) swabbing the blister with methylated spirit; (2) pricking the blister in two places with a needle sterilised by being held in a candle or match flame; (3) pressing the fluid out of the blister; (4) applying an Elastoplast dressing. Do not remove the loose skin as this acts as an additional dressing.

BRUISES, *including* BLACK EYE

First counteract the swelling and discoloration of every kind of bruise, including Black Eye, by gently dabbing with Witch Hazel. Then apply with a moderately tight bandage a compress made of cotton wool or lint steeped in cold water. To any unbroken surface, except near the eye, the application of a pad soaked in lead lotion (from the Chemist) is useful. When bruised all over and feeling shaken but not faint there is much relief in a hot bath.

BURNS: MINOR

To burns (including slight sun-burn) causing no more damage than a reddening of the skin, apply calamine lotion. For oven burns, and others which have broken the skin or may raise a blister, immerse or bathe the part immediately in luke warm water to which salt has been added. This excludes air, and so stops pain. Dress with normal saline solution (see p.502).

CUTS: MINOR

Stop the bleeding by pressing hard with your thumb, covered by a clean handkerchief, directly on the cut. Apply either a normal saline dressing (see p.502) or a dry dressing. Fix the dressing in place with Elastoplast.

DIARRHOEA *and/or* VOMITING

(1) Do not eat. (2) Drink during twenty-four hours up to six pints of normal saline (see p.502) to which has been added half an ounce of glucose to the pint.

FAINTING

When this threatens prevent it by (1) laying the patient down, or sitting him down with his head between his knees; (2) providing fresh air; (3) loosening all tight clothing; (4) giving a teaspoonful of sal volatile in a medicine glass of water, or a sip of brandy, or a sniff of smelling-salts.

If, after all, the patient loses consciousness, keep him warm and, when he comes round, which should be in a few moments, dose him again with sal volatile or brandy.

If the patient is not conscious within five minutes this is not a faint but some more serious condition, and a doctor must be called.

503

Never attempt to give an unconscious patient anything to drink, as he might inhale the fluid and thus drown.

FISH HOOK

If a fish hook should become embedded in a fleshy part of the anatomy, push the hook further on, so that the embedded end, that with the barb, protrudes through the skin. Cut off the barb and withdraw the hook, back the way that it went in. Cover the wound with a clean dry dressing. Later, apply a quadruple saline fomentation (see pp.501 and 502). The dressing should be changed every four hours except at night.

FOREIGN BODY IN THE EYE

There are three methods of removal. (1) Grasp the lashes of the upper lid and pull it down over the lower lashes, leave go, and allow the inside of the upper lid to be swept by the lower lashes as it returns to position. (2) Bathe the eye with luke warm normal saline (see p.502), using an eye bath. (When bathing the eyes it is safer to use a different eye bath for each eye to avoid spreading possible infection from one eye to the other. Have two eye baths of different colours.) (3) Stand behind the patient, tilt his head back against your chest, and, holding the affected eye open with your first and second fingers, irrigate the eye by pouring normal saline (see p.502) from a jug across the eye, from the inner corner to the outer. (Use the hand on the same side as the patient's injured eye to hold the eye open, otherwise his nose gets in the way.) The eye may now be sore, so put in a drop of castor oil. This must not be more than six months old or it will smart.

HICCUPS

To stop hiccups drink water backwards. This consists of applying the lips to the far side of the glass and bending forward the head and body till drinking becomes possible. Another method is to sip slowly a glass of water with both ears and nostrils stopped. Sucking a lump of sugar sprinkled with a few drops of essence of peppermint is very effective if water cannot be swallowed.

NOSE BLEEDING

When anyone over forty has a severe attack a doctor must be sent for, as it may be haemorrhage due to high blood pressure: in other words, a stroke, saved from being dangerous because the blood has an outlet. When the sufferer is a child there is usually no cause for alarm. Sit the child in front of an open window, pinch the nostrils until the bleeding stops. Afterwards instruct the patient to breathe through the mouth for a few minutes to allow the blood clot to harden. The nose must not be blown.

PARTY-DRINKING
Before party-drinking swallow a half to one ounce of Olive Oil or drink a glass of milk.

SEA-SICKNESS
There is no effective first aid but before sailing sufferers should get Dramamine on a prescription from their doctor or "Marzine", available without a prescription.

SPRAINED ANKLE
Remove the shoe before the foot becomes too swollen to allow this to be done. Pad all round the foot and ankle with cotton wool. Apply a firm figure-of-eight bandage over the padding. Keep the foot up, resting on a cushion which is protected by a mackintosh. Wet the dressing with cold water. Seek medical advice before attempting to walk; the ankle may be fractured, not sprained.

STINGS
Bee. Remove the sting by pressing the hole at the handle end of a small key over the puncture. The sting of a bee is acid, therefore neutralise this by the application of bicarbonate of soda solution (see p.501).
Wasp. The wasp does not leave its sting in its victim. Its sting is alkaline, therefore neutralise with acetic acid (see p.501).
In rare cases an allergy to these stings is present. Therefore if headache, nausea, dizziness, or any other symptoms of general malaise arise, a doctor must be seen at once.

TOOTHACHE
Whiskey or brandy held in the mouth may alleviate the pain.

¶ MAJOR ACCIDENTS
BLEEDING
Bleeding is classified according to the vessel or vessels from which it occurs: *Capillary*, bleeding without rhythm;

Venous, more profuse and usually darker in colour, also without rhythm; *Arterial,* spurting in rhythm with the heart-beat.

The first two can be controlled by the application of a firm pad and bandage over the bleeding point. *Arterial bleeding may be exceedingly dangerous.* A doctor must be sent for: but there is need for immediate first-aid action. Apply a tourniquet (see p. 502) and treat for shock (see p. 507). When the application of a tourniquet is impossible (*e.g.* in bleeding of the head) apply a hard pad and bandage firmly, or press with your thumb, directly over the cut artery so that it is compressed against the bone over which it passes.

BURNS: EXTENSIVE

Exclude all air from the injured surface by wrapping in a clean sheet or towel. Send for a doctor as the patient will need hospital treatment. Treat for shock (see p.507) which will be severe. Do not apply any medicament whatever.

DROWNING

The first and imperative necessity is to induce respiration as described below. While you are attempting this send the first available person for a doctor and set the second to prepare treatment for shock (see p.507).

Place the patient on dry land, face downwards. Stand astride him, place your hands under his waist and lift him to empty the water out of him. Remove any foreign matter from his mouth. Raise his arms and place them so that his forehead is resting on the back of his crossed hands. While you are doing this kneel at the patient's head and apply artificial respiration as follows: Place your hands on the patient's shoulder-blades, fingers spread, and thumbs meeting. Keeping your elbows straight, swing slightly forward so that about thirty pounds of your weight is placed on the patient's back. Do this to the count of 1.2.3. (each count being about one second). Lift your hands at the count of 4. Place your hands under the patient's arm-pits, and slide them down to his elbows, slightly lifting the patient's arms to expand his chest, to the count of 5.6.7. Lower his arms, and return your hands to the patient's shoulder-blades, at the count of 8.

Repeat this cycle for at least three hours, or until the patient starts to breathe. If the operator is changed during this time, the continuity of the movements must never be interrupted.

Note that the amount of weight placed upon the patient must vary according to his build. When resuscitating an infant only the arm raising and lowering movement (5.6.7.8.) is used.

FRACTURED BONES
Immobilise the injury in the position in which you find it by filling in the natural hollows with padding, and fixing with triangular bandages or scarves. Treat for shock (see below) and send for the doctor.

POISONING
In all cases of poisoning send immediately for the doctor. Preserve for the doctor's examination all vomited matter and excreta and all suspect food, etc.

In general follow this procedure: (1) give an emetic (see p.501); (2) give copious draughts of water to dilute the poison; (3) treat for shock (see below).

In cases where there are stains or burns around the mouth no emetic must be given. The probability is that they are evidence of a corrosive having been swallowed. If the patient is made to vomit, the poison which has burned the mouth and throat on its way down would do so again on its way up. Further burning might well cause asphyxia. These corrosives are either acid or alkaline, and should be neutralised by giving, for an acid poison, bicarbonate of soda solution (see p.501); and for an alkaline poison, acetic acid (see p.501). Any splashes of poison seen on the skin should be dabbed off, and then the skin must be flooded with water. Finally the suitable antidote should be applied to the skin. If there is no means of knowing whether an acid or alkaline corrosive has been taken, give the patient nothing but water and await the doctor.

Food Poisoning
(1) Do not eat. (2) Take an emetic (see p.501). (3) Take a 2 oz. dose of castor oil. (4) Stay in bed, and generally treat for shock (see below). Send for the doctor.

SHOCK
All accidents are accompanied by a more or less severe shock. Shock is a sudden depression of the vital functions of the body. The blood pressure and temperature are lowered and,

in an attempt to compensate for this, the pulse and respiration rates increase and the patient sweats profusely. All this occurs when there is a sudden and adverse change in bodily circumstances. This condition is most dangerous to the elderly and the very young. In many cases of serious injury it is shock, and not the actual injury, which causes the death of the victim. The First Aid worker cannot treat the serious injury, but he can treat the shock, and hand over to professional skill a patient in better general condition than would otherwise be the case.

Shock Treatment

(1) Lay the patient down, and afford him absolute rest.
(2) Make the patient warm. Place coats or blankets under and over him. Place covered hot water bottles at his sides, *outside* the covering blanket.
(3) Give him hot drinks, both for warmth and to replace fluid lost by sweating, provided that there is no abdominal injury and that the patient is conscious.
(4) If the patient is on a bed or a stretcher raise the foot of it a little to facilitate the return of the blood to the heart.
(5) Reassure the patient.
(6) As far as possible allay his pain: in the case of a fracture, by immobilising the part injured, finding a comfortable body position and supporting the patient in it; in the case of burns by the application of an air-excluding covering.

SNAKE BITE

Apply tourniquet (see p.502) just on the heart side of the bite. (2) Keep the limb hanging down. (3) Send for the doctor. (4) If no doctor is immediately available, sterilise a razor blade by passing it through a flame and cut the area just enough to make it bleed. Rub permanganate of potash crystals into the wound. Get medical aid.

SUNSTROKE

Prevent this by covering the head and the spine (which includes the neck) and by wearing dark glasses. Remember that the spine, being hairless, is more vulnerable than the head.
If sunstroke does occur, keep the patient lying down in a darkened room. If possible apply ice to the forehead. Treat for shock (see p.507). Send for the doctor.

508

FOR YOUR FIRST AID BOX

Bandages
Bicarbonate of Soda
Brandy
Calamine Lotion
Castor Oil
Cotton Wool
Elastoplast: dressings and
    $2\frac{1}{2}''$ strip
Eye Baths
Gauze Dressing
Glucose
Lead Lotion
Lint, plain white
Matches
Methylated Spirit

Mustard
Needle
Oiled Silk or Grease-proof
    paper
Peppermint, Essence of
Permanganate of Potash
    crystals
Salt
Sal Volatile
Scissors
Smelling Salts
Stick for tightening
    tourniquet
Vinegar
Witch Hazel

THE LAW AND HOW YOU BREAK IT

Who to himself is law, no law doth need,
Offends no law, and is a king indeed.
George Chapman.

Never make a defence of apology before you
be accused.
Charles I.

I have no great regard for The Law.
Samuel Butler.

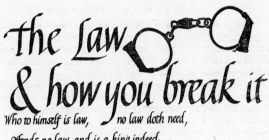

the Law & how you break it

Who to himself is law, no law doth need,
Offends no law, and is a king indeed.

OF 'CIVIL' AND 'CRIMINAL' LAW

You can divide English law into two main parts: civil and criminal, or private and public. If you are the victim of some breach of civil law, whether by tort or breach of contract, the remedy lies with you. You can sue for damages, or 'specific performance', or what not; or you can shrug the whole thing off. But if you are the victim of some breach of criminal law (theft, fraud, malicious damage, assault, and so on) you are a public sufferer: your sorrow is everyone's, your injury is supposed to hurt us all. The criminal law will protect and avenge you whether you want it to or not; and because every 'crime' is really a private wrong erected into a public one, you have a public duty to perform in reporting it and helping to find out who did it.

OF ARRESTING AND BEING ARRESTED

The 'civil' and 'criminal' distinction used to be important in relation to arrest. In Dickens' time you could be arrested by your creditors, or at their instance, and kept in prison until you paid your debts; and there was a long list of 'privileged' people (clergymen, lawyers, M.P.s and so on) who could claim immunity. There is no 'civil' arrest today (except on a warrant for failure to obey some Court order for the payment of money); all other arrests are for criminal matters, and there are no immunities.

A policeman's powers of arrest are not much wider than the ordinary citizen's: the policeman being, in fact, little more (or less) than an ordinary citizen, oddly dressed and doing for payment what it is everyone's duty to do for nothing. His

513

strength is that he usually knows what his powers are, while the ordinary citizen has never looked them up. Do not, therefore, resist him with violence when you think he is arresting you mistakenly. Warn him, by all means, that you will 'have the law on him' afterwards; but go quietly.

There are times when you may, and others when you must, make an arrest yourself. When you know that someone has committed murder, burglary, rape, theft, arson, espionage or coining (this is an arbitrary list – there are a good many more), you are required by the law to arrest him. It may be easier, and will pass, if you find out where he is going and then tell the police via '999'.

OF SETTING THE LAW IN MOTION

If you want redress from the civil, or private, law, you had best seek a lawyer. If that sounds too expensive, find out the address of your local Legal Aid Committee (the Town Hall will know) and see what help you are entitled to. If the matter is criminal – anything from a servant embezzling your money to a man continually parking his car in front of your house – tell the police.

There are times when the police won't take any action: you have no case, they say, or it is not really a police matter. This can even happen where you have been assaulted, if it occurred a day or two ago and there is nothing to show for it. But you can still go to the Magistrates' Court (you could have done this anyway), ask to see the Clerk, tell him you want a summons issued, and (perhaps the next morning) go into Court before the public business starts and ask the Magistrate to issue one. If he does, you don't need any police help from then on.

OF GETTING A LAWYER

But if you prefer to seek out a lawyer and 'have it all done proper', there are many ways of finding out where to get a good one. Is it a 'civil' case – rent, breach of contract, nuisance? Go to the County Court (you'll find it in the 'phone book) and ask one of the Clerks to recommend a solicitor who practises there. A 'criminal' case? Go to the Magistrates' Court and put the same question there – or to the police station if you like. Do you want to buy a house, make a will? Ask your bank manager – he knows all the good solicitors. And two don'ts are worth mention: don't ask the porter at a hospital, who is likely to recommend (perhaps unwittingly) an 'ambulance-chaser'; and don't have anything to do with any solicitor who offers to work on a 'no cure, no pay' basis or to accept a percentage of any damages you get as a result of litigation. He's a crook: walk straight out of his office, and report him to the Law Society.

OF DEFENDING YOUR OWN CASE

A layman who defends himself is said to have a fool for a client. It isn't necessarily true, but in spite of all that can be done to protect him in Court, the dice are loaded against him. It can be slightly easier in a civil case than in a criminal one, where the pitfalls are many and you may go down one while no one happens to be looking. In all but the simplest cases (parking too long, forgetting that rear lamp, letting the dog get out with no collar?), it's best to be defended – except, of course, where you plead guilty. Then there's not much point in being defended at all, unless there's a lot that is worth saying in mitigation.

You can sue on your own account, too, in a civil case. And you can prosecute a criminal – in a Magistrates' Court only: once the case gets before a Judge and Jury, you can no longer carry the prosecution yourself but *must* have a lawyer and the Crown must provide him free . . . And if your income doesn't exceed certain limits (for a civil case they are surprisingly high), you can get legal aid for a 'civil' case through the Public Assistance Authority and your local Legal Aid Committee. But whichever of all these things it is that you do, don't refer to any of the lawyers in Court as 'my learned friend': they can only say that about each other, and you will get yourself laughed at.

OF PLEADING GUILTY

If you *have* overstayed your two hours on a parking place, if the dog *did* run out without a collar, if . . . well, you can't always help these things; but if you don't want to attend Court in answer to the summons, it is not enough *merely* to write to the Magistrate's Clerk and plead guilty. You must also ask, rather nicely, that the case be dealt with in your absence; and you must not embark on any kind of challenge or defence to the charge, for that amounts to a plea of 'Not

Guilty' and the case will automatically be adjourned for you to be there in person.

But in case you discover later that you are for some reason *not* really guilty, don't make any admissions when the police first speak to you, or when they come to serve the summons on you, or at any other time. Don't make any admission about anything, ever, until you've seen your solicitor or at least had time to think things over. And only your own lawyer (certainly not the police, whether you have a lawyer or not) can properly advise you to plead guilty at all.

OF BEING A WITNESS

One is tempted not to be a witness, not to know anything: the Courts can take up so much of one's time. But the Courts are as considerate as they can contrive, 'releasing' witnesses as often and soon as possible. Some day, one may desperately need witnesses oneself.

In the witness box, never give an opinion unless asked for it. Only facts. Don't let anyone make you angry, or the facts will get confused. If you don't know whether to call the man on the Bench 'My Lord', 'Your Honour', or 'Your Worship', call him 'Sir' and everyone will be satisfied, including him.

OF BEING A JUROR

You are liable for jury service if you are under sixty and paying rates (or an inclusive rent) for premises assessed at £20 (in London it's £30). There is a 'J' against your name on the register of voters – you can see it at the municipal library or the Town Hall. All the time it is there you can go on getting jury summonses – or never getting them, it's quite a lottery. It shouldn't be there if you are over 60, or a lawyer, doctor, clergyman, policeman, chemist, peer – a host of occupations; but you are the only person who can get it taken off, because no one else troubles to find out what you are or what your age is.

If you get a jury summons just as you are strapping the holiday bags on to your luggage grid, don't panic. Ring up the office it came from, and explain. They'll always postpone your turn, in a good cause.

On the jury, don't talk to anyone off it about the case you're trying; don't try to make notes about the cases; and don't eat big lunches.

OF DRIVING AND STOPPING

By the time you know the Highway Code your motoring knowledge seems monumental; but you could go on learning your rights and duties from the Acts and Regulations about the licensing, taxation, use, and maintenance of motor vehicles and their drivers until you feared to unlock your garage door. Few people know them all: fewer drive as though they did. A week-end can be the happier for knowing a few of these rights and duties that the Highway Code leaves out.

YOUR EXCISE LICENCE

In law, there are no 'days of grace' for renewing your car licence. There's an administrative arrangement that lets you drive for fourteen days at the beginning of *each* licensing quarter with a freshly-expired licence on the windscreen, but only if you take out the new one within the fourteen days. This is not, moreover, a concession to you and your procrastination: it's a device to spread the work at the local taxation offices.

YOUR DRIVING LICENCE

Sign it at once: your 'usual signature in ink' is the second thing the policeman looks for. The first is the date of expiry, which admits of *no* 'days of grace'. The third is your name and address, which should be up to date. He will also look for endorsements (for speeding offences, etc.) if you let him, but you need not let him – you can hold the licence while he reads it. Always have it with you: the policeman must allow you five days for producing it at any police station you care to name, but this can be a great nuisance.

THIRD PARTY INSURANCE

Carry your insurance certificate (or cover note): if you forget, and a policeman wants to see it, the five-day interval for production applies here too, except where you have caused personal injury to someone, in which event you must produce the document either to the other party or to a policeman, *as soon as possible;* the outside limit in this case is twenty-four hours, but that might not help you if you could conveniently have done it sooner.

HAVING AN ACCIDENT

Stop at once after every accident, whether or not anyone requires you to. An 'accident' means one involving 'damage or injury to any person, vehicle, or animal'; and 'vehicle' seems to include anything on wheels or 'caterpillar' tracks, while 'animal' means any horse, cattle, ass, mule, sheep, pig, goat, or dog. Injury to deer, cats, rabbits, stoats, birds of all kinds, snakes and monkeys *need* not, therefore, be reported to anyone; nor need damage to telegraph posts, walls, street refuges, or other roadside property. But don't try to work this out when the occasion arises. Stop first; and report everything, either to the other party if he is there, or to the police *as soon as possible* – the outside limit, again, being twenty-four hours.

'Report' means give the bare details for identification purposes – numbers, names and addresses, place of accident. The less you add to these, at that stage, the better it may well prove to be for you.

LIGHTS

The requirements as to 'obligatory' lights are under constant review. Precept seems in many cases to follow practice. During the war-time black-out it was made an offence to park on the off-side at night. This provision has now been made permanent, and a breach of it (except in a one-way street) could cost you a £20 fine.

PARKING FOR A PICNIC

You must not, without valid permission, drive on any footway or bridleway, or more than fifteen yards from the road on to any common, moor, or 'other land of whatsoever description'. Nor must you (nor, indeed, would you) park on a road 'in such a position or in such condition or in such circumstances as to be *likely* to cause danger'.

OUTSIDE THE INN

A hotel is an inn, and the proprietor is liable for any theft of your car from the forecourt or car-park if, in order perhaps merely to get a drink, you have locked it and removed the ignition key. A pub is not an inn unless guests can sleep there, and the theft at an ordinary pub would be your loss (or your insurance company's), not the publican's. 'Traveller', once a Common Law expression with a restricted dignity, has come to include a man who pushes open the inn door for a drink, though he may live across the road.

518

OF RAILWAY TRAVEL

A railway ticket does not guarantee you a seat, and the time-tables don't guarantee that your train will be on time. The cloakroom ticket for your luggage, although you have paid for it, does not mean that the Railway will pay you any compensation if it loses your luggage – unless *you* prove that the loss was due to negligence in the cloakroom. (And if the luggage was worth more than £5, you should have 'declared the true nature and value thereof' and paid a special price for the cloakroom ticket.) If a porter drops your luggage off the platform and it gets run over by a train, the Railway can repudiate your claim for damages because, under the bye-laws, the porter is your personal agent until the luggage is actually inside the van. But the Railway is responsible for damage done by sparks falling from its engines.

The bye-laws do not deal with the window-up-or-window-down dispute, except by empowering the guard to turn the disputants out of the compartment if they get too excited.

Do you wish for more information about the bye-laws? Buy a strong magnifying glass, borrow a ladder, and read them at your local station. There is one respect in which they may sometimes help you. If the ones printed on the back of your ticket are too smudged to read, they have no force and you can put your feet up on the seat opposite.

OF COMMONS

The few remaining pieces of uncultivated land known as commons are not, as you might suppose, common property. You cannot do as you like on them. The common *rights* belong to local tenants and farmers, and cover the grazing of cattle and a few other things that the general public are only tepidly interested in. Some rights are held by 'immemorial custom' – the use of wells or ponds, or the erection of may-poles and the touching habit of dancing round them. Other rights can be acquired in 60 years, others in 30. One of the rights now being acquired, because no one complains, is the right to use model speedboats that make conversation impossible within a quarter of a mile; and another is the right to fly model aeroplanes within a few inches of a passer-by's face.

R

OF RIGHTS OF WAY

A right of way can be acquired by grant from the landowner, or by 'continuous undisputed use' for twenty years. But it can be lost by disuse after an indefinite number of years – no one quite knows how long. If a landlord puts an obstruction where there is a right of way, anyone entitled to the right of way can lawfully remove it; and if no one removes it for 20 years, the right of way is lost.

OF ANCIENT LIGHTS

Lawyers and antiquarians are not at one about the meaning of 'ancient'. To the lawyer, it means 'anterior', or 'prior'. (An 'ancient writing' is a document accepted by the Courts without proof of its authorship because it is more than twenty years old.) 'Ancient lights' are windows that have 'enjoyed uninterrupted access of light' for 20 years or more, even if the building has all that time been unoccupied. And everyone may build upon his own land, regardless of the fact that he is interfering with the light that would otherwise reach his neighbours – unless that neighbour can prove that the light has been enjoyed for 20 years and is now 'substantially' reduced (he has to put up with *some* reduction).

Windows are not the only openings protected: skylights, unglazed openings in walls, glazed doors, greenhouse roofs, church arches all come into it. But not land: your neighbour can ruin your gardening prospects with a high brick wall, and you have no legal remedy.

OF BEACHES

Not even the seashore is public property. Above high water level, the beach always belongs to someone – usually to the person who owns the land adjoining it, but very often to the Town Council, who can therefore make rules about what you can do on it. Below high water level it belongs to the Crown. So unless there is a highway, the beach cannot be reached without trespassing; and it's always doubtful whether the public have any *right* to bathe.

OF LOST PROPERTY AND TREASURE TROVE

Findings are not keepings. The finder of a lost article has an absolute right to it against everyone but the true owner, but if he thinks there is the slightest chance of that owner's being traced he must do something about it. The easiest way is to tell the police. You can leave the article with them if you like, or hold it yourself while their enquiries are going on. If the owner is traced you must give it up – and he is not bound to reward you. If he is not traced, you can keep it, *but it never becomes your absolute property*. The loser can claim it from you after a lifetime.

Treasure trove is gold or silver, in money, plate, or bullion, found hidden, the owner being unknown. Most of this kind of treasure was buried by the Romans when the Danes and Saxons drove them out, and most of it has been found. But because the Saxon Kings wanted it so much, they executed all citizens finding it without saying anything; and we still have to report the finding of it to the Coroner. He decides whether it *is* treasure trove. If it is, the British Museum will usually pay us its full market value. If not, we can keep it.

OF FLOTSAM, JETSAM AND LIGAN

Goods which float on the sea after a shipwreck are called 'flotsam'; but if they are thrown out to lighten the ship they are 'jetsam', and if sunk, with a buoy attached, then 'ligan'. When it cannot be ascertained who is owner of such goods, then, if they are found in the sea, they belong to the finder. But all wrecks and wreckage cast ashore are in general the perquisites of the Crown, unless the owner of the land on which they are found has a legitimate 'grant of wreck'.

Week-enders (and other persons) who happen to find a corpse on the shore are obliged to notify the police within six hours. The reward for fulfilling this obligation is five shillings: the penalty for not doing it is five pounds.

OF MONEY AND LEGAL TENDER

In the absence of any different agreement, a debtor can be required to pay his debts in cash – and the creditor must take any cash which is 'legal tender' or forfeit his claim.

But copper coins are legal tender only up to a shilling's worth and silver up to forty shillings' worth. Foreign coins are not legal tender at all.

An I.O.U. is evidence of a debt, and will support a legal claim. If it bear a *date* of payment, it is a promissory note and

521

must be stamped to have any value as evidence. Otherwise no stamp is needed.

OF NEIGHBOURLINESS

If you habitually repair the fence or wall between your garden and your neighbour's, that may become evidence that it belongs to you – so that you'll be held responsible for it. You can usually tell whose fence it is by looking at the house deeds – but not always. The 'working rule' that your fence is the one with the nails driven in towards you does not always work, because some house deeds show the contrary.

If your fruit trees overhang the neighbour's property, you have a right to any fruit that falls on to his land. If he won't give it up you can go upon his land without his permission (but not with any force or damage) and take it. He can cut the roots and branches of your trees penetrating or overhanging his land without giving you notice or asking your permission.

OF TRESPASS

Every invasion of private property is a trespass, whether there is damage or not. You acquire no immunity or other status by giving or offering a farmer money when he complains. He can turn you off his land, as you can turn anyone out of your house; but he can't 'prosecute', and neither can you, for trespass is not a criminal offence (except on railways, airports, military stations, and 'in pursuit of game'). When a farmer tells you that you are trespassing you should first look horrified: then contrite: and then about to go back the way you came. But you should closely watch the effect of all this upon him, and be ready to go gracefully on if he says it's all right this time provided you shut the gates and light no fires.

OF DOGS

Contrary to common – and fostered – belief, a dog is not allowed two bites. If you keep a savage dog you do it at your peril – one bite can bring a summons, either for the offence of 'suffering a ferocious dog to be at large' or to 'show cause why it should not be destroyed or kept under control'. But if the person bitten wants damages – money – he has to sue you in a County Court as distinct from prosecuting you before a Magistrate. In this case he must prove that the dog had a known propensity to bite, because the law thinks dogs are peaceable by nature; and he does this by calling evidence that it has bitten someone before.

Your dog licence is not transferable: the man who buys your dog must take out his own seven-and-sixpenny licence, which will last for 12 months from then.

The law has never regarded a dog as a 'chattel'. Therefore, although it is an offence to steal a dog, it is no offence to obtain one by false pretences.

If you find a stray dog you are not required by law to do anything about it; but if you do take possession of it for the time being, you must either find its owner or take it to the Police Station at once. If you want to keep it, the police will give you a certificate, the effect of which is that it becomes yours in a month if still unclaimed. You have to take out a licence at once, and the police come round to see that you do.

OF CATS

The law is more concerned about cats than it was a few years ago. It protects them against cruelty, and will not allow them to be stolen, or sold in the street (except on market stalls) or to children under twelve, or operated on without drugs, or killed without their owners' consent. But there is no ground for the belief that it is unlawful to kill your own cat more than six weeks (or months?) old. If you want to dispose of a cat, only a vet can really be relied on to do it without cruelty; but there is no law to say that you must not do it yourself.

OF CATTLE

'Cattle' can include pigs; and if, in a private field, you should happen to be gored or trampled by a bull or cow, or savaged by pigs (which *can* be dangerous), you have no remedy in law. If it happens on the highway you are better off: but you will have to prove, in the case of a cow or pigs, that the owner of the animals could and should have foreseen what they were going to do. This may be easy with a bull, but cows and pigs have a better reputation. Trust neither.

OF NUISANCES

Any human activity causing noise, smell, dirt or other unhealthy affront to the senses can be treated by the law as a nuisance. If it is a 'common nuisance', affecting the public at large (like a rotting elephant on the highway), it is a crime

THE LAW AND HOW YOU BREAK IT

and can result in fine or imprisonment on conviction of the person responsible for it by a jury. If the annoyance is that of a particular person or group, there can be an action in the County Court to get the nuisance stopped or abated. Indeed, the victims may themselves take some action to abate it, and go on to the offender's land for the purpose of doing so – this is not a trespass.

If some unneighbourly nuisance afflicts you, do not delay too long: once it has gone on for twenty years, the man doing it may have acquired a Common Law right to continue.

OF ADVERTISEMENTS

The Town and Country Planning (Control of Advertisements) Regulations, 1948, provide for the control of advertisements by the Local Planning Authority, limit the size and placing of great and ugly hoardings, and allow for the establishment of 'areas of special control' to keep places of particular beauty, especially in rural areas, from being spoilt by advertisements. So if your favourite view has been hidden by a large sign urging you to drink someone's beer, eat someone's cereal, or use someone's soap, appeal to the Local Authority. If it grants your appeal the advertisement, after a certain period of toleration, must go.

If your political opponents stick election posters on your side wall without asking you, you can have them prosecuted and fined. Anyone wishing to advertise on your property must first get your consent to do so, and if the advertisement is big and conspicuous they must also have permission from the Local Planning Authority. However, you may have advertisements on your own property about the local dog show or cricket match, or any other local activity of a non-commercial character, without express permission from the Local Planning Authority as long as the advertisement is no bigger than six square feet.

If you want to display the number of your house, or its name – whether it be Pook's Corner, Kozy Kot, or Ashton Hall – keep the sign smaller than two square feet or you will need the consent of the Local Planning Authority.

OF INNS AND REFRESHMENT

Every hotel is an inn, whether it has a licence to sell intoxicants or is a temperance hotel. Boarding houses, lodging houses, and restaurants are not. The Innkeepers' Liability

Act, 1863, defines an inn as 'any hotel, inn, tavern, public house, or other place of refreshment, the keeper of which is *by law* responsible for the goods and property of his guests'. By what law? The ancient Common Law of England, which used to regard all innkeepers as rogues in league with the local highwaymen; it defined an innkeeper as 'one who holds himself out as being prepared to receive and accommodate any traveller', and it still binds him to 'accommodate' every traveller who is ready – at any hour – to pay his way, provided he is well-conducted *and there is room for him*.

What is a 'traveller'? It may be yourself, away for the week-end; or it may even be a man on his way home from work – the old three-mile stint that used to establish the *'bona fide* traveller' is a thing of the past. What is 'accommodation'? Bed and board for 'man and beast'; and the word beast, appropriately or not, now includes his car.

But no innkeeper, no publican, no bar-tender, no club steward, is bound by law to serve you with intoxicants if he doesn't want to. You can demand 'refreshment' in an inn, and the innkeeper, who must supply it, can interpret the word to please himself. Elsewhere, you can't *demand* anything, at any time. But a publican who declines to serve drinks to people he doesn't like is not quite in the same position as a man who declines to sell pins or pianos to people he doesn't like. The publican (who may also be an innkeeper) needs a Justices' licence, and must renew it every year. It is when he applies for the renewal that you can effectively complain to the Justices about the way he runs his business.

So long as he keeps a copy of the Innkeepers Act exhibited where you can read it, an innkeeper is not liable to a greater extent than £30 for the loss or injury of any goods – *except* (1) a car, a carriage, a horse and its harness, (2) anything stolen, lost or damaged through his or his servant's carelessness, and (3) anything he has accepted for safe custody. He has a 'lien' on his guests' goods, and can sell your luggage after six weeks if you have left it with him and omitted to pay your bill – but he must first have advertised for you in one London and one local newspaper.

He is not bound to keep for an indefinite time anyone who comes as a traveller and then settles down with no apparent intention of moving on.

OF THE ENGLISH SUNDAY

If you belong to the Church of England, you are bound to go to church on Sunday, the penalty being 'ecclesiastical censure'. This is still important, because the duty to go is the foundation of the *right* to go, which you can enforce against a churchwarden who tries to keep you out – even if the church is full. If you are a dissenter, the law merely shrugs its shoulders about you.

But there are many things that you are not allowed to do. No public billiards (except in the club). No public stage plays. No fairs or circuses. No bear-baiting, bull-baiting, interludes or common players, even in your own parish. Outside the parish, no public games at all. No taking of any kind of game, whether with a dog, a net, a gun, or other instrument. No salmon-fishing. No bookmaking or 'tote' betting. No boxing or all-in wrestling. But look at the things that *may* be sold and the business that *may* be done in shops: meals (this does *not* include fish and chips), newly cooked provisions and dressed tripe, sweets, minerals and ices, flowers, fruit and vegetables, milk and cream, new bread and rolls, medicines, cycle and motor accessories, smokers' needs, newspapers and magazines, books and stationery from main line bookstalls, guide books, postcards and souvenirs in the art galleries and parks, passport photographs, sporting requisites at a place where the sport is actually going on, fodder for horses, and post office business.

It is true that the only places of entertainment open to you are cinemas (where the local residents are in favour of Sunday picture-going), museums, waxworks, picture galleries, zoos, aquaria, lecture halls, and concert halls for the provision of 'music with or without singing or recitation'.

ETIQUETTE

Of Courtesy, it is much less
Than Courage of Heart or Holiness,
Yet in my Walks it seems to me
That the Grace of God is in Courtesy.
                    Hilaire Belloc.

It isn't etiquette to cut any one you've been
introduced to. Remove the joint.
                    Lewis Carroll.

Etiquette

*'Of Courtesy, it is much less
Than Courage of Heart, or Holiness,
Yet in my Walks it seems to me
That the Grace of God is in Courtesy.'*

LETTERS OF THANKS

(From 'The Art of Letter-Writing', 1762.)

We should always endeavour to testify our Gratitude according to the Obligation we are under. Let us never be wanting to examine the Favour received, and the Merit of the Person who conferred it. If a Friend has been of Service to us, we may thank him familiarly; but we must thank in very submissive Terms a great Lord, to whom we are indebted for a settled Condition of Life, or some considerable Present. Whatever may be the Quality of the Benefit and Benefactor, it is necessary we should seem sensible of it, and withal exaggerate its Circumstances, making appear the Utility or Honour that has accrued to us from it, and protesting, in concluding our Letter, that we shall preserve it in perpetual Remembrance.

An Example
LETTER OF THANKS FOR A SEAL

The Seal you sent me is the prettiest Thing I ever saw, and I am vexed I cannot praise it sufficiently. But, let me tell you, that the Poet who would fain seal up his Mistress's Mouth, because not very reserved in keeping his Secrets, ought to have had such an agreeable Seal, to be worthy of so nice an Application. The most excellent Engravers are Botchers to your's; nay, I may say, *Apelles's* Pencil never delineated any Thing with the Art and Delicacy of your Figures. But as I do not so much regard your Present as a Master-piece in its Kind, than as a Pledge of your Friendship; I cannot thank you enough for it, nor express to what a Degree I am, &c.

ETIQUETTE

¶

A MODERN BREAD AND BUTTER LETTER OR COLLINS*

Dear Molly,

What a week-end! A household like yours shows us stuffy town-mice just what we miss. All those endless gossips over the washing-up! The romps with the children – dear things, so ready to accept one as their equal! The *smugness* of toasting one's toes at a blaze one has *laboured* to provide. Then that glorious windy climb to your quaint little market town and the lovely long *scribbler's eavesdrop* in the queue before plunging *headlong* home again! (Did I remember to tell you your back brake was broken?) And never did I *dream* I'd be present at the return of a real *prodigal* – so well-timed too, with Vicar there to tea!

Back in my little flat I realise how *right* my doctor was when he said I should enjoy life again after a complete change. Thank you a thousand times for that change.

Yours affectionately,
Margaret Usborne

ANOTHER EXAMPLE OF THE SAME

Dear Pandora,

I got back all right. That was the *slow* train. They took the fast one off last May. My wire hadn't arrived. So Jocelyn must have put 'Highbury' instead of 'Highgate' after all.

Excuse uneven writing – it's the bandage. Which reminds me, could you possibly see if I dropped my bangle in the wood-shed – either there or by the sink? Sorry – it was the rush at the end and the confusion of seeing Francis again after all those years. He's got very Australian, hasn't he?

Hope peace reigns in the nursery today. Sebastian and Sary Ann certainly are wonderfully lively! And I shall always remember my 'Dick Turpin's last ride' on Saturday afternoon. And he wasn't carrying six of gran. and two of lump.

Well, thanks so much, Pandora. It was sweet of you to ask me, especially with no help.

Love,
Audrey Morris

* '*Collins*': *although letters of thanks are called after Jane Austin's character, in fact the terms of his letter are not given in 'Pride and Prejudice'.*

530

FROM A LADY RECENTLY MARRIED (1860)

My dearest Edith,

I have now been married six months, and not one little visit have you paid me yet! Do come and spend a fortnight with us, that you may see how happy we are. I am as happy as the days are long, and one look at dear Willie's face will satisfy you as to his contentment. He is the best and dearest of husbands, grants all my wishes, and loves me as foolishly as ever.

Our house is not a mansion, but happiness is not always found in splendid dwellings. I will not describe our little snuggery, as I wish you to come and judge for yourself if I have not every cause to be a happy woman. I have been so spoilt lately that I cannot bear a disappointment; so do not refuse my request. Hoping that you will come very soon (and with best love),

> Believe me,
> Your affectionate old friend,
> *Milly Le Briton*

LETTER FROM A LADY TO HER HUSBAND AT THE ARMY IN GERMANY

(From 'The Art of Letter-Writing', 1762. N.B. Wife and husband should not use the same Letter Book.)

Dear Husband,

I cannot express how much I suffered when you set out for the Army in *Germany*. God alone knows the Grief my Heart has been pierced with. The Hopes of Peace we were flattered with, seemed to mitigate my Anxieties, and calm the Disturbances of my Mind. The Campaign opens, the War begins a-new; and I know not where I am, nor what I am doing. You might have lived happy and contented in the Bosom of your Country, with your Family, and with your Friends. But you have preferred Troubles, Fatigues, and Alarms, to the Repose and Tranquility of Life. What a cruel Destiny is this! How melancholy are the Reflections that weigh down my Heart! I spend the Days and Nights amidst continual Fears. Dread and Despair agitate continually my dejected Mind, and plunge me into an Ocean of Afflictions. Take Care of your Health, write to me often, love me as much as I love you; I cannot say more. Farewell, my dear Husband! I am the most disconsolate Wife living.

ETIQUETTE

– AND HIS ANSWER

The Enemy does not give me half the Uneasiness you do, Madam! In the Name of God compose yourself, if you have any real Love for me. Misfortunes are only great in Imagination. I have happily passed through all former Campaigns; this will be attended with the same Success. Hardships and Labour are inseparable from a military Life; and it is at this Expense we must gather Laurels: Such is my State, such my Profession; I must gloriously discharge the Duties annexed to it. What are you afraid of? I am in perfect Health. Every Thing bodes us a favourable Campaign. We are almost sure of Victory. Cease your Alarms, my dear Spouse! I am sensible of your Tenderness; I love you to the Extent of your Wishes. Love, and a Husband's Fidelity, have the most engaging Charms, and afford the sweetest Consolation to your Sex. Hark! The drums now beat, and the Trumpets sound, *March!* Glory calls me forth. The Affections of my Heart rest upon you: It is you alone that does possess it intirely. What will you have more? Farewell, my dearer Half; every Thing, I hope, will succeed to the Wish of, &c.

MODERN LETTERS TO CREDITORS

Dear Sirs:

It is with deep regret that I note the tone of your last ten communications. If you will be good enough to examine your books you will find that I have been a customer of some value to you for a matter of many years, and, though without commercial training myself, I cannot think that this policy of oblique insinuation and covert threat is the best way to insure the good will and continued custom of your patrons.

You hold me responsible for the purchase of 5 pairs of socks (or 5 tins of ginger biscuits, or 5 bottles of gin, as the case may be or may not be, as the case may be) in the year 1903 (or 1913, or 1923). It is not often that a firm of your standing commits itself to so gross an error, and I must request you to go into this matter of the socks (or biscuits or gin) at your leisure, as I have not the faintest recollection of having made any such purchase. Kindly acquaint me with the colour of the socks (or the brand of biscuits or kind of gin) with which you are under the misapprehension of having supplied me, and I will be glad to reconsider your uncouth demands for prompt payment.   Yours faithfully,

Dear Sir,
We beg to inform you that according to the Bank's Books, your
account appears to be overdrawn to the extent of £105 7s. 2d.
We think it advisable to inform you of this, in case a remittance
intended for your credit has not reached the Bank.
                                        Yours faithfully,

Dear Sir,
I am greatly obliged to you for the information contained in
your letter. I will hasten to glance through all the remittances
intended for my credit and ascertain why they have not
reached the Bank.
                        Yours faithfully,

Sir,
We have been instructed by our clients, Messrs. Clapperclaw
and Carp, to apply for payment of £25 4s. 0d., the amount of
their account against you.
Kindly see that this reaches us within five days of the date of
this letter, failing which we shall instruct our solicitors to com-
mence legal proceedings for the recovery of the debt.
                                    We are,
                                        Yours faithfully,

Sirs,
You are cordially invited to commence legal proceedings
against me, as there is nothing which would give me greater
pleasure than to expose to the British Bench the perfidy of
Messrs Clapperclaw and Carp. Do you realise the nature of
your clients ? Debt collectors cannot be too careful in these
matters, and it is with real sorrow and surprise that I see an
old city firm like yours, which, I note on your letter head,
was established in and has no doubt flourished since 1875,
receiving instructions from Messrs. Clapperclaw and Carp.
Were I to describe in detail the shabby treatment and
shabbier suiting which I have received at the hands of your
clients, I doubt not that your Principal, as a man of judgment
and respectability, would shudder away in horror at the very
idea of acting on their behalf and would indeed reconsider
the peremptory tone he pleases to take to me in his letter.
No, Sirs. In withholding prompt payment, which is quite contrary to my usual custom, from Messrs. C. and C., I am
merely following the dictates of an outraged sense of justice

and moral indignation. That they should have been able to impose upon so worthy a firm of debt collectors as yourselves is a matter for grave and disturbing reflection. My answer to them, as to you, Sirs, is, without hesitation, sue and be damned.

Yours faithfully,

THE BOOK-BORROWER

Charles Lamb was an honest borrower, returning the volumes as soon as he had read them. On one occasion he had borrowed from H. F. Carey a copy of Phillips' *Theatrum Poetarum* which he temporarily mislaid:

To Mrs George Dyer   Dec. 22nd, 1834.
Dear Mrs Dyer,
I am very uneasy about a *Book* which I either have lost or left at your house on Thursday. It was the book I went out to fetch from Miss Buffam's, while the tripe was frying. It is called Phillip's Theatrum Poetarum; but it is an English book. I think I left it in the parlour. It is Mr Carey's book, and I would not lose it for the world. Pray, if you find it, book it at the Swan, Snow Hill, by an Edmonton stage immediately, directed to Mr Lamb, Church-street, Edmonton, or write to say you cannot find it. I am quite anxious about it. If it is lost, I shall never like tripe again.

With kindest love to Mr Dyer and all.
Yours truly,
C. Lamb

'To lend Bysshe a book,' says Hogg, 'was to bid it a long farewell, to take leave of it forever; but the pain of parting was often spared, for he bore away silently, reading it as he went, any work that caught his attention.'

'Of those who borrow some read slow; some mean to read and don't read; and some neither read nor mean to read, but borrow to leave you an opinion of their sagacity.'
Charles Lamb

Lady Dorothy Nevill, so Sir Edmund Gosse tells, preserved her library by pasting in each volume the legend: 'This book has been stolen from Lady Dorothy Nevill'.

The owner of a country house was showing some visitors over a superb library. 'Do you ever lend books?' he was asked. 'No,' he replied promptly, 'only fools lend books.' Then, waving his hand to a many-shelved section filled with handsomely bound volumes, he added, 'All those books once belonged to fools.' *A correspondent to 'The Times'.*

> Say, little book, what furtive hand
> Thee from thy fellow books conveyed?
> > *W. Cowper.*

> Prince, hear a hopeless Bard's appeal;
> Reverse the rules of Mine and Thine;
> Make it legitimate to steal
> The Books that never can be mine!
> > *Andrew Lang.*

RETORTS COURTEOUS

A *Blue-Mould Fancier*, by looking too long at a Stilton cheese, was at last completely overcome, by his Eye exciting his Appetite, till it became quite ungovernable; and unconscious of every thing but the *mity* object of his contemplation, he began to pick out in no small portions, the primest parts his eye could select from the centre of the Cheese.
The good-natured Founder of the Feast, highly amused at the Ecstasies each morsel created in its passage over the palate of the enraptured *Gourmand*, thus encouraged the perseverance of his Guest –'Cut away my dear sir, cut away, use no Ceremony, I pray: – I hope you will pick out all the best of my Cheese – *don't you think* that T H E R I N D *and the* R O T T E N *will do very well for my Wife and Family?'*
> *William Kitchiner, MD, 1838.*

As a matter of course young ladies do not eat cheese at dinner parties. *From 'Manners and Rules of Good Society', 1888.*

By his host to Beau Brummel, who in his usual fashion arrived very late at dinner, which was not delayed for him: 'I hope you like cheese'.

When the Duke of Wellington was at Paris, as Commander of the allied armies, he was invited to dine with Cambaceres, one of the most distinguished statesmen and *gourmands* of the time of Napoleon. In the course of the dinner, his host having helped him to some particularly *recherché* dish, expressed a hope that he found it agreeable. 'Very good', said the hero of Waterloo, who was probably speculating upon what he would have done if Blucher had not come up: 'Very good; but I really do not care what I eat.' 'Heavens!' exclaimed Cambaceres, – as he started back and dropped his fork, quite frightened from his propriety,–'Don't care what you eat! What *did* you come here for, then?'

From 'Etiquette for Gentlemen', 1841.

There was once-upon-a-time – or, because we have heard the story ascribed to three different Dukes, perhaps thrice-upon-a-time – a Duke who did not tolerate smoking during dinner, though he had many American acquaintances. Once, and once only, one of these lit a cigarette as soon as the soup-plates were removed. The Duke called his butler. 'You will now serve coffee' he commanded, and that was the end of the meal.

1876 HINT ON TRAVELLING

For Ladies: In travelling, you need not refuse to speak to a gentleman who addresses you politely, as some foolish girls do. But by no means encourage random conversation in such a case. Your best plan, however, is to think as little as possible of gentlemen *as gentlemen*. Think of them as fellow-creatures of the same God, and treat them with respect and with self-respect. Your woman's heart should teach you the rest.

ON MUSIC AND WALTZING

A lady must never sing a song that is of a decidedly masculine character, nor if the words describe masculine action or passion. Imagine an interesting woman taking a part in 'All's well', or 'Here's a health to all good lasses', or singing 'Pretty star of the night'; yet, can such things be, for they have been. Glees and catches should rarely be sung by a lady . . . there is something so boisterous in the practice, most particularly of the latter, that, as a general principle, they ought to be avoided, especially at parties. . . Choruses, in many instances, are still more objectionable. I can hardly imagine a chorus-loving lady, except, indeed, she be a listener only.

I will leave the subject of waltzing in the hands of my fair
readers, with this simple request, viz., that whenever the
waltz is proposed, they will think of its tendency,– of the
indelicacy of the exhibition; and then I am quite certain that
this anti-English dance will very soon be banished from
society. *From 'The Ladies Pocket-Book of Etiquette', 1840.*

CONVERSATIONAL MANNERS: I

Table Talk is so natural to man, that the mouth is the organ
both of eating and speaking. The tongue is set flowing by the
bottle. Dr Johnson talked best when he dined; and Addison
could not talk at all till he had drunk. Table and conversation interchange their metaphors. We *devour* wit and argument, and *discuss* a turkey and chine. That man must be very
much absorbed in reflection, or stupid, or sulky, or unhappy,
or a mere hog at his trough, who is not moved to say something when he dines. The two men who lived with no other
companions in the Eddystone Light-house, and who would
not speak to one another during their six months, must have
been hard put to it, when they tapped a fresh barrel. To be
sure, the greater the temptation, the greater the sulk; but the
better-natured of the two must have found it a severe
struggle on a very fine or very foggy day.

Table-talk, to be perfect, should be sincere without bigotry,
differing without discord, sometimes grave, always agreeable, touching on deep points, dwelling most on seasonable
ones, and letting everybody speak and be heard. During the
wine after dinner, if the door of the room be opened, there
sometimes comes bursting up the drawing-room stairs a
noise like that of a tap-room. Everybody is shouting in order
to make himself audible; argument is tempted to confound
itself with loudness; and there is not one conversation going
forward, but six, or a score. This is better than formality and
want of spirits; but it is no more the right thing, than a
scramble is a dance, or the tap-room chorus a quartette of
Rossini. The perfection of conversational intercourse is when
the breeding of high life is animated by the fervour of genius.
Nevertheless, the man who cannot be loud, or even vociferous on occasion, is wanting on the jovial side of good-
fellowship. Chesterfield, with all his sense and agreeable-
ness, was but a solemn fop when he triumphantly asked,

537

whether anybody had 'ever seen him laugh?' It was as bad as the jealous lover in the play who says, 'Have *I* been the life of the company? Have *I* made you all die with merriment?' And there were occasions, no doubt, when Chesterfield might have been answered as the lover was, 'No: to do you justice, you have been confoundedly stupid.'

Luckily for table-talkers in general, they need be neither such fine gentlemen as Chesterfield, nor such oracles as Johnson, nor such wits as Addison and Swift, provided they have nature and sociability, and are not destitute of reading and observation. *Leigh Hunt.*

CONVERSATIONAL MANNERS: II

When there are no more than four people at table let there not be two conversations at the same time; for one of the four people will always want to forsake his conversation for the other. *F.M.*

CONVERSATIONAL MANNERS: III

Every denial of, or interference with, the personal freedom or absolute rights of another, is a violation of good manners. He who presumes to censure me for my religious belief, or want of belief; who makes it a matter of criticism or reproach that I am a Theist or Atheist, Trinitarian or Unitarian, Catholic or Protestant, Pagan or Christian, Jew, Mohammedan or Mormon, is guilty of rudeness and insult. If any of these modes of belief make me intolerant or intrusive, he may resent such intolerance or repel such intrusion; but the basis of all true politeness and social enjoyment is the mutual tolerance of personal rights. (*19th century*).

CONVERSATIONAL MANNERS: IV

Conversation is but carving;
Give no more to every guest
Than he is able to digest;
Give him always of the prime
And but little at a time;
Carve to all, but not enough,
Let them neither starve nor stuff.
And that each may have its due,
Let your neighbour carve for you.

Sir Walter Scott.

ON THE HANDSHAKE

Have you noticed how people shake your hand? There is the
high-official – the body erect, and a rapid, short shake, near
the chin. There is the *mortmain* – the flat hand introduced
into your palm, and hardly conscious of its contiguity. The
digital – one finger held out, much used by the high clergy.
There is the *shakus rusticus*, where your hand is seized in an
iron grasp, betokening rude health, warm heart, and distance from the Metropolis; but producing a strong sense of
relief on your part when you find your hand released and
your fingers unbroken. The next to this is the *retentive shake*
– one which, beginning with vigour, pauses as it were to take
breath, but without relinquishing its prey, and before you
are aware begins again, till you feel anxious as to the result,
and have no shake left in you. Worst, there is the *pisces* –
the damp palm like a dead fish, equally silent, equally clam-
my, and leaving its odour in your hand. *Sydney Smith, 1820.*

ON SAYING GRACE

It is not creditable to a 'thinking people' that the two things
they most thank God for should be eating and fighting. We
say grace when we are going to cut up lamb and chicken, and
when we have stuffed ourselves with both to an extent that
an ourangoutang would be ashamed of; and we offer up our
best praises to the Creator for having blown and sabred his
'images', our fellow-creatures, to atoms, and drenched them
in blood and dirt. This is odd. Strange that we should keep
our most pious transports for the lowest of our appetites and
the most melancholy of our necessities! that we should never
be wrought up into paroxysms of holy gratitude but for
bubble and squeak, or a good-sized massacre! that we should
think it ridiculous to be asked to say grace for a concert or a
flower-show, or the sight of a gallery of pictures, or any other
of the divinest gifts of Heaven, yet hold it to be the most
natural and exalted of impulses to fall on our knees for having
kicked, beaten, torn, shattered, drowned, stifled, exenterated,
mashed, and abolished thousands of our neighbours, whom
we are directed to 'love as ourselves!'
A correspondent of the *Times*, who had of course been doing
his duty in this respect, and thanking Heaven the first thing
every morning for the carnage in the Punjaub, wished the
other day to know 'what amount of victory was considered,

539

by the Church or State, to call forth a public expression of
thankfulness to Almighty God.' He was angry that the
Bishops had not been up and stirring at the slaughter; that
Sir Robert Peel was not as anxious to sing hymns for it, as
to feed the poor; that Lord John Russell, with all his piety,
was slower to call for rejoicings over the Sikh widows, than
attention to hapless Ireland. *Leigh Hunt.*

THE LANGUAGE OF FLOWERS

In ancient Athens, the flowers consecrated to the gods were
the symbols of their character and power; so that the Poppy
was for Ceres, the Laurel for Apollo, the Ivy for Bacchus, the
Cypress for Pluto and so on. The Romans used flowers for
festive decoration even more than the Greeks. And in the
mediæval codes of chivalry, the language of flowers was
developed as part of the ritual of courtship.

Fortunately the language of flowers and the etiquette of
giving them are not too generally understood; and flowers
today will be acceptable for themselves apart from their
significance. But if, like a modern poet, you wish to indulge
in a private meaning, these are the terms that you can use:
Acacia: Platonic Love; the acacia was brought here from
Canada, where it was venerated by the Indians as a symbol of
chaste love. *Aloe:* Grief and Bitterness. *Amaranth:* Immortality; it was supposed to adorn the brows of the gods.
Amaryllis: Pride; a meaning which comes from the nature of
the flower for it is very difficult to cultivate. *Bramble:* Envy;
because it hates its neighbours. *Carnation:* Pure Love.
Columbine: Folly. *Cypress:* Mourning. *Daffodils:* Regret.
Daisy: Innocence. *Eglantine:* Poetry. *Fennel:* Strength;
Roman gladiators mixed it with their food to give them more
power. *Fern:* Sincerity. *Field Daisy:* 'I will think of it'; a
wreath worn round the head is an answer to a lover. *Gilly
Flower:* Unfading Beauty; because they flower for so long,
from early spring through the summer. *Hawthorn:* Hope.
Holly: Foresight. *Holly-hock:* Fecundity; because of the
great number of its flowers. *Honeysuckle:* The Bonds of
Love. *Iris:* A Message; from its many colours resembling the
rainbow, which was regarded by the ancients as a messenger
of the gods. *Ivy:* Friendship. *Laurel:* Glory. *Lettuce:* Cold-
ness; Venus, after the death of Apollo, slept on a couch
of lettuce, to banish her passion. *Lilac:* First Emotions of

Love: 'I am falling in love with you.' *Marigold:* Distress of Mind or Grief. *Orange Blossom:* Chastity. *Rose:* Beauty, Joy, and Fragrance; those who dream of roses will have especially good fortune. *Snapdragon:* Presumption; because it often goes where it is not wanted. *Snowdrop:* Consolation. *Thistle:* Fearlessness. *Tulip:* Intense Affection; 'Will you marry me?'

But if you lack both flowers and the power of speech, here are two signs: A little shake of the left ear-lobe with the left hand means that the person or object under discussion is very nice indeed. A little shake of the right ear-lobe with the left hand (the left hand being taken over the top of your head) means that she, or he, or it, is superb, gorgeous, sonic.

Lady Mary Wortley Montagu reported that in Turkey in the 18th century the lover's sentiments were not written but expressed by gift:
Pearl: Fairest of the young. *Clove:* You are as slender as the clove; you are an unblown rose! I have loved you, and you have not known it. *Jonquil:* Have pity on my passion! *Paper:* I faint every hour! *Pear:* Give me some hope. *Soap:* I am sick with love. *Coal:* May I die, and all my years be yours! *A Rose:* May you be pleased, and your sorrows mine! *A Straw:* Suffer me to be your slave. *Cloth:* Your price is not to be found. *Cinnamon:* But my fortune is yours. *A Match:* I burn! I burn! my flame consumes me! *Gold Thread:* Don't turn away your face from me. *Hair:* Crown of my head! *Grape:* My two eyes! *Gold Wire:* I die – come quickly.

A MIXTY MAXTY OF HINTS

PRECEDENT FOR THOSE ENTERTAINING ROYALTY AT THE SEASIDE

'Weymouth. The King (George III) bathes and with great success; a machine follows the Royal one into the sea filled with fiddlers who play 'God save the King' as His Majesty takes his plunge.' *Fanny Burney.*

OF CHILDREN'S RECITATIONS

A doating father once proposed to Dr Johnson, that his two sons should, alternately, repeat Gray's 'Elegy', that he might judge which had the happiest cadence. 'No', said the doctor, beseachingly, 'pray, sir, let the dears both speak it at once; more noise will by that means be made, but it will be the sooner over.' *From 'Etiquette for Ladies', 1837.*

PUNCTUALITY

Punctuality to the hour of dinner cannot be too much insisted on . . .'*Le grand Boileau*' has a shrewd observation on this subject. 'I have always been punctual to the hour of dinner,' he says, 'for I knew that those I kept waiting would employ those unpleasant moments to sum up all my faults. "Boileau", they will say, "is a man of genius – a very honest man; but that dilatory and procrastinating way he has got into would mar the virtues of an angel!" ' *From 'Etiquette for Ladies', 1837.*

Be punctual – especially for breakfast. Your hostess is almost certain to have much work to do and a breakfast later than she intended can dislocate the work of the day.

Do not put ash, and *a fortiori* cigarette ends, in your saucer or plate.
As a corollary, the hostess should see that there are ash-trays on the table.

Assemble your cocktail glasses and coffee cups to the general tray: it is tiresome to find strays after the washing-up has been done.

COMPLIMENTS

At thy friend's table forget not to praise the cook, and the same shall be reckoned unto thee even as the praise of the mistress. *Dr Kitchener, 'Etiquette for Ladies', 1837.*

In the old days a compliment to the cook was taken as a compliment by the hostess. Today a compliment to the hostess is almost always a compliment to the cook.

If you are being entertained by an Arab Sheik and he gives you, as in duty bound, his most beautiful horse because you admired it, remember to give it back to him forthwith. The eye of the sheep however has to be swallowed.

TIPS

English guests do not need to be told that it is customary to leave a tip for the hired help, even if she comes in only by the hour. But Americans will welcome the hint.

ETIQUETTE

OF MEAN-NOTHING

Mere general invitations mean nothing; they are only the small coin of good society. 'Sorry you're going. Hope we shall soon meet again. Hope we shall have the pleasure of seeing you to dinner some day', is a very common mean-nothing form of politeness. *From 'Ask Mamma', 1858.*

OF DURATION

Don't presume on his (your host's) kindness by attempting to stay beyond what he presses you to do, for two short visits tell better than one long one, looking as though you have been approved of. You can easily find out from the butler or the groom of the chambers, or some of the upper servants, how long you are expected to stay. *From the same.*

TRUMPETERS

A valet is absolutely indispensible for a young gentleman. Bless you! you would be thought nothing of among the servants if you hadn't one. They are their masters' trumpeters. *From the same.*

OF STEALTHINESS

Goloshes are capital things. They keep the feet warm, and prevent your footsteps from being heard. *From the same.*

A POWERFUL NEW PROVERB

It's the careful step that makes the stairs squeak. *F.M. 1910.*

OF CARVING

'As it occurs at least once in *every day*, it deserves some attention. *It is ridiculous* not to carve well. A man who tells you that he cannot carve, may as well tell you that he cannot blow his nose: it is both as *necessary* and as *easy*.' *Chesterfield, 1751.*

APOLOGIES

I: FOR MY DAUGHTER

You mustn't mind Caroline, she's –
  – going through a phase
  – taken a real liking to you
  – still got to learn there are things one doesn't say

ETIQUETTE

– all Audrey Hepburn just now
– just read a book on your subject
– going to bed soon, we hope
– best if you just ignore her
– always a one for the men
– due to grow out of it soon
– a bit uninhibited but we don't like to repress her
– got very high standards
– rather worried about her exam
– going to fetch it in a minute, aren't you, darling?
– just been promoted to grown-up dinner
– never been able to resist a moustache
– trying to be nice in her own way
– got a very strong will of her own
– never cared for milk, cocoa, fish, cake, green vegetables
    or anything but ice-cream
– had such a good time, really.

II: FOR MY HOSPITALITY

I'm afraid it's only a scratch meal but –
– my daily walked out on me
– Caroline's been an absolute little devil
– the butcher didn't send
– I wasn't quite sure if we'd said tonight
– when you think that, before the war, we –
– I forgot it was half-closing
– something went wrong with the stew
– personally I can never manage anything before a lecture
– there's plenty of macaroni; I've only to open a tin
– we usually have our big meal at lunchtime
– I simply loathe cooking
– it's all the less to wash up
– I do hope you can eat eel
– we're vegetarians ourselves
– what I say is, it's not the food but the company
– home's always nicer than a restaurant
– we *are* having it in the dining-room
– the turnips are our very own
– it won't be long now
– I knew you wouldn't mind.

Marghanita Laski.

DRIVING MANNERS

EASY GALLICO METHOD FOR DEFLATING
THE PUMPKIN AND RESTORING THE
HUMANITIES TO DRIVING

If you care to experiment with the Easy Gallico Method for Deflating the Pumpkin and Restoring the Humanities to Driving, you might try out some of these simple canons. They will kill you at first until you begin to get the hang of them but after a while you will find you will have no difficulty in becoming a member of the human race again.

1. When you come across a bunch of pedestrians trying to cross a street, come to a dead stop and wave them across, particularly if there are baby carriages, old people and fat women involved. Any chump can stop for a pretty girl, but try being kind to a few scarecrows. Never mind the maniac behind you with his finger on the horn button. His blood pressure will eventually kill him and then there will be one less. If you have managed to contribute to this, it is your good deed for the day.

2. Slow down whenever you are in the vicinity of children. Pass them with your foot on the brake, not on the gas.

3. When a guy in a car is trying to enter a line of traffic from the side and nobody will let him in, giving him the old too-bad-for-you-Jack-hooray-for-me treatment, stop your car and let him in. The dazed expression on his puss will be worth the couple of seconds you lose. Again, you may help to kill off a couple of hysterics behind you.

4. If the light changes from red to green and pedestrians are caught in the middle of the street, wait until they are over before starting, instead of trying to unzip their garments with your wing. What great contribution to humanity are you making that demands that you save those extra three and a half seconds with a lightning getaway?

5. On the open road when somebody wants to get by, pull over and slow down. Make it easy for him instead of difficult.

6. If for any reason your jalopy won't do better than thirty on the open road, or you are a Caspar Milquetoast who likes to putter along on a Sunday, when you come to a straight stretch of road *pull over to the side, stop for a few seconds and let the queue go by*. This is the Millennium Department. It

hasn't happened yet, but the blessings that would be impelled your way by the passing motorists would bring you good luck for a week.

7. Whatever the other monkey wants to do, let him do it. Give him a smile and wave him on. It won't cure him, but it *will* cure you.

8. Stop hating women drivers. Appreciate the miracle taking place before your eyes that this bundle of contradictions is actually handling a ton or so of complicated machinery and doing it darned well. There's nothing wrong with women drivers. The trouble goes much further back to their being women. You'll never fix that.

9. Stop hating other drivers, whether male or female, just on sight. Did you ever have the embarrassment of having a bumper hook or wing scrape, and you get out of your car jawing and howling only to discover the driver of the other car is your best friend, a client, somebody you owe money to, or the wife of the boss? Think of other drivers as friend and not enemy. They could be someone just like you – God forbid.

10. Relax. Be grateful. Be humble. Be kind. Be human. Mind your manners. Enjoy this wonderful machine and help others to do the same. *Paul Gallico.*

9
PENMANSHIP

'It doesn't matter what you write but how you write it'.

Let the 'how' in this phrase refer not to the wording, the composition, of your thank-you letter but to its penmanship. Remember that Charles Kingsley once received a letter from Dean Stanley, the illegibility of whose hand was notorious, at a time when Mrs Kingsley lay very ill. Kingsley examined the letter for many minutes in vain. At last he said: 'I have every reason to believe this is a very kind letter of sympathy from Stanley – I feel sure it is. Yet the only two words I can even guess at are 'heartless devil'. But I pause – I pause to accept that suggestion as a likely one under the circumstances.'

We now have less excuse than ever for writing badly. The Italian Cursive, or Italic, Hand, first used by the Papal Chancery Scribes in the XV Century, is now widely used

LITTERA DA BREVI

A a b c d e e' f g g h i k l m n o p q r s s t u x y z

~: *Marcus Antonius Casanoua* :~
Pierij vates, laudem si opera ista merentur,
Praxiteli nostro carmina pauca date'.
Non placet hoc; nostri pietas laudanda Coryti est;
Qui dicat hæc; nisi vos forsan utcroq monet ;
Debetis saltem Dijs carmina, ni quoqs, et istis
Illa datis, iam nos mollia saxa sumus .

A A B B C C D D E E F F G G H H J I
K L L M M N N O P P Q R R S
S T T U V V X X Y Z & c' R & R

Ludouicus Vicentinus scribebat Roma' anno
salutis M·D XXIII

and properly admired. There are several books of examples
and instruction, and a Society of enthusiasts; and there are
fountain pens made specially without the usual bump on
the underside of the nib, which must be flat. From the be-

ginning to write with a flat, edged pen (or pencil) is pleasure, is fun. And anyone at any age can with a little diligence write a good hand at speed within six months.

To make a start all you need is paper and a pencil sharpened to a flat chisel edge. Now follow these few hints:

1. Hold the pencil lightly, the shaft pointing in the direction of the right forearm.

2. Make sure that the edge of the pencil is at the correct angle to the paper: it should make its thickest and thinnest strokes at a 45° angle to the writing line. The thickest stroke should be the downward diagonal stroke \; the thinnest, the upward diagonal /. For the diagonal strokes practice /\/\/. The vertical and horizontal strokes will be slightly less thick than the downward diagonal.

3. The arches of '*m*' and '*n*' should be curved. Let there be no doubt as to whether you write *n* (joined, like *m*, at the top) or *u* (joined at the bottom).

4. Note that: (a) the key letters are '*a*' and '*m*'. Begin the '*a*' with a push-stroke to the left at its top; (b) '*t*' is not a full ascender; cross it at the height of '*a*.' (c) Turn the right-hand stroke of '*v*' in and of '*r*' out. As an aid to legibility it is as well not to join '*r*' to a following letter. (d) Capitals should be two-thirds the height of an ascender.

5. See that your letters are close one to the other: the italic is a compressed and cursive (that is running-one-letter-into-the-next) hand. Keep the space between words even and not too wide. Keep neat margins both left and right.

6. Now write out the alphabet; small letters and capitals. The example on p. 547 by Arrighi, the first Master Scribe to write a manual, should inspire you. But note that it is inevitably thickened in the reproduction, which is itself reproduced from an inevitably thickened 16th century reproduction.

7. After the week-end buy one or more of the excellent contemporary manuals on calligraphy – notably by Alfred Fairbank and Philip A. Burgoyne: they are not only excellent 'tutors' but they also list the best makes of pens and nibs. *And resolve* that before the present season has twice changed you will be writing a fair italic hand.

P.S. To those who say that italic has no 'character' point out (a) that Chinese faces look alike to a European only until he becomes familiar with the general physiognomy; and (b) that what is called 'character' nearly always means illegibility, and is often begotten by swank (unsure or vain people tend to develop the most illegible secret signatures).

P.P.S. W. R. Lethaby once wrote: 'A common interest in the improvement of ordinary handwriting would be an immense disciplinary force; we might reform the world if we began with our own handwriting but we certainly shall not unless we begin somewhere.'

"QUALITIES"

OR THE NEW CONFESSIONS BOOK

No one should assess other people before he has assessed himself. Full marks are 20 for each quality. See page 449.

	BEAUTY	BRAINS	CHARM	PERSONALITY
on				
on				
on				
on				
on				
on				
on				
on				
on				
on				
on				
on				
on				
on				
on				
on				
on				
on				
on				
on				

SENSE OF HUMOUR	TASTE	SENSIBILITY	INTEGRITY	HUMILITY	GENEROSITY	ORIGINALITY	ADJUSTMENT	DETERMINATION	GOOD TEMPER	JOIE DE VIVRE

"QUALITIES"

OR THE NEW CONFESSIONS BOOK

No one should assess other people before he has assessed himself. Full marks are 20 for each quality.

	BEAUTY	BRAINS	CHARM	PERSONALITY
on				
on				
on				
on				
on				
on				
on				
on				
on				
on				
on				
on				
on				
on				
on				
on				
on				
on				
on				
on				

SENSE OF HUMOUR	TASTE	SENSIBILITY	INTEGRITY	HUMILITY	GENEROSITY	ORIGINALITY	ADJUSTMENT	DETERMINATION	GOOD TEMPER	JOIE DE VIVRE

"QUALITIES" OR THE NEW CONFESSIONS BOOK No one should assess other people before he has assessed himself. Full marks are **20** for each quality.	BEAUTY	BRAINS	CHARM	PERSONALITY
_____ on _____				
_____ on _____				
_____ on _____				
_____ on _____				
_____ on _____				
_____ on _____				
_____ on _____				
_____ on _____				
_____ on _____				
_____ on _____				
_____ on _____				
_____ on _____				
_____ on _____				
_____ on _____				
_____ on _____				
_____ on _____				
_____ on _____				
_____ on _____				
_____ on _____				
_____ on _____				
_____ on _____				
_____ on _____				

SENSE OF HUMOUR	TASTE	SENSIBILITY	INTEGRITY	HUMILITY	GENEROSITY	ORIGINALITY	ADJUSTMENT	DETERMINATION	GOOD TEMPER	JOIE DE VIVRE

ACKNOWLEDGEMENT

For poems added to this edition the editor owes his thanks to the literary executors of Hilaire Belloc; Stephen Vincent Benét; Mary Coleridge; Wilfrid Meynell; Robert Nichols (Mr Milton Waldman); Edward Thomas (Mrs Helen Thomas); Katharine Tynan (Miss Pamela Hinkson). 'All ignorance toboggans into know' from *Poems* by E. E. Cummings (copyright 1944 by E. E. Cummings) is printed by permission of Harcourt, Brace & Co. Inc. 'At a Lunar Eclipse' by Thomas Hardy is printed by permission of the Hardy Estate, Macmillan & Co. Ltd. of London and Macmillan & Co. of New York. 'The Leaden Echo and The Golden Echo' by Gerard Manley Hopkins from *The Poems of Gerard Manley Hopkins* is printed by permission of the Oxford University Press. The three poems by A. E. Housman are printed by permission of The Society of Authors, as the literary representative of the Trustees of the Estate of the late A. E. Housman, Jonathan Cape, Ltd., publishers of *A. E. Housman's Collected Poems* and Henry Holt & Co. Inc., New York. 'Cities and thrones and powers' from *Puck of Pook's Hill* by Rudyard Kipling, copyright in the U.S.A. in 1906, is printed by permission of Doubleday & Co. Inc., New York, Macmillan & Co. Ltd., London and Mrs George Bambridge. 'Our Story' by Thomas Mac-Donagh is printed by permission of Ernest Benn Ltd. 'Happiness' by Wilfred Owen is printed by permission of the heirs of Wilfred Owen, Chatto & Windus and New Directions, New York. 'The force that thro' the green fuse' by Dylan Thomas is printed by permission of J. M. Dent and Sons, Ltd. and New Directions, New York. 'Address to my Soul' by Elinor Wylie is printed by permission of Alfred A. Knopf, Inc.

The editor also thanks the following poets and their publishers: John Betjeman and John Murray (Publishers) Ltd., for 'Essex' from *A Few Late Chrysanthemums;* Edmund Blunden for 'Forefathers'; Gerald Bullett for 'To a Certain Archbishop'; Gerald Bullett and the Cambridge University Press for 'So still the world this winter noon'; Roy Campbell for 'Not only did he lose his life', 'Who forced the muse', 'The Soldier's Reply' and 'The Flower'. Richard Church for 'The Shower'; R. N. Curry and Routledge & Kegan, Paul,

557

Ltd. for 'There is no joy in water'; Walter De la Mare and
Henry Holt & Co., U.S.A., for 'The Scribe'; Walter De la
Mare for 'Slim Cunning Hands' and 'Blessed Mary, pity
me'; T. S. Eliot, Faber & Faber Ltd. and Harcourt, Brace
& Co. Inc. for 'Whispers of Immortality'; Colin Ellis for
nine epigrams; David Gascoyne and Macdonald & Co.
(Publishers) Ltd., for 'A tough Generation'; Robert Graves,
Cassell & Co. Ltd. and Doubleday & Co. Inc. for 'Thunder
at Night' and 'Flying Crooked' from *Collected Poems of
Robert Graves 1914-1947;* G. Rostrevor Hamilton and Wm.
Heinemann Ltd. for 'Time upon my Wrist'; Kenneth Hare
and Ernest Benn Ltd. for 'The Puritan'; Frank Kendon and
John Lane, The Bodley Head Ltd. for 'The Immigrants'
from *Poems and Sonnets;* Laurie Lee and André Deutsch
Ltd. for 'The Abandoned Shade' from *My many-coated man;*
Louis MacNeice, Faber & Faber Ltd. and Random House,
Inc., New York for 'Meeting Point'; Viola Meynell for 'The
Sick Boy'; Edwin Muir and Faber & Faber Ltd. for 'The
Return'; Ogden Nash, J. M. Dent & Sons, Ltd. and Little,
Brown & Co., U.S.A. for three epigrams and 'Parsley for
Vice-President'; Norman Nicholson and Faber & Faber Ltd.
for 'Poem for Epiphany'; Alfred Noyes for 'Cats and Kings';
Ruth Pitter and The Cresset Press Ltd. for 'Matron Cat's
Song' from *Ruth Pitter on Cats,* 'The Comet' from *Urania,*
and 'Time' from *A Trophy of Arms;* Kathleen Raine,
Hamish Hamilton, Ltd. and Farrar, Straus & Young Inc.,
U.S.A. for 'Prayer'; J. Crowe Ranson and Alfred A. Knopf,
Inc., New York for 'Winter Remembered'; Henry Reed,
Jonathan Cape, Ltd. and Harcourt, Brace & Co. Inc. for
'Judging Distances' from *A Map of Verona;* Anne Ridler and
Faber & Faber Ltd. for 'At Richmond'; W. R. Rodgers,
Secker & Warburg, Ltd. and Farrar, Straus & Young, Inc.,
U.S.A. for 'Pan and Syrinx'; Siegfried Sassoon and Wm.
Heinemann Ltd. for 'To an old lady dead'; V. Sackville-
West for extracts from 'The Land'; E. J. Scovell for 'The
February Hedge'; Stephen Spender, Faber & Faber Ltd.
and Random House, Inc., New York for 'Since we are what
we are'; Sylvia Townsend Warner, Chatto & Windus and the
Viking Press Inc., New York for 'After long thirty years';
Vernon Watkins, Faber & Faber Ltd. and New Directions,
New York for 'The Shell'; Andrew Young for 'Killed by a
Hawk' from *Winter Harvest* (Nonesuch Press); Morton

ACKNOWLEDGEMENT

Zabel and *The Times Literary Supplement* for 'The Traitors'. For poems and two songs which were in previous editions and are here retained the editor records again his obligation to the literary executors of Rupert Brooke, Samuel Butler, James Elroy Flecker, Richard Garnett, Alice Meynell, Walter Raleigh and Francis Thompson; and to all the living authors and to the publishers in the following list, in which the titles of books from which poems have been taken are printed in italics. G. Bell & Sons Ltd.: *The Unknown Eros*, by Coventry Patmore. Ernest Benn Ltd.: *The Unknown Goddess*, by Humbert Wolfe; *Beauty the Pilgrim*, by Gerald Gould. Burns Oates & Washbourne Ltd.: *Poems* by G. K. Chesterton; *Collected Poems of Alice Meynell*; *Collected Works of Francis Thompson*; *The Flower of Peace*, by Katharine Tynan; *Poems*, by J. B. Tabb. Jonathan Cape Ltd.: *Collected Poems* of W. H. Davies; *Samuel Butler's Notebooks*; *Poems*, by Muriel Stuart. Chatto and Windus: *Leda*, by Aldous Huxley; *Argonaut and Juggernaut*, by Osbert Sitwell. The Clarendon Press, Oxford: *The Shorter Poems of Robert Bridges, 1931*. Constable & Co. Ltd.: *Collected Works of George Meredith*; *Poems* by W. Raleigh. J. M. Dent & Sons, Ltd.: *The Wild Knight*, by G. K. Chesterton. Gerald Duckworth & Co. Ltd.: *Sonnets and Verse*, by Hilaire Belloc; *Troy Park*, by Edith Sitwell. Elkin Mathew & Marrot: *Poems*, by Mary Coleridge. Faber & Faber Ltd.: *Poems* by W. H. Auden. Wm. Heinemann Ltd.: *Selected Poems*, by Robert Frost; *Collected Poems*, by John Masefield; *Poems, 1914-1926* by Robert Graves. Hodder & Stoughton Ltd.: *Poems*, by J. C. Squire. The Hogarth Press: *Collected Poems, 1929-1933* by C. Day Lewis. Longmans, Green & Co. Ltd.: *Child's Garden of Verses*, by R. L. Stevenson; *Songs of Childhood*, by Walter De la Mare. Erskine Macdonald & Co.: 'And When I Die' from *More Tommy's Tunes*. Macmillan & Co. Ltd: *Collected Poems of T. E. Brown; Late Lyrics* and *Collected Poems* by Thomas Hardy; *Poems*, by Ralph Hodgson; *Songs of England*, by Alfred Austin; *Songs from the Clay* and *The Hill of Vision* by James Stephens; *Later Poems*, by W. B. Yeats. Elkin Mathews Ltd.: *Poems*, by Lionel Johnson. Elkin Mathews and Mr Martin Secker: *Collected Poems of J. E. Flecker*. Methuen and Co. Ltd.: *Collected Poems*, by W. H. Davies. E. J. Moeran: 'Mrs Dyer'. Oxford University Press: *Fifty Poems*,

ACKNOWLEDGEMENT

by A. D. Godley. The Poetry Bookshop: *Spring Morning* and *Autumn Midnight*, by Frances Cornford; *Strange Meetings*, by Harold Monro; The *Georgian Poetry* anthologies. Grant Richards: *Little Poems*, by Walter Leaf. Mr Martin Secker: *Pier Glass*, by Robert Graves; *Verses*, by Viola Meynell; *Complete Poems*, by Emily Dickinson; *Poems*, by Edna St. Vincent Millay. Sidgwick & Jackson Ltd.: *Collected Poems of Rupert Brooke.*

The following American permissions to print poems are also to be acknowledged once again: Doubleday Doran & Co.: *Beauty the Pilgrim*, by Gerald Gould. Harper and Brothers: *Poems*, copyright by Edna St. Vincent Millay 1917; *Second April*, copyright by Edna St. Vincent Millay 1921. Little, Brown & Co.: *Poems*, by Emily Dickinson. Longmans, Green & Co. Ltd.: *The Traveller's Curse*, by Robert Graves; *The Fly*, by Walter De la Mare. The Macmillan Co. of New York: *Collected Poems* and *Later Lyrics* by Thomas Hardy; *Poems* by Ralph Hodgson; 'The Daniel Jazz', by Nicholas Vachel Lindsay; *Poems*, by John Masefield; *Later Poems*, by W. B. Yeats. Random House Inc.: *Collected Poems, 1929-1933*, by C. Day Lewis; *Poems* by W. H. Auden. *The New Yorker*: 'Trial and Error' by Phyllis McGinley; 'Too Bad' by Clarence Day.

Thanks are also due to Rupert Hart-Davis Ltd. for a poem by Mary Coleridge; Wm. Heinemann Ltd. for quotations from James Boswell's *London Journal;* Paul Gallico for 'Driving Manners'; E. L. Hawke and the Royal Meteorological Society for a selection from Ralph Inwards' *Weather Lore* (newly edited by E. L. Hawke); Marghanita Laski and *The Observer* for 'Apology for my daughter' and 'Apology for my hospitality'; *The New Statesman & Nation* for two letters from one of their admirable competitions; John Lane, The Bodley Head, Ltd. for 'Letters to Creditors' from *Creditors and How to Escape Them.*

INDEX OF POEMS (FIRST LINES)

571

575

578

INDEX OF ROUNDS AND SONGS

VIOLET FAMILY

Sand Violet · Dog Violet · Hearts-ease · Sweet Violet

Foxglove FAMILY

Ivy-leaved · Toad flax · Mimulus

SNAPDRAGON

Louse-wort

SIMPLE

linear · lobed · palmate

pinnate · perfoliate · COMPOUND

TYPES OF LEAVES

PINK FAMILY

Cheddar Pink · Soap wort · Ragged Robin

DICOTYLEDONS